Spain Travel Guide 2025

Spain Travel Guide 2025   1

Also by Phil Tang   7

Welcome to your guide to a Luxury Trip to Spain on a budget!   9

The Magical Power of Bargains   10

Who this book is for and why anyone can enjoy luxury travel on a budget 11

Discover Spain   13

Some of Spain's Best Bargains   15

Free Tapa   17

Government Subsidized Entertainment   19

Super Cheap Accommodations   21

Freebies from Institutions   22

Ferry Travel   25

Completely free tours   27

National Parks Pass   29

Markets   31

Spanish Wine   32

Olives and Olive Oil   34

See Cave Paintings   36

Second-Hand Designer Clothing   39

Go Outlet shopping   40

Be in a TV audience   41

Buy Discount Passes   43

Loyalty cards that save you huge amounts   45

Free Festivals   46

Why is so Spain expensive and how can I save money   49

Weird and wonderful facts about that most people don't know about Spain
50

Know Before you Go   53

Money mistakes to Avoid   61

Accommodation   62

Best day passes to five star hotels in with prices   64

Cheapest hotel chains	64
Unique and Cheap Places to Stay:	66
Is It Still Cheap to Stay in an Airbnb in Spain?	66
Top 25 Attractions in Spain for Cheap or Free	68
Common Tourist Taxes in Spain	79
How to Enjoy ALLOCATING Money in Spain	80
How to feel RICH in Spain	82
How to use this book	83
Planning your trip	84
When to visit	84
Freebies month-by-month	84
Booking Flights	86
How to Fly Business Class to Spain cheaply	86
How to ALWAYS Find Super Cheap Flights to Spain	86
Saving money on Spanish Food	90
Food Culture	90
Saving Money on Food in Spain	91
Cheap Michelin-starred restaurants in Spain	91
Cheapest Breakfasts in Spain	97
Cheap Snackfoods in Spain	98
Street Food	99
First-day Itinerary for first time visitor to Spain	103
7-Day Itinerary for Luxury on a Budget	105
Unique bargains we love in Spain	107
OUR SPECIFIC SUPER CHEAP TIPS…	111
Arriving	111
Getting around cheaply	113
Spain's Top 25	117
Barcelona	118
Madrid	126

Valencia	136
Seville	144
Granada	150
San Sebastián	156
Bilbao	162
Santiago de Compostela	168
Toledo	174
Málaga	181
Córdoba	188
Ibiza	195
Tenerife	202
Ronda	209
Regions	216
Catalonia	218
Andalusia	222
Valencian	227
Balearic Islands	232
Canary Islands	235
Basque Country	240
Galicia	243
Aragon	248
Murcia	253
Truly weird and wonderful things to do in Spain	257
Best beaches	258
Best public swimming pools with prices	260
Best Hikes	261
What to do at night for free in Spain	263
Getting Out Cheaply	264
Cheapest Airport lounges in Spain	267
Spain's Quirks	268

100 useful phrases Spanish with english pronunciation 271

Spanish Slang 276

Common complaints of tourists visiting 279

Checklist of top 20 things To Do 280

History 281

How to Have a $10,000 Trip to Spain for $500: A Detailed Breakdown 283

The secret to saving HUGE amounts of money when travelling to Spain is… 286

Thank you for reading 289

Bonus Travel Hacks 292

Common pitfalls when it comes to allocating money to your desires while traveling 293

Hack your allocations for your Spain Trip 295

MORE TIPS TO FIND CHEAP FLIGHTS 297

What Credit Card Gives The Best Air Miles? 300

Frequent Flyer Memberships 303

How to get 70% off a Cruise 304

Relaxing at the Airport 305

How to spend money 306

How I got hooked on luxury on a budget travelling 309

A final word… 310

Copyright 311

"Spain is a country that has a soul of its own."
— Joaquín Sorolla

Also by Phil Tang

Making expensive destinations SUPER CHEAP since 2017 with a 4.1 ★★★★★ average rating on Amazon.

Super Cheap AUSTRALIA
Super Cheap CANADA
Super Cheap DENMARK
Super Cheap FINLAND
Super Cheap FRANCE
Super Cheap GERMANY
Super Cheap ICELAND
Super Cheap ITALY
Super Cheap IRELAND
Super Cheap JAPAN
Super Cheap LUXEMBOURG
Super Cheap MALDIVES
Super Cheap MEXICO
Super Cheap NEW ZEALAND
Super Cheap NORWAY
Super Cheap Spain
Super Cheap SWITZERLAND

Super Cheap ADELAIDE 2025
Super Cheap ALASKA 2025
Super Cheap AUSTIN 2025
Super Cheap Banff
Super Cheap BANGKOK 2025
Super Cheap BARCELONA 2025
Super Cheap BELFAST 2025
Super Cheap BERMUDA 2025
Super Cheap BORA BORA 2025
Super Cheap Great Barrier Reef 2025
Super Cheap CAMBRIDGE 2025
Super Cheap CANCUN 2025
Super Cheap CHIANG MAI 2025
Super Cheap CHICAGO 2025
Super Cheap DOHA 2025
Super Cheap DUBAI 2025
Super Cheap DUBLIN 2025
Super Cheap EDINBURGH 2025
Super Cheap GALWAY 2025
Super Cheap LAS VEGAS 2025
Super Cheap LIMA 2025
Super Cheap LISBON 2025
Super Cheap MALAGA 2025
Super Cheap Machu Pichu 2025
Super Cheap MIAMI 2025
Super Cheap Milan 2025

Super Cheap NASHVILLE 2025
Super Cheap NEW ORLEANS 2025
Super Cheap NEW YORK 2025
Super Cheap PARIS 2025
Super Cheap SEYCHELLES 2025
Super Cheap SINGAPORE 2025
Super Cheap ST LUCIA 2025
Super Cheap TORONTO 2025
Super Cheap TURKS AND CAICOS 2025
Super Cheap VENICE 2025
Super Cheap VIENNA 2025
Super Cheap YOSEMITE 2025
Super Cheap ZURICH 2025
Super Cheap ZANZIBAR 2025

Welcome to your guide to a Luxury Trip to Spain on a budget!

This travel guide is your step-by-step manual for unlocking luxury hotels, enjoying the best culinary offerings and once-in-a-lifetime luxury experiences in Spain at a fraction of the usual cost.

Everyone's budget is different, but luxury is typically defined by first or business class seats on the airplane, five-star hotels, chauffeurs, exclusive experiences, and delectable fine dining. Yes, all of these can be enjoyed on a budget.

Finding luxury deals in Spain simply requires a bit of research and planning, which this book has done for you. We have packed this book with local insider tips and knowledge to save you tens of thousands.

If the mere mention of the word luxury has you thinking things like "Money doesn't grow on trees," "I don't need anything fancy," "I don't deserve nice things," or "People who take luxury trips are shallow and materialistic/environmentally harmful/lack empathy, etc.," then stop. While we all know travel increases our happiness, research on the effects of luxury travel has proven even better results:

Reduced stress: A study published in the Journal of Travel Research found that individuals who visited luxury hotels reported feeling less stressed than those who in standard hotels.[1]

Increased happiness: A study conducted by the International Journal of Tourism Research found that luxury travel experiences lead to an increase in happiness and overall life satisfaction.[2] Researchers also found that luxury travel experiences can improve individuals' mental health by providing a sense of escape from daily stressors and enhancing feelings of relaxation and rejuvenation.

Enhanced creativity: Researchers found engaging in luxury travel experiences can stimulate creativity and lead to more innovative thinking.[3]

While all of this makes perfect sense; it feels much nicer to stay in a hotel room that's cleaned daily than in an Airbnb where you're cleaning up after yourself. What you might not know is that you can have all of that increased happiness and well-being without emptying your bank account. Does it sound too good to be true? This book will prove it isn't!

---

[1] Wöber, K. W., & Fuchs, M. (2016). The effects of hotel attributes on perceived value and satisfaction. Journal of Travel Research, 55(3), 306-318.

[2] Ladhari, R., Souiden, N., & Dufour, B. (2017). Luxury hotel customers' satisfaction and loyalty: An empirical study. International Journal of Hospitality Management, 63, 1-10.

[3] Kim, S., Kim, S. Y., & Lee, H. R. (2019). Luxury travel, inspiration, and creativity: A qualitative investigation. Tourism Management, 71, 354-366.

The Magical Power of Bargains

Have you ever felt the rush of getting a bargain? And then found good fortune just keeps following you?

Let me give you an example. In 2009, I graduated into the worst global recession for generations. One unemployed day, I saw a suit I knew I could get a job in. The suit was £250. Money I didn't have. Imagine my shock when the next day I saw the exact same suit (in my size) in the window of a second-hand shop (thrift store) for £18! I bought the suit and after three months of interviewing, without a single call back, within a week of owning that £18 suit, I was hired on a salary far above my expectations. That's the powerful psychological effect of getting an incredible deal. It builds a sense of excitement and happiness that literally creates miracles.

I have no doubt that the wonders of Spain will uplift and inspire you but when you add the bargains from this book to your vacation, not only will you save a ton of money; you are guaranteed to enjoy a truly magical trip to Spain.

Who this book is for and why anyone can enjoy luxury travel on a budget

Did you know you can fly on a private jet for $500? Yes, a fully private jet. Complete with flutes of champagne and reclinable creamy leather seats. Your average billionaire spends $20,000 on the exact same flight. You can get it for $500 when you book private jet empty leg flights.This is just one of thousands of ways you can travel luxuriously on a budget. You see there is a big difference between being cheap and frugal.

When our brain hears the word "budget" it hears deprivation, suffering, agony, even depression. But budget travel need not be synonymous with hostels and pack lunches. You can enjoy an incredible and luxurious trip to Spain on a budget, just like you can enjoy a private jet flight for 10% of the normal cost when you know how.

Over 20 years of travel has taught me I could have a 20 cent experience that will stir my soul more than a $100 one. Of course, sometimes the reverse is true, my point is, spending money on travel is the best investment you can make but it doesn't have to be at levels set by hotels and attractions with massive ad spends and influencers who are paid small fortunes to get you to buy into something you could have for a fraction of the cost.

This book is for those who love bargains and want to have the cold hard budget busting facts to hand (which is why we've included so many one page charts, which you can use as a quick reference), but otherwise, the book provides plenty of tips to help you shape your own Spain experience.

We have designed these travel guides to give you a unique planning tool to experience an unforgettable trip without spending the ascribed tourist budget.

This guide focuses on Spain's unbelievable bargains. Of course, there is little value in traveling to Spain and not experiencing everything it has to offer. Where possible, we've included super cheap workarounds or listed the experience in the Loved but Costly section.

When it comes to luxury budget travel, it's all about what you know. You can have all the feels without most of the bills. A few days spent planning can save you thousands. Luckily, we've done the planning for you, so you can distill the information in minutes not days, leaving you to focus on what matters: immersing yourself in the sights, sounds and smells of Spain, meeting awesome new people and feeling relaxed and happy.

This book reads like a good friend has travelled the length and breadth of Spain and brought you back incredible insider tips.

So, grab a cup of tea or coffee, put your feet up and relax; you're about to enter the world of enjoying Spain on the Super Cheap. Oh, and don't forget a biscuit. You need energy to plan a trip of a lifetime on a budget.

Discover Spain

Spain, a land steeped in history, adorned with captivating landscapes, and brimming with vibrant culture, beckons travelers with promises of unforgettable experiences. From the ancient ruins of Moorish fortresses to the sun-kissed beaches of the Mediterranean coast, Spain's allure lies in its rich tapestry of influences, where the echoes of past civilizations resonate harmoniously with modern-day vibrancy.

Nestled on the Iberian Peninsula in southwestern Europe, Spain boasts a storied past that dates back millennia. Phoenicians, Greeks, Romans, Moors, and Visigoths have all left their indelible marks on this land, shaping its architecture, cuisine, and customs. The legacy of these diverse cultures is evident in Spain's bustling cities, where Gothic cathedrals stand alongside Moorish palaces, and medieval alleyways lead to modern boulevards.

One cannot explore Spain without encountering its crown jewels: the historic cities of Madrid, Barcelona, Seville, and Granada. Madrid, the nation's capital, pulses with energy and sophistication, offering world-class museums, elegant boulevards, and a vibrant nightlife. Barcelona, nestled on the shores of the Mediterranean, captivates visitors with its whimsical architecture, including the iconic Sagrada Familia and Park Güell.

Seville, with its labyrinthine streets and ornate Moorish architecture, embodies the essence of Andalusia's rich heritage. The Alcazar Palace, a UNESCO World Heritage site, transports visitors back in time to the era of Moorish splendor, while the flamenco tablaos resonate with the passionate rhythms of Spanish music and dance.

Granada, nestled at the foot of the Sierra Nevada mountains, exudes an aura of mystique and romance. The crowning jewel of Granada is the Alhambra, a breathtaking fortress-palace that embodies the pinnacle of Moorish art and architecture. As the sun sets over the Alhambra, casting a golden glow over its intricate arabesques and lush gardens, visitors cannot help but be transported to a bygone era of enchantment and opulence.

Beyond its historic cities, Spain boasts a diverse array of landscapes, from the sun-drenched beaches of the Costa del Sol to the rugged mountains of the Pyrenees. The Camino de Santiago, a network of ancient pilgrimage routes that crisscross the country, offers intrepid travelers the chance to embark on a transformative journey of self-discovery.

For those seeking luxury on a budget, Spain offers a plethora of options to indulge in opulence without breaking the bank. Boutique hotels nestled in historic buildings offer personalized service and stylish accommodations at affordable prices. Dining experiences abound, from Michelin-starred restaurants serving innovative cuisine to tapas bars and markets offering authentic flavors at budget-friendly prices.

To truly experience the essence of Spanish culture, travelers should immerse themselves in the local customs and traditions. Joining a flamenco performance or attending a bullfight provides insight into Spain's rich cultural heritage, while exploring local markets and festivals offers the chance to sample regional delicacies and mingle with locals.

Spain captivates the senses and nourishes the soul. In this land of contrasts, where the past intertwines with the present, every corner reveals a new facet of its timeless allure. So, pack your bags, immerse yourself in the magic of Spain, and embark on a journey of discovery that will leave an indelible mark on your heart and soul and not your bank balance!

Some of Spain's Best Bargains

Spain is filled with luxurious experiences that you can enjoy without breaking the bank, here are just a few:

Savor Affordable Michelin-Star Flavors

- **Michelin Bib Gourmand Restaurants:** Look for restaurants with the Michelin Bib Gourmand designation, which indicates high-quality food at a reasonable price. These places often feature exceptional regional dishes without the Michelin star price tag.
- **Lunch Menus:** Many Michelin-starred restaurants offer more affordable tasting menus at lunchtime. Places like **Barcelona** and **San Sebastián** have Michelin-starred spots where lunch is a fraction of the dinner price.

Explore Rooftop Bars with Stunning Views

- **Rooftop Bars for Happy Hour:** Many rooftop bars in cities like **Madrid** and **Barcelona** have happy hours where you can enjoy a drink with a view for less. Some options include **Azotea del Círculo** in Madrid or **Sky Bar** in Barcelona.
- **Stay at Boutique Hotels:** Book a night or two at boutique hotels with rooftop bars. Many let you access the rooftop amenities as a guest, so you can enjoy the ambiance and views without paying extra.

Enjoy Luxurious Pastries on a Budget

- **Traditional Bakeries:** Visit bakeries like **La Mallorquina** in Madrid or **Escribà** in Barcelona for authentic pastries like *ensaimadas* and *napolitanas* at reasonable prices. These pastries are decadent and feel like a treat from a fancy café, but they're affordable.
- **Churros with Chocolate:** Indulge in a Spanish classic for a low price. Head to **San Ginés** in Madrid or **Granja M. Viader** in Barcelona for a traditional experience that feels luxurious without the high cost.

Catch a Flamenco Show Without the Premium

- **Free Flamenco Shows:** Some bars in **Seville** and **Granada** offer free Flamenco shows with the purchase of a drink. Bars like **La Carbonería** in Seville or **Le Chien Andalou** in Granada provide a chance to experience this art form in an intimate setting for just the cost of a drink.

- **Flamenco Festivals:** If you're traveling during festival season, keep an eye out for free Flamenco performances, especially in Andalusia. Festivals like the **Bienal de Flamenco** often feature free events around the city.

Indulge in Seafood Without a heavy price tag

- **Tapas Bars:** For fresh and affordable seafood, visit local *marisquerías* (seafood tapas bars) rather than high-end restaurants. Try *boquerones* (marinated anchovies), *pulpo a la gallega* (Galician-style octopus), and *gambas al ajillo* (garlic shrimp) at spots favored by locals.
- **Markets:** Head to food markets like Barcelona's **La Boqueria** or Madrid's **Mercado de San Miguel**, where you can enjoy a wide range of seafood tapas at various stalls. You'll often find high-quality seafood for much less than at restaurants.
- **Coastal Towns:** Smaller towns along the coast offer incredibly fresh seafood at more reasonable prices than big cities. Head to places like **Cadiz**, **A Coruña**, or **Sanlúcar de Barrameda** where you can find seafood dishes like fried fish (*pescaíto frito*) for a fraction of the price.

Free Tapa

Sampling free tapas is one of the best ways to enjoy Spanish cuisine while keeping your budget in check. Each of these cities has its own unique tapas culture, so take the time to explore various bars and discover the delightful flavors that await you. Don't forget to engage with the locals, as they can offer great recommendations and insights into the best places to enjoy free tapas! Enjoy your culinary adventure across Spain!

1. Seville

- **Best Free Tapa: Pork Belly (Panceta)**
- **Where to Go: La Taverna de Alvaro** – This bustling bar serves excellent pork belly as a complimentary tapa with your drink.
- **Tip**: Arrive during peak hours (around 8 PM) for the best atmosphere and variety of tapas options.

2. Granada

- **Best Free Tapa: Patatas Bravas**
- **Where to Go: Bodegas Castañeda** – Known for its generous portions, this bar offers delicious patatas bravas when you order a beer or wine.
- **Tip**: Try pairing your drink with a selection of their other tapas for a full meal experience!

3. Barcelona

- **Best Free Tapa: Bread with Tomato (Pa amb tomàquet)**
- **Where to Go: Cervecería Catalana** – A popular spot among locals and tourists alike, you'll receive a slice of delicious bread topped with fresh tomato and olive oil.
- **Tip**: Visit during off-peak hours to avoid long waits, as it can get crowded.

4. Madrid

- **Best Free Tapa: Chorizo al Vino**
- **Where to Go: Casa de la Cerveza** – Order a drink here, and you'll be treated to their tasty chorizo cooked in wine as a complimentary tapa.
- **Tip**: Try visiting during "horas felices" (happy hours) for better deals on drinks!

5. Valencia

- **Best Free Tapa: Olives**
- **Where to Go: Casa Montaña** – This traditional bar serves a bowl of marinated olives with each drink, making it a delightful and easy snack.
- **Tip**: Pair your olives with a glass of local wine for an authentic Valencian experience.

6. Bilbao

- **Best Free Tapa: Bacalao (Cod)**
- **Where to Go: La Olla** – When you order a drink, enjoy a small serving of bacalao, a local favorite, as a complimentary tapa.
- **Tip**: Explore the nearby **Casco Viejo** for more bars offering free tapas with drinks.

7. San Sebastián

- **Best Free Tapa: Pintxos (Basque Tapas)
- **Where to Go: Bar Nestor** – While some pintxos require payment, ordering a drink often gets you a small, delightful sample of their offerings.
- **Tip**: Walk through the **Old Town** (Parte Vieja) to discover other bars offering free pintxos with drinks.

8. Málaga

- **Best Free Tapa: Tortilla Española (Spanish Omelette)**
- **Where to Go: Taberna La Tita** – This cozy tavern serves a slice of their delicious tortilla with your drink, making it a perfect pairing.
- **Tip**: Try their selection of local wines to enhance your tapa experience.

9. Toledo

- **Best Free Tapa: Zorzal (Thick Soup)**
- **Where to Go: El Trébol** – Enjoy a small bowl of zorzal, a traditional thick soup, as a free tapa with your drink order.
- **Tip**: Visit during lunch hours for a more relaxed atmosphere and to enjoy their full menu.

10. Alicante

- **Best Free Tapa: Fried Fish**
- **Where to Go: La Taverna del Puerto** – Order a drink and savor the fried fish, a popular tapa among locals.
- **Tip**: Head here for dinner, as the lively atmosphere in the evenings enhances the experience.

Government Subsidized Entertainment

Spain offers several government-subsidized activities that allow you to enjoy culture and the arts at a fraction of the cost, including opera, museums, and performances. Here's a guide to some of the top affordable cultural experiences in Spain:

1. Subsidized Opera Performances

- **Teatro Real (Madrid):** Spain's premier opera house, **Teatro Real**, offers subsidized tickets for students, young people (under 30), and seniors. There are also "Last Minute Tickets," which are often heavily discounted. Tickets can go as low as €15 for some performances. Keep an eye out for special government-backed events where admission is free or significantly reduced.
- **Gran Teatre del Liceu (Barcelona):** Barcelona's famed opera house offers similar discounts, with special prices for youth and seniors, and occasionally hosts free or very affordable performances as part of cultural promotion initiatives. They also have day-of-show discount tickets.

2. Government-Subsidized Museums

- **Museo del Prado (Madrid):** One of the most famous art museums in the world, **Museo del Prado**, offers free entry during the last two hours of the day (typically from 6:00 p.m. to 8:00 p.m. on weekdays and from 5:00 p.m. to 7:00 p.m. on Sundays). The museum is subsidized by the Spanish government to promote access to culture.
- **Museo Reina Sofia (Madrid):** Home to Picasso's *Guernica*, **Museo Reina Sofia** also offers free admission on select days and times (usually from 7:00 p.m. to 9:00 p.m. on weekdays and 1:30 p.m. to 7:00 p.m. on Sundays). This museum is part of Spain's national heritage and receives government funding to support public access to art.
- **Museo Nacional Thyssen-Bornemisza (Madrid):** Offers free entry on Mondays from 12:00 p.m. to 4:00 p.m. as part of a government initiative to promote cultural access.

3. Affordable Classical Music and Ballet

- **Auditorio Nacional de Música (Madrid):** The National Auditorium offers subsidized tickets for many performances, including classical concerts and ballet. You can often find tickets starting at around €15, particularly for weekday performances.
- **Teatro de la Zarzuela (Madrid):** Known for its Spanish operettas (zarzuela), this theater offers affordable tickets, with many government-subsidized options starting as low as €10. They also have discounted prices for younger audiences and seniors.

4. Free and Affordable Entry to Historic Sites

- **The Alhambra (Granada):** The **Alhambra**, one of Spain's most iconic sites, offers free entry on specific days for EU citizens, particularly during the **Jornadas Europeas del Patrimonio** (European Heritage Days). There are also reduced-price tickets available for students, seniors, and large groups.
- **Alcázar of Seville:** This historic palace, subsidized by the Spanish government, offers discounted tickets for students and seniors. In addition, it is free for EU citizens on Mondays from 4:00 p.m. to 5:00 p.m. in winter, and from 6:00 p.m. to 7:00 p.m. in summer.

5. Subsidized Cultural Events and Festivals

- **Flamenco Biennial (Seville):** This major flamenco festival often includes subsidized tickets for performances, as well as free public events, to promote cultural heritage.
- **Noche en Blanco (Various Cities):** During **La Noche en Blanco** (White Night), cities like **Madrid** and **Malaga** host a wide range of free cultural activities — museums stay open late, there are concerts, art installations, and performances — all government-supported to foster public engagement in the arts.

6. Subsidized Cinema

- **Filmoteca Española (Madrid):** The **Filmoteca Española** is a government-subsidized cinema that screens classic films and Spanish cinema at a very low price, often as little as €2-€3 per ticket. It's a fantastic way to enjoy Spain's rich film history on a budget.
- **Filmoteca de Catalunya (Barcelona):** Similarly, **Filmoteca de Catalunya** offers subsidized screenings of classic films, many for under €5.

Super Cheap Accommodations

Spain offers a variety of affordable accommodations run by government entities, particularly in natural parks and rural areas. You can find huts, and other budget-friendly accommodations managed by government or regional authorities with exceptional views from $10!

Cabañas (Cabins) in Natural Parks

Many national and regional parks in Spain offer rustic cabins or huts for rent, often at lower prices than traditional hotels.

- **Locations**: These cabins can be found in stunning natural settings, such as **Picos de Europa National Park**, **Sierra de Guadarrama**, and **Ordesa y Monte Perdido National Park**.
- **Cost**: Prices for cabins vary, but you can often find options for €40 to €80 per night, depending on the location and amenities.
- **Example: Cabañas de la Sierra de Cazorla** are eco-friendly cabins located within the Cazorla, Segura, and Las Villas Natural Park, providing a great base for hiking and nature activities.

Refugios (Mountain Huts)

For hikers and outdoor enthusiasts, refugios are mountain huts located in various national parks and along popular trekking routes.

- **Locations**: You can find refugios in the **Picos de Europa**, **Sierra Nevada**, and along the **Camino de Santiago**.
- **Cost**: Prices usually range from €10 to €30 per night, often including meals.
- **Example: Refugio de la Caldera** in the Sierra Nevada provides basic accommodation for hikers and a communal atmosphere.

Freebies from Institutions

In Spain you can enjoy free public lectures, workshops, and other cultural offerings with zero cost!

1. Free Public Lectures at Universities

- **What it is:** Many Spanish universities offer free public lectures, particularly on history, literature, science, and current affairs. These are often open to anyone interested, not just students.
- **Where to find them:**
  - **Universidad Complutense de Madrid (UCM):** Offers regular lectures and talks on a variety of academic subjects. Check their website or bulletin for upcoming events.
  - **Universitat de Barcelona (UB):** Hosts a wide range of free academic lectures, including those from visiting scholars. Many are open to the public.
  - **Universidad de Salamanca:** One of Spain's oldest universities, it often hosts open conferences and discussions on history, culture, and modern social issues.
- **Practical Tips:** Universities often have public calendars where you can find details of upcoming free lectures. You may need to register in advance, especially for more popular events.

2. Free Museums on Certain Days

- **What it is:** Many national museums in Spain offer free entry on specific days or times, allowing visitors to explore art, history, and culture without spending anything.
- **Examples:**
  - **Museo del Prado (Madrid):** Free entry Monday to Saturday from 6 to 8 p.m., and Sundays and holidays from 5 to 7 p.m.
  - **Museo Reina Sofía (Madrid):** Free entry Monday, Wednesday to Saturday from 7 to 9 p.m., and Sundays from 1:30 to 7 p.m.
  - **Museu Picasso (Barcelona):** Free entry Thursday afternoons from 6 to 9:30 p.m. and the first Sunday of every month.
- **Practical Tips:** Arrive early, as free admission periods can draw large crowds. Also, check the museum's website in advance for any registration requirements.

3. Casa Encendida (Madrid)

- **What it is:** A social and cultural center that hosts free workshops, lectures, art exhibitions, and screenings on subjects ranging from contemporary art to sustainability.
- **What's free:** Regular free events include public talks, exhibitions, and art installations.
- **Practical Tips:** Many events require advance registration, and tickets can go quickly. Visit their website to browse upcoming free offerings.

4. Cultural Centers (Centro Cultural)

- **What it is:** Most cities in Spain have municipal cultural centers that offer free workshops, concerts, art exhibits, and lectures. These centers are often run by local governments to promote cultural engagement.
- **Where to find them:**
  - **Círculo de Bellas Artes (Madrid):** Offers free entry to public debates, lectures, and film screenings on certain days.
  - **Ateneu Barcelonès (Barcelona):** Hosts a range of free cultural events including talks on literature, politics, and science.
- **Practical Tips:** Cultural centers usually have monthly event calendars available online or at their location. Some events may require prior registration, so check ahead.

5. Libraries and Reading Rooms

- **What it is:** Public libraries in Spain often host free cultural and educational events such as book launches, readings, and public lectures. Libraries are also free to enter and offer quiet spaces for reading and working.
- **Where to find them:**
  - **National Library of Spain (Madrid):** Offers free exhibitions and occasional public talks on literature and history.
  - **Library of Catalonia (Barcelona):** Hosts free cultural programs, including exhibitions and literary discussions.
- **Practical Tips:** Many libraries list their free events on notice boards or websites. Public lectures often don't require registration, but it's worth checking event details in advance.

6. CaixaForum Centers

- **What it is:** CaixaForum cultural centers, located in cities like Madrid, Barcelona, and Seville, regularly host free exhibitions, public talks, and cultural events related to art, science, and social issues.
- **What's free:** While some exhibitions have an entry fee, CaixaForum often offers free public lectures and screenings. There are also free admission days for exhibitions.
- **Practical Tips:** Check the CaixaForum website for event schedules and free entry times.

7. Matadero Madrid

- **What it is:** A former slaughterhouse turned cultural hub, **Matadero Madrid** is known for its free workshops, talks, and exhibitions on urbanism, sustainability, and contemporary art.
- **What's free:** Many of the art installations, film screenings, and public debates are free to attend.
- **Practical Tips:** Matadero often requires advance registration for popular workshops and events. Visit their website for details.

8. Athenaeums (Ateneos)

- **What it is:** **Ateneos** are cultural institutions in many Spanish cities, offering public lectures, literary readings, and political debates. These institutions aim to foster intellectual and artistic exchange.
- **Examples:**

- o **Ateneo de Madrid:** Offers free or low-cost public lectures on topics like literature, history, and philosophy.
- o **Ateneo de Barcelona:** A space for public intellectual debate, often hosting free talks on current events, literature, and politics.
- **Practical Tips:** Many events are free, but some popular events may require you to become a member of the institution to attend regularly.

9. Town Hall (Ayuntamiento) Events

- **What it is:** Town halls in Spain's cities and smaller towns often organize free public events, including lectures, concerts, workshops, and guided tours.
- **Where to find them:**
  - o **Madrid City Hall:** Offers free guided tours of historical city sites and organizes cultural events in public squares.
  - o **Barcelona City Hall:** Hosts free events, including lectures on urban planning and cultural heritage, as well as free city tours.
- **Practical Tips:** Many town halls have event calendars posted online. You can also check tourist information centers for a list of free activities.

10. Free Open-Air Cinema (Veranos de la Villa in Madrid)

- **What it is:** Every summer, the **Veranos de la Villa** festival in Madrid offers free or very low-cost open-air cinema screenings, concerts, and cultural performances in parks and public spaces across the city.
- **What's free:** A wide variety of events, including concerts and outdoor cinema screenings, are free to attend.
- **Practical Tips:** Bring a blanket and snacks for outdoor screenings. Check the festival's schedule for dates and locations of free events.

11. Museo Nacional Centro de Arte Reina Sofía (Madrid)

- **What it is:** In addition to free entry during certain hours, this museum offers free public programs like art lectures, discussions, and film screenings.
- **What's free:** Entry is free Monday through Friday from 7 p.m. to 9 p.m. and on Saturdays from 2:30 p.m. to 9 p.m. Also, check for free lectures and film screenings that the museum regularly hosts.
- **Practical Tips:** Try to arrive early for free entry periods to avoid long lines.

Ferry Travel

Spain's extensive coastline and numerous islands make it an ideal destination for ferry travel. Here are some of the cheapest ferry routes around Spain that offer budget-friendly options for exploring both the mainland and its islands:

1. Barcelona to Mallorca

- **Operator**: Balearia, Trasmediterranea
- **Duration**: Approximately 7-8 hours (overnight options available)
- **Cost**: Prices can start as low as €30-€50 for a one-way ticket, especially if booked in advance.

2. Valencia to Ibiza

- **Operator**: Balearia, Trasmediterranea
- **Duration**: About 2-3 hours
- **Cost**: Tickets typically range from €35-€60 one way, depending on the season and how early you book.

3. Alicante to Mallorca

- **Operator**: Balearia, Trasmediterranea
- **Duration**: Approximately 5-6 hours
- **Cost**: Prices can start at around €30-€40 for a one-way ticket.

4. Cadiz to Tenerife (Canary Islands)

- **Operator**: Trasmediterranea
- **Duration**: Approximately 40-45 hours (overnight ferry)
- **Cost**: Expect prices around €60-€80 for a one-way ticket, though it can vary based on season and availability.

5. Huelva to Canary Islands

- **Operator**: Trasmediterranea
- **Duration**: About 32 hours
- **Cost**: One-way fares generally range from €50-€70, depending on booking time and season.

6. Algeciras to Tangier (Morocco)

- **Operator**: Balearia, Trasmediterranea, FRS
- **Duration**: About 1.5 hours
- **Cost**: One-way tickets can be as low as €30-€40.

7. Barcelona to Menorca

- **Operator**: Balearia, Trasmediterranea
- **Duration**: Approximately 3-4 hours
- **Cost**: Prices usually start at €20-€40, particularly during the off-peak season.

8. Santander to Plymouth (UK)

- **Operator**: Brittany Ferries
- **Duration**: About 20 hours
- **Cost**: Prices for a one-way ticket can start around €100, depending on how far in advance you book.

Tips for Finding Cheap Ferry Tickets:

- **Book in Advance**: Prices are usually lower when tickets are booked early, especially for popular routes.
- **Travel Off-Peak**: If possible, travel during the off-peak season or midweek to find cheaper fares.
- **Check Different Operators**: Several companies operate on popular routes, so compare prices to find the best deal.
- **Look for Special Offers**: Keep an eye on promotions or discounts offered by ferry operators, especially during holiday seasons.

Completely free tours

While some tours ask for a tip at the end, there are many in Spain that are volunteer-led free, particularly in government buildings and cultural institutions, allowing you to explore the country's rich history and architecture with an insider for free!

1. Palacio del Parlamento de Andalucía (Andalusian Parliament)

- **Location**: Seville
- **Tour Details**: This beautiful parliament building offers guided tours that provide insight into the history and function of the Andalusian government.
- **When**: Tours are typically available on weekdays, but it's best to check the official website for specific times.
- **Where to Meet**: The main entrance of the Palacio del Parlamento, located in **Calle José de Gálvez, s/n, 41003 Seville**.
- **Website**: Parlamento de Andalucía

2. Congreso de los Diputados (Congress of Deputies)

- **Location**: Madrid
- **Tour Details**: The Spanish Parliament offers guided tours that explore the history of Spanish democracy and the architecture of the building.
- **When**: Tours are available on weekdays, with time slots usually around 10 AM, 11 AM, and 12 PM.
- **Where to Meet**: Visitors should meet at the entrance to the Congress building, located at **Calle de Floridablanca, 3, 28014 Madrid**.
- **Booking**: Advance booking is required; you can reserve tickets via their official website.
- **Website**: Congreso de los Diputados

3. Palacio de la Moncloa (Moncloa Palace)

- **Location**: Madrid
- **Tour Details**: The official residence of the Prime Minister of Spain, Moncloa Palace offers guided tours highlighting its history and the political significance of the site.
- **When**: Tours are typically offered on Thursdays and Fridays, usually at 11 AM and 12 PM.
- **Where to Meet**: At the entrance gate of the palace, located at **Avenida de la Moncloa, 9, 28071 Madrid**.
- **Booking**: Tours must be booked in advance through their official website.
- **Website**: La Moncloa

4. Museo de la Ciudad (City Museum)

- **Location**: Valencia
- **Tour Details**: While not a government building per se, this museum offers free guided tours that discuss Valencia's history and governance.
- **When**: Check the museum's schedule for specific times; tours often run from 10 AM to 1 PM on weekdays.

- **Where to Meet**: Meet at the museum entrance, located at **Calle de la Nave, 1, 46001 Valencia.**
- **Website**: Museo de la Ciudad

5. Ajuntament de Barcelona (Barcelona City Hall)

- **Location**: Barcelona
- **Tour Details**: The City Hall offers guided tours that delve into the history of Barcelona's municipal government and the building itself.
- **When**: Tours are generally available on weekdays, often starting at 10 AM and 11 AM.
- **Where to Meet**: Visitors should meet at the main entrance of the City Hall, located at **Plaça de Sant Jaume, 1, 08002 Barcelona.**
- **Website**: Ajuntament de Barcelona

6. Palacio Real de Madrid (Royal Palace of Madrid)

- **Location**: Madrid
- **Tour Details**: While primarily a royal residence, the palace often hosts government functions and offers guided tours exploring its history and architecture.
- **When**: Tours are available daily, with time slots typically between 9:30 AM and 8 PM, depending on the season.
- **Where to Meet**: At the main entrance of the Royal Palace, located at **Calle de Bailén, s/n, 28071 Madrid.**
- **Booking**: While the palace charges an entry fee, free guided tours may be available during specific events.
- **Website**: Palacio Real

7. Capitoline Museum of Córdoba (Museo Arqueológico de Córdoba)

- **Location**: Córdoba
- **Tour Details**: This museum offers free guided tours that focus on the archaeological history of Córdoba and its ancient Roman influence.
- **When**: Tours are generally offered on weekends, but it's best to check the schedule.
- **Where to Meet**: Meet at the museum entrance, located at **Plaza de Jerónimo Páez, s/n, 14003 Córdoba.**
- **Website**: Museo Arqueológico de Córdoba

National Parks Pass

Spain is home to some of the most breathtaking national parks in Europe, each offering a unique tapestry of landscapes, ecosystems, and wildlife. From rugged mountains to serene wetlands, these parks are a testament to the country's natural beauty and biodiversity. Here's a chart outlining some of the national parks in Spain, along with their pros and cons regarding entrance fees:

As of now, the **National Parks Pass** (Abono de Parques Nacionales) in Spain is priced at approximately **€18** per person for a one-year validity. This pass grants unlimited access to most national parks across Spain, making it a cost-effective option for nature enthusiasts.

National Park	Location	Pros	Cons	Entrance Fee (Starting Price)
Ordesa y Monte Perdido	Aragon	Stunning mountain scenery, hiking trails, wildlife	Limited facilities, crowded during peak season.	4,50 €
Picos de Europa	Asturias/ Cantabria	Dramatic landscapes, hiking, rock climbing, wildlife.	Limited accessibility, crowded trails in summer.	6,00 €
Teide National Park	Tenerife	UNESCO World Heritage Site, volcanic landscapes,	Crowded at the summit, parking can be difficult.	€27.00 (cable car included)
Doñana National Park	Andalusia	Important wetland habitat, birdwatching, guided tours available.	Limited public access, some areas closed to visitors.	8,00 €
Tablas de Daimiel	Castilla-La Mancha	Unique wetland ecosystem, birdwatching, walking trails.	Seasonal flooding may limit access, limited visitor facilities.	4,00 €

Aigüestortes i Estany de Sant	Mnt. Catalonia	Scenic lakes, hiking trails, alpine scenery.	Limited parking, some trails can be	5,00 €
Garajonay National Park	La Gomera	Ancient laurel forest, hiking, UNESCO World Heritage Site.	Rainy weather can limit visibility, limited accommodation options on	Free
Sierra de Grazalema	Andalusia	Spectacular limestone landscapes, hiking, birdwatching.	Limited public transportation, some trails can be strenuous.	Free
Cabrera Archipelago	Balearic Islands	Marine reserve, snorkeling, boat tours.	Limited access, requires a boat trip from the mainland.	€15.00 (boat trip included)
Sierra Nevada	Andalusia	Spain's highest peaks, skiing (in winter), hiking.	Crowded during ski season, limited facilities in	€17.00 (ski pass not included)

Markets

Spain boasts a rich and vibrant market culture that reflects its diverse regional heritage and artistic flair. From bustling city centers to quaint villages, markets are a staple of daily life, offering everything from fresh produce to artisanal crafts. Each market has its unique character, often showcasing local specialties, handmade goods, and traditional products. The atmosphere is lively, with locals mingling, vendors haggling, and the aroma of street food wafting through the air, creating an immersive experience that invites both locals and tourists to explore.

Best Flea Markets in Spain

1. **El Rastro (Madrid)**: One of the most famous flea markets in Spain, El Rastro is held every Sunday in the La Latina district. It features a vast array of antiques, vintage clothing, and unique trinkets. Arrive early to beat the crowds and snag the best deals.

2. **Mercat de Sant Antoni (Barcelona)**: This revitalized market is not only a hub for fresh food but also hosts a flea market every Sunday. You can find a mix of second-hand clothes, antiques, and collectibles here.

3. **Mercadillo de las Ranas (Granada)**: Held on the first Saturday of each month in the Realejo neighborhood, this market features local artisans selling handmade crafts, vintage items, and delicious street food.

4. **Mercado de las Pulgas (Bilbao)**: This flea market, located in the old town, is a treasure trove of antiques, vintage clothing, and handmade goods. It's a great place to discover local crafts and unique souvenirs.

5. **Flea Market at Parque de la Ciudadela (Barcelona)**: Known as "Lost & Found," this market occurs on select Sundays and showcases a mix of vintage items, crafts, and local food stalls.

Budget Tips for Shopping at Spanish Markets

- **Bargain Wisely**: Haggling is part of the shopping experience in many markets. Don't be afraid to negotiate prices, especially for antiques or handmade crafts. Start lower than what you're willing to pay and work your way up.

- **Cash is King**: While some vendors may accept cards, many prefer cash. Carry small bills to make transactions easier, and it can sometimes lead to better deals.

- **Shop Early or Late**: Arriving at the market early can help you find the best selection and prices. Alternatively, visiting closer to closing time may result in vendors offering discounts to clear out their remaining stock.

-

Spanish Wine

Spanish wine has a rich history dating back over 3,000 years, with the Phoenicians introducing viticulture to the Iberian Peninsula around 1100 BC. Today, Spain is one of the world's largest wine producers, renowned for its diverse regions like Rioja and Ribera del Duero, where traditional methods blend seamlessly with modern innovations to create exceptional wines. Look for bargain bottles of local Spanish wines, including Rioja, Ribera del Duero, and Priorat, at supermarkets or specialty wine shops.

1. Visit Local Wine Bars (Tabernas)

- **What to Do**: Look for local wine bars or "tabernas," especially in regions like La Rioja, Ribera del Duero, and Catalonia, where wine culture is deeply ingrained.
- **Budget Tip**: Order a "copa de vino" (glass of wine) instead of a bottle, as many places offer excellent regional wines by the glass for as low as €2-€4.
- **Pro Tip**: Ask for the "vino de la casa" (house wine), which is usually a local option and often represents great value.

2. Explore Supermarket Selections

- **What to Do**: Major supermarkets like Mercadona, Carrefour, and Lidl offer a range of quality Spanish wines at budget-friendly prices.
- **Budget Tip**: You can find good-quality bottles of wine for €5-€10. Look for labels from lesser-known wine regions such as Jumilla, Utiel-Requena, or Montsant, which often have high-quality wines at lower prices than those from more famous regions.
- **Pro Tip**: Spanish supermarkets frequently offer wine tastings, especially in larger locations, giving you a chance to sample and select without spending much.

3. Attend a Wine Festival

- **What to Do**: Plan your visit around local wine festivals, where you can sample various wines from regional producers.
- **Budget Tip**: Festivals like La Rioja Wine Harvest Festival or Jerez's Sherry Festival often have entry passes for as low as €10-€20, which includes tastings.
- **Pro Tip**: Bring a reusable glass; many festivals charge a deposit for tasting glasses, so having your own can save money.

4. Join a Budget Wine Tasting Tour

- **What to Do**: Look for budget-friendly wine tours, particularly those focusing on smaller, family-owned wineries (bodegas) rather than the big-name brands.
- **Budget Tip**: In regions like La Rioja or Penedès, you can find tours for around €15-€25, which often include several tastings and a vineyard tour.
- **Pro Tip**: Opt for group tours rather than private ones to lower costs, and check for online discounts on platforms like Groupon or Viator.

5. Try Wines from Spanish Cooperatives (Cooperativas)

- **What to Do**: Many Spanish wine regions have cooperatives where local winemakers pool their resources. These places often offer wines at very affordable prices.
- **Budget Tip**: Cooperative wines can cost as little as €3-€7 per bottle, and the quality is often comparable to more expensive wines.
- **Pro Tip**: Look for cooperatives in smaller wine regions, such as Yecla or Rueda, where you can find excellent bargains.

6. Opt for Tapas and Wine Deals

- **What to Do**: Many tapas bars offer deals where a glass of wine is included with tapas for a set price.
- **Budget Tip**: In cities like Madrid or Seville, you can find deals starting at €3-€5, which includes both a tapa and a glass of local wine.
- **Pro Tip**: Ask for local wines specific to that region to get an authentic experience, often at no extra cost.

7. Buy Direct from Wineries (Bodegas)

- **What to Do**: Many wineries offer direct sales, often at lower prices than retail shops.
- **Budget Tip**: By buying directly, you can find bottles starting from €5, and some wineries even offer discounts for purchasing multiple bottles.
- **Pro Tip**: Check for "Vino Joven" (young wine) labels, as these wines are made for early drinking and tend to be more affordable.

8. Sample Cava in Catalonia

- **What to Do**: Cava, Spain's sparkling wine, is affordable and excellent for celebratory experiences. Most of the production takes place in Catalonia, where it's widely available.
- **Budget Tip**: In Barcelona or other Catalan cities, you can find cava bars (Cavaerías) that offer glasses for €3-€6.
- **Pro Tip**: For an affordable bottle, look for Brut or Brut Nature Cava from smaller producers, which often cost €5-€10.

Olives and Olive Oil

Spain is the largest producer of olive oil in the world, accounting for nearly 30% of the global market. Here is how you can experience the liquid gold cheaply!

1. Visit Local Markets

- **Where to Go**: Explore local markets like **Mercat de Sant Josep de la Boqueria** in Barcelona or **Mercado de San Miguel** in Madrid. These markets often have vendors selling high-quality olive oil and a variety of olives at reasonable prices.
- **What to Look For**: Sample different varieties of olives and olive oils, many of which are sold in smaller quantities, allowing you to taste before buying. You might also find local producers selling directly, often at lower prices than larger retailers.

2. Tour Olive Oil Mills

- **Budget-Friendly Tours**: Look for olive oil mills offering free or low-cost tours, especially in regions like **Andalusia** (specifically Jaén, the world's largest producer of olive oil). Many mills provide informative tours about the production process and the health benefits of olive oil.
- **Examples**: Places like **Oleoestepa** in Seville or **Finca La Torre** in Málaga often offer affordable tours and tastings. Check their websites for group discounts or special events.

3. Participate in Olive Oil Tasting Events

- **Local Festivals**: Participate in local olive oil festivals, which often take place in the autumn during the olive harvest season. These events typically feature tastings, workshops, and sometimes free entry to producers' farms.
- **Wine and Olive Oil Pairings**: Some vineyards and olive farms host pairing events where you can taste olives and olive oil alongside local wines, usually at a reasonable price.

4. Join a Guided Tour

- **Budget Tours**: Seek out budget-friendly guided tours that focus on olive oil production. Many tours offer transportation to rural areas and include tastings at multiple farms or mills. Prices vary, but some can be found for under €50 per person.
- **Examples**: Companies like **Eating Europe** and **Devour Tours** offer experiences in cities like Madrid and Barcelona that include visits to local producers.

5. DIY Olive Oil Experience

- **Rent a Car**: If you're in regions known for olive oil production, consider renting a car for a day trip to explore smaller towns and local producers. Look for places offering direct sales, where you can often buy fresh products at lower prices.
- **Explore Countryside**: Take scenic drives through olive groves in Andalusia or Extremadura, where you can stop at roadside stalls or family-run farms selling their products directly to consumers.

More deliciousness to delight in:

- **Spanish Ham (Jamón):** Sample and purchase delicious Spanish cured ham, such as Jamón Serrano or Jamón Ibérico, from local markets or specialty shops for a taste of authentic Spanish cuisine.
- **Saffron:** Spain produces some of the world's finest saffron. Look for bargain packs of saffron threads, known as "azafrán," at markets or specialty food stores for a taste of Spanish luxury.
- **Gourmet Spanish Cheeses:** Sample and purchase a variety of Spanish cheeses, such as Manchego, Cabrales, or Idiazabal, at local cheese shops or markets for a delicious bargain.

See Cave Paintings

Spain is home to some of the **oldest cave paintings in the world**, including some that date back over 40,000 years. These prehistoric artworks provide a fascinating glimpse into early human creativity and symbolism. The most famous of these ancient cave paintings are found in several regions of Spain, particularly in **Cantabria, Asturias, and Andalusia.**

Visiting original cave paintings in Spain is a fantastic way to step back in time and explore some of the earliest human art. While the most famous sites, like Altamira, have restricted access, there are still opportunities to view original prehistoric cave paintings without breaking the bank. Here's a detailed guide on how to see these ancient artworks on a budget, including practical tips, entry prices, and travel advice.

Cueva de Altamira (Cantabria) – Replica Viewing

- **About the Site:** Altamira, often called the "Sistine Chapel of Prehistoric Art," is home to some of the world's most impressive Paleolithic paintings, dating back over 36,000 years. However, due to preservation concerns, the original cave is closed to regular visitors.

- **How to See It on a Budget:**

    o **Museum & Replica:** The **Museo de Altamira** features a detailed replica of the cave known as the **Neocueva**. Here, you can experience a full-scale reconstruction of the original paintings for a fraction of the price of a private tour.
    o **Entry Fees:** Museum admission costs around **€3–€5**, and entry is **free** on Saturdays after 2 p.m. and all day on Sundays.
    o **Practical Tips:** To see the original cave, a **weekly lottery** grants access to a very limited number of visitors (5 people) on Fridays. Entrance to the actual cave is extremely rare, so plan ahead if you're hoping to win a spot.
    o **Getting There:** The cave is located near **Santillana del Mar**, and the nearest major city is **Santander**, about 30 km away. Buses run from Santander to Santillana for about **€5–€7**.
- **More Info:** Museo de Altamira

Cueva de Tito Bustillo (Asturias)

- **About the Site:** Located in the coastal town of **Ribadesella**, the **Cueva de Tito Bustillo** is one of the most important Paleolithic art sites in Europe. The cave is famous for its paintings of animals, particularly horses and deer, dating back over 15,000 years.

- **How to See It on a Budget:**

- o **Entry Fees:** The standard ticket price is **€7**, and **free entry** is offered on certain designated days, typically on International Museum Day (May 18) and during other local celebrations. For students and seniors, reduced rates are available.
- o **Practical Tips:** Access to the cave is seasonal, and during the summer, you'll need to book in advance as entry is limited to small groups to protect the artwork. The cave is closed from November to February.
- o **Getting There:** Ribadesella is well-connected by bus and train. From **Oviedo** or **Gijón**, buses run to Ribadesella for around **€6–€10**. The cave is about a 15-minute walk from the town center.
- **More Info:** Cueva de Tito Bustillo

Cueva de las Ventanas (Granada)

- **About the Site:** Nestled in the **Sierra Arana** near **Píñar**, **Cueva de las Ventanas** offers a unique mix of prehistoric cave paintings and geological formations. This cave is thought to have been inhabited since the Neolithic period.

- **How to See It on a Budget:**

  - o **Entry Fees:** Entrance costs €7, but group discounts are available, and children under 12 enter for free. Sometimes free or reduced-entry days are offered during local festivals.
  - o **Practical Tips:** The cave tour is guided, lasting about 1.5 hours, and includes an exploration of the archaeological significance of the area. Wear comfortable shoes, as the terrain is rugged.
  - o **Getting There:** The town of **Píñar** is about an hour's drive from **Granada**. There are no direct buses, but you can take a bus from Granada to nearby towns and then a taxi or car to the cave.
- **More Info:** Cueva de las Ventanas

Cueva de Nerja (Andalusia)

- **About the Site:** Located near the coastal town of **Nerja** in Andalusia, the **Cueva de Nerja** is famous for its massive chambers and impressive prehistoric paintings, including depictions of animals and abstract shapes. Some of these paintings may date back over 42,000 years, potentially making them the oldest in Europe.

- **How to See It on a Budget:**

  - o **Entry Fees:** Standard entry is €12, but there are discounts for students, seniors, and large groups. Check for free entry days during local holidays or special cultural events.
  - o **Practical Tips:** If you're visiting in the summer, book your ticket online in advance, as the caves are a popular tourist destination. The cave also hosts music concerts during the **Nerja Cave Festival**, which is a unique way to experience the site.
  - o **Getting There:** Nerja is easily accessible from **Málaga** via buses for around €4–€7 each way. The cave is a short bus ride or walk from the town center.
- **More Info:** Cueva de Nerja

7. La Sarga Cave Paintings (Alicante)

- **About the Site:** Located near **Alcoy** in **Alicante**, the **La Sarga cave paintings** depict ancient Neolithic hunting scenes and are one of the lesser-known prehistoric art sites in Spain. The paintings are considered some of the best examples of **Levantine rock art**.

- **How to See It on a Budget:**
    - **Entry Fees:** Entry to La Sarga is **free**, but you must book a guided tour in advance, as visits are only possible at certain times of the year.
    - **Practical Tips:** The best time to visit is during **Heritage Days** in Spain when many archaeological sites, including La Sarga, offer free guided tours. Wear hiking shoes, as the path to the cave is steep.
    - **Getting There:** Alcoy is about an hour from Alicante by car or bus (tickets cost around €5–€7). The site is located a short drive from Alcoy, and it's best to rent a car for easier access.
- **More Info:** Contact Alcoy tourism for details on tours and availability.

Second-Hand Designer Clothing

Fashion in Spain is vibrant and influential, with cities like **Barcelona** and **Madrid** being fashion hubs. Spanish designers are celebrated for their creativity and craftsmanship, with brands like **Zarà**, **Mango**, and **Desigual** gaining international recognition. Finding second-hand designer clothing in Spain at budget-friendly prices can be a treasure hunt! Spain has a growing market for pre-owned luxury fashion, with many shops and online platforms dedicated to affordable second-hand designer pieces. Here's your guide to scoring the best deals on second-hand designer clothing across the country:

1. Explore Local Thrift and Vintage Stores

- **Where to Look**: Cities like Madrid and Barcelona have a vibrant vintage shopping scene. Look for stores in trendy neighborhoods such as Malasaña in Madrid and El Raval or Gràcia in Barcelona.
- **Budget Tip**: Many shops offer discounts for bulk purchases, so consider buying multiple items to maximize savings. Prices can start as low as **€15-€50** for designer pieces in some stores.

2. Visit Flea Markets and Pop-Up Markets

- **Where to Go**: Flea markets like *El Rastro* in Madrid and *Mercantic* in Barcelona often feature vendors selling designer pieces at a fraction of retail prices.
- **When to Go**: Visit on weekdays or off-peak hours for the best selection and fewer crowds. Prices are typically lower compared to weekends.
- **Budget Tip**: Haggle with vendors, as it's common at these markets. Look for items in mixed stalls where designer pieces are mixed with other clothing, as they may be overlooked and sold cheaper.

3. Check Out Consignment Stores

- **What They Are**: Consignment stores specialize in gently-used luxury goods, including clothing, accessories, and handbags. Popular stores include *Le Swing* and *The Storage* in Barcelona, and *Siglo Vintage* in Madrid.
- **How It Works**: Consignment stores often rotate stock quickly, so visit regularly to catch new arrivals.
- **Budget Tip**: Many stores offer discounts during sales or clearance events, where items can be up to **50% off**.

Go Outlet shopping

Outlet shopping is a popular activity for both locals and visitors in Spain, offering the opportunity to find discounted prices on a wide range of products from popular brands. Here are some of the best outlet shopping destinations in Spain:

- **Las Rozas Village, Madrid:**
    - Located just outside Madrid, Las Rozas Village is one of Spain's premier outlet shopping destinations. The village-style complex features over 100 boutiques offering discounts of up to 60% off on luxury fashion, accessories, home goods, and more. Brands include Burberry, Gucci, Prada, and Hugo Boss, among others.
- **La Roca Village, Barcelona:**
    - Situated near Barcelona, La Roca Village is another upscale outlet shopping destination in Spain. Visitors can explore over 130 boutiques offering discounts on designer fashion, sportswear, accessories, and homeware. Brands include Versace, Michael Kors, Lacoste, and Diesel, among others.
- **The Style Outlets, Madrid:**
    - With locations in Las Rozas, San Sebastián de los Reyes, and Getafe, The Style Outlets offer a wide range of fashion and lifestyle brands at discounted prices. Visitors can enjoy savings of up to 70% off retail prices on clothing, footwear, accessories, and more.
- **La Noria Outlet Shopping, Murcia:**
    - La Noria Outlet Shopping is the largest outlet center in the Region of Murcia, offering over 50 stores with discounts on fashion, footwear, accessories, and home goods. Located in the town of Cartagena, the outlet features brands such as Nike, Levi's, Mango, and Desigual.
- **Málaga Designer Outlet, Málaga:**
    - As the first designer outlet in Andalusia, Málaga Designer Outlet offers a selection of international and Spanish brands at discounted prices. Visitors can shop for fashion, sportswear, footwear, and accessories from brands like Polo Ralph Lauren, Calvin Klein, Adidas, and Tommy Hilfiger.
- **Factory Bonaire, Valencia:**
    - Factory Bonaire is one of the largest outlet centers in Valencia, offering a diverse range of fashion, sportswear, accessories, and home goods. The outlet features over 100 stores with discounts on brands such as Guess, Pepe Jeans, Converse, and Desigual.
- **Factory San Sebastián de los Reyes, Madrid:**
    - Located in the outskirts of Madrid, Factory San Sebastián de los Reyes is a popular outlet shopping destination with discounts on fashion, footwear, accessories, and home goods. The outlet features brands like Adidas, Nike, Puma, and Levi's, among others.
- **Factory Sevilla, Seville:**
    - Factory Sevilla is one of the largest outlet centers in Seville, offering discounts on a wide range of products from fashion and footwear to electronics and home goods. Visitors can find brands such as Zara, Mango, Pull&Bear, and Bershka at discounted prices.

Be in a TV audience

If you're looking for an engaging way to enhance your Spanish language skills while immersing yourself in the vibrant culture of Spain, attending a live TV show recording can be a fantastic experience! Not only will you be entertained, but you'll also have the chance to hear the language in action, learn colloquial phrases, and interact with locals. Here's how to make the most of this unique opportunity.

1. "El Hormiguero" (Antena 3)

- **What it is:** One of Spain's most popular talk shows, featuring celebrity interviews, comedy sketches, live music performances, and science experiments. Hosted by Pablo Motos, "El Hormiguero" regularly features A-list international and Spanish stars.

- **How to get tickets:** You can request free tickets through the show's official website. Tickets are in high demand, so you may need to apply several weeks in advance.

- **Location:** Taped in Madrid at the **Neox TV Studios**.

- **Practical Tips:** Arrive early as seating is on a first-come, first-served basis, even with a ticket. The show is often taped live, so dress well and be prepared to clap and cheer a lot!

- **Website for tickets:** El Hormiguero - Audience Tickets

2. "La Resistencia" (Movistar+)

- **What it is:** A late-night talk show hosted by David Broncano, known for its irreverent humor and interviews with famous athletes, actors, and musicians. It's one of Spain's most unique talk shows, with a younger, more rebellious vibe.

- **How to get tickets:** Apply for tickets by contacting the show via its social media channels (particularly **Twitter**) or checking for availability through Movistar+.

- **Location:** Taped at **Teatro Arlequín** in Madrid.

- **Practical Tips:** This show is immensely popular among younger audiences, so tickets are snapped up quickly. Be on the lookout for announcements on social media for ticket availability.

- **Twitter for tickets updates:** La Resistencia on Twitter

3. "El Intermedio" (La Sexta)

- **What it is:** A satirical news show hosted by the famous comedian **El Gran Wyoming**, blending political commentary with humor. It's one of Spain's most beloved political satire shows.
- **How to get tickets:** Free tickets are available by emailing the show's production team at **publicointermedio@globomedia.es** or checking La Sexta's website for updates.
- **Location:** Taped in **San Sebastián de los Reyes**, near Madrid.
- **Practical Tips:** Since it's a political satire show, it's important to have a basic understanding of current events and politics in Spain to fully enjoy the taping. You'll be expected to laugh and participate in the show's energy.

Buy Discount Passes

When exploring Spain, snagging the right discount pass can turn your adventure into a wallet-friendly escapade! For instance, the **Barcelona Pass** is a gem, offering free entry to iconic attractions like La Sagrada Familia and Park Güell, plus unlimited public transport—perfect for those who want to hop around the city. If Madrid is on your itinerary, the **Madrid Tourist Travel Pass** provides unlimited metro and bus access, making it a breeze to discover the city's gems. For a taste of Andalusia, the **Seville Card** grants free access to must-see sites like the stunning Cathedral of Seville and the Real Alcázar, while the **Valencia Tourist Card** is a winner for public transport lovers keen on visiting the City of Arts and Sciences. If you're hitting the Basque Country, don't miss the **Bilbao Card**, which offers discounts on museums and public transport. For art aficionados, buying a specific ticket for the Picasso Museum can save you time, letting you skip the line. And for families enjoying the Costa del Sol, the **Costa del Sol Pass** is your ticket to fun, offering access to various attractions. No matter where you roam in Spain, these passes can help you save a pretty penny while soaking in the rich culture and stunning sights!

Discount passes can be a fantastic way to save money while exploring Spain, especially if you plan to visit multiple attractions or use public transportation. Here are some of the most popular discount passes available in major cities and regions, along with how they can help you save a fortune:

Pass Name	Coverage	Pros	Cons	Starting Price
Barcelona Card	Museums, attractions, transport	- Offers free admission to top attractions in Barcelona- Includes unlimited public transportation	- Limited to Barcelona area- Not valid for all attractions- Limited duration (24, 48, or 72 hours)	45 €
Madrid Card	Museums, attractions, transport	- Provides free entry to major museums and monuments in Madrid- Includes unlimited use of public transportation	- Limited to Madrid area- Not valid for all attractions- Limited duration (24, 48, or 72 hours)	47 €

Andalusia Tourist	Museums, monuments, transport	- Covers admission to top attractions in Andalusia, including Alhambra in Granada and Mezquita-Catedral in Cordoba-Includes unlimited use of public transport in select cities	- Limited to Andalusia region- Not valid for all attractions-Limited duration (2, 4, or 6 days)	40 €
Spain Museum Pass	Museums	- Provides free entry to over 300 museums across Spain, including Prado Museum in Madrid and Picasso Museum in Barcelona	- Does not include transport- Not valid for all museums-Limited duration (1 year from activation)	50 €
National Parks Pass	National parks	- Grants access to all national parks in Spain, including Picos de Europa, Sierra Nevada, and Teide National Park	- Limited to national parks- Not valid for all activities within parks-Limited duration (1 year)	30 €

Loyalty cards that save you huge amounts

- **Youth Hostel Association (YHA) Membership**: If you're planning on staying in hostels during your travels, a YHA membership can provide substantial savings on accommodation costs. Members typically receive discounts on room rates, as well as additional perks like free Wi-Fi and laundry facilities.
- **International Student Identity Card (ISIC)**: Designed for students, the ISIC card offers discounts on a wide range of goods and services, including transportation, accommodation, attractions, and dining. With the card, students can enjoy significant savings on their travels throughout Spain.
- **Youth Card (Carné Joven)**: Available to young people aged 14 to 30, the Carné Joven offers discounts on a variety of products and services, including transportation, entertainment, shopping, and more. With this card, young travelers can save money on everything from train tickets to museum admissions.
- **Senior Citizen Card (Tarjeta Dorada)**: For travelers aged 60 or older, the Tarjeta Dorada provides discounts on train travel throughout Spain, including high-speed and long-distance trains operated by Renfe. Cardholders can enjoy savings of up to 40% on train tickets, making it an excellent option for seniors looking to explore the country by rail.
- **Family Card (Tarjeta Familia Numerosa)**: Families with three or more children can apply for the Tarjeta Familia Numerosa, which offers discounts on a variety of products and services, including transportation, leisure activities, and cultural events. With this card, families can save money on everything from flights to theme park tickets, making it easier to travel together.
- **Amigo Card (Renfe)**: Frequent travelers on Renfe trains can sign up for the Amigo Card, which offers discounts on train tickets and other benefits, such as free cancellations and changes. With this card, frequent train travelers can save money on their journeys throughout Spain.
- **Airline Loyalty Programs**: Many airlines offer loyalty programs that allow members to earn points or miles for their travels, which can be redeemed for free flights, upgrades, and other rewards. By joining a loyalty program and accruing points, travelers can save money on future flights to and from Spain.
- **Hotel Loyalty Programs**: Similarly, many hotel chains offer loyalty programs that provide members with benefits such as discounted room rates, complimentary upgrades, and free nights. By joining a hotel loyalty program and earning points or elite status, travelers can save money on their accommodations during their stay in Spain.

Free Festivals

Spain's vibrant festival culture has roots that stretch back centuries, with some of the earliest celebrations linked to ancient agricultural rituals and religious observances. The first recorded festival is believed to be the **Feria de Abril**(April Fair) in Seville, which dates back to 1847 and was originally established as a livestock fair but has since evolved into a colorful celebration of Andalusian culture, complete with flamenco dancing, traditional attire, and delicious local cuisine. Other significant festivals, such as **Las Fallas** in Valencia, can trace their origins to the 18th century, where they began as a celebration of St. Joseph's Day, featuring the burning of wooden structures called "fallas." Today, these festivals not only honor historical traditions but also promote local pride and community, drawing millions of visitors each year to partake in the exuberance and joy that define Spanish culture.

1. Las Fallas

- **Location**: Valencia
- **Dates**: March 15-19, 2025
- **Description**: A spectacular celebration featuring large, intricate sculptures made of wood and cardboard. The festival culminates in a grand finale where the sculptures are burned.

2. Feria de Abril (April Fair)

- **Location**: Seville
- **Dates**: April 22-27, 2025 (Exact dates may vary)
- **Description**: This famous fair features flamenco dancing, traditional music, and vibrant costumes. While there are paid events, many performances and activities are free to the public.

3. San Juan Night

- **Location**: Various coastal cities, notably Alicante and Barcelona
- **Dates**: June 23-24, 2025
- **Description**: Celebrated on the summer solstice, locals gather on beaches to light bonfires, enjoy fireworks, and celebrate with music and dancing.

4. La Tomatina

- **Location**: Buñol, Valencia
- **Date**: August 27, 2025
- **Description**: Known as the world's largest food fight, participants throw tomatoes at each other. While there are fees for participation, the atmosphere in town is vibrant and free to enjoy.

5. Semana Santa (Holy Week)

- **Location**: Seville and other cities
- **Dates**: April 13-20, 2025
- **Description**: This deeply religious festival includes processions featuring elaborate floats and traditional music. Many processions are free to watch, allowing visitors to experience this cultural event.

6. Carnival

- **Location**: Cádiz, Tenerife, and Sitges
- **Dates**: February 8-11, 2025 (varies by city)
- **Description**: One of the most colorful festivals in Spain, featuring parades, costumes, and street parties. While some events may charge admission, many street performances and parties are free.

7. Festa Major de Gràcia

- **Location**: Gràcia neighborhood, Barcelona
- **Dates**: August 15-21, 2025
- **Description**: A week-long festival featuring street decorations, live music, and various cultural activities. The streets are adorned with colorful and creative decorations, creating a festive atmosphere.

8. Nochevieja (New Year's Eve)

- **Location**: Madrid (Puerta del Sol)
- **Date**: December 31, 2025
- **Description**: Celebrate New Year's Eve at Puerta del Sol, where locals and tourists gather to eat 12 grapes at midnight, marking the start of the new year. The event is free to attend and features music and fireworks.

9. Festival Internacional de Jazz de Madrid

- **Location**: Madrid
- **Dates**: November 2025 (Exact dates TBA)
- **Description**: A month-long celebration of jazz music featuring free concerts in various venues across the city, as well as street performances and events.

10. Fiesta de San Isidro

- **Location**: Madrid
- **Date**: May 15, 2025
- **Description**: This festival celebrates Madrid's patron saint with parades, traditional music, and food stalls. Many events are free, including outdoor concerts and activities in Retiro Park.

11. Fallas de San José

- **Location**: Valencia
- **Dates**: March 15-19, 2025
- **Description**: This festival includes the famous "mascletà," a series of loud firecracker displays, and the burning of the Fallas sculptures. Many activities and street performances are free.

12. Festa de la Mercè

- **Location**: Barcelona
- **Dates**: September 24, 2025
- **Description**: This festival honors the patron saint of Barcelona, featuring free concerts, parades, and cultural activities throughout the city.

13. Almond Blossom Festival

- **Location**: Valle del Jerte, Extremadura
- **Dates**: Late February to early March (exact dates vary)
- **Description**: Celebrate the blooming of almond trees with local festivities, free concerts, and activities showcasing the region's culture.

14. Málaga Film Festival

- **Location**: Málaga
- **Dates**: March 2025 (Exact dates TBA)
- **Description**: While some events may have fees, there are often free screenings and activities celebrating Spanish cinema.

15. Día de los Reyes (Three Kings' Day)

- **Location**: Nationwide
- **Date**: January 6, 2025
- **Description**: Celebrated across Spain, this day features parades, festivities, and traditional treats. Many events, such as the parades, are free to attend.

16. Fira de Santa Llúcia

- **Location**: Barcelona
- **Dates**: November 30 - December 23, 2025
- **Description**: This traditional Christmas market takes place in front of the Barcelona Cathedral, featuring free concerts and activities during the festival.

17. Zaragoza's Fiestas del Pilar

- **Location**: Zaragoza
- **Dates**: October 5-14, 2025
- **Description**: A major festival featuring processions, music, and performances, with many events and activities offered for free.

18. International Festival of Gastronomy

- **Location**: Various cities, including Madrid and Barcelona
- **Dates**: November 2025 (Exact dates TBA)
- **Description**: Experience free tastings and workshops showcasing local cuisine from around Spain.

19. Festival de Jazz de San Sebastián

- **Location**: San Sebastián
- **Dates**: July 2025 (Exact dates TBA)
- **Description**: While some concerts may charge for entry, there are often free performances and jam sessions throughout the city.

20. Festival de la Luz

- **Location**: Santiago de Compostela
- **Dates**: November 2025 (Exact dates TBA)
- **Description**: A festival of light that transforms the city with light installations and projections, many of which are free to enjoy.

Why is so Spain expensive and how can I save money

- **High Demand**: Spain is one of the most visited countries in the world, attracting millions of tourists each year. The high demand for accommodations, dining, and attractions can drive prices up, especially in popular destinations like Barcelona and Madrid.
- **Tourist Areas**: Areas heavily frequented by tourists tend to have inflated prices compared to more off-the-beaten-path locations. For example, accommodations, restaurants, and souvenirs in tourist hotspots like La Rambla in Barcelona or Puerta del Sol in Madrid may be pricier compared to neighborhoods where locals live and work.
- **Peak Season**: Traveling during peak seasons, such as summer months (June to August) and major holidays, can significantly increase costs. Accommodation prices are often higher, and attractions may be more crowded, leading to longer wait times and potentially higher expenses.
- **Dining and Entertainment**: Dining out and experiencing nightlife in Spain can also add up, especially if you frequent high-end restaurants or popular bars and clubs.
-

Despite these challenges, there are several strategies you can employ to save money while visiting Spain:

- **Travel Off-Season**: Consider visiting Spain during the shoulder seasons (spring and fall) when the weather is still pleasant, but tourist crowds are thinner, and prices are lower. Accommodation and flights are often more affordable during these times.
- **Explore Alternative Destinations**: Instead of sticking to major cities, consider exploring smaller towns and villages, where accommodation and dining options may be more budget-friendly. These destinations often offer a more authentic experience and allow you to stretch your budget further.
- **Eat Like a Local**: Venture away from touristy areas and seek out neighborhood eateries, where you can enjoy authentic Spanish cuisine at lower prices. Menu del dia (menu of the day) offers affordable fixed-price meals at many restaurants during lunchtime. Additionally, shop at local markets and supermarkets for picnic supplies or to prepare your meals.
- **Use Public Transportation**: Opt for public transportation, such as buses and trains, instead of taxis or rental cars, which can be expensive. Many cities in Spain have efficient and affordable public transportation systems that make getting around easy and cost-effective.
- **Take Advantage of Free Activities**: Spain offers many free or low-cost activities, including exploring parks, visiting museums on free admission days, and taking self-guided walking tours of historic neighborhoods. Research free events and attractions in the cities you plan to visit to make the most of your budget.

Weird and wonderful facts about that most people don't know about Spain

Let's dive deeper into the origins, weird facts, and some hidden gems behind these fascinating Spanish traditions and quirks:

1. Siesta Tradition:

- **Origin:** The siesta isn't just about a midday nap—it dates back to ancient Roman times. The word "siesta" comes from the Latin "sexta," referring to the sixth hour of the day (around noon), when Romans would take a break from work to avoid the intense heat. This practice later became common in Spain due to its hot climate and agrarian lifestyle.
- **Weird Fact:** While it's a stereotype that all Spaniards nap in the afternoon, in reality, only about 18% of the population still takes siestas today. The concept is more about enjoying a leisurely lunch with family than actually napping.
- **Hidden Gem:** In small Spanish towns like **Málaga** or **Granada**, you'll still see shops close from 2 p.m. to 5 p.m., creating an eerie stillness in the streets—a modern homage to the siesta tradition.

2. Strange Festivals: Baby Jumping Festival (El Colacho)

- **Origin:** Dating back to 1620, this bizarre festival in **Castrillo de Murcia** has its roots in Catholicism. The men, dressed as devils, symbolically leap over babies to protect them from evil and ensure they are free of sin.
- **Weird Fact:** What's even stranger? The babies are laid out on mattresses in the street, and the "devils" jump right over them while bystanders cheer. This practice is said to ward off bad luck and bring blessings to the newborns.
- **Hidden Gem:** Despite its age-old traditions, the festival is often misunderstood by outsiders as dangerous. However, it's surprisingly safe—no baby has ever been harmed in the making of this strange custom!

3. Unusual Cuisine: Calçotada

- **Origin: Calçots**, a type of green onion, are celebrated in **Catalonia** with the **Calçotada festival**, which takes place every winter. It's a communal event where locals gather to grill the onions, peel off their burnt outer layers, and dunk them in **romesco sauce**.
- **Weird Fact:** Eating calçots is a messy affair. Diners are given bibs and encouraged to get their hands dirty. It's one of the few foods where the messier you are, the more you're enjoying it!
- **Hidden Gem:** If you're visiting **Valls**, the home of the calçotada, during festival time, don't miss the **Calçot Eating Contest**, where participants devour dozens of these onions as quickly as they can. Record? Over 300 calçots eaten in under 45 minutes!

4. Unique Architecture: Casa Milà (La Pedrera)

- **Origin:** Designed by the visionary architect **Antoni Gaudí**, Casa Milà (also known as La Pedrera, or "The Quarry") was completed in 1912. It was revolutionary for its organic, flowing lines and whimsical chimneys that look like abstract sculptures.
- **Weird Fact:** Gaudí's designs were so unconventional that some locals initially hated Casa Milà. They mocked it as resembling an open-pit quarry due to its unusual undulating façade.
- **Hidden Gem:** Look closer at the rooftop sculptures—they're not just decorative. Gaudí designed these figures to serve as air vents and chimneys, proving his genius in merging functionality with art.

5. Mystery of the Dalí Museum

- **Origin:** The **Dalí Theatre-Museum** in **Figueres** was conceived by Salvador Dalí himself as a surrealistic experience for visitors. Opened in 1974, it houses some of his most iconic works, and Dalí personally oversaw the museum's design until his death.
- **Weird Fact:** Dalí's body is buried beneath the stage of the museum's main hall, making it both a museum and his crypt. Visitors walk above his tomb, symbolically entering Dalí's dreamlike world.
- **Hidden Gem:** In true Dalí fashion, his grave was designed to allow for one final surrealist twist—his resting place is unmarked, blending into the floor of the museum. You can visit the museum a dozen times and still not realize you're standing right above him.

6. Whistling Language (Txistu)

- **Origin:** In the **Pyrenees** mountains of Spain, especially in the Basque Country, locals developed a unique whistling language known as **txistu** to communicate across the steep valleys. It's thought to be one of the oldest forms of long-distance communication, predating mobile phones by centuries!
- **Weird Fact:** The language isn't just random whistling—it's a full-fledged system with tonal variations that convey complex messages. For centuries, it was a lifeline for shepherds, allowing them to share critical information over miles of mountainous terrain.
- **Hidden Gem:** While the language is fading due to modern communication tools, there are efforts to preserve it. You can still hear **txistu** whistles during local festivals in the Pyrenees if you visit remote villages like **Aas** or **Gorbea**.

7. Eccentric Festivities: Festival of Santa Marta de Ribarteme

- **Origin:** Held in the village of **As Neves** in Galicia, this festival celebrates those who have had near-death experiences. The festival honors **Santa Marta**, the patron saint of resurrection, and involves participants being carried in coffins to the local church.
- **Weird Fact:** The festival is like attending your own funeral—people who survived close calls ride in coffins, paraded through the streets as family and friends follow, often wailing in faux grief.
- **Hidden Gem:** Despite its morbid nature, the event is deeply joyous, as it celebrates life and the second chances granted to participants. It's also an opportunity for locals to reflect on their own mortality.

8. Running of the Bulls (Pamplona)

- **Origin:** The Running of the Bulls, or **Encierro**, is part of the annual **San Fermín** festival in **Pamplona**, which dates back to the 14th century. Originally, bulls were herded through the streets to the bullring for the afternoon bullfights, but over time, it became a daredevil challenge for locals to join them.
- **Weird Fact:** Though thousands participate each year, only about 10% are Spaniards. The event has gained international fame, drawing thrill-seekers from all over the world to test their bravery.
- **Hidden Gem:** Locals have a secret route through the old city's side streets, allowing them to join the run midway or avoid the most dangerous sections. If you befriend a Pamplonan, you might get a few insider tips!

9. Island of Rabbits (Isla de los Conejos)

- **Origin: Isla de los Conejos** is a small, uninhabited island off the coast of **Alicante**, where hundreds of wild rabbits roam free. Legend has it that the island was once used as a laboratory for rabbit testing, and after the tests were discontinued, the rabbits multiplied unchecked.
- **Weird Fact:** The rabbits on the island have adapted to live completely independent of humans. Unlike most wild rabbits, they have little fear of visitors and are known to curiously approach tourists who visit by boat.
- **Hidden Gem:** Despite its overrun population of rabbits, Isla de los Conejos is a pristine spot for nature lovers, with crystal-clear waters perfect for snorkeling and stunning views of the mainland.

Know Before you Go

- **Entry Requirements**: Make sure to check the entry requirements for your nationality. Most travelers from the EU, EEA, and some other countries do not need a visa for short visits, but it's essential to verify the latest requirements before traveling.
- **Health Insurance**: While Spain has excellent healthcare facilities, it's advisable to have travel insurance that covers medical expenses in case of emergencies. European Health Insurance Cards (EHIC) may provide coverage for EU citizens, but additional insurance is still recommended.
- **Currency**: Spain uses the euro (€) as its currency. Be aware of exchange rates and banking fees if you plan to withdraw cash or use your credit/debit cards.
- **Language**: While Spanish is the official language, English is widely spoken in tourist areas. Learning a few basic Spanish phrases can be helpful and appreciated by locals.
- **Safety**: Spain is generally a safe country for tourists, but it's essential to remain vigilant, especially in crowded tourist areas where pickpocketing can occur. Keep valuables secure and be cautious of scams. In Barcelona, the police will not investigate a robbery unless the items taken are over $500.
- **Weather and Seasons**: Spain experiences a Mediterranean climate, with hot, dry summers and mild winters. However, climate variations exist across regions. Coastal areas are typically milder, while inland regions can experience more extreme temperatures. Be prepared for weather fluctuations depending on your destination and the time of year.
- **Health Concerns**: Common health complaints for tourists visiting Spain include sunburn, dehydration, and gastrointestinal issues. It's crucial to stay hydrated, use sunscreen, and practice good hygiene, especially when dining out.
- **Local Customs and Etiquette**: Spaniards are known for their warm hospitality, but it's essential to respect local customs and etiquette. Dress modestly when visiting religious sites, greet people with a handshake or kiss on the cheek (depending on the region), and avoid discussing sensitive topics like politics or religion.
- **Transportation**: Spain has an extensive and efficient transportation network, including trains, buses, and metros in major cities. Consider purchasing transportation passes or tickets in advance to save money and avoid long queues.
- **Cultural Events and Festivals**: Spain is renowned for its vibrant festivals and cultural events throughout the year. Check local event calendars to see if any festivals coincide with your visit and immerse yourself in the local culture.

Practical Tips for First-Time Visitors to Spain

1. Embrace the Siesta Culture

You've probably heard of the siesta, but did you know that it's a real thing? Many shops and restaurants close in the early afternoon for a couple of hours, usually from around 2 PM to 5 PM.

- **What to Do**: If you find yourself in a small town or village during siesta time, take this opportunity to relax! Find a local café, grab a coffee or a cold drink, and soak up the atmosphere. It's a perfect time to plan your next adventure or just enjoy a leisurely break.

- **Pro Tip**: In larger cities, many tourist attractions remain open during siesta hours, but restaurants might be quieter. Use this time to visit sites like museums or parks, where you can avoid the crowds.

2. Master the Art of Tipping

Tipping in Spain can be a bit different from what you might be used to. While it's appreciated, it's not obligatory, and the amount tends to be smaller.

- **How to Tip**: In restaurants, it's common to round up the bill or leave a euro or two if you received good service. For bars, leaving your change is often sufficient.

- **Pro Tip**: If you're enjoying tapas at a bar, simply leave the small change from your bill on the counter. This is a polite way to show appreciation without making a big deal out of it.

3. Don't Skip the "Menú del Día"

Eating out in Spain can be a delightful experience, especially with the "menú del día" (menu of the day).

- **What It Is**: This fixed-price menu typically offers a starter, main course, dessert, and a drink for a very reasonable price, usually around €10-€15.

- **Where to Find It**: Most restaurants and cafés offer this special during lunchtime, typically from 1 PM to 3 PM. It's a fantastic way to try traditional dishes without breaking the bank.

- **Pro Tip**: Look for restaurants filled with locals—this is usually a good sign that the food is both authentic and affordable.

4. Learn Some Basic Spanish Phrases

While many people in Spain speak English, especially in tourist areas, learning a few basic Spanish phrases can go a long way.

- **Useful Phrases**:
    - "**¿Dónde está...?**" (Where is...?)
    - "**¿Cuánto cuesta?**" (How much does it cost?)
    - "**Me gustaría...**" (I would like...)
    - "**La cuenta, por favor.**" (The bill, please.)
- **Pro Tip**: Using even a little Spanish can make your interactions more pleasant. Don't worry about making mistakes—locals appreciate the effort!

5. Navigate Public Transportation Like a Local

Spain has an extensive public transportation system, and knowing how to use it can save you time and money.

- **Metro Systems**: Major cities like Madrid and Barcelona have efficient metro systems. Buy a multi-trip ticket (like the 10-trip ticket in Madrid) to save money.

- **Trains**: If you plan to travel between cities, look into Spain's high-speed trains (AVE). Booking in advance can yield significant savings, and tickets can sometimes start as low as €20 if you catch a good deal.

- **Pro Tip**: Download apps like **Google Maps** or **Citymapper** to help you navigate public transport. They provide real-time directions and schedules, making it easier to find your way around.

6. Watch Out for Tourist Traps

Spain is teeming with tourists, and unfortunately, that means there are plenty of tourist traps as well.

- **Avoiding Traps**: Be cautious of restaurants that have menus in multiple languages displayed prominently outside. Instead, seek out places that have a local vibe and are frequented by locals.

- **Pro Tip**: Use travel forums or apps like **Yelp** or **TripAdvisor** to find hidden gems. You can also ask locals for recommendations; they often know the best spots!

7. Experience the Local Markets

Spain's local markets are a feast for the senses and a great way to experience the culture.

- **What to Look For**: Head to **Mercado de La Boqueria** in Barcelona or **Mercado de San Miguel** in Madrid for fresh produce, artisanal cheeses, cured meats, and local wines.

- **Bargain Tip**: Many vendors offer samples, so don't hesitate to ask. You can often grab a bite to eat at market stalls without spending much.

- **Pro Tip**: Visiting markets is a fantastic way to mingle with locals and enjoy authentic flavors. Plus, it's an inexpensive way to enjoy lunch!

8. Try the Free Tapas

In many cities, especially in Andalusia, ordering a drink at a bar can get you a free tapa.

- **Where to Experience**: In places like Granada and Seville, order a beer or a glass of wine, and enjoy a complimentary tapa with your drink.

- **Pro Tip**: Don't be afraid to ask for recommendations from the bartender! They might have special items or local favorites that you wouldn't find on the menu.

9. Plan Your Museum Visits

Many museums in Spain have specific days or times when entry is free.

- **Examples**: The **Prado Museum** in Madrid offers free entry from 6 PM to 8 PM on weekdays and all day on certain days. Similarly, the **Museo del Rey** in Barcelona has free entry on the first Sunday of every month.

- **Pro Tip**: Check museum websites for special offers, discounts, and free entry days before your visit.

10. Enjoy the Beaches

Spain is known for its stunning beaches, and many of them are free to access!

- **Where to Go**: Popular beaches like **Playa de la Malvarrosa** in Valencia and **Playa de la Barceloneta** in Barcelona are perfect for sunbathing and swimming.

- **Bargain Tip**: Bring your own snacks and drinks to avoid overpriced beachside vendors. Pack a picnic to enjoy while soaking up the sun!

- **Pro Tip**: Arrive early to secure a good spot on the beach, especially during peak summer months when crowds can get large.

11. Attend Local Festivals and Events

Spain is famous for its vibrant festivals, many of which are free to attend.

- **Examples**: Events like **La Tomatina** in Buñol (a giant tomato fight) and **Fallas** in Valencia (a celebration with large sculptures) are iconic and often free to participate in.

- **Pro Tip**: Check local tourism websites for a calendar of events happening during your visit. You might stumble upon lesser-known festivals that offer unique experiences!

Money mistakes to Avoid

Mistake	Solution
Renting Sun Loungers on the Beach	Solution: Bring your own beach towel and find a spot on the sand or look for free public beaches without fees.
Eating at Tourist Trap Restaurants	Solution: Venture off the beaten path and dine at local cafes or tapas bars where prices are more reasonable.
Overpaying for Transportation	Solution: Use public transportation instead of taxis, or consider purchasing multi-day transportation passes.
Booking Last-Minute Accommodations	Solution: Book accommodations in advance to secure lower prices and better options, especially during peak seasons.
Falling for Scams or Pickpocketing	Solution: Stay vigilant, keep belongings secure, and avoid engaging with strangers offering unsolicited assistance.
Exchanging Currency at Tourist Spots	Solution: Exchange currency at banks or use ATMs to withdraw cash, avoiding excessive fees and poor exchange rates.
Overspending on Souvenirs	Solution: Set a budget for souvenirs and prioritize items that are unique and meaningful, avoiding impulse purchases.
Paying Full Price for Attractions	Solution: Look for discounts or free admission days at museums and attractions, or consider purchasing city attraction passes.

Accommodation

Traveling to Spain and staying in luxury accommodations doesn't have to be a pipe dream. With the right strategies, you can enjoy the indulgence of five-star hotels while keeping your expenses in check. Here's a comprehensive guide packed with tips and strategies, including last-minute bookings, day passes, and more, to help you save money while experiencing the best that Spain has to offer.

1. Last-Minute Booking: The Spontaneous Traveler's Advantage

One of the best ways to secure affordable rates at five-star hotels is through last-minute bookings. Many luxury hotels would rather fill their rooms at a reduced rate than let them sit empty. This strategy works best if you're flexible with your travel plans.

How to Utilize Last-Minute Booking:

- **Apps and Websites**: Utilize apps like HotelTonight, Last Minute Travel, and even Booking.com to find exclusive last-minute deals. These platforms specialize in offering discounts for last-minute stays.
- **Timing is Key**: The best time to book is typically within a few days of your desired check-in date. Hotels often start slashing prices in the late afternoon of the day before or the morning of your stay.
- **Be Prepared to Act Fast**: When you see a deal that's too good to pass up, be ready to book immediately. Last-minute deals can disappear quickly, so have your payment information handy to secure your room.

Example: Imagine you're in Madrid, and you decide last minute to treat yourself to a luxury stay at the Ritz. Checking the app just before dinner might reveal a discounted room rate that allows you to experience five-star luxury for half the price!

2. Same-Day Booking: Embrace the Flexibility

Similar to last-minute bookings, same-day bookings can also yield incredible savings. If you find yourself in a city with luxury hotels and the itch to indulge in a pampered night, check prices for same-day bookings.

Tips for Same-Day Booking:

- **Search When You Arrive**: Upon arriving in your destination, take a moment to explore available luxury accommodations for the night. Many hotels will have reduced prices for same-day stays.
- **Consider Off-Peak Times**: If you're traveling during a less busy season, hotels are more likely to offer significant discounts to fill rooms. If you're exploring a popular destination like Barcelona in January, you may find amazing last-minute deals.
- **Utilize Online Resources**: Use hotel booking apps or websites to filter for same-day deals. This can often lead you to incredible discounts for last-minute luxury stays.

Example: If you're wandering through the streets of Seville and decide to extend your stay, checking for same-day booking opportunities could lead to a plush stay at Hotel Alfonso XIII for significantly less than the usual rate.

3. Off-Peak Travel: Timing Your Stay Right

Traveling during the off-peak season can save you substantial amounts on accommodations. In Spain, the peak tourist season is typically summer (June to August), with many cities seeing a surge in visitors.

Benefits of Off-Peak Travel:

- **Lower Hotel Rates**: Luxury hotels often lower their rates during off-peak seasons to attract guests. For example, visiting Barcelona in late November or early February could see substantial savings.
- **Availability of Rooms**: With fewer tourists, you have a better chance of snagging those coveted luxury rooms that might otherwise be booked solid in the summer.
- **Unique Experiences**: Traveling off-peak means you can explore cities at a leisurely pace, enjoy fewer crowds, and have a more authentic experience.

Example: If you visit Valencia in late fall during the Las Fallas festival, you may still enjoy luxury accommodations at reduced prices compared to spring.

4. Use Loyalty Programs: The Long-Term Strategy

If you frequently travel or plan to stay in the same hotel chain, signing up for a loyalty program can provide incredible benefits. Many five-star hotels have loyalty programs that offer perks like free nights, upgrades, and exclusive discounts.

How to Maximize Loyalty Programs:

- **Sign Up Before Your Trip**: If you haven't already, sign up for loyalty programs of hotel chains you plan to stay at. Common luxury chains include Marriott Bonvoy, Hilton Honors, and Hyatt World.
- **Track Your Points**: Keep track of your points to know when you can redeem them for free stays or upgrades. Some programs also offer double points during specific promotional periods, so time your stays accordingly.
- **Use Credit Cards with Travel Rewards**: Many credit cards offer bonus points for hotel bookings and travel-related expenses. Look for cards that partner with hotel loyalty programs to maximize your savings.

Example: If you're a member of Marriott Bonvoy and accumulate points through your stays, you might be able to redeem enough for a free night at the luxurious Hotel Arts Barcelona.

5. Book Directly with the Hotel

Booking directly through a hotel's official website can sometimes provide the best rates and perks. Many hotels offer exclusive deals for direct bookings, including complimentary breakfast, upgrades, or spa credits.

Benefits of Direct Booking:

- **Price Match Guarantees**: Some hotels will match lower rates from third-party sites, ensuring you get the best price.
- **Exclusive Offers**: Look for "members only" rates or promotions that are available only through direct booking.

- **Personalized Service**: Booking directly allows you to communicate special requests or preferences, enhancing your stay.
Example: If you find a great deal on a five-star hotel in Madrid through a third-party site, check the hotel's official website to see if they can match the rate or offer added perks.

Best day passes to five star hotels in with prices

Day passes to five-star hotels in Spain can grant you access to five-star hotels at a 10th of the cost. Sleep somewhere cheap and enjoy luxury in your waking hours with these hotel passes:

- **Barcelona**:
  - W Barcelona: Day passes for access to the hotel's beach club and pool facilities typically range from €50 to €100 per person.
- **Madrid**:
  - The Westin Palace Madrid: Day passes for access to the hotel's spa and fitness center start at around €80 per person.
- **Marbella (Costa del Sol)**:
  - Marbella Club Hotel: Day passes for access to the hotel's beach club, pool, and spa facilities start at approximately €150 per person.
- **Mallorca**:
  - St. Regis Mardavall Mallorca Resort: Day passes for access to the hotel's pools, beach, and wellness facilities start at around €120 per person.
- **Tenerife (Canary Islands)**:
  - The Ritz-Carlton, Abama: Day passes for access to the hotel's pools, beach, and amenities start at approximately €100 per person.

Cheapest hotel chains

In Spain, several budget hotel chains offer affordable accommodations for travelers. Some of the cheapest hotel chains in Spain include:

- **ibis Budget**: Part of the AccorHotels group, ibis Budget offers basic yet comfortable accommodations at budget-friendly prices. With locations in major cities and near transportation hubs, ibis Budget hotels provide convenient stays for budget-conscious travelers.
- **B&B Hotels**: B&B Hotels offers affordable accommodations with modern amenities and convenient locations across Spain. With a focus on providing value for money, B&B Hotels are popular among budget travelers looking for comfortable stays without breaking the bank.

- **Premiere Classe**: Premiere Classe is another budget hotel chain that offers simple and affordable accommodations in Spain. With clean rooms and essential amenities, Premiere Classe hotels provide a no-frills option for travelers on a budget.
- **Travelodge**: Travelodge operates several budget hotels in Spain, offering comfortable rooms and convenient locations at competitive prices. With a focus on providing value and quality service, Travelodge hotels are a popular choice for budget travelers.
- **Campanile**: Campanile hotels offer affordable accommodations with a focus on comfort and convenience. With locations in major cities and near transportation hubs, Campanile hotels provide budget-friendly stays for travelers seeking quality accommodations at affordable prices.

Best Boutique Hotels:

- **Cotton House Hotel, Barcelona:**
  - Located in the heart of Barcelona, this boutique hotel offers elegant rooms, a rooftop pool, and stylish decor inspired by its former life as a textile factory. Prices start at around €200 per night.
- **Hotel Hospes Palacio del Bailío, Cordoba:**
  - Set in a restored 16th-century palace, this boutique hotel features luxurious rooms, a spa, and a beautiful courtyard with orange trees. Prices start at around €150 per night.
- **Hotel Mercer Sevilla:**
  - Situated in the historic center of Seville, this boutique hotel offers stylish rooms, a rooftop terrace, and a Michelin-starred restaurant. Prices start at around €250 per night.
- **Hotel Casa 1800, Granada:**
  - Located near the Alhambra, this boutique hotel offers charming rooms, a rooftop terrace with views of the city, and complimentary afternoon tea. Prices start at around €120 per night.
- **Hotel Marqués de Riscal, Elciego:**
  - Set in the heart of La Rioja wine country, this avant-garde hotel features futuristic architecture, luxurious rooms, and a Michelin-starred restaurant. Prices start at around €400 per night.

Cheapest Guesthouses:

- **Pension Loli, Madrid:**
  - Located in the city center, this guesthouse offers affordable rooms with basic amenities. Prices start at around €40 per night.
- **Hostal San Vicente II, Barcelona:**
  - Situated near the Gothic Quarter, this guesthouse offers simple rooms with shared bathrooms. Prices start at around €50 per night.
- **Hostal La Fonda, Granada:**

- Located in the Albaicín neighborhood, this guesthouse offers budget-friendly rooms with a traditional Andalusian vibe. Prices start at around €60 per night.
- **Hostal Avenida, Valencia:**
  - Situated near the train station, this guesthouse offers clean and comfortable rooms at affordable prices. Prices start at around €45 per night.
- **Hostal Bia, Seville:**
  - Located in the historic center, this guesthouse offers budget-friendly accommodations with a friendly atmosphere. Prices start at around €50 per night.

Unique and Cheap Places to Stay:

- **Camping Sites**: Spain offers numerous camping sites in picturesque locations, including national parks, coastal areas, and mountain regions. Camping is often an affordable option for travelers seeking budget-friendly accommodations with access to nature.
- **Farm Stays (Agriturismo)**: Experience rural life in Spain by staying at a farm or agriturismo accommodation. These properties offer a unique opportunity to immerse yourself in agricultural activities, such as harvesting fruits and vegetables, feeding animals, and participating in farm-to-table dining experiences.
- **Rural Guesthouses (Casas Rurales)**: Casas rurales are rural guesthouses located in charming villages and countryside settings. These accommodations offer cozy rooms, traditional decor, and homemade meals at affordable prices, providing a peaceful retreat away from the hustle and bustle of city life.
- **Hostels and Backpacker Accommodations**: Hostels are a budget-friendly option for travelers seeking affordable accommodations in Spain. Many hostels offer dormitory-style rooms with shared facilities, as well as private rooms at competitive prices.
- **Budget Hotels and Guesthouses**: Look for budget hotels and guesthouses in less touristy areas or smaller cities and towns, where prices tend to be lower compared to popular tourist destinations. These accommodations may offer basic amenities but provide good value for money.
-

Is It Still Cheap to Stay in an Airbnb in Spain?
If you're considering a trip to Spain and wondering whether Airbnb is a good option for accommodations, you're not alone! Many travelers are drawn to the idea of staying in unique spaces, having a kitchen to prepare meals, and often finding better deals than traditional hotels. However, with the evolving regulations surrounding short-term rentals, it's essential to understand what's happening in the Airbnb landscape in Spain. Let's break it down!

Finding Affordable Airbnb Listings

To make sure you're getting the best deals, here are some tips for finding affordable Airbnb options in Spain:

- **Book Early**: If you have fixed travel dates, booking early can help you secure lower rates, as last-minute prices can increase significantly.

- **Search for Registered Listings**: Look for properties that are legally registered with the local government. These listings often adhere to local regulations, providing peace of mind regarding your stay.

- **Flexibility with Dates**: If possible, be flexible with your travel dates. Prices can fluctuate based on demand, so shifting your stay by a day or two may lead to better deals.

- **Consider Different Neighborhoods**: While you may want to stay in a central location, exploring neighborhoods slightly outside the main tourist areas can yield more affordable options without sacrificing too much convenience.

Cheapest Areas to Rent an Airbnb:

- **Valencia**: The third-largest city in Spain, Valencia offers a wide range of affordable Airbnb options, especially in neighborhoods like Ruzafa and El Cabanyal.
- **Granada**: Known for its rich history and stunning architecture, Granada offers budget-friendly Airbnb accommodations in neighborhoods like Albaicín and Realejo.
- **Seville**: The capital of Andalusia, Seville has plenty of affordable Airbnb options, particularly in neighborhoods like Triana and La Macarena.
- **Malaga**: Located on the Costa del Sol, Malaga offers affordable Airbnb accommodations near the beach as well as in the city center.
- **Bilbao**: The largest city in the Basque Country, Bilbao has affordable Airbnb options, particularly in neighborhoods like Casco Viejo and Abando.

Top 25 Attractions in Spain for Cheap or Free

1. Sagrada Familia, Barcelona

Sagrada Familia, Barcelona's iconic basilica, was designed by the famous architect **Antoni Gaudí**. Construction began in **1882** and, even today, the basilica remains unfinished, with completion expected by **2030**. Known for its stunning combination of **Gothic and Art Nouveau styles**, it represents Gaudí's devotion to nature and spirituality. The intricate facades tell biblical stories, while the interior mimics a natural forest with tree-like columns and mesmerizing light through stained-glass windows.

- **Opening Times:** Daily from 9:00 a.m. to 6:00 p.m. (closing hours may vary depending on the season)
- **Money-Saving Tip:** Book tickets online in advance to skip the line and secure a discounted rate. Visiting during off-peak hours (early morning or late afternoon) may offer lower ticket prices.
- **Creative Freebie:** Enjoy a picnic in Plaça de Gaudí while admiring the basilica's exterior.
- **Discount Pass:** Barcelona City Pass or Articket BCN includes Sagrada Familia and other major attractions.
- **Visit the Crypt for Free:** You can access the crypt during religious services at no cost, located at the back of the building.

2. Park Güell, Barcelona

Park Güell, another masterpiece by **Antoni Gaudí**, was built between **1900 and 1914**. Originally intended as a private residential estate, it was transformed into a public park in **1926**. The park is known for its **whimsical architecture**, colorful mosaics, and unique integration with nature. Its famous **serpentine bench** and **multicolored lizard statue (El Drac)** have made it one of Barcelona's most iconic attractions.

- **Opening Times:** Daily from 9:30 a.m. to 7:30 p.m.
- **Money-Saving Tip:** Access free areas of the park, and book Monumental Zone tickets online for discounted rates. Weekdays are less crowded.
- **Creative Freebie:** Sketch the colorful mosaics for a creative outing.
- **Discount Pass:** Articket BCN covers Park Güell and other sites.

3. Alhambra, Granada

The **Alhambra**, a stunning palace and fortress complex in **Granada**, was originally constructed in **889 AD** as a small fortress and later transformed into a royal palace in the mid-13th century by the Nasrid emir **Mohammed ben Al-Ahmar**. The Alhambra became a symbol of the powerful Islamic rulers in Spain, featuring intricate **Islamic architecture**, beautiful **courtyards**, and impressive **gardens**. After the Christian Reconquista in **1492**, it became the royal court of **Ferdinand and Isabella**.

- **Opening Times:** Daily from 8:30 a.m. to 6:00 p.m.
- **Money-Saving Tip:** Buy tickets directly from the official website to avoid third-party fees. Visit in the afternoon for cheaper last-time slots.
- **Creative Freebie:** Explore the Generalife Gardens for free during off-peak times.
- **Discount Pass:** The Granada Card includes Alhambra and other attractions in the city.
- **Night Visits:** If you're looking for a magical experience, book a night visit to see the Alhambra beautifully illuminated with fewer crowds.
- **Generalife Gardens for Free:** If you're on a budget, the gardens and surrounding areas sometimes offer free access during specific times.
- **Albaicín Views:** For a free, fantastic view of the Alhambra, head to the **Mirador de San Nicolás** in the Albaicín neighborhood, where you can take stunning photos of the fortress with the Sierra Nevada mountains in the background.
-

4. Prado Museum, Madrid

The **Prado Museum**, opened in **1819**, is Spain's premier art museum and one of the finest in the world. Originally commissioned by King **Charles III** as a natural science museum, it was later converted into an art museum by **Ferdinand VII**. The Prado houses an unparalleled collection of **European art** from the 12th to the early 20th century, featuring masterpieces by **Velázquez**, **Goya**, **El Greco**, and **Rubens**. Its crown jewel is **Las Meninas** by Velázquez.

- **Opening Times:** Monday to Saturday 10:00 a.m. to 8:00 p.m., Sundays 10:00 a.m. to 7:00 p.m.
- **Money-Saving Tip:** Visit during free hours (6:00 p.m. to 8:00 p.m. on weekdays and 5:00 p.m. to 7:00 p.m. on Sundays).

- **Discount Pass:** Madrid Art Walk Pass covers Prado, Reina Sofia, and Thyssen-Bornemisza. Explore the Prado with a **free audio guide** (available online), which allows you to enjoy an informative self-guided tour at your own pace.

Tips

- **Visit During Free Hours:** Arrive 30 minutes early during free entry times to beat the queues, especially on weekends.
- **Plan Your Route:** The museum is large, so plan ahead to see the highlights like **Las Meninas**, **The Garden of Earthly Delights**, and **The Third of May 1808**.
- **Picnic in Retiro Park:** After your visit, head to **Retiro Park**, just a short walk away, for a peaceful and free picnic to unwind.

5. Royal Palace of Madrid

The **Royal Palace of Madrid**, also known as **Palacio Real**, is the largest functioning royal palace in Europe. Construction began in **1735** on the orders of King **Philip V** and was completed in **1764**. Built on the site of a former Moorish fortress, the palace has served as the official residence for Spanish monarchs, though today it is used primarily for state ceremonies. It boasts **2,800 rooms** filled with art, tapestries, and stunning architecture, and is surrounded by the beautiful **Sabatini Gardens** and **Campo del Moro**.

- **Opening Times:** Daily from 10:00 a.m. to 6:00 p.m.
- **Money-Saving Tip:** Book tickets in advance online or purchase combo tickets with nearby attractions.
- **Creative Freebie:** Stroll through the Sabatini Gardens for free.
- **Discount Pass:** Madrid Card includes the Royal Palace and other landmarks.

- **Free Entry Days:** EU citizens can visit for free from **Monday to Thursday** from 4:00 p.m. to 6:00 p.m. (October to March) or 5:00 p.m. to 7:00 p.m. (April to September). Free entry is also available for students and seniors.
- **Book Tickets Online:** Save time by purchasing your tickets online in advance to skip long lines.
- **Combination Tickets:** Opt for combo tickets that include entry to nearby attractions like the **Almudena Cathedral**or the **Royal Armory** for additional savings.

- **Changing of the Guard:** Witness the **Changing of the Guard** ceremony, which takes place every Wednesday and Saturday at noon, free of charge.

6. Park de la Ciutadella, Barcelona

Park de la Ciutadella is one of the most significant green spaces in Barcelona. Built on the site of a former 18th-century military fortress, the park was transformed into a public space in **1888** for the **Universal Exhibition**. It houses **Barcelona's zoo**, the **Catalan Parliament**, the beautiful **Cascada Monumental fountain**, and several museums. The park's design features sculptures, serene gardens, and expansive walking paths, making it a favorite among locals and tourists alike.

- **Opening Times:** Open 24 hours daily
- **Money-Saving Tip:** Enjoy the park's gardens, lake, and monuments for free. Bring your own picnic.
- **Creative Freebie:** Rent a rowboat for a low fee or play frisbee with friends.
- **Discount Pass:** N/A (Free attraction)

7. Plaza Mayor, Madrid

- **Opening Times:** Open 24 hours daily
- **Money-Saving Tip:** Wander and people-watch for free. Avoid eating at the plaza's restaurants.
- **Creative Freebie:** Participate in free festivals or street performances.
- **Discount Pass:** N/A (Free attraction)

8. La Rambla, Barcelona

- **Opening Times:** Open 24 hours daily
- **Money-Saving Tip:** Stroll and enjoy the street performances without buying souvenirs.
- **Creative Freebie:** Visit the nearby Mercat de Sant Josep de la Boqueria to sample local delicacies for free.
- **Discount Pass:** N/A (Free attraction)

9. Montserrat Monastery, Catalonia

The **Montserrat Monastery**, perched high in the **Montserrat Mountains** of Catalonia, was founded in **1025**. It became a significant pilgrimage site, home to the revered statue of the **Black Madonna (La Moreneta)**, the patron saint of Catalonia. Throughout history, it has been a center of cultural, spiritual, and religious importance in the region. The stunning location offers breathtaking views, and the monastery continues to be an active site of worship, drawing visitors for its religious, cultural, and natural significance.

- **Opening Times:** Daily from 9:00 a.m. to 5:45 p.m.
- **Free Access to the Monastery:** Entry to the basilica and to view the **Black Madonna** is free, though donations are appreciated.
- **Creative:** Hike the trails for free and enjoy a scenic picnic.

10. La Concha Beach, San Sebastián

- **Opening Times:** Open 24 hours daily
- **Money-Saving Tip:** Bring your own snacks to avoid pricey beachfront eateries.
- **Creative Freebie:** Enjoy beach activities like volleyball or frisbee for free.
- **Discount Pass:** N/A (Free attraction)

11. Seville Cathedral and Giralda Tower

- **Opening Times:** Monday to Saturday 10:45 a.m. to 5:00 p.m., Sunday 2:30 p.m.

The **Seville Cathedral**, completed in **1507**, is the largest Gothic cathedral in the world and a UNESCO World Heritage Site. It was built on the site of a former **Almohad mosque**, and its bell tower, **La Giralda**, was originally the mosque's minaret, which dates back to the **12th century**. The cathedral houses the tomb of **Christopher Columbus** and is known for its breathtakingly ornate interiors, vast size, and historical significance. **La Giralda Tower** offers panoramic views of the city and stands as a symbol of Seville's rich history.

Why Visit

- **World's Largest Gothic Cathedral:** The sheer size and grandeur of the cathedral's Gothic architecture are awe-inspiring.
- **Historical Significance:** Home to the tomb of **Christopher Columbus**, it's a key landmark in Spanish history.
- **Stunning Views:** Climb **La Giralda Tower** for panoramic views of Seville, one of the best viewpoints in the city.

How to Save on Entrance Costs

- **Free Entry on Sundays:** The cathedral offers free entry on **Sundays** from 2:30 p.m. to 6:00 p.m. for visitors, although it can get crowded.

24. Guggenheim Museum, Bilbao

The **Guggenheim Museum** in Bilbao, designed by **Frank Gehry** and opened in **1997**, has rapidly become one of Spain's most iconic modern art museums. Its **curvaceous titanium structure** and avant-garde exhibitions have drawn attention worldwide. Now, it's becoming more popular with modern art enthusiasts and architecture lovers.

Why Visit:

- **Stunning Architecture:** The building itself is a work of art, with its innovative design and reflective surfaces.
- **World-Class Exhibits:** Explore cutting-edge contemporary art exhibitions from international artists.
- **Outdoor Sculptures:** The museum grounds feature famous sculptures like **Jeff Koons' Puppy** and **Louise Bourgeois' Maman**.

How to Save on Entrance Costs:

- **Free for Under-12s:** Children under 12 can enter the museum for free.
- **Discounted Tickets:** Reduced rates for students, seniors, and large families.
- **Bilbao Bizkaia Card:** This pass offers discounts on the Guggenheim and other local attractions.

Insider Tips:

- **Exterior Art for Free:** You can enjoy much of the museum's outdoor sculptures and architecture without purchasing a ticket.
- **Visit the Rooftop:** The museum's upper levels offer panoramic views of Bilbao, often without extra charge.

13. Plaza de España, Seville

- **Opening Times:** Open 24 hours daily
- **Money-Saving Tip:** Explore the plaza and take photos for free.
- **Creative Freebie:** Participate in photo scavenger hunts.
- **Discount Pass:** N/A (Free attraction)

14. Aqueduct of Segovia

- **Opening Times:** Open 24 hours daily
- **Money-Saving Tip:** Admire the aqueduct for free from the outside.
- **Creative Freebie:** Picnic in the nearby park with views of the aqueduct.
- **Discount Pass:** N/A (Free attraction)

15. Tibidabo Amusement Park, Barcelona

- **Opening Times:** Vary by season; generally 11:00 a.m. to 6:00 p.m. on weekends
- **Money-Saving Tip:** Enjoy free panoramic views of Barcelona from the park's hilltop.
- **Creative Freebie:** Hike up the hill for free scenic views.
- **Discount Pass:** N/A

16. Casa Batlló, Barcelona

- **Opening Times:** Daily from 9:00 a.m. to 8:15 p.m.
- **Money-Saving Tip:** Admire the exterior for free, and consider buying combined tickets with other Gaudí attractions.
- **Creative Freebie:** Explore other nearby Gaudí buildings for free.
- **Discount Pass:** Articket BCN covers Gaudí attractions.

17. Toledo Cathedral

- **Opening Times:** Monday to Saturday 10:00 a.m. to 6:30 p.m., Sunday 2:00 p.m. to 6:30 p.m.
- **Money-Saving Tip:** Attend a religious service for free access to the cathedral interior.
- **Creative Freebie:** Stroll through Toledo's streets and admire the cathedral's exterior.
- **Discount Pass:** Toledo Card includes the cathedral and other attractions.

18. Montserrat Funicular, Catalonia

- **Opening Times:** Daily from 9:00 a.m. to 6:00 p.m.
- **Money-Saving Tip:** Use group or family discounts for the funicular.
- **Creative Freebie:** Hike up the mountain for free.
- **Discount Pass:** N/A

19. Valencia City of Arts and Sciences

The **City of Arts and Sciences** (Ciudad de las Artes y las Ciencias) is a futuristic architectural complex in **Valencia**, designed by the renowned architect **Santiago Calatrava** and opened in **1998**. It is one of the most iconic modern landmarks in Spain, comprising several buildings dedicated to science, nature, and art. Key attractions include the **Hemisfèric** (IMAX cinema), the **Prince Felipe Science Museum**, the **Oceanogràfic** (Europe's largest aquarium), and the stunning **Palau de les Arts Reina Sofia** (opera house).

- **Opening Times:** Open daily; individual attractions vary
- **Visit the Gardens and Reflecting Pools for Free:** Stroll around the outdoor areas, such as **L'Umbracle**—a garden promenade, and admire the futuristic landscape without spending a penny.
- **Best Time for Photos:** Visit early in the morning or during sunset for the best lighting and fewer crowds, making it the perfect time for photography.
- **Bring Snacks:** There are picnic-friendly areas around the complex, allowing you to save on meals by bringing your own food.
- **Discounts on Weekdays:** Tickets for some attractions are cheaper during weekdays, especially outside peak tourist seasons, so plan your visit accordingly.

20. Costa del Sol Beaches, Malaga

- **Opening Times:** Open 24 hours daily
- **Money-Saving Tip:** Enjoy the beach for free and bring your own gear.
- **Creative Freebie:** Play beach games or enjoy the sunset.
- **Discount Pass:** N/A (Free attraction)

21. Museo Nacional de Arte de Cataluña (MNAC), Barcelona

Located in the impressive **Palau Nacional** on **Montjuïc Hill**, the **Museu Nacional d'Art de Catalunya (MNAC)** was established in **1934**. It houses a vast collection of **Catalan art**, including Romanesque church paintings, Gothic art, and works by modern masters like **Dalí** and **Picasso**. It's gaining popularity due to its comprehensive representation of Catalan culture and art.

Why Visit:

- **Extensive Art Collection:** The MNAC spans a wide range of artistic styles, from medieval art to modernism.
- **Spectacular Location:** Situated on **Montjuïc Hill**, the museum offers incredible views of Barcelona.
- **Cultural Immersion:** Get a deep dive into the history and evolution of Catalan art.

How to Save on Entrance Costs:

- **Free Entry Saturdays:** Free entry on Saturdays after 3:00 p.m. and on the first Sunday of every month.
- **Discounts for Young People and Seniors:** Students, seniors, and large families can enjoy discounted tickets.
- **Articket BCN Pass:** Includes access to MNAC and other top museums in Barcelona, offering savings if you plan to visit multiple sites.

Insider Tips:

- **Combine with Magic Fountain Show:** Visit in the evening and enjoy the nearby **Magic Fountain of Montjuïc**show, a free water and light spectacle.
- **Panoramic Views:** The museum's terrace provides fantastic views of the city and is free to access.

22. Basilica of San Isidoro, León

The **Basilica of San Isidoro** is located in **León** and is becoming increasingly popular for its incredible collection of **Romanesque frescoes** and historical significance. Built in the **11th century**, it's known as the **Sistine Chapel of Romanesque Art** due to its beautifully preserved murals.

Why Visit:

- **Historical Significance:** This basilica is one of the finest examples of Romanesque architecture and art in Europe.
- **Royal Pantheon:** Houses the tombs of the kings of León and is renowned for its frescoed ceilings.
- **Romanesque Art:** The frescoes are some of the best-preserved examples from the Middle Ages.

How to Save on Entrance Costs:

- **Guided Tour Included:** Admission typically includes a guided tour of the Royal Pantheon and the museum.
- **Discounted Tickets:** Reduced prices for students, seniors, and large families.

- **Free Entry:** Check for special free entry days during public holidays or religious celebrations.

Insider Tips:

- **Visit Early:** Go early to avoid crowds and have a more peaceful visit.
- **Stay Nearby:** Combine your visit with a stay in the **Parador de León**, a historic hotel in a former monastery.

23. Picos de Europa National Park, Asturias/Cantabria/León

Picos de Europa, Spain's first national park, established in **1918**, is now becoming a popular destination for nature enthusiasts. Located across the regions of **Asturias, Cantabria**, and **León**, this stunning park is famous for its dramatic peaks, deep gorges, and rich wildlife.

Why Visit:

- **Natural Beauty:** The park boasts breathtaking landscapes, including jagged peaks, lush valleys, and glacial lakes.
- **Outdoor Activities:** A paradise for hiking, birdwatching, and adventure sports like rock climbing.
- **Cultural Heritage:** Explore traditional mountain villages that retain their historical charm.

How to Save on Entrance Costs:

- **Free Entry:** The park itself is free to enter and explore.
- **Paid Attractions Inside:** Some visitor centers or guided experiences within the park, such as the **Covadonga Lakes** or **Cable Car of Fuente Dé**, may require a fee.
- **Public Transportation:** Use local buses to reach the park rather than booking an expensive tour.

Insider Tips:

- **Hiking Trails:** Many free hiking trails provide stunning views without the need for paid guides.
- **Early Morning or Late Evening Visits:** To avoid crowds, visit the most popular spots like **Covadonga Lakes**early or late in the day.
- **Pack a Picnic:** Bring your own food, as options within the park can be pricey and limited.

-

25. Palau de la Música Catalana, Barcelona

Designed by **Lluís Domènech i Montaner**, the **Palau de la Música Catalana** opened in **1908** and is one of the finest examples of **Catalan Modernism**. Known for its intricate mosaic work, stained glass, and innovative design, it has become a favorite destination for those seeking to explore Barcelona's artistic heritage.

Why Visit:

- **Architectural Masterpiece:** The concert hall's colorful interior, including its **stained-glass skylight**, is a sight to behold.
- **Cultural Hub:** It regularly hosts performances ranging from classical music to modern concerts.
- **UNESCO World Heritage Site:** Recognized for its contribution to Catalan culture and architecture.

How to Save on Entrance Costs:

- **Guided Tours:** A guided tour of the building is often cheaper than attending a concert and allows you to appreciate the full architectural details.
- **Discounted Concert Tickets:** Check for discounted last-minute tickets, especially for lesser-known performances.
- **Articket BCN Pass:** Includes access to several Modernist landmarks in Barcelona, including Palau de la Música Catalana.

Insider Tips:

- **Visit During the Day:** Even if you're not attending a concert, the guided tour offers excellent insight into the building's history and design.
- **Photographer's Dream:** The stunning interior is perfect for photography, but check the rules before snapping away.
- **Combine with Nearby Attractions:** The **Gothic Quarter** and **Barcelona Cathedral** are within walking distance, allowing you to maximize your day in the city.

Common Tourist Taxes in Spain

1. **Tourist Tax (Tasa Turística)**:

   ○ **Where It Applies**: This tax is common in popular tourist destinations such as Barcelona, Mallorca, and the Canary Islands.

   ○ **How It Works**: The tax usually applies per person, per night, and the amount varies by region and the type of accommodation. For example, in Barcelona, it can range from €0.75 to €2.25 per night, depending on the star rating of your hotel.

   ○ **Exemptions**: Children under 17 years old are typically exempt, and some regions may waive the tax after a certain number of nights.

2. **City Tax**:

   ○ **Where It Applies**: Cities like Valencia and San Sebastián have their own city taxes.

   ○ **How It Works**: Similar to the tourist tax, this fee is applied per person, per night. In Valencia, it can be around €0.50 to €2.00, depending on accommodation type.

   ○ **Exemptions**: Again, children under 16 are usually exempt, and some cities offer discounts for long stays.

3. **Sustainable Tourism Tax**:

   ○ **Where It Applies**: Particularly in Balearic Islands (Mallorca, Menorca, Ibiza).

   ○ **How It Works**: This is a specific fee aimed at promoting sustainable tourism. It generally applies to all visitors staying in tourist accommodation.

   ○ **Exemptions**: Children under 16 are usually exempt, as well as locals.

Tips to Save on Tourist Taxes

1. **Choose Accommodations Wisely**:

   ○ **Look for Hotels with No Tourist Tax**: Some smaller hotels, hostels, or guesthouses may not charge a tourist ta

How to Enjoy ALLOCATING Money in Spain

'Money's greatest intrinsic value—and this can't be overstated—is its ability to give you control over your time.' - Morgan Housel

Notice I have titled the chapter how to enjoy allocating money in Spain. I'll use saving and allocating interchangeably in the book, but since most people associate saving to feel like a turtleneck, that's too tight, I've chosen to use wealth language. Rich people don't save. They allocate. What's the difference? Saving can feel like something you don't want or wish to do and allocating has your personal will attached to it.

And on that note, it would be helpful if you considered removing the following words and phrase from your vocabulary for planning and enjoying your Spain trip:

- Wish

- Want

- Maybe someday

These words are part of poverty language. Language is a dominant source of creation. Use it to your advantage. You don't have to wish, want or say maybe someday to Spain. You can enjoy the same things millionaires enjoy in Spain without the huge spend.

'People don't like to be sold-but they love to buy.' - Jeffrey Gitomer.

Every good salesperson who understands the quote above places obstacles in the way of their clients' buying. Companies create waiting lists, restaurants pay people to queue outside in order to create demand. People reason if something is so in demand, it must be worth having but that's often just marketing. Take this sales maxim 'People don't like to be sold-but they love to buy and flip it on its head to allocate your money in Spain on things YOU desire. You love to spend and hate to be sold. That means when something comes your way, it's not 'I can't afford it,' it's 'I don't want it' or maybe 'I don't want it right now'.

Saving money doesn't mean never buying a latte, never taking a taxi, never taking vacations (of course, you bought this book). Only you get to decide on how you spend and on what. Not an advice columnist who thinks you can buy a house if you never eat avocado toast again.

I love what Kate Northrup says about affording something: "If you really wanted it you would figure out a way to get it. If it were that VALUABLE to you, you would make it happen."

I believe if you master the art of allocating money to bargains, it can feel even better than spending it! Bold claim, I know. But here's the truth: Money gives you freedom and options. The more you keep in your account and or invested the more freedom and options you'll have. The principal reason you should save and allocate money is TO BE FREE! Remember, a trip's main purpose is relaxation, rest and enjoyment, aka to feel free.

When you talk to most people about saving money on vacation. They grimace. How awful they proclaim not to go wild on your vacation. If you can't get into a ton of debt enjoying your once-in-a-lifetime vacation, when can you?

When you spend money 'theres's a sudden rush of dopamine which vanishes once the transaction is complete. What happens in the brain when you save money? It increases feelings of security and peace. You don't need to stress life's uncertainties. And having a greater sense of peace can actually help you save more money.' Stressed out people make impulsive financial choices, calm people don't.'

The secret to enjoying saving money on vacation is very simple: never save money from a position of lack. Don't think 'I wish I could afford that'. Choose not to be marketed to. Choose not to consume at a price others set. Don't save money from the flawed premise you don't have enough. Don't waste your time living in the box that society has created, which says saving money on vacation means sacrifice. It doesn't.

Traveling to Spain can be an expensive endeavor if you don't approach it with a plan, but you have this book which is packed with tips. The biggest other asset is your perspective.

Winning the Vacation Game
The inspiration for these books struck me during a Vipassana meditation retreat. As I contemplated the excitement that precedes a vacation, I couldn't help but wish that we could all carry that same sense of anticipation in our daily lives. It was from this introspection that the concept of indulging in luxurious trips on a budget was born. The driving force behind this idea has always been the prevalence of disregarded inequalities.

A report from the Pew Charitable Trusts unveiled a stark reality: only about 4% of individuals born into the lowest income quintile, the bottom 20%, in the United States manage to ascend to the top income quintile during their lifetime. This trend is mirrored in many parts of Europe, underscoring the immense hurdles faced by those from disadvantaged backgrounds, including myself, in their pursuit of financial security.

To compound this, a comprehensive study conducted by researchers at Stanford University and published in the Journal of Personality and Social Psychology illuminated a compelling connection between career choices, personal fulfillment, and income. It revealed that individuals who prioritize intrinsic factors like passion often find themselves with lower average incomes, highlighting the intricate dynamics at play in the pursuit of one's dreams. Either you're in a low-income career, believing you can't afford to travel, or you're earning well but desperately need a vacation due to your work being mediocre at best. Personally, I believe it's better to do what you love and take time to plan a luxury trip on a budget. Of course, that, in itself, is a luxurious choice not all of us have. I haven't even mentioned Income, education, and systemic inequalities that can lock restrict travel opportunities for many.

Despite these challenging realities, I firmly believe that every individual can have their dream getaway. I am committed to providing practical insights and strategies that empower individuals to turn their dream vacations into a tangible reality without breaking the bank.

How to feel RICH in Spain

You don't need millions in your bank account to feel rich while exploring Spain. What "feeling rich" means can vary from person to person. Researchers have pooled data from over 1.6 million individuals across 162 countries and found that wealthier people often experience more positive "self-regard emotions," such as confidence, pride, and determination.

Here are some experiences to see, do, and taste in Spain that will leave you overflowing with gratitude for your luxurious trip without breaking the bank.

Michelin-Star Dining on a Budget
Achieving a Michelin Star is the pinnacle of culinary achievement, often associated with high prices. However, Spain boasts Michelin-starred restaurants that offer lunch menus for as low as €15! For an unforgettable treat, visit **Restaurante Egaña-Oriza** in San Sebastián, where you can indulge in exquisite local dishes crafted from seasonal ingredients. If fine dining isn't your thing, don't worry—further in this guide, you'll find a range of affordable eats across Spain that could easily earn a Michelin Star for their quality and flavor.

Sweet Indulgence
While money can't buy happiness, it can buy cake—and isn't that close enough? Jokes aside, **Patisserie Holtkamp** in Madrid has transformed cakes and pastries into edible masterpieces. Stop by to taste their renowned buttery croissants, hailed as some of the best in Spain, or indulge in a slice of their decadent cakes. Your taste buds will thank you!

Stunning Views from Rooftop Bars
Even if you're not staying in a penthouse, you can still enjoy breathtaking views. Check out **Terraza 360** in Barcelona for a stunning sunset view while sipping on a delicious cocktail for the price of just one drink. For a more budget-friendly experience, head over to **La Terraza de Cine** in Madrid, where you can enjoy fantastic city views without spending a fortune.

Happy Hour Fun
If you want to keep the good times rolling, make your way to **Cervecería 100 Montaditos**, which has locations throughout Spain. Their happy hour offers a selection of beers and montaditos (small sandwiches) for as low as €1 each! This is a great way to experience local flavors without emptying your wallet.

These are just a few ideas to remind you that visiting Spain on a budget doesn't have to feel like a sacrifice. Now, let's dive into the nuts and bolts of experiencing Spain without spending a fortune!

How to use this book

Google and TripAdvisor are your on-the-go guides while traveling, a travel guide adds the most value during the planning phase, and if you're without Wi-Fi. Always download the google map for your destination - having an offline map will make using this guide much more comfortable. For ease of use, we've set the book out the way you travel, booking your flights, arriving, how to get around, then on to the money-saving tips. The tips we ordered according to when you need to know the tip to save money, so free tours and combination tickets feature first. We prioritized the rest of the tips by how much money you can save and then by how likely it was that you could find the tip with a google search. Meaning those we think you could find alone are nearer the bottom. I hope you find this layout useful. If you have any ideas about making Super Cheap Insider Guides easier to use, please email me philgattang@gmail.com

A quick note on How We Source Super Cheap Tips
We focus entirely on finding the best bargains. We give each of our collaborators $2,000 to hunt down never-before-seen deals. The type you either only know if you're local or by on the ground research. We spend zero on marketing and a little on designing an excellent cover. We do this yearly, which means we just keep finding more amazing ways for you to have the same experience for less.

Now let's get started with juicing the most pleasure from your trip to Spain with the least possible money!

Planning your trip

When to visit

The first step in saving money on your trip to Spain is timing. If you're not tied to school holidays, the best time to visit is during the shoulder season months of March, April, and October through November.

Traveling in the off-season offers a wealth of benefits. You'll encounter fewer crowds, making it easier to explore popular sights without feeling jostled. Additionally, hotel bookings will be significantly cheaper, and you won't need to buy skip-the-line tickets for many attractions. Plus, during these shoulder months, you can enjoy the beautiful fall foliage in parks and gardens across the country.

The high season runs from late April through September, during which prices can double. If you plan to visit during this time, it's essential to book accommodations well in advance to avoid steep price hikes.

If you find yourself in Spain during the peak season, expect to pay higher rates for hotels and airfare, along with long lines at some of the most popular attractions. But don't despair—there are countless hacks to save on accommodations in Spain that we'll delve into later. Additionally, if you visit in summer, Spain bursts with vibrant free festivals, from the Feria de Abril in Seville to La Tomatina in Buñol, ensuring there's something for everyone to enjoy.

Freebies month-by-month

Here's a month-by-month guide to free events and festivals happening across Spain, offering an array of cultural experiences without the cost. Each month features unique celebrations that showcase Spain's rich heritage, vibrant culture, and local traditions.

January

- **Día de Reyes (Three Kings' Day)**: Celebrated on January 6th, this festival includes parades across the country, especially in cities like Madrid and Barcelona, with festive music, performances, and sweets.

February

- **Carnival Celebrations**: Various cities, such as Cádiz and Tenerife, host vibrant carnival celebrations featuring parades, music, and dancing. While some events might have a fee, many street parties and performances are free to attend.

March

- **Las Fallas**: From March 15-19 in Valencia, experience the famous festival with free events, parades, and fireworks. The burning of the fallas sculptures is a highlight of this lively celebration.

April

- **Semana Santa (Holy Week)**: Held in various cities like Seville and Málaga, free processions take place throughout the week, showcasing traditional music and elaborate floats from April 1-7, 2025.

May

- **Feria de Abril (April Fair)**: Although it usually occurs in April, the spirit continues into May with free events in Seville featuring flamenco music, dance, and cultural performances.

June

- **San Juan Night**: Celebrated on June 23rd, this festival marks the summer solstice with bonfires and fireworks on the beaches, particularly in cities like Barcelona and Alicante.

July

- **Festa Major de Gràcia**: This street festival in Barcelona, held in mid-August, features free live music, dancing, and beautifully decorated streets. The festivities are free to enjoy.

August

- **San Fermín Festival**: While the famous running of the bulls in Pamplona might have ticketed events, many of the surrounding celebrations and street parties from July 6-14 are free.

September

- **La Mercè**: This festival in Barcelona takes place in late September and includes free concerts, parades, and cultural activities celebrating the city's patron saint.

October

- **Fiestas del Pilar**: Held in Zaragoza from October 5-14, this festival features free concerts, traditional dances, and parades celebrating the Virgin of the Pillar.

November

- **Día de los Muertos**: Celebrated across Spain, especially in places like Granada, this day involves free cultural events honoring deceased loved ones, including altars and performances.

December

- **Christmas Markets**: Throughout December, many cities host free Christmas markets filled with festive lights, decorations, and local artisan goods. Cities like Madrid, Barcelona, and Málaga feature elaborate displays and activities.

Special Notes

- **Free Museum Days**: Many museums in Spain offer free admission on certain days of the month, so check local listings for specific dates.
- **Cultural Events**: Various towns host free cultural events and workshops throughout the year, so it's worth checking local tourism websites or community boards during your visit.

Booking Flights

How to Fly Business Class to Spain cheaply

TAP Air Portugal is a popular airline that operates flights from New York City to Spain with the cheapest business class options. In low season this route typically started at around $1,000-$1,500 per person for a round-trip ticket.

The average cost for a round-trip flight from New York City to Spain typically ranged from around $400 to $1200 for an economy seat, so if travelling business class is important to you, TAP Air Portugal is likely to be the best bang for your buck.

To find the best deals on business class flights to Spain, follow these steps:

1. Use travel search engines: Start by searching for flights on popular travel search engines like Google Flights, Kayak, or Skyscanner. These sites allow you to compare prices from different airlines and book the cheapest available business option.
2. Sign up for airline newsletters: Airlines often send out exclusive deals and promotions to their email subscribers. Sign up for TAP Air Portugal's newsletter to receive notifications about special offers and discounts on business class flights.
3. Book in advance: Booking your flight well in advance can help you secure a better deal on business class tickets. Aim to book your flight at least two to three months before your travel date.

How to ALWAYS Find Super Cheap Flights to Spain

If you're just interested in finding the cheapest flight to Spain here is here to do it!

Luck is just an illusion.

Anyone can find incredible flight deals. If you can be flexible you can save huge amounts of money. In fact, the biggest tip I can give you for finding incredible flight deals is simple: find a flexible job. Don't despair if you can't do that theres still a lot you can do.

Book your flight to Spain on a Tuesday or Wednesday

Tuesdays and Wednesdays are the cheapest days of the week to fly. You can take a flight to Spain on a Tuesday or Wednesday for less than half the price you'd pay on a Thursday Friday, Saturday, Sunday or Monday.

Start with Google Flights (but NEVER book through them)

I conduct upwards of 50 flight searches a day for readers. I use google flights first when looking for flights. I put specific departure but broad destination (e.g Europe) and usually find amazing deals.

The great thing about Google Flights is you can search by class. You can pick a specific destination and it will tell you which time is cheapest in which class. Or you can put in dates and you can see which area is cheapest to travel to.

But be aware Google flights does not show the cheapest prices among the flight search engines but it does offer several advantages

1. You can see the cheapest dates for the next 8 weeks. Other search engines will blackout over 70% of the prices.
2. You can put in multiple airports to fly from. Just use a common to separate in the from input.
3. If you're flexible on where you're going Google flights can show you the cheapest destinations.
4. You can set-up price tracking, where Google will email you when prices rise or decline.

Once you have established the cheapest dates to fly go over to skyscanner.net and put those dates in. You will find sky scanner offers the cheapest flights.

Get Alerts when Prices to Spain are Lowest

Google also has a nice feature which allows you to set up an alert to email you when prices to your destination are at their lowest. So if you don't have fixed dates this feature can save you a fortune.

Baggage add-ons

It may be cheaper and more convenient to send your luggage separately with a service like sendmybag.com Often the luggage sending fee is cheaper than what the airlines charge to check baggage. Visit Lugless.com or luggagefree.com in addition to sendmybag.com for a quotation.

Loading times

Anyone who has attempted to find a cheap flight will know the pain of excruciating long loading times. If you encounter this issue use google flights to find the cheapest dates and then go to skyscanner.net for the lowest price.

Always try to book direct with the airline

Once you have found the cheapest flight go direct to the airlines booking page. This is advantageous because if you need to change your flights or arrange a refund, its much easier to do so, than via a third party booking agent.

That said, sometimes the third party bookers offer cheaper deals than the airline, so you need to make the decision based on how likely you think it is that disruption will impede you making those flights.

More Fight Tricks and Tips

www.secretflying.com/usa-deals offers a range of deals from the USA and other countries. For example you can pick-up a round trip flight non-stop from from the east coast to johannesburg for $350 return on this site

Scott's cheap flights, you can select your home airport and get emails on deals but you pay for an annual subscription. A free workaround is to download Hopper and set search alerts for trips/price drops.

Premium service of Scott's cheap flights.
They sometime have discounted business and first class but in my experience they are few and far between.

JGOOT.com has 5 times as many choices as Scott's cheap flights.

kiwi.com allows you to be able to do radius searches so you can find cheaper flights to general areas.

Finding Error Fares

Travel Pirates (www.travelpirates.com) is a gold-mine for finding error deals. Subscribe to their newsletter. I recently found a reader an airfare from Montreal-Brazil for a $200 round trip (mistake fare!). Of course these error fares are always certain dates, but if you can be flexible you can save a lot of money.

Things you can do that might reduce the fare to Spain:

• Use a VPN (if the booker knows you booked one-way, the return fare will go up)
• Buy your ticket in a different currency

If all else fails...

If you can't find a cheap flight for your dates I can find one for you. I do not charge for this nor do I send affiliate links. I'll send you a screenshot of the best options I find as airlines attach cookies to flight links. To use this free service please review this guide and send me a screenshot of your review - with your flight hacking request. I aim to reply to you within 12 hours. If it's an urgent request mark the email URGENT in the subject line and I will endeavour to reply ASAP.

A tip for coping with Jet-lag

Jetlag is primarily caused by disruptions to the body's circadian rhythm, which is the internal "biological clock" that regulates many of the body's processes, including sleep-wake cycles. When you travel across multiple time zones, your body's clock is disrupted, leading to symptoms like fatigue, insomnia, and stomach problems.

Eating on your travel destination's time before you travel can help to adjust your body's clock before you arrive, which can help to mitigate the effects of jetlag. This means that if you're traveling to a destination that is several hours ahead of your current time zone, you should try to eat meals at the appropriate times for your destination a few days before you leave. For example, if you're traveling from New York to Spain, which is seven hours ahead, you could start eating dinner at 9pm EST (which is 3am Spain time) a few days before your trip.

By adjusting your eating schedule before you travel, you can help to shift your body's clock closer to the destination's time zone, which can make it easier to adjust to the new schedule once you arrive.

Saving money on Spanish Food

Food Culture

Spain is renowned for its vibrant and diverse food culture, influenced by a rich history and a wide range of regional ingredients and traditions. From hearty stews to flavorful tapas, Spanish cuisine offers a delightful array of dishes that reflect the country's cultural heritage. In this exploration of Spanish food culture, we'll delve into some of the most popular dishes, their histories, and the culinary traditions that define them.

Paella:

One of Spain's most iconic dishes, paella originated in the Valencia region on the eastern coast of Spain. Traditionally cooked over an open flame in a wide, shallow pan called a paellera, this flavorful rice dish is typically made with ingredients such as saffron, chicken, rabbit, seafood, and vegetables. The name "paella" refers to the pan itself, which is derived from the Latin word "patella," meaning shallow pan. Paella has become synonymous with Spanish cuisine and is enjoyed by locals and visitors alike.

Tapas:

Tapas are small, savory dishes that are typically served as appetizers or snacks in Spain. The tradition of serving tapas dates back to the 19th century when bartenders would place a slice of bread or cheese over the mouth of a wine glass to prevent insects from entering. Over time, these small bites evolved into a culinary tradition of their own, with a wide variety of tapas now available across Spain. Popular tapas include patatas bravas (fried potatoes with spicy tomato sauce), tortilla española (Spanish omelette), and gambas al ajillo (garlic shrimp). Tapas are often enjoyed with a glass of wine or beer and are a social and convivial part of Spanish dining culture.

Gazpacho:

Gazpacho is a refreshing cold soup that originated in the Andalusian region of southern Spain. Made with ripe tomatoes, cucumbers, bell peppers, onions, garlic, olive oil, vinegar, and bread, gazpacho is a perfect dish for hot summer days. The soup is typically blended until smooth and served chilled, sometimes garnished with diced vegetables or croutons. Gazpacho is not only delicious but also nutritious, as it is packed with vitamins and antioxidants from the fresh vegetables.

Jamón Ibérico:

Jamón Ibérico is a type of cured ham made from the meat of Iberian pigs, which are native to Spain and Portugal. Considered a delicacy, Jamón Ibérico is prized for its rich flavor, melt-in-your-mouth texture, and complex aroma. The pigs are raised in specific regions of Spain, where they are allowed to roam freely and feed on acorns, giving the meat its distinctive nutty flavor. The curing process can take several years, during which the ham develops its unique taste and character. Jamón Ibérico is often served thinly sliced as a tapa or accompanied by crusty bread and a glass of wine.

Saving Money on Food in Spain

While dining out in Spain can be a delightful experience, it's also possible to enjoy delicious meals without breaking the bank. Here are some tips for saving money on food in Spain:

- · **Menu del Día:**
- · Many restaurants in Spain offer a menu del día (menu of the day), which typically includes a starter, main course, dessert, bread, and a drink at a fixed price. This is a great way to enjoy a three-course meal at a reasonable price, especially during lunchtime when many restaurants offer special deals.
- · **Tapas Bars and Markets:**
- · Tapas bars and food markets are excellent places to sample a variety of dishes without spending a lot of money. Many bars offer free tapas with the purchase of a drink, allowing you to try different flavors and specialties without ordering a full meal. Food markets, such as Mercado de San Miguel in Madrid or La Boqueria in Barcelona, are also great places to find affordable and delicious snacks and meals.
- · **Cooking at Home:**
- · If you're staying in self-catering accommodation or a hostel with a kitchen, consider cooking some of your meals at home. Visit local markets or supermarkets to purchase fresh ingredients and cook traditional Spanish dishes yourself. Not only is this a budget-friendly option, but it also allows you to immerse yourself in the local culinary culture.
- · **Picnics:**
- · Take advantage of Spain's beautiful outdoor spaces by having a picnic in a park or on the beach. Pick up some bread, cheese, cured meats, olives, and fresh fruit from a local market and enjoy a leisurely meal alfresco. This is a budget-friendly and enjoyable way to dine like a local while taking in the sights and sounds of your surroundings.
- · **Discount Websites and Apps:**
- · Several websites and apps offer discounts and deals on dining experiences in Spain. Websites like ElTenedor (TheFork) and Groupon often have special offers and promotions for restaurants across the country. Additionally, consider using apps like Yelp or TripAdvisor to find highly-rated restaurants that offer good value for money.

Cheap Michelin-starred restaurants in Spain

Finding Michelin-starred restaurants that offer affordable dining options can be a challenge, as these establishments typically prioritize high-quality ingredients and exceptional service, which often come with higher price tags. However, some Michelin-starred restaurants in Spain do offer more affordable options, especially during lunchtime or with set menus. Here are a few examples:

- **Casa Gerardo (Asturias):**
  - Located in Prendes, Asturias, Casa Gerardo holds one Michelin star and is known for its traditional Asturian cuisine. While not necessarily cheap, Casa Gerardo offers a lunch menu at a more accessible price point compared to its dinner menu, making it a more affordable option for experiencing Michelin-starred dining.
- **El Xato (Alicante):**
  - Situated in La Nucía, Alicante, El Xato is a Michelin-starred restaurant offering Mediterranean cuisine with a modern twist. The restaurant offers a "Menu of the Day" for lunch, which includes a selection of dishes at a fixed price, providing an opportunity to enjoy Michelin-starred dining at a more affordable cost.
- **El Molino de Urdániz (Navarre):**
  - Located in Urdaitz, Navarre, El Molino de Urdániz is a Michelin-starred restaurant housed in a renovated mill. The restaurant offers a set lunch menu featuring seasonal ingredients and creative dishes at a relatively affordable price compared to its à la carte options.
- **La Tasquería (Madrid):**
  - La Tasquería, located in Madrid, holds one Michelin star and is known for its innovative approach to traditional Spanish cuisine. The restaurant offers a lunch menu featuring offal-based dishes and other creative creations at a more accessible price, allowing diners to experience Michelin-starred dining without breaking the bank.
- **Els Casals (Barcelona):**
  - Situated in Sagàs, near Barcelona, Els Casals is a Michelin-starred restaurant known for its farm-to-table approach and emphasis on seasonal ingredients. The restaurant offers a weekday lunch menu featuring dishes inspired by Catalan cuisine at a reasonable price, making it a more affordable option for experiencing Michelin-starred dining in the region.

Cheapest Tasting Menus:

- **La Tana (Madrid):**
  - La Tana offers a budget-friendly tasting menu featuring creative dishes inspired by Mediterranean and international cuisine. Prices start at around €30 per person, making it one of the cheapest tasting menu options in Madrid.
- **Restaurant Xerta (Barcelona):**
  - Restaurant Xerta, located in the Monument Hotel in Barcelona, offers a tasting menu highlighting traditional Catalan flavors with a modern twist. Prices for the tasting menu start at around €40 per person, making it an affordable option for experiencing Michelin-starred dining.
- **Quinto (Seville):**
  - Quinto offers a budget-friendly tasting menu featuring a selection of Andalusian specialties and creative dishes. Prices for the tasting menu start at around €35 per person, making it one of the cheapest options for tasting menus in Seville.

Unusual Restaurants with Great Prices:

- **Bodega la Puntual (Barcelona):**
  - Bodega la Puntual is a traditional tapas bar located in the Born district of Barcelona. The restaurant offers a wide selection of tapas and pintxos at affordable prices, making it a great option for a casual and budget-friendly dining experience.
- **Taberna La Sacristía (Seville):**
  - Taberna La Sacristía is a quirky restaurant located in the historic center of Seville. The restaurant offers traditional Andalusian dishes with a modern twist at reasonable prices, along with a cozy atmosphere and friendly service.
- **La Bombilla (Madrid):**
  - La Bombilla is a hidden gem located in the Lavapiés neighborhood of Madrid. The restaurant offers a menu of Spanish and international dishes at affordable prices, along with a unique and eclectic ambiance that reflects the neighborhood's multicultural vibe.

Cheapest Take Away Coffee in Spain:

- **Cafetería HD (Madrid):**
  - Cafetería HD offers affordable take away coffee options in Madrid, with prices starting at around €1 for a small coffee. The café also offers a selection of pastries and snacks at budget-friendly prices, making it a popular choice for locals and visitors alike.
- **Cafetería del Centro (Barcelona):**
  - Cafetería del Centro is a budget-friendly café located in the heart of Barcelona. The café offers take away coffee options starting at around €1.20 for a small coffee, along with a selection of sandwiches and pastries at affordable prices.

Must-Try Cheap Eats in Spain and Tips:

- **Bocadillos (Sandwiches):**
  - Look for local sandwich shops or street vendors selling bocadillos filled with a variety of ingredients such as ham, cheese, chorizo, or grilled vegetables. These sandwiches are affordable and portable, making them perfect for a quick and budget-friendly meal on the go.
- **Menu del Día (Menu of the Day):**
  - Many restaurants offer a menu del día during lunchtime, which typically includes a starter, main course, dessert, bread, and a drink at a fixed price. This is an excellent way to enjoy a three-course meal at an affordable price and sample traditional Spanish dishes.
- **Street Food Markets:**
  - Visit local street food markets or food trucks for a diverse selection of affordable and delicious eats. You'll find everything from traditional Spanish tapas to international cuisine, all at budget-friendly prices.
- **Pintxos Bars:**
  - In cities like Barcelona and San Sebastian, explore pintxos bars offering a variety of small bites skewered on toothpicks. These bite-sized snacks are often displayed on the bar counter, allowing you to choose your favorites and pay by the toothpick, making it easy to control your spending.
- **Supermarket Picnics:**

- Save money on dining out by purchasing fresh ingredients from local supermarkets and enjoying a picnic in a nearby park or scenic spot. Pick up bread, cheese, cured meats, olives, and fresh fruit for a budget-friendly and delicious meal on the go.

Use 'Too Good To Go'

Spain offers plenty of food bargains if you know where to look. The app **Too Good To Go** connects you with local restaurants and bakeries selling "magic bags" of unsold food at a fraction of the price. For example, you can often pick up €15 worth of baked goods for as low as €2.99!

How it works: Simply pay for a magic bag through the app and pick it up during the designated time. This way, you can score cheap breakfast, lunch, dinner, and even groceries. Download the app and select "my current location" to find deals near you in Spain. Not only will you save money, but you'll also help reduce food waste.

Some of the best chain restaurants and food businesses available on **Too Good To Go** in Spain include popular options offering great deals on surplus food. Here are a few top chains commonly featured on the app:

1. **Dunkin'**
   Famous for its doughnuts and coffee, Dunkin' often has leftover pastries, donuts, and sandwiches at reduced prices. It's a favorite for those looking for a quick snack or sweet treat.

2. **Foster's Hollywood**
   A popular American-style chain in Spain that offers a variety of comfort foods, including burgers, ribs, and fries. Too Good To Go customers can often score a mix of their favorite dishes.

3. **Panaria**
   This café and bakery chain is known for fresh bread, pastries, and light meals such as salads and sandwiches. Panaria often offers deals on baked goods near the end of the day.

4. **Vips**
   A popular casual dining chain offering everything from breakfast to dinner. Through Too Good To Go, you can find discounted ready-made meals, sandwiches, and desserts.

5. **Pans & Company**
   Known for its sandwiches, Pans & Company frequently offers discounted baguettes, wraps, and snacks through Too Good To Go.

6. **Rodilla**
   A beloved sandwich shop chain, Rodilla specializes in cold and hot sandwiches, salads, and light bites. It often offers packages with a variety of leftover sandwiches.

7. **Muerde La Pasta**
   This all-you-can-eat Italian chain often has surplus pasta, pizza, and salads available at discounted prices.

8. **Starbucks**
   With Too Good To Go, you can often grab sandwiches, wraps, or pastries at the end of the day, offering a great deal on their expensive snacks.

9. **Paul**
   A French-style bakery chain with branches across Spain, Paul offers artisan bread, pastries, and coffee. Their leftovers make for an indulgent treat at a fraction of the cost.

10. **La Tagliatella**
    Offering a selection of Italian dishes, particularly pasta and pizzas, La Tagliatella often features reduced-price options via Too Good To Go, perfect for an easy, hearty meal.

Emphasizing Nutrition

An often-quoted saying suggests that "there is no such thing as cheap food," but that dismisses the fact that good nutrition is a choice we make every time we eat. The great thing about using **Too Good To Go** is that you can enjoy nutritious food—fruits, vegetables, fish, and nut dishes—at a fraction of their supermarket cost.

Opt for Prix-Fixe Lunch Menus

Many restaurants in Spain offer prix-fixe lunch menus, which typically feature three courses for under €20. For instance, places like **Casa Mono** in Madrid and **El Xalet de Montjuïc** in Barcelona offer fantastic set menus that let you indulge in delicious local cuisine without overspending.

Take Advantage of Food Delivery Discounts

If you prefer dining in, utilize food delivery services like **Just Eat** or **Uber Eats**, which often have promotions for first-time users, typically offering discounts of €10 off your first order.

Cheapest Supermarkets in Spain

When shopping for groceries, look for discount supermarkets such as **Lidl** and **Aldi**, commonly found in residential areas. These stores usually offer better prices than traditional supermarkets. If you're in larger cities, consider shopping at local markets for fresh produce and lower prices.

Timing Your Grocery Shopping

Supermarkets often mark down fresh produce near closing time. Check stores like **Mercadona** or **Carrefour** around 5 PM for discounts on items nearing their sell-by date. You can often find great deals during this time!

Affordable Coffee Options

Start your day with a delicious coffee without splurging at cafes like **Café de Oriente** or **Café A Bicyclette**, where you can enjoy a cup for around €1.50. Many local cafés offer affordable breakfast deals, so keep an eye out for those!

IKEA for Budget Meals
For an exceptionally affordable breakfast, head to an **IKEA** store, where you can get a €1 breakfast that includes a boiled egg, croissant, jam, and filter coffee. Just sign up for their **FAMILY CARD** to access the restaurant and enjoy free coffee during your visit!

Cheapest Breakfasts in Spain

Here's a list of some of the cheapest breakfasts you can enjoy in Spain, along with approximate prices and where to find them:

1. Pan con Tomate and Coffee

- **Price**: Around €2-€3
- **Where to Buy**: **Local Cafés** – Most cafés in Barcelona and other parts of Catalonia offer this traditional breakfast of toasted bread with ripe tomato and olive oil. Try places like **Café de Oriente** in Madrid for a great experience.

2. Tostada with Butter and Jam

- **Price**: Approximately €1.50-€2
- **Where to Buy**: **Bar Tomas** in Barcelona – This popular spot offers a simple yet delicious tostada, perfect for a light breakfast.

3. Churros with Hot Chocolate

- **Price**: About €3-€4
- **Where to Buy**: **Chocolatería San Ginés** in Madrid – Famous for their churros, this place is a must-visit for a sweet breakfast treat.

4. Café con Leche and Croissant

- **Price**: Around €2-€3
- **Where to Buy**: **Bakeries and Cafés** – You can find this breakfast combo at nearly any bakery or café throughout Spain, like **Panadería La Mallorquina** in Madrid.

5. Breakfast Menu at Local Bars

- **Price**: Typically €3-€5
- **Where to Buy**: **Local Bars** – Many local bars offer breakfast menus that include a coffee and a small pastry or sandwich. For example, check out **Cafetería El Cangrejo** in Valencia for good deals.

6. IKEA Breakfast

- **Price**: €1
- **Where to Buy**: **IKEA** – The IKEA restaurant offers a €1 breakfast that includes a boiled egg, croissant, jam, and coffee. Visit any IKEA location in Spain, such as **IKEA Madrid**.

7. Spanish Omelette (Tortilla Española) with Bread

- **Price**: Around €3-€4
- **Where to Buy**: **Cafés and Tapas Bars** – Many places serve tortilla as a breakfast option, including **La Taverna** in Seville.

8. Bocadillo (Sandwich) with Coffee

- **Price**: About €3-€4

- **Where to Buy**: **Cafés** – You can find bocadillos filled with cheese or cured meats at many local cafés like **Casa Mingo** in Madrid.

9. Fruit and Yogurt

- **Price**: Approximately €2-€3
- **Where to Buy**: **Local Markets or Supermarkets** – Pick up some fresh fruit and yogurt at local markets like **Mercat de Sant Josep de la Boqueria** in Barcelona.

10. Porras (Thicker Churros)

- **Price**: Around €3-€4
- **Where to Buy**: **Chocolatería San Ginés** in Madrid – Another great spot for churros, where you can enjoy them with chocolate for dipping.

Cheap Snackfoods in Spain

1. Tortilla Española (Spanish Omelette)

- **Price**: Around €2-€3 per slice
- **Where to Buy**: **Local Tapas Bars** – Many bars serve tortilla as a snack. Try **Casa González** in Madrid for a delicious version.

2. Churros

- **Price**: Approximately €1-€3 for a serving
- **Where to Buy**: **Chocolatería San Ginés** in Madrid – Famous for their churros, you can enjoy them with hot chocolate for dipping.

3. Patatas Bravas

- **Price**: About €3-€4
- **Where to Buy**: **Tapas Bars** – Enjoy this classic dish at local bars like **Bar Tomás** in Barcelona, where they serve some of the best in the city.

4. Bocadillo (Sandwich)

- **Price**: Around €3-€5
- **Where to Buy**: **Local Cafés or Bakeries** – Look for bocadillos filled with jamón (ham) or cheese at places like **Casa Mingo** in Madrid.

5. Pimientos de Padrón

- **Price**: Approximately €4-€5
- **Where to Buy**: **Tapas Bars** – Sample these small green peppers, usually fried and salted, at places like **Bar Lobo** in Barcelona.

6. Croquetas

- **Price**: About €2-€4 for a few
- **Where to Buy**: **Tapas Bars** – Many bars serve these creamy fritters. Try **La Casa de las Croquetas** in Madrid for a variety of flavors.

7. Empanadas

- **Price**: Around €2-€3 each
- **Where to Buy**: Bakeries – Look for delicious empanadas filled with meat, cheese, or vegetables at **La Mallorquina** in Madrid.

8. Chips (Papas Fritas)

- **Price**: Approximately €1-€2
- **Where to Buy: Local Supermarkets or Convenience Stores** – Grab a bag of local potato chips from **Mercadona**or **Carrefour**.

9. Olives

- **Price**: About €2-€4 for a small bowl
- **Where to Buy: Tapas Bars** – Enjoy a selection of olives at bars like **Bodega de la Ardosa** in Madrid.

10. Tortas de Aceite (Oil Cakes)

- **Price**: Around €1 each
- **Where to Buy: Local Bakeries** – These sweet pastries are often found in bakeries across Spain, such as **Patisserie Holtkamp** in Madrid.

Street Food

Street food in Spain can be traced back to the **medieval period,** influenced heavily by the **Moorish occupation** of the Iberian Peninsula (711–1492). The Moors introduced new agricultural practices and ingredients such as citrus, spices, almonds, and rice. These new flavors became integral to Spanish cuisine, and many foods traditionally sold in the streets were inspired by Moorish dishes.

1. Madrid

- **Bocadillo de Calamares**: A Madrid classic, this fried calamari sandwich is typically served with lemon wedges and may have a dollop of aioli. You can find it in markets and stalls around Plaza Mayor.
  - **Price**: €3-€5
- **Churros con Chocolate**: Freshly fried churros dipped in thick hot chocolate are a street food favorite, particularly for breakfast or a late-night snack.
  - **Price**: €2-€4 for churros, €1-€2 extra for chocolate dipping.
- **Tortilla Española**: The famous Spanish omelet, made with potatoes and onions, is often sold by the slice at street stalls and food trucks.
  - **Price**: €2-€3 per slice

2. Barcelona

- **Bomba**: A potato croquette filled with meat and served with spicy sauce, originating in Barceloneta, this is one of the city's most beloved tapas-turned-street-food dishes.
  - **Price**: €2-€4 per bomba
- **Coca**: A flatbread, similar to pizza, topped with various ingredients like roasted peppers, onions, and sausage. Often sold at market stalls.

- **Price**: €3-€5 per slice
- **Pintxos**: These small, skewered bites originated in the Basque region but are popular in Barcelona's food markets. Pintxos come with various toppings like fish, meat, or vegetables.
  - **Price**: €1.50-€3 per pintxo

3. Seville

- **Montaditos**: These small sandwiches are typically filled with a variety of ingredients like jamón, cheese, or chorizo. Perfect as an on-the-go snack, you'll find them in food trucks and markets.
  - **Price**: €1-€2 each
- **Pescaito Frito**: This is a fried fish dish, including small fish like anchovies, squid, or shrimp, served in paper cones from street vendors, especially near the Guadalquivir River.
  - **Price**: €3-€6 per cone
- **Torrijas**: Similar to French toast, this sweet dish is made from stale bread soaked in milk, fried, and sprinkled with sugar. It's popular during Semana Santa (Holy Week) but can be found year-round.
  - **Price**: €1.50-€3 per slice

4. Valencia

- **Empanadas**: Stuffed pastry filled with tuna, vegetables, or meat, a popular grab-and-go snack at street stalls.
  - **Price**: €1.50-€3 per empanada
- **Buñuelos de Calabaza**: Sweet pumpkin fritters, often sold in the streets during Las Fallas festival, but available in food markets year-round.
  - **Price**: €1-€2 per buñuelo
- **Horchata**: A refreshing drink made from tiger nuts (chufas) served cold, often accompanied by fartons (a soft pastry) for dipping.
  - **Price**: €2-€4 for horchata, €1-€2 for fartons

5. San Sebastián

- **Gildas**: A pintxo consisting of olives, anchovies, and pickled green peppers skewered on a toothpick. Found in local markets and street food fairs.
  - **Price**: €1.50-€2.50 per skewer
- **Txistorra**: A Basque-style sausage similar to chorizo, often grilled and served in a baguette or as a pintxo.
  - **Price**: €2-€4 per portion
- **Pimientos de Padrón**: Small green peppers fried in olive oil and sprinkled with sea salt. You can find them at many food markets.
  - **Price**: €3-€5 per portion

6. Granada

- **Tapas**: While tapas are more commonly enjoyed in bars, in Granada, free tapas are offered with every drink. You can find street stalls offering similar small plates of croquetas, jamón, and more.
  - **Price**: Free with a drink purchase (usually around €2-€3 for beer or wine)
- **Migas**: Made from fried breadcrumbs and usually served with chorizo or fried eggs, migas is a hearty street food dish, often found at festivals.

- Price: €2-€4 per portion
- **Tortas de Aceite**: Thin, crispy sweet cakes made with olive oil and often sprinkled with sugar and anise. They're popular at markets.
  - Price: €1.50-€3 per torta

7. Bilbao

- **Talos con Chorizo**: A Basque-style flatbread filled with chorizo, cheese, or bacon. Found at street fairs and food trucks throughout the region.
  - Price: €3-€6 depending on the filling
- **Bacalao a la Vizcaína**: Salted codfish in a tomato-based sauce, served in portions at food markets and street food stands.
  - Price: €4-€6 per portion
- **Txangurro**: Spider crab served stuffed in its shell, a Basque specialty found in food markets.
  - Price: €4-€8 per serving

8. Málaga

- **Espetos**: Skewers of sardines grilled over an open fire, a coastal specialty that you'll find all along Málaga's beaches, especially from small food carts.
  - Price: €3-€5 per skewer
- **Gazpacho**: A refreshing cold tomato soup, served in cups to go from street vendors and food stalls, perfect for the hot Andalusian climate.
  - Price: €2-€3 per cup
- **Borrachuelos**: A sweet pastry filled with pumpkin or sweet wine, particularly popular during Christmas but found in markets year-round.
  - Price: €1-€2 each

9. Galicia

- **Pulpo a la Gallega**: Grilled octopus served on wooden plates with olive oil, paprika, and sea salt. You'll find this dish in food markets and festivals.
  - Price: €4-€8 per portion
- **Empanada Gallega**: A large savory pie filled with tuna, cod, or meat, available by the slice at local food stalls.
  - Price: €3-€5 per slice
- **Percebes**: Goose barnacles, a Galician delicacy that can be pricey in restaurants but more affordable at street food markets.
  - Price: €6-€12 per portion, depending on the market

10. Canary Islands

- **Papas Arrugadas**: Small, wrinkled potatoes boiled in salt water and served with mojo sauce (red or green). A popular street food in Tenerife and Gran Canaria.
  - Price: €2-€4 per portion
- **Churros de Pescado**: Fried fish churros, typically cod, served with lemon and found at food stalls near beaches.
  - Price: €3-€5 per portion
- **Ropa Vieja**: A stewed dish of chickpeas, potatoes, and shredded beef or pork, often served as a tapa from street vendors.
  - Price: €3-€6 per portion

Street Food Festivals and Markets

- **Mercado de San Miguel (Madrid)**: A popular market offering a wide variety of street food, including everything from seafood to churros.
- **La Boqueria (Barcelona)**: One of the most famous food markets in Spain, offering pintxos, croquetas, and fresh seafood.
- **Calle Feria Market (Seville)**: Known for local specialties like montaditos and pescaito frito.
- **Ribeira Market (Lisbon)**: For those traveling nearby, this market offers a blend of Portuguese and Spanish street food options.

First-day Itinerary for first time visitor to Spain

First-Day Itinerary in Barcelona: Luxury on a Budget

Morning:

1. **Breakfast at Café de Oriente**

   - **Time**: 8:30 AM
   - **Details**: Start your day with a delicious breakfast at **Café de Oriente**, where you can enjoy a coffee and a freshly baked croissant for around €3. The café offers stunning views of the Royal Palace, setting a luxurious tone for your day.

2. **Explore La Sagrada Familia**

   - **Time**: 9:30 AM
   - **Details**: Head to **La Sagrada Familia** to marvel at Gaudí's masterpiece. Purchase your tickets online in advance to skip the line (€26). Spend time exploring the intricate details of this iconic basilica.

Midday:

3. **Stroll Through Park Güell**

   - **Time**: 11:30 AM
   - **Details**: Make your way to **Park Güell** (€10 entry for the Monumental Zone). Spend a leisurely hour exploring Gaudí's colorful mosaics and unique architecture. The views of the city from the park are breathtaking.

4. **Lunch at La Paradeta**

   - **Time**: 1:00 PM
   - **Details**: Enjoy a fresh seafood lunch at **La Paradeta**, where you can select your fish and have it cooked on the spot. Expect to spend around €15-€20 for a satisfying meal in a casual setting.

Afternoon:

5. **Visit Casa Batlló**

   - **Time**: 2:30 PM
   - **Details**: Head to **Casa Batlló** and experience another of Gaudí's masterpieces. Book your tickets online for around €25. Take your time exploring the whimsical architecture and rich history.

6. **Coffee Break at El Nacional**

   - **Time**: 4:00 PM

- o **Details**: Stop for a coffee at **El Nacional**, a beautifully designed space with multiple dining options. Enjoy a café con leche and a light pastry for about €4-€6 while soaking in the atmosphere.

Evening:

7. **Walk Down La Rambla**

   - o **Time**: 5:00 PM
   - o **Details**: Take a leisurely stroll down **La Rambla**, a bustling street filled with shops, street performers, and local markets. It's a great place to people-watch and soak in the vibrant culture.

8. **Dinner at Cervecería 100 Montaditos**

   - o **Time**: 7:00 PM
   - o **Details**: For dinner, visit **Cervecería 100 Montaditos**, known for its variety of affordable montaditos (small sandwiches) starting at €1 each. Enjoy their lively atmosphere and happy hour specials for budget-friendly dining.

9. **Evening Views at Bunkers del Carmel**

   - o **Time**: 9:00 PM
   - o **Details**: End your day with a visit to **Bunkers del Carmel** for stunning panoramic views of the city as the sun sets. This spot is free to enter and offers a perfect backdrop for photos.

7-Day Itinerary for Luxury on a Budget

Day 1: Madrid – Exploring the Capital

- **Accommodation**: Stay at a budget-friendly boutique hotel like **Hostal Central Palace Madrid** ($40/night).
- **Morning**: Visit **Retiro Park** for free. Rent a rowboat on the lake ($8).
- **Afternoon**: Explore the **Prado Museum** during free entry hours (Monday to Saturday from 6-8 p.m.).
- **Evening**: Have tapas at **El Tigre** (€10 or $11 for drinks and free tapas).

Daily Total: ~$60

Day 2: Madrid – History and Art

- **Morning**: Visit **The Royal Palace** (free on weekdays for EU citizens after 4 p.m., or $12 for non-EU).
- **Lunch**: Enjoy an affordable lunch menu (menu del día) at **Casa Labra** (~€12 or $13).
- **Afternoon**: Walk through **Gran Via** and shop for souvenirs or enjoy window shopping.
- **Evening**: Watch a flamenco show in **Casa Patas** (tickets start at €20 or $21).

Daily Total: ~$50

Day 3: Seville – Andalusian Charm

- **Travel**: Take a budget train from Madrid to Seville (starting at €25 or $26).
- **Accommodation**: Stay in a stylish hostel like **For You Hostel Seville** ($30/night).
- **Morning**: Visit **Plaza de España** and **Maria Luisa Park** (free).
- **Lunch**: Have a budget-friendly Andalusian meal at **Bodeguita Romero** (~€10 or $11).
- **Afternoon**: Visit **Seville Cathedral** and **Giralda Tower** during free entry hours (Mondays from 4:30 p.m. to 6 p.m.).
- **Evening**: Enjoy tapas in **El Rinconcillo** (~€15 or $16).

Daily Total: ~$60

Day 4: Seville – Immersing in Culture

- **Morning**: Visit the **Real Alcázar** (free entry for students or under $15 for general entry).
- **Lunch**: Have tapas at **La Azotea** (~€15 or $16).
- **Afternoon**: Take a free walking tour through Seville's old town and the Jewish quarter.

- **Evening**: Wander around **Triana** and enjoy the riverside views with affordable tapas (~€10 or $11).

Daily Total: ~$50

Day 5: Granada – The Alhambra Experience

- **Travel**: Take a budget bus from Seville to Granada (starting at €15 or $16).
- **Accommodation**: Stay at **Hostel Lima** or a similar budget hostel ($35/night).
- **Morning**: Visit the **Alhambra** with a general ticket (~$16). Book tickets in advance.
- **Afternoon**: Explore the **Albayzín** and enjoy tea in a Moroccan-style tetería (~€5 or $5.50).
- **Evening**: Have tapas at **Bar Los Diamantes** (~€10 or $11).

Daily Total: ~$60

Day 6: Granada – Moorish Beauty

- **Morning**: Walk through the **Sacromonte** and enjoy views of the Alhambra from **Mirador San Nicolás** (free).
- **Lunch**: Have a budget lunch in **Café 4 Gatos** (~€12 or $13).
- **Afternoon**: Visit the **Granada Cathedral** (free entry or under €5/$5.50).
- **Evening**: Enjoy a flamenco performance in a cave in **Sacromonte** (€15 or $16).

Daily Total: ~$50

Day 7: Barcelona – A Day of Gaudí

- **Travel**: Budget flight or bus from Granada to Barcelona (~€30 or $32).
- **Accommodation**: Stay at **Yeah Hostel** or a similar budget-friendly yet chic spot ($40/night).
- **Morning**: Visit **Park Güell** (entry is under €10 or $11).
- **Lunch**: Enjoy a budget meal at **La Boqueria Market** (~€12 or $13).
- **Afternoon**: Walk through **Las Ramblas** and visit **Barcelona Cathedral** (free entry).
- **Evening**: Visit **La Barceloneta** beach and have tapas in **Can Ramonet** (~€15 or $16).

Daily Total: ~$65

Budget Breakdown:

- **Accommodation**: ~$250 for 7 nights.
- **Meals and activities**: ~$200 total.
- **Transport**: ~$50 (budget trains, buses, and local transport).

Grand Total: ~$500

Unique bargains we love in Spain

Spain is a treasure trove of unique bargains that cater to food lovers, culture enthusiasts, and savvy travelers alike. Whether you're searching for exquisite saffron, discount passes for attractions, or free shows, Spain has a lot to offer. This guide will explore some of the most enticing bargains that will enhance your experience while keeping your budget intact.

1. Culinary Delights: Unique Food Bargains

Saffron from La Mancha

One of the most renowned culinary treasures of Spain is saffron, particularly the saffron produced in the region of La Mancha. Known for its vibrant color and distinct flavor, saffron is a key ingredient in traditional dishes like paella.

- **Where to Buy**: Head to local markets such as **Mercado de San Miguel** in Madrid or **La Boqueria** in Barcelona. You can find authentic La Mancha saffron for around €5-€10 per gram, significantly cheaper than in most grocery stores.

- **Bargain Tip**: Look for small artisanal shops specializing in spices, where you might find even better deals. Purchasing saffron directly from producers during your travels can often result in savings and a fresher product.

Tapas and Menú del Día

When in Spain, indulging in tapas is a must. These small plates allow you to sample a variety of flavors without spending much.

- **Price**: Most tapas range from €2 to €5, and many bars offer a "menú del día," which is a fixed-price lunch menu that includes multiple courses for as little as €10-€15.

- **Where to Eat**: Try **El Tigre** in Madrid for generous portions of free tapas with your drink, or **Bar Tomás** for some of the best patatas bravas in Barcelona.

- **Bargain Tip**: Enjoying tapas at lunchtime often offers better deals compared to dinner. Plus, many bars offer happy hour specials, making it an ideal time to sample more dishes without breaking the bank.

Cheap Churros and Chocolate

Churros, fried dough pastries often enjoyed with thick hot chocolate, are a delightful treat found all over Spain.

- **Price**: You can find churros and chocolate for around €3-€5.

- **Where to Buy**: Visit **Chocolatería San Ginés** in Madrid, famous for its churros and chocolate. In Barcelona, try **Churrería Laietana** for delicious options.

- **Bargain Tip**: Look for local bakeries or churrerías that offer breakfast deals. Some cafés serve churros as part of a breakfast combo that includes coffee for a very low price.

Fresh Produce at Local Markets

Spain's local markets are brimming with fresh fruits, vegetables, and artisanal products at prices often lower than supermarkets.

- **Where to Buy**: Markets like **Mercado de La Boqueria** in Barcelona and **Mercado de San Miguel** in Madrid are excellent places to explore.

- **Bargain Tip**: Buy seasonal produce, which is often cheaper and fresher. Also, try bargaining with vendors for bulk purchases or end-of-day discounts.

2. Discount Passes for Attractions

Barcelona Pass

The **Barcelona Pass** offers significant savings for travelers looking to explore the city's top attractions.

- **Cost**: Prices start at around €100 for a two-day pass.

- **What's Included**: The pass includes free entry to major attractions like **La Sagrada Familia**, **Park Güell**, and **Casa Batlló**, along with public transportation and discounts at select restaurants.

- **Bargain Tip**: If you plan to visit several attractions, this pass can save you money and time, allowing you to skip lines at popular sites.

Madrid Tourist Travel Pass

If you're planning to explore Madrid extensively, the **Madrid Tourist Travel Pass** is a worthwhile investment.

- **Cost**: Prices start at around €8.40 for one day.

- **What's Included**: The pass grants unlimited travel on public transportation (metro, bus, and train) within the chosen zones, as well as discounts at various attractions.

- **Bargain Tip**: The pass is particularly valuable if you're visiting multiple areas of the city. Combining it with free or discounted entrance days at museums, such as the **Prado Museum** (free on certain days), maximizes your savings.

Seville Card

In Seville, the **Seville Card** is an excellent option for budget-conscious travelers.

- **Cost**: The card costs around €40 for a 24-hour pass.

- **What's Included**: It provides free access to key attractions, including the **Cathedral of Seville** and **Giralda Tower**, plus discounts on guided tours.

- **Bargain Tip**: The card often includes a hop-on, hop-off bus tour, allowing you to explore the city at your own pace.

3. Free Shows and Cultural Experiences

Flamenco Shows

Flamenco is an essential part of Spanish culture, and many venues offer free or low-cost performances.

- **Where to Experience**: In Seville, **Casa de la Memoria** frequently features flamenco shows with ticket prices starting at €20, but you can often find free shows in local bars and during festivals.

- **Bargain Tip**: Check local event listings for free flamenco performances at festivals, local fiestas, or in less touristy neighborhoods.

Free Walking Tours

One of the best ways to explore Spanish cities is by joining free walking tours, which are available in most major cities.

- **Where to Find Them**: Look for companies like **Sandemans New Europe** or **Free Tour Madrid** that offer comprehensive tours led by knowledgeable guides.

- **Bargain Tip**: While these tours are free, it's customary to tip your guide based on your experience (typically around €10-€15).

Cultural Festivals

Spain is known for its vibrant festivals, many of which are free to attend.

- **Examples**: Events like **La Tomatina** in Buñol and **Las Fallas** in Valencia are not only exciting but also offer free participation.

- **Bargain Tip**: Plan your visit around local festivals for unique cultural experiences. Many towns have smaller celebrations throughout the year that provide a glimpse into local traditions without any entry fees.

4. Unique Local Products

Spanish Olive Oil

Spain is one of the world's largest producers of olive oil, and purchasing directly from local producers can yield significant savings.

- **Where to Buy**: Visit local farmers' markets or specialty shops in regions like **Andalusia** or **Catalonia**.

- **Bargain Tip**: Look for brands that sell directly to consumers, often at a lower price than retail. You can find high-quality extra virgin olive oil for as low as €5-€10 per liter.

Wine Tasting Experiences

Spain is renowned for its wines, and many wineries offer affordable tasting experiences.

- **Where to Visit**: In regions like **La Rioja** or **Ribera del Duero**, many wineries charge as little as €10-€15 for tours and tastings.

- **Bargain Tip**: Look for package deals that include multiple tastings at different wineries. Some tours offer transportation and a comprehensive experience for around €50.

Handmade Crafts and Souvenirs

Support local artisans by purchasing handmade crafts, which often cost less than mass-produced items.

- **Where to Buy**: Markets such as **Mercado de Artesanía** in Granada or **El Raval** in Barcelona feature local artisans selling unique items.

- **Bargain Tip**: Bargaining is often acceptable in markets. Don't hesitate to negotiate prices, especially when buying multiple items.

OUR SPECIFIC SUPER CHEAP TIPS...

Here are our specific super cheap tips for enjoying a $10,000 trip to Spain for just $500

Arriving

Here's a guide to the cheapest public transport routes from the top ten airports in Spain, including prices and estimated travel times. Prices can vary based on time and demand, so it's a good idea to check official transport websites or apps for the latest information.

1. Adolfo Suárez Madrid-Barajas Airport (MAD)

- **Route:** Metro Line 8 to Nuevos Ministerios, transfer to Line 10.
- **Price:** €4.50
- **Time:** ~30-40 minutes

2. Barcelona-El Prat Airport (BCN)

- **Route:** Aerobus to Plaça Catalunya or Metro Line L9 to Zona Universitària, then transfer to L1 or L3.
- **Price:** €5.90 (Aerobus) / €4.60 (Metro)
- **Time:** ~35-45 minutes

3. Málaga-Costa del Sol Airport (AGP)

- **Route:** Train (C1) to Málaga Centro-Alameda.
- **Price:** €1.80
- **Time:** ~12 minutes

4. Alicante-Elche Airport (ALC)

- **Route:** C-6 bus to Alicante city center.
- **Price:** €3.85
- **Time:** ~30 minutes

5. Valencia Airport (VLC)

- **Route:** Metro Line 3 or 5 to Colón station.
- **Price:** €4.90
- **Time:** ~25 minutes

6. San Pablo Airport (SVQ) in Seville

- **Route:** EA bus to Plaza de Armas.
- **Price:** €4.00
- **Time:** ~30 minutes

7. Bilbao Airport (BIO)

- **Route:** Bizkaibus A3247 to Bilbao city center.
- **Price:** €3.00
- **Time:** ~30 minutes

8. Gran Canaria Airport (LPA)

- **Route:** Global bus line 60 to Las Palmas.
- **Price:** €4.40
- **Time:** ~30-40 minutes

9. Fuerteventura Airport (FUE)

- **Route:** Bus line 3 to Puerto del Rosario.
- **Price:** €3.00
- **Time:** ~30 minutes

10. Ibiza Airport (IBZ)

- **Route:** Bus line 10 to Ibiza Town.
- **Price:** €3.50
- **Time:** ~30 minutes

Additional Tips:

- **Tickets:** Purchase tickets from machines at the airport or on the bus.
- **Check Times:** Be sure to check the latest schedules as they may vary by day and time.
- **Apps:** Consider using apps like Google Maps, Moovit, or local transport apps for real-time information.

Getting around cheaply

1. Buses:

Buses are a cost-effective way to travel within cities and between towns and regions in Spain. They are often cheaper than trains and offer extensive coverage throughout the country. Here's a breakdown of bus travel in Spain:

- **City Buses:** Most cities in Spain have an efficient and affordable bus network that covers major tourist attractions, neighborhoods, and suburbs. Tickets can be purchased directly from the driver or at designated ticket machines.
- **Intercity Buses:** Several bus companies operate intercity routes connecting major cities and towns across Spain. Companies like ALSA, Avanza, and FlixBus offer comfortable coaches with amenities such as Wi-Fi and air conditioning. Booking tickets online in advance can often result in discounted fares.

2. Trains:

Trains are another popular mode of transportation in Spain, offering both high-speed and regional services. While high-speed trains (AVE) can be more expensive, regional trains are often budget-friendly. Here's what you need to know about train travel in Spain:

- **High-Speed Trains (AVE):** Renfe operates high-speed trains that connect major cities like Madrid, Barcelona, Seville, and Valencia. While these trains offer fast and efficient service, tickets can be expensive if not booked in advance. Look for promotional fares and discounts on the Renfe website.
- **Regional Trains:** Renfe also operates regional trains (Cercanías) that serve smaller towns and suburbs. These trains are usually cheaper than high-speed services and offer a more scenic journey. Tickets can be purchased at the station or online.

3. Ferries:

For travel between mainland Spain and the Balearic or Canary Islands, ferries are a common mode of transportation. While not always the cheapest option, ferries offer a unique travel experience and can be budget-friendly if booked in advance. Here's what you need to know about ferry travel in Spain:

- **Balearic Islands:** Ferry companies like Trasmediterranea, Balearia, and Acciona Trasmediterranea operate routes between mainland Spain (Barcelona, Valencia, Denia) and the Balearic Islands (Mallorca, Menorca, Ibiza). Prices vary depending on the season and the type of accommodation (e.g., seats, cabins).
- **Canary Islands:** Ferry companies such as Naviera Armas and Fred. Olsen Express offer routes between mainland Spain (Cadiz, Huelva) and the Canary Islands (Tenerife, Gran Canaria, Lanzarote). Prices can vary significantly, so it's advisable to compare fares and book early.

4. Car Rentals:

Renting a car can be an affordable option for exploring rural areas and remote destinations in Spain. While rental costs vary depending on the type of vehicle and rental period, there are ways to save money:

- **Firefly** is far and away the cheapest operator in Spain for rental cars.
- **Comparison Websites:** Use comparison websites like Rentalcars.com or Kayak to compare prices from different car rental companies. Look for deals and promotions to secure the best rate.
- **Off-Peak Travel:** Rental rates tend to be cheaper during off-peak periods, so consider traveling outside of peak tourist seasons if possible.
- **Fuel Efficiency:** Choose a fuel-efficient car to save money on fuel costs during your journey. Opting for a smaller car can also result in lower rental fees and insurance premiums.

5. Bike Rentals:

Many cities in Spain offer bike rental services, providing an eco-friendly and budget-friendly way to explore urban areas. Here's what you need to know about bike rentals:

- **City Bike Share Programs:** Major cities like Barcelona, Madrid, Seville, and Valencia have bike share programs that allow users to rent bikes for short periods. Prices are typically based on usage time, with the first 30 minutes often included in the initial fee.
- **Private Bike Rental Companies:** In addition to city bike share programs, there are private bike rental companies in many Spanish cities. These companies offer a variety of bikes for rent, including electric bikes, mountain bikes, and city bikes. Prices vary depending on the type of bike and rental duration.

Travel Passes and Discounts:

- **Renfe Spain Pass:** Renfe offers the Spain Pass, which allows travelers to take multiple journeys on the Renfe network within a set period. Passes are available for 4, 6, 8, or 10 journeys and can result in significant savings compared to individual ticket purchases.
- **InterRail Pass:** For travelers exploring multiple European countries, an InterRail pass can be a cost-effective option. The InterRail Global Pass allows unlimited travel on trains in up to 33 European countries, including Spain, for a set number of days within a specified period.
- **City Tourist Cards:** Many cities in Spain offer tourist cards that provide discounts on transportation, attractions, and activities. These cards often include unlimited use of public transportation within the city, making them a convenient and budget-friendly option for travelers.

Renfe Spain Pass

The **Renfe Spain Pass** allows travelers to make multiple journeys across Spain on the Renfe network within a set period. Prices depend on the number of journeys:

- **4 journeys**: ~€200 ($210)
- **6 journeys**: ~€250 ($263)
- **8 journeys**: ~€300 ($315)
- **10 journeys**: ~€350 ($368)
  Pass is valid for 1 month from the first journey.

InterRail Global Pass (for Spain and other European countries)

The **InterRail Global Pass** allows unlimited train travel across up to 33 European countries, including Spain, for a set number of travel days within a period. Here are the approximate prices:

- **4 days within 1 month**: ~€246 ($260)
- **7 days within 1 month**: ~€335 ($355)
- **10 days within 2 months**: ~€450 ($475)
- **15 days within 2 months**: ~€568 ($600)
  Discounts available for youth, seniors, and families.

City Tourist Cards (Spain)

Each city offers its own tourist card, and the cost varies by city. Here are examples from popular cities in Spain:

- **Madrid City Pass** (includes transportation, fast-track museum entry): ~€50 ($53) for 24 hours.
- **Barcelona Card** (includes unlimited transport, attraction discounts): ~€46 ($48) for 72 hours.
- **Seville Card** (includes transport and entry to top sites): ~€35 ($37) for 24 hours.

There are **bus passes** for intercity travel in Spain that offer an economical way to explore the country by bus. Spain has an extensive bus network connecting cities and towns, often at cheaper rates compared to trains. Here are some of the options:

ALSA FlexiPass

ALSA, Spain's largest intercity bus company, offers the **ALSA FlexiPass**, which allows multiple journeys within a set number of days. This pass can be used for any route within the ALSA network, offering significant savings for travelers who plan to visit multiple cities.

- **5 trips**: ~€95 ($100)
- **10 trips**: ~€180 ($190)
- **20 trips**: ~€340 ($360)
  The pass is valid for 1 year from the date of purchase, and trips can be booked as needed.

FlixBus Intercity Travel

FlixBus offers affordable intercity bus travel with routes across Spain and Europe. While they don't offer a traditional pass, their tickets are generally cheap and can be bought in bulk through the

FlixBus DiscoverEU Pass (intended for travelers up to 27 years old). Prices vary, but generally, intercity travel can cost:

- **Single trips**: ~€10-€30 ($11-$32), depending on distance and time of booking.

Movelia Multi-Journey Pass

Movelia is a platform that aggregates tickets from various bus companies in Spain, offering a **Multi-Journey Pass** for frequent travelers. This allows for discounted travel on select routes across Spain. The price and conditions depend on the bus company and the number of journeys purchased.

Eurolines Pass (for broader European travel)

While Eurolines mainly focuses on international travel across Europe, they offer passes that can also be used for travel within Spain.

- **15-day Eurolines Pass**: ~€205 ($215)
- **30-day Eurolines Pass**: ~€340 ($360)

Transportation Mode	Description	Starting Prices
Buses	City and intercity buses	€1-€20
Trains	High-speed and regional trains	€5-€100
Ferries	Ferries to Balearic and Canary Islands	€20-€200
Car Rentals	Rental cars for exploring rural areas	€20-€100 per day
Bike Rentals	City bike share programs and private rental companies	€5-€20 per day

Spain's Top 25

Barcelona

Barcelona's rich and varied history spans over 2,000 years, blending Roman, medieval, and modern influences into the vibrant metropolis it is today. Its origins date back to **Barcino**, the Roman colony established around **15 BC**, remnants of which can still be seen in the **Gothic Quarter**, particularly at the **Placa del Rei** and **Barcelona's History Museum**.

During the **Middle Ages**, Barcelona became a flourishing maritime power, the capital of the Crown of Aragon, with strong connections across the Mediterranean. The **Gothic Quarter** and structures like the **Cathedral of Barcelona** and **Basilica of Santa Maria del Mar** showcase the grandeur of this era.

By the 19th century, **Barcelona experienced a cultural renaissance** called the **Renaixença**, which reignited Catalan identity and led to a flowering of **Modernisme** (Catalan Art Nouveau). This period gave rise to the works of **Antoni Gaudí**, including his masterpiece, the **Sagrada Família**, as well as **Casa Batlló**, **Casa Milà**, and **Park Güell**.

Barcelona also played a significant role during the **Spanish Civil War** (1936–1939). As a Republican stronghold, it suffered greatly from bombings and fascist occupation, leaving a lasting impact on its architecture and political identity.

In the late 20th century, Barcelona reinvented itself, particularly when hosting the **1992 Summer Olympics**, which spurred a wave of urban regeneration. Today, Barcelona stands as a symbol of **Catalan pride** and is one of Europe's most visited cities, blending historical depth with cutting-edge modernity.

Insider Tips for Visiting Barcelona

Here are some **key insider tips** to make the most of your trip to Barcelona:

1. **Visit Sagrada Família Early or Late**
    The **Sagrada Família** can get extremely crowded. Book your tickets in advance and aim for the first or last entry slots of the day to avoid the bulk of the crowds. The light hitting the stained glass windows in the morning or evening adds a magical touch to the visit.

2. **Skip La Rambla for Authentic Experiences**
    While **La Rambla** is a well-known tourist hub, it's often overpriced and packed. Instead, wander through the **Raval** or **El Born** neighborhoods for authentic local tapas bars, street art, and unique boutiques.

3. **Free Museum Days**
    Many of Barcelona's museums offer free entry at certain times. For example, the **Picasso Museum** is free on Thursdays after 6:00 p.m. and the first Sunday of each month. Check the official websites for free hours at other major museums.

4. **Use the T10 Metro Ticket for Cheap Transport**
   Instead of buying single metro tickets, get a **T-Casual (T10)** ticket, which gives you 10 rides for about €11.35 ($12) and works across buses, trams, and metros. This is much cheaper than buying individual tickets, especially if you plan to move around the city.

5. **Take in the Views at Bunkers del Carmel**
   For one of the best panoramic views of the city, head to the **Bunkers del Carmel**, a former anti-aircraft battery with 360-degree views over Barcelona. It's a local favorite for sunsets and less touristy than **Park Güell**.

6. **Enjoy Free Walking Tours**
   Several companies offer free walking tours (just tip your guide). These tours give great insight into the history, architecture, and culture of Barcelona. Explore the **Gothic Quarter**, **Raval**, or even do a specialized **Gaudí walking tour**.

7. **Avoid Restaurants with Tourist Menus**
   In popular areas like **La Rambla**, many restaurants cater to tourists with overpriced and inauthentic "tourist menus." Instead, look for places offering a **menu del día** (daily menu) – a multi-course lunch for around €12-15 ($13-16) – popular with locals.

8. **Explore El Born for Hidden Gems**
   El Born is a neighborhood rich in medieval charm, known for its winding streets and trendy atmosphere. Don't miss the **Born Cultural Center**, and enjoy the cozy cafes and artisan shops along **Carrer de l'Argenteria**.

9. **Visit Park Güell for Free Before 9 a.m.**
   While the monumental zone of **Park Güell** charges an entry fee, the rest of the park is free to explore at any time. Arriving before 9 a.m. also grants free access to the monumental area without the crowds.

10. **Beat the Beach Crowds**
    Instead of heading to **Barceloneta**, one of the city's most famous but overcrowded beaches, take the metro to **Ocata Beach** (30 minutes from Barcelona). It's quieter, with golden sands and clear waters, offering a much more relaxed experience.

11. **Book Attractions Online**
    For popular attractions like **Casa Batlló**, **Casa Milà**, or **Camp Nou**, booking tickets online in advance often saves you money and allows you to skip the lines. Look for package deals or combined tickets to save even more.

12. **Explore Montjuïc for Free**
    The **Montjuïc** area offers many free attractions, including the **Magic Fountain** show (running on select evenings) and the grounds of **Montjuïc Castle**. The **Joan Miró Foundation** and **Poble Espanyol** are also nearby, with occasional free admission days.

13. **Take Advantage of Tapas Hours**
    Some bars offer free tapas with a drink during specific hours, especially in **Gràcia** or **Poble Sec**. It's a great way to sample authentic food without breaking the bank.

14. **Beware of Pickpockets**
    Barcelona is notorious for pickpocketing, especially in crowded areas like **La Rambla** and the **Gothic Quarter**. Keep an eye on your belongings, avoid carrying valuables, and use a secure bag.

15. **Check Out Alternative Gaudí Sites**
    While **La Sagrada Família** and **Park Güell** are must-sees, consider visiting less crowded Gaudí works like the **Casa Vicens** or **Torre Bellesguard** for a quieter and equally stunning experience of his architectural genius.

1. Sagrada Família

No visit to Barcelona would be complete without a pilgrimage to Antoni Gaudí's magnum opus, the Sagrada Família. This basilica has been under construction since 1882 and is expected to be completed by 2026. Its stunning facades and intricate interiors are a testament to Gaudí's genius. To save on fees, consider booking your tickets online in advance and visiting during off-peak hours. For a free alternative, take a stroll around the surrounding park, where you can admire the basilica from different angles. Don't forget to bring your camera; the light filtering through the stained glass is a sight to behold!

2. Park Güell

Another of Gaudí's masterpieces, Park Güell is a whimsical park filled with colorful mosaics, serpentine benches, and fantastical structures. Originally intended as a residential project, it's now a public park with breathtaking views of the city. You can save money by exploring the free areas of the park, which are just as stunning as the paid zone. For a creative alternative, visit the nearby Carmel Bunkers for panoramic views without the entry fee. Pro tip: go early in the morning to avoid the crowds!

3. Casa Batlló

This iconic building on Passeig de Gràcia is renowned for its organic shapes and vibrant colors. Casa Batlló, another Gaudí gem, is a brilliant example of modernist architecture. To save on admission, visit on Wednesdays, when they often have discounts. If you're looking for a free alternative, simply admire the facade from the street—it's a showstopper! Don't miss the intriguing dragon motif that runs throughout the design, symbolizing the legend of Saint George.

4. Casa Milà (La Pedrera)

Famous for its undulating stone facade and wrought-iron balconies, Casa Milà, also known as La Pedrera, is another of Gaudí's landmarks. The rooftop offers fantastic views of the city, adorned with whimsical chimney sculptures. Buy a combined ticket for Casa Batlló and Casa Milà to save some euros. Alternatively, enjoy a leisurely walk along Passeig de Gràcia, where you'll encounter plenty of other architectural wonders for free. Don't forget to check out the guided night tours for a magical experience!

5. Camp Nou

For football enthusiasts, Camp Nou is hallowed ground. As the home of FC Barcelona, this stadium has hosted countless memorable matches. The museum offers a deep dive into the club's illustrious history. To save on fees, look for family tickets or visit during the week when the crowds are thinner. If you're not a football fan, consider the nearby Parc de la Espanya Industrial for a relaxed stroll and a chance to see the iconic Mosaico de Miró, a large outdoor mosaic.

6. Picasso Museum
Dive into the world of Pablo Picasso at the Picasso Museum, which boasts one of the most extensive collections of his works, focusing on his formative years. To save on admission, visit on Thursdays after 5 PM when entry is free. A great alternative is to wander through the nearby El Born neighborhood, where you can soak in the artistic vibe and enjoy street performances. Don't forget to explore the museum's lovely courtyard!

7. Gothic Quarter (Barri Gòtic)
Wandering through the Gothic Quarter feels like stepping back in time. The narrow medieval streets are filled with history, from the Roman walls to the stunning Barcelona Cathedral. Although it's a free attraction, consider joining a guided tour for a deeper understanding of its history. Alternatively, find a quiet plaza to enjoy a coffee and people-watch. Fun fact: this area is said to have inspired George R.R. Martin while he was writing "Game of Thrones."

8. Montjuïc Castle
Perched atop Montjuïc Hill, this 17th-century fortress offers breathtaking views of the city and the Mediterranean Sea. To save on entry fees, hike up the hill rather than taking the cable car. You can also explore the surrounding gardens for free. If you're interested in history, don't miss the military museum inside the castle, which tells the story of Barcelona's past. Pro tip: the sunset views from the castle are absolutely magical!

9. Palau de la Música Catalana
This concert hall is a UNESCO World Heritage site known for its stunning stained glass and elaborate mosaics. Catch a performance for an unforgettable experience, or simply take a guided tour of the building. To save on tickets, check for last-minute deals on performances. For a free alternative, wander through the nearby streets to admire other modernist buildings and grab a drink at a local café.

10. Magic Fountain of Montjuïc
The Magic Fountain is a stunning display of water, light, and music that comes alive in the evenings. While it's free to watch, consider dining at a nearby restaurant for a lovely view while you wait for the show to start. If you're looking for a creative alternative, visit the Poble Espanyol nearby for a more immersive experience of Spanish culture and architecture without the admission fee.

11. Fundació Joan Miró
This museum is dedicated to the works of the surrealist artist Joan Miró, showcasing a fantastic collection of his paintings, sculptures, and tapestries. To save on fees, check for free entry days or reduced prices for students. For a free alternative, stroll around Montjuïc Park and discover more of Miró's works in the public space. The museum's garden is a lovely spot for a quiet moment, surrounded by art and nature.

12. National Art Museum of Catalonia (MNAC)

Housed in the Palau Nacional, the MNAC boasts an impressive collection of Catalan art from the Romanesque period to the mid-20th century. Admission is free on the first Sunday of each month, making it a great time to visit. If you prefer to save even more, enjoy the stunning view of the museum from the nearby Magic Fountain area without stepping inside. Be sure to explore the rooftop terrace for some of the best views of the city!

13. Aquarium Barcelona

Perfect for families, the Aquarium offers a fascinating look at marine life, featuring the largest oceanarium in Europe. To save on tickets, consider buying them online in advance or visiting during off-peak times. For a free alternative, explore the Barceloneta beach and enjoy the sun, sea, and sand. It's also a great spot for picnics and casual beach games!

14. Barcelona Zoo

Located in the heart of the Parc de la Ciutadella, the Barcelona Zoo is home to a wide variety of animals and focuses on conservation. Save on entry by purchasing tickets online. Alternatively, enjoy the beautiful park itself for free, where you can stroll among the trees, have a picnic, or rent a paddleboat on the lake. Keep an eye out for the famous Cascada Monumental, a stunning fountain designed by Gaudí.

15. La Rambla

This iconic street is a must-see for any visitor, bustling with life, street performers, and shops. While it's free to walk along La Rambla, consider taking a guided tour to learn more about its history. For a creative free alternative, explore the adjacent Gothic Quarter's lesser-known alleys for hidden gems, cafes, and charming boutiques. Grab some local snacks at La Boqueria market, where the vibrant colors and aromas are sure to excite your senses.

16. Poble Espanyol

This open-air museum showcases replicas of traditional Spanish architecture and crafts from various regions of Spain. To save on tickets, check for discounts on certain days or consider purchasing a combined ticket with other attractions. For a free alternative, visit the nearby Montjuïc Park, where you can explore beautiful gardens and enjoy panoramic views without spending a cent. Pro tip: Poble Espanyol often hosts cultural events and markets, adding to its charm!

17. L'Aquarium de Barcelona

Dive into the wonders of the ocean at L'Aquarium de Barcelona, which features a vast array of marine life and an impressive underwater tunnel. To save on fees, book your tickets online and visit during quieter hours. If you're looking for a creative alternative, enjoy a leisurely stroll along the waterfront, where you can find free art installations and lively street performances. Don't miss the nearby Maremagnum shopping center for some shopping and dining options!

18. Hospital de Sant Pau

This architectural gem, a UNESCO World Heritage site, is a stunning example of Catalan modernism designed by Lluís Domènech i Montaner. Admission to the site offers a unique glimpse into its history as a hospital. To save on fees, visit on the first Sunday of the month when entry is free. If you're on a budget, simply admire the stunning exterior and gardens from the outside for a taste of its beauty without spending a dime.

19. Torre Glòries (formerly Torre Agbar)

This modern skyscraper has become a symbol of Barcelona's skyline. While you can't go inside, visiting at night when it lights up is a treat for the eyes. Save on fees by skipping the interior and instead take a leisurely walk around the area to enjoy the architecture and perhaps grab a drink at a nearby bar. For a free alternative, check out the nearby Encants Vells market,

Affordable Luxury Accommodation in Barcelona

Accommodation	Description	Starting Price (Approx.)
H10 Casa Mimosa	Chic hotel with a rooftop pool near La Sagrada	120 €
Hotel Barcelona 1882	Eco-friendly hotel with stylish interiors and a pool.	100 €
Hotel Neri	Boutique hotel in the Gothic Quarter with a	150 €
The Wittmore	Elegant hotel with a rooftop pool and stunning	160 €
Hotel 1898	Luxurious hotel on La Rambla with a spa and rooftop terrace.	140 €
Catalonia Passeig de Gràcia	Upscale hotel in a prime location with a pool.	110 €
Ohla Barcelona	Modern hotel with a Michelin-starred restaurant	200 €
Hotel El Palace	Opulent hotel with historical charm and luxurious	200 €
Majestic Hotel & Spa	Five-star hotel with a rooftop terrace and spa	180 €
Hotel Astoria	Stylish hotel with a prime location and elegant	120 €

Free Events and Experiences in Barcelona That Most People Don't Know About

Barcelona is teeming with hidden gems and unique experiences that don't require spending a dime. One of the best-kept secrets is the **free concerts at the Parc de la Ciutadella**, especially during the summer months. Local musicians often perform, creating a vibrant atmosphere perfect for a picnic. Additionally, you can explore the **Art Nouveau architecture**of the hospital complex at **Hospital de Sant Pau**, which often hosts free guided tours on certain days, showcasing its stunning mosaics and unique structures.

Another hidden treasure is the **Magic Fountain of Montjuïc**, where visitors can enjoy a mesmerizing light and music show. Although it's known among locals, many tourists miss

out on its beauty. The show typically runs from Thursday to Sunday evenings, so plan to arrive early to grab a good spot. For those who love art, **Nits d'Estiu** is a lesser-known event during the summer, featuring outdoor film screenings in parks around the city— bring a blanket and snacks for a relaxed night under the stars.

Don't forget to check out local festivals such as **La Mercè** in September, celebrating the city's patron saint with parades, fireworks, and free concerts. These events are an excellent way to experience the local culture without spending a cent!

Practical Tips to Save Money in Barcelona

1. **Public Transport**: Purchase a **T-10 transport card** for €11.35, which gives you ten journeys on the metro, tram, and bus. This card saves you nearly 50% compared to buying individual tickets (€2.40 each).

2. **Picnic in the Park**: Instead of dining out, visit a local market like **Mercat de Sant Antoni** to buy fresh produce, cheeses, and bread. You can prepare a delightful picnic for around €10, compared to spending €20-€30 in a restaurant.

3. **Free Museum Days**: Many museums, including the **Picasso Museum** and **National Art Museum of Catalonia**, offer free entry on the first Sunday of each month. If you visit on this day, you can save up to €12-€17 per ticket.

4. **Discounted Tickets**: Look for combined tickets that include multiple attractions, such as the **Barcelona Card**. Starting at €46, it provides entry to various sites and unlimited public transport, allowing you to save on both admission fees and transportation.

5. **Local Markets**: Eating at local markets instead of restaurants can save you a significant amount. A meal at **Mercat de Sant Josep de la Boqueria** costs about €5-€10, whereas a sit-down meal in a nearby restaurant can easily exceed €20.

6. **Free Walking Tours**: Join a **free walking tour** where you pay what you can at the end. It's an excellent way to learn about the city's history and culture while saving on guided tour fees.

7. **Explore Beaches**: Barcelona's beaches are free to access, so spend a day sunbathing and swimming instead of paying for expensive beach clubs.

Practical Information for Visiting Barcelona

Getting There: Barcelona is well connected through **Barcelona El Prat Airport**, approximately 15 km from the city center. You can take the Aerobús for around €6 to Plaça Catalunya or use the train for about €4.60.

Crowd Times: The city can get crowded, especially from late June to early September and during major holidays like **La Mercè**. To avoid the rush, aim to visit popular sites early in the morning or late in the afternoon.

Tickets: For attractions like the **Sagrada Família** and **Park Güell**, it's wise to purchase tickets online in advance to avoid long lines and guarantee your entry time. Tickets for the Sagrada Família are around €17, while Park Güell is €10.

What to Do: Besides the major attractions, explore the lesser-known **Bunkers del Carmel** for stunning city views and the peaceful **Parc del Laberint d'Horta**, where you can get lost in a charming maze and enjoy the tranquil gardens for just €2.

Secret Spots: For an off-the-beaten-path experience, visit **El Laberint d'Horta**, the oldest garden in the city, featuring a beautiful neoclassical maze. It's a hidden gem compared to the more popular parks and is perfect for a peaceful afternoon. Another secret spot is the **Carmel Bunkers**, a former anti-aircraft defense that offers one of the best panoramic views of Barcelona, especially at sunset.

Madrid

Madrid's origins can be traced back to the **9th century**, when the Moors, led by **Muhammad I**, established a small fortress on the banks of the Manzanares River. This settlement was initially called **Mayrit** (meaning 'place of abundant water'). The Moors built the city as a strategic military outpost to protect the region from Christian forces. Today, remnants of Moorish Madrid can still be seen in the **Almudena** area, where parts of the old city walls remain.

The Christian Reconquest and Growth

In **1085**, Madrid was conquered by King **Alfonso VI** during the Christian Reconquista. Over time, Madrid began to grow as a small yet significant trading center. It was during this period that the city began to develop its characteristic narrow, winding streets, many of which still exist in the **La Latina** and **El Rastro** neighborhoods.

From Small Town to Capital

Madrid's big break came in **1561**, when King **Philip II** moved the Spanish court from Toledo to Madrid, making it the capital of his vast empire. This shift brought new importance to the city, transforming it into the center of political and cultural life in Spain. With this royal endorsement, Madrid grew rapidly, and grand architectural projects began, such as the **Royal Palace** and the **Plaza Mayor**, which became the stage for celebrations, markets, and even public executions.

The Bourbon Influence

In the **18th century**, under the reign of the **Bourbon kings**, Madrid underwent significant modernization. **King Charles III** was a key figure in shaping Madrid into the elegant European city it is today. His reign saw the construction of the **Puerta de Alcalá**, the **Prado Museum**, and the beautiful **Retiro Park**. Often referred to as the "best mayor of Madrid," Charles III's reforms modernized the city's infrastructure and expanded its cultural offerings.

The Spanish Civil War and Franco Era

Madrid played a central role in the **Spanish Civil War** (1936-1939), enduring heavy bombing and fierce fighting between Republican and Nationalist forces. After the victory of **General Franco**, Madrid became a symbol of the dictatorship's power. During the Franco era, the city's political life was suppressed, but it remained a hub for arts and culture, particularly after Franco's death in **1975**, when Madrid blossomed into a thriving cultural epicenter during the **La Movida Madrileña**—a countercultural movement in the 1980s characterized by freedom of expression, art, music, and the rise of a vibrant nightlife scene.

Modern Madrid

Today, Madrid is a bustling metropolis that blends its historical roots with modern life. It's known for its world-class museums, stunning architecture, lively plazas, and endless tapas bars. The city remains the political, economic, and cultural heart of Spain.

Insider Tips for Visiting Madrid

Madrid is full of hidden gems and local secrets. To truly experience the city like a local, consider these insider tips:

1. Best Time to Visit

- **Avoid the Summer Heat**: Madrid can get scorching in the summer, with temperatures often exceeding 35°C (95°F). The best times to visit are **spring (March-May)** and **fall (September-November)**, when the weather is more pleasant, and the city is full of life.
- **Fiestas and Festivals**: Time your visit with local festivals like **San Isidro** (mid-May), where the streets fill with parades, traditional music, and food stalls. It's Madrid's biggest celebration in honor of its patron saint, San Isidro.

2. Explore Hidden Markets

- While the **Mercado de San Miguel** is a tourist favorite, try exploring more **authentic markets** where locals shop, like **Mercado de la Cebada** in La Latina or **Mercado de Antón Martín** in Lavapiés. These markets offer cheaper, fresher food, and an opportunity to interact with Madrileños in their daily routines.

3. Tapas Like a Local

- In some traditional bars, particularly in neighborhoods like **La Latina**, **Lavapiés**, or **Malasaña**, **free tapas** are often served with a drink (a caña—small beer—or glass of wine). Look for spots where locals gather, like **El Tigre** or **Casa Julio**, to enjoy this custom.
- **Go for the bocadillo de calamares** (calamari sandwich) in **Plaza Mayor**, but for a better and more local experience, try smaller taverns around **Calle de Toledo**.

4. Enjoy the Art Scene for Free

- Madrid is home to three world-renowned art museums: **Prado**, **Reina Sofía**, and **Thyssen-Bornemisza**. However, you can visit these for free during specific hours. For example:
  - **Prado Museum**: Free Monday-Saturday from 6-8 p.m. and Sundays from 5-7 p.m.
  - **Reina Sofía Museum**: Free Monday-Saturday from 7-9 p.m. and Sundays from 12:30-2:30 p.m.

5. Walk Through History in Retiro Park

- **El Retiro Park**, once the royal gardens of the Spanish monarchy, is the perfect place to relax. Besides walking or renting a rowboat on the lake, you can visit the **Palacio de Cristal** (Crystal Palace) and **Palacio de Velázquez**, which often host free art exhibitions. The park also has free walking tours that cover the park's historical significance.

6. Get Lost in Lavapiés

- One of Madrid's most culturally diverse neighborhoods, **Lavapiés** is a melting pot of global influences. The area is full of street art, bohemian bars, and affordable international cuisine. Try Indian, Senegalese, or Middle Eastern dishes in small, family-run restaurants. Visit **Tabacalera**, an old tobacco factory turned into an underground art space that hosts free exhibitions and events.

7. Visit the Royal Palace on Wednesdays

- The **Royal Palace** is the largest functioning royal palace in Europe. Although you have to pay for entry, on **Wednesdays and Thursdays** from 3-6 p.m., entry is **free for EU** residents. For a local experience, don't miss the **changing of the guard** on **Wednesdays at noon**.

8. Catch a Flamenco Show Without Breaking the Bank

- Flamenco is an essential part of Spanish culture, and while some tourist shows can be expensive, you can find **affordable or even free performances** in traditional bars. Check out **Las Tablas**, which offers reasonable prices, or **Candela**, a flamenco bar where locals and artists mingle.

9. Sunset at the Temple of Debod

- One of Madrid's most unique landmarks is the **Temple of Debod**, an ancient Egyptian temple gifted to Spain. It's located in a park near the Royal Palace and offers some of the best views of Madrid's sunset—completely free of charge.

10. Discover Madrid's Rooftop Bars

- Madrid has some stunning rooftop terraces where you can enjoy a drink and panoramic views of the city. For a local favorite, head to the **Círculo de Bellas Artes** rooftop for sunset views of **Gran Vía**. Alternatively, visit **Azotea del Círculo** or **Ginkgo Sky Bar** for chic, relaxed atmospheres.

11. Off-the-Beaten-Path Museums

- While the main museums are must-sees, Madrid also has some quirky, less-known spots, like the **Museum of Romanticism**, which showcases 19th-century art, or the **Sorolla Museum**, housed in the artist's former mansion, which is often less crowded but equally fascinating.

12. Take a Day Trip

- If you have time, take a day trip to nearby historic towns like **Toledo** (only 30 minutes by train), **Segovia**, or **El Escorial**. Each offers incredible history, stunning architecture, and a slower pace than the bustling capital.

Top 20 Paid Attractions in Madrid

1. **Museo del Prado**
   The Prado Museum is a must-visit for art lovers, housing works by masters like Velázquez, Goya, and El Greco. To save on fees, visit on free entry days, typically on weekdays after 6 PM. If you can't get in for free, consider visiting the nearby **Museo Thyssen-Bornemisza**, which often offers a combo ticket at a discount. For a creative alternative, explore the art scattered throughout the city, like street murals in Lavapiés. Practical tip: use the audio guide app to enhance your visit. The Prado's history dates back to the 18th century when it was established as a royal museum.

2. **Palacio Real**
   The Royal Palace is the official residence of the Spanish royal family, and it's opulent! Save money by opting for a guided tour rather than the more expensive private ones. If you're looking for a free alternative, stroll through the beautiful Campo del Moro gardens that surround the palace. Make sure to check out the changing of the guard, which is free and happens every Wednesday and Saturday.

Did you know that this palace was built in the 18th century on the site of a Moorish castle?

3. **Parque del Retiro**
    This expansive park is perfect for a leisurely day out, and while entry is free, consider renting a rowboat on the lake for a small fee. Alternatively, pack a picnic and enjoy it on the grass. To save on time, go early in the morning to avoid crowds. The park has a rich history, once being a royal retreat, and is now a beloved public space where locals and tourists alike come to unwind.

4. **Museo Reina Sofía**
    Home to Picasso's Guernica, this modern art museum is a highlight of Madrid's cultural scene. To save on admission, visit on Mondays or from 7 PM on weekdays when it's free. If you can't make it, explore the nearby **Atocha Station**, which houses a beautiful indoor garden for a lovely stroll. Pro tip: take advantage of the guided tours that provide in-depth insights into the exhibits. The museum was originally a hospital before becoming a home for contemporary art.

5. **Estadio Santiago Bernabéu**
    Football fans can't miss a tour of Real Madrid's iconic stadium. To save on fees, check for discounts for students and seniors. If you're not keen on the fee, enjoy the atmosphere in the surrounding area and catch a match in a nearby bar. Pro tip: plan your visit around a game day for the ultimate experience. Opened in 1947, the stadium has witnessed countless memorable matches and moments in football history.

6. **Thyssen-Bornemisza Museum**
    This museum boasts a diverse collection of artworks spanning centuries. To save on admission, combine your ticket with the nearby Prado Museum for a discount. Alternatively, admire the art displayed on the streets of Madrid, especially in the Malasaña neighborhood. Practical tip: don't miss the café in the museum for a delightful break. The museum originated from the private collection of the Thyssen-Bornemisza family, showcasing their exquisite taste in art.

7. **Teleférico de Madrid**
    The Madrid Cable Car offers breathtaking views of the city. To save, purchase a round-trip ticket online for a discount. If you prefer a free alternative, walk up to the **Casa de Campo** for panoramic views of the city. Pro tip: go during sunset for the most stunning views. The cable car was opened in 1968 and provides a unique perspective of Madrid from above.

8. **Mercado de San Miguel**
    This vibrant market is a food lover's paradise, but it can get pricey. To save, share tapas with friends and sample smaller portions. Alternatively, check out local street food stalls in neighborhoods like Lavapiés for a more budget-friendly experience. Make sure to try local specialties like jamón ibérico! The market has a rich history, having been established in 1916, and retains its historic charm.

9. **Museo Nacional de Ciencias Naturales**
    This natural history museum is great for families and offers discounts for children and students. To save money, visit on Sundays when entry is free. For a creative alternative, head to the nearby **Parque de la Cuña Verde** for a nature walk. Pro tip:

the dinosaur exhibits are a must-see! The museum has been promoting the study of natural history since the 18th century.

10. **Catedral de la Almudena**
Madrid's stunning cathedral is both an architectural gem and a spiritual site. Admission is free, but consider paying for a guided tour to gain deeper insights. If you're looking for something free, enjoy the view from the nearby **Mirador de la Almudena**. Practical tip: don't miss the crypt and the rooftop views of the city. The cathedral's construction took over a century, finally completed in 1993.

11. **Palacio de Cibeles**
The stunning City Hall offers an impressive viewpoint from its observation deck for a small fee. To save, visit during the week when admission is often discounted. A creative alternative is to take pictures of the building from the stunning Plaza de Cibeles. Pro tip: check out the exhibitions often held inside the palace for a cultural experience. Originally built as a post office, the palace showcases a beautiful blend of architectural styles.

12. **Atención al Cliente de Madrid**
This unique attraction allows you to learn about the city's history and services. It's free to enter, but consider signing up for a guided walking tour that includes this stop. If you're not keen on tours, use your time to explore **Plaza Mayor**, another historic site nearby. Pro tip: grab a coffee from a nearby café while soaking in the atmosphere. The building has been a part of Madrid's history since the early 20th century.

13. **Círculo de Bellas Artes**
This cultural center hosts art exhibitions, concerts, and films, and offers a panoramic rooftop terrace for a fee. To save, check their schedule for free events or discounted student tickets. If you're looking for a free alternative, explore the cultural spaces around the **Gran Vía**. Practical tip: the rooftop terrace provides some of the best sunset views in the city. Established in 1880, the Círculo has been a cornerstone of Madrid's cultural life.

14. **Museo del Romanticismo**
This museum showcases the Romantic period's art and artifacts. To save, visit on weekends when it offers free entry. For a creative alternative, explore the nearby **Barrio de Las Letras**, known for its literary history. Practical tip: take your time in the museum's charming garden café. The museum is housed in a beautiful 18th-century mansion that tells the story of Spain's romantic past.

15. **Casa de Campo**
This sprawling park is perfect for outdoor enthusiasts, offering attractions like a zoo and amusement park. To save, opt for a picnic instead of dining at the park's restaurants. For a free alternative, explore the hiking trails or rent a bike. Pro tip: don't miss the stunning lake area! Originally a royal hunting ground, Casa de Campo has transformed into a recreational haven for locals.

16. **Fundación MAPFRE**
This cultural institution hosts rotating art exhibitions, with a focus on photography and painting. To save, check for free exhibition days and student discounts. For a creative alternative, visit the outdoor sculptures in the surrounding area. Pro tip:

combine your visit with a stroll through the nearby **Retiro Park**. The foundation has played a significant role in promoting the arts in Madrid since its establishment.

17. **Museo de la Ciudad**

    Dive into the history of Madrid at this city museum. To save, visit on the first Sunday of the month when entry is free. For a free alternative, explore the streets of the historic center, soaking in the architecture. Pro tip: join a free walking tour that includes this museum. The museum has a collection that showcases Madrid's evolution through the ages.

18. **La Tabacalera**

    This former tobacco factory has been transformed into a cultural space filled with art installations and community projects. Entry is free, but check for guided tours that might have a small fee. For a creative alternative, enjoy street art in the surrounding neighborhood. Pro tip: explore the exhibitions and take part in workshops. The building dates back to the 18th century and has been a hub for creativity since its renovation.

19. **Museo del Ferrocarril**

    Train enthusiasts will love this railway museum, showcasing historic trains and memorabilia. Save by visiting on Sundays when it's free. If you're looking for a free alternative, visit the nearby **Madrid Rio** park for a lovely stroll. Pro tip: the museum hosts special events and exhibitions, so check the schedule. The museum is located in a beautiful old train station that dates back to the late 19th century.

20. **National Archaeological Museum**

    This museum boasts an impressive collection of artifacts

Insider Tips for Madrid

1. **Get a Transport Card**: If you're planning to use public transport, consider getting a Transport Card. It's a cost-effective way to travel on the metro and buses throughout the city. You can choose between single journeys or unlimited travel for a specific number of days.

2. **Tapas Time**: Enjoy the tradition of tapas by opting for bars that offer free tapas with your drink. Head to **La Latina**or **Malasaña** for a vibrant atmosphere and delicious options.

3. **Plan for Siesta**: Many shops and restaurants close for a few hours in the afternoon for siesta. Embrace the culture by taking a break, then venture out later for dinner when the city comes alive!

4. **Explore Neighborhoods**: Each neighborhood in Madrid has its unique vibe. Spend time in **Chueca** for LGBTQ+ culture, **Malasaña** for trendy shops and cafes, and **Lavapiés** for a multicultural experience.

5. **Local Markets**: Don't miss the local markets like **Mercado de San Miguel** or **Mercado de San Antón**. They offer an array of gourmet food and local produce, perfect for sampling without breaking the bank.

6. **Free Museums**: Many museums have free entry on specific days. The **Prado Museum** and **Reina Sofía** offer free visits, so plan accordingly to save on admission fees.

7. **Walk or Bike**: Madrid is a walkable city with beautiful parks and plazas. Rent a bike or walk to discover hidden gems, especially in **Retiro Park**.

8. **Cultural Festivals**: If you visit during one of Madrid's many festivals, such as **San Isidro** in May, you'll get to experience the city's vibrant culture for free, with parades, music, and food stalls.

Getting Around Madrid Cheaply

1. **Metro System**: Madrid's metro is one of the most efficient and extensive in Europe. A single journey costs €1.50, but if you plan to use public transport frequently, consider buying a **10-trip ticket** (Metrobús) for around €12.20. This ticket can be shared among multiple passengers, making it a cost-effective option for groups.

2. **Public Buses**: Buses are another excellent way to navigate the city and are included in the same ticketing system as the metro. With frequent service and a vast network, buses can take you to areas that might not be easily reached by metro.

3. **Walking**: Many of Madrid's main attractions are within walking distance of each other, especially in the city center. Strolling through the streets allows you to

experience the vibrant atmosphere of the city and discover charming shops and cafes along the way—plus, it's completely free!

4. **Bicycle Rentals**: Madrid is increasingly bike-friendly, with bike lanes and rental options available. You can rent a bike through the **BiciMAD** system. A single ride costs around €2, and a day pass is approximately €8, allowing unlimited rides for 24 hours.

5. **Electric Scooters**: Electric scooters have become a popular mode of transport in Madrid. You can find them throughout the city, and they typically cost around €1 to unlock and €0.15 per minute. They offer a fun and quick way to get around.

6. **Taxi and Ride-Sharing**: While taxis can be expensive, ride-sharing apps like Uber and Cabify may offer more competitive prices. Always check for promotional offers, especially for new users, which can help you save money.

7. **Tourist Travel Pass**: If you plan to explore multiple attractions, consider purchasing the **Madrid Tourist Travel Pass**. It provides unlimited travel on public transport for 1, 2, 3, 5, or 7 days, allowing you to hop on and off as you explore the city.

8. **Free Walking Tours**: Madrid offers numerous free walking tours that allow you to learn about the city's history and culture. While these tours are free, it's customary to tip your guide based on your satisfaction.

9. **Discounted Tickets for Attractions**: Many attractions offer discounted entry for students, seniors, or large groups. Always ask if discounts are available, which can often save you a substantial amount on admission fees.

10. **Plan Your Routes**: Utilize apps like Google Maps or the official Madrid transport app to plan your routes efficiently. This will help you avoid unnecessary travel, saving both time and money.

Affordable Luxury Accommodation in Madrid

Hotel Name	Location	Average Nightly	Description
Hotel	Gran	150 €	A chic hotel located on the iconic Gran Vía, offering stylish
Hotel	Gran	120 €	Features a rooftop pool and luxurious amenities, with a
The Principal Madrid	Gran Vía	200 €	A luxurious boutique hotel with stunning views, offering personalized service in the heart of Madrid.
Hotel Villa Real	Plaza de Cibeles	130 €	Offers a classic atmosphere with art-filled rooms and a rooftop terrace for a touch of luxury.
H10 Casa de	La	110 €	A stylish hotel with modern decor and a cozy rooftop
Hotel Quatro Puerta del Sol	Puerta del Sol	130 €	Nestled in the heart of Madrid, this hotel features modern amenities with a touch of elegance.
Room Mate Oscar	Chueca	120 €	A trendy hotel known for its vibrant design and welcoming atmosphere, close to major attractions.
Hotel Zenit Abeba	Salamanca	110 €	This contemporary hotel offers luxurious amenities at an affordable price, with easy access to the city center.

Free Events or Experiences in Madrid That Most People Don't Know About

1. **Cultural Festivals**: Madrid hosts various cultural festivals throughout the year that many tourists overlook. For example, the **San Isidro Festival** in May celebrates the city's patron saint with parades, concerts, and traditional dances. Attending these events is completely free, providing a fantastic way to immerse yourself in local culture while enjoying vibrant performances and delicious food stalls.

2. **Rooftop Views**: While many tourists flock to popular lookout points, several lesser-known rooftops offer stunning views for free or at a minimal cost. For instance, the rooftop of **Círculo de Bellas Artes** charges a small fee for entry, but the views are well worth it. Alternatively, head to **Terraza del Urban** for cocktails that don't require an entry fee, all while enjoying picturesque views of the city.

3. **Street Art Tours**: Madrid is home to an impressive street art scene, particularly in neighborhoods like **Malasaña**and **Lavapiés**. While formal street art tours may charge a fee, you can explore these neighborhoods yourself for free. Keep an eye out for works by local artists and enjoy the vibrant, ever-changing urban landscape.

4. **Public Concerts and Performances**: Many parks and public squares host free concerts, particularly during the summer months. The **Madrid Summer Festival** often features free live music and performances in parks like **Retiro Park**. Check local listings to find out what's happening during your visit.

5. **Free Entry to Museums**: While many museums charge an entry fee, several offer free admission on certain days. For instance, the **Prado Museum** has free entry from 6 PM to 8 PM on weekdays, while the **Reina Sofía** offers free admission on Mondays from 7 PM to 9 PM. This is a great way to explore these incredible collections without spending a cent.

Practical Things to Remember to Save Money in Madrid

1. **Use Public Transport**: A single metro or bus ticket costs €1.50, but consider purchasing a **10-trip ticket**(Metrobús) for €12.20 to save money. This ticket can be shared among multiple travelers.

2. **Dining Smart**: Instead of dining in touristy restaurants, opt for local tapas bars where you can enjoy a drink and get a free tapa. Many bars in neighborhoods like **La Latina** or **Malasaña** offer this, saving you money while providing an authentic experience.

3. **Explore Markets**: Visit local markets like **Mercado de San Miguel** or **Mercado de San Antón** for affordable food options. Instead of dining in restaurants, you can grab small bites at various stalls. Expect to spend around €10-15 for a meal compared to €20-30 at sit-down restaurants.

4. **Take Advantage of Discounts**: Many attractions offer discounted entry for students, seniors, and large groups. Always ask if discounts are available, which can often save you around 20-50% on admission fees.

5. **Free Activities**: Explore the numerous parks in Madrid, such as **Casa de Campo** or **Retiro Park**, where you can enjoy a picnic, rent a rowboat (around €6 for 45 minutes), or simply stroll through the beautiful landscapes without spending anything.

Practical Information for Visiting Madrid

1. **Getting There**: Madrid-Barajas Airport is well-connected to the city center by metro (Line 8) and bus. A metro ticket to the city center costs around €5. Alternatively, taxis are available, with a flat rate of about €30 from the airport to the city center.

2. **Best Times to Visit**: The best times to visit are during spring (March to May) and fall (September to November) when the weather is pleasant. Avoid July and August if you're not a fan of heat, as temperatures can soar above 35°C (95°F), and many locals are on holiday, leading to quieter streets.

3. **Crowds**: Major tourist attractions, such as the **Prado Museum** and **Royal Palace**, can get crowded, especially during weekends and holidays. Aim to visit these sites early in the morning or late in the afternoon to avoid the heaviest crowds.

4. **Tickets for Attractions**: Most attractions, such as the **Royal Palace** and **Museo del Prado**, offer online ticket sales that can save you time and sometimes money. Look for combo tickets for multiple attractions, which can provide a discount.

5. **What to Do There**: Besides visiting major sites, don't miss local experiences like attending a flamenco show or enjoying a local festival. Explore neighborhoods like **Chueca** and **La Latina** for nightlife and authentic dining.

6. **Secret Spots**: Seek out hidden gems like **Calle del Cuchilleros** near Plaza Mayor, a charming street lined with restaurants and bars that offer a more local feel. **Tabacalera** in Lavapiés, an old tobacco factory turned cultural space, is also worth a visit for its street art and exhibitions.

7. **Safety Tips**: While Madrid is generally safe, be cautious of pickpockets in crowded areas, especially on public transport and tourist sites. Keep your belongings secure and be aware of your surroundings.

Valencia

Valencia, the third-largest city in Spain, boasts a rich and complex history that dates back over 2,000 years. Founded in 138 BC as a Roman colony, it was named *Valentia* (meaning "strength" or "valor"). The city has been shaped by numerous civilizations, including the Romans, Visigoths, and Moors, each leaving their mark on its culture and architecture.

The Moors, who ruled Valencia from 711 to 1238, significantly influenced the city, introducing advanced agricultural techniques like irrigation systems that are still in use today. They also built mosques, bathhouses, and palaces, remnants of which can still be explored.

In 1238, King James I of Aragon reconquered Valencia for the Christians. This period saw the construction of iconic structures like the Valencia Cathedral, a beautiful mix of Gothic, Baroque, and Romanesque styles. The city's famed *Miguelete* bell tower is a striking symbol of this era. Over time, Valencia became a key Mediterranean trading hub, especially during the 15th century, known as its *Siglo de Oro* (Golden Age). This economic boom led to the construction of many Gothic masterpieces, such as the *Lonja de la Seda* (Silk Exchange), now a UNESCO World Heritage Site.

In the 19th and 20th centuries, Valencia experienced industrial growth, and its port became one of Spain's most important. The Spanish Civil War left its scars, but Valencia has since recovered and modernized. Today, it's known for its futuristic *Ciudad de las Artes y las Ciencias* (City of Arts and Sciences), designed by Valencian architect Santiago Calatrava, which symbolizes the city's forward-looking spirit.

Insider Tips for Visiting Valencia

1. **Best Time to Visit**: Late spring (May) and early autumn (September-October) offer pleasant weather without the crowds of high summer. March is also special, as Valencia hosts *Las Fallas*, an extravagant festival of fire and fireworks.

2. **Explore Barrio del Carmen**: This historic quarter is perfect for a leisurely stroll, filled with narrow, winding streets, vibrant street art, and charming medieval architecture. Visit the Torres de Serranos, one of the ancient gates that once protected the city, for panoramic views.

3. **Albufera Natural Park**: Located just 10 kilometers south of the city, this natural paradise is a great spot for birdwatching, boat trips, or sampling traditional *paella*, which was invented in Valencia. The park's calm, reflective lagoon is particularly stunning at sunset.

4. **Paella Tip**: While most people associate Spain with *paella*, Valencia is its true birthplace. Skip the tourist traps near the beach and instead head to local favorites like *La Pepica* or *Casa Carmela* for authentic *paella Valenciana* (made with rabbit, chicken, and beans).

5. **Visit the Central Market**: The Mercado Central, one of the largest and oldest markets in Europe, is a feast for the senses. Grab some local produce, such as *horchata* (a traditional drink made from tiger nuts) or fresh seafood. It's also a great place to interact with locals.

6. **Cheap Art & Culture**: The City of Arts and Sciences offers multiple types of tickets for different attractions, but one of the best deals is purchasing a combo pass for the Hemisfèric, Science Museum, and Oceanogràfic, Europe's largest aquarium. You can also visit the nearby *Gulliver Park*, a whimsical playground free of charge.

7. **Horchatarias**: After a day of sightseeing, cool off with *horchata* and *fartons* (sweet pastries). Visit Horchatería Santa Catalina, one of the city's oldest establishments, to try this refreshing drink.

8. **Beach Tip**: Malvarrosa Beach is the most famous, but if you want a quieter beach experience, head to the nearby *Playa de la Patacona*. It's more relaxed and less crowded, perfect for a peaceful beach day.

9. **Turia Gardens**: After the catastrophic flood of 1957, the river Turia was rerouted, and its former riverbed was turned into a beautiful green park. Stretching over 9 kilometers, the Turia Gardens offer lush landscapes, playgrounds, and bicycle paths. It's a wonderful place to relax, jog, or rent a bike and explore.

10. **Fiestas**: Valencia's festivals are legendary, with *Las Fallas* being the most famous. This fiery celebration sees large, satirical statues (called *ninots*) paraded through the streets before being burned on the final night. Other notable festivals include *La Tomatina* (just outside Valencia in Buñol) and *La Virgen de los Desamparados*, the patron saint festival in May.

Top 20 Paid Attractions in Valencia

1. **City of Arts and Sciences (Ciudad de las Artes y las Ciencias)**
   This architectural marvel is a must-see! It houses a science museum, planetarium, aquarium, and more. To save on fees, consider visiting on a weekday when tickets are often discounted. If you're looking for a creative alternative, stroll through the stunning gardens surrounding the complex—perfect for a picnic! A fun fact: the design was inspired by the ocean and the human body, showcasing Valencia's connection to nature.

2. **Valencia Cathedral**
   This stunning cathedral is said to house the Holy Grail. Explore its intricate architecture and climb the Miguelete Tower for panoramic views. To save on entry fees, visit during free entry hours, typically on Sundays. If you're not keen on climbing, enjoy the serene atmosphere in the surrounding Plaza de la Virgen. Fun historical tidbit: the cathedral combines Romanesque, Gothic, and Baroque styles, symbolizing the city's diverse history.

3. **Bioparc Valencia**
   A unique zoo experience that immerses you in the animals' natural habitats. Buy tickets online for discounts, and opt for a weekday visit to avoid crowds. Alternatively, take a stroll in the nearby Turia Gardens, where you can enjoy the greenery for free. Fun fact: the Bioparc emphasizes conservation and education, making it a fantastic choice for families.

4. **L'Oceanogràfic**
   The largest aquarium in Europe, home to thousands of marine species. Look for combo tickets that include other attractions for savings. If you're short on cash, spend time at the nearby beach, enjoying the sun and surf without spending a dime. Interesting note: the building's design resembles a water lily, reflecting Valencia's relationship with water.

5. **Mercado Central**
   While entry is free, you may want to sample the delicious local produce. Bring cash for a true local experience and visit early for the best selection. As a free alternative, you can browse the nearby streets filled with local boutiques and cafes. This market is one of the largest in Europe and is a feast for the senses!

6. **Torres de Serranos**
   These medieval towers offer a glimpse into Valencia's past. Climb to the top for a small fee and enjoy spectacular views. For a free experience, explore the Turia Gardens right next to the towers. Did you know these towers were once part of the city's defensive walls?

7. **Valencia's Silk Exchange (La Lonja de la Seda)**
   A UNESCO World Heritage Site, this stunning Gothic building is a must-visit. Tickets are inexpensive, but you can save by visiting during free hours. If you're looking for a free alternative, check out the nearby Mercado Central for its beautiful architecture and lively atmosphere. The Silk Exchange was once the center of Valencia's silk trade, showcasing the city's economic history.

8. **Museo de Bellas Artes**
   Home to an impressive collection of Spanish art, including works by Goya and Velázquez. Admission is free on Sundays, and you can save by checking their website for special exhibitions. Instead of spending on entrance fees, explore the beautiful gardens surrounding the museum. Fun fact: it houses the second-largest collection of paintings in Spain after the Prado!

9. **Central Park of Valencia**
   An urban oasis in the heart of the city, perfect for a leisurely stroll or picnic. While it's free to enter, consider renting a bike to explore more efficiently. Alternatively, you can visit the nearby Turia Gardens for a longer, scenic walk. The park was once a riverbed that transformed into a lush green space, showcasing Valencia's innovative urban planning.

10. **IVAM (Institut Valencià d'Art Modern)**
    A modern art museum featuring contemporary works. Admission is discounted on certain days, so check the website before you go. If art isn't your thing, wander the streets nearby to discover street art and local galleries for free! The museum plays a vital role in promoting modern art in Valencia.

11. **Bioparc Valencia**
    This immersive zoo experience allows you to explore wildlife in a naturalistic setting. To save on admission, look for combo tickets with other attractions or visit on weekdays. If you're looking for a free alternative, take a walk in the Turia Gardens. Bioparc emphasizes conservation, providing a unique educational experience.

12. **Palacio de las Artes Reina Sofia**
    A stunning opera house showcasing impressive performances. To save on tickets, attend matinee shows, which are often cheaper. Alternatively, catch a free outdoor performance during summer months. The design of the building is inspired by the waves of the sea, reflecting Valencia's maritime heritage.

13. **Parque de la Albufera**
A beautiful natural park just outside the city, perfect for birdwatching and boat rides. Entrance is free, but boat rides require a small fee. Instead of spending on boat rides, pack a picnic and enjoy the stunning views of the lake and surrounding wetlands. This park is home to Valencia's famous rice fields, essential for authentic paella!

14. **Museo Fallero**
This museum is dedicated to Valencia's famous Fallas festival, showcasing the incredible artistry behind the festival's sculptures. Tickets are affordable, but consider visiting during off-peak hours for a quieter experience. For a free alternative, stroll through the streets during the Fallas festival to see the sculptures before they're burned! The museum captures the spirit and creativity of this unique Valencian tradition.

15. **Parque Gulliver**
A giant playground inspired by "Gulliver's Travels." While entrance is free, activities within the park may have fees. For a budget-friendly alternative, bring your own snacks and enjoy a picnic on the grass. This whimsical park is a hit with families, providing a fantastic space for children to play and explore.

16. **Museo de Historia de Valencia**
This museum offers an engaging look at Valencia's rich history. Tickets are reasonably priced, but free entry is available on certain days. Instead of spending money, take a guided walking tour of the historic center to learn more about the city's past. The museum is located in a former fish market, adding to its historical charm!

17. **Parque Natural de la Albufera**
A beautiful park just outside the city, famous for its rice fields and stunning sunsets. Entrance is free, but boat rides have a small fee. For an affordable option, rent a bike and explore the trails around the park. The Albufera is also home to many migratory birds, making it a paradise for nature lovers.

18. **Oceanogràfic**
This vast aquarium is part of the City of Arts and Sciences, housing a diverse range of marine life. Save money by purchasing tickets online or visiting during weekdays. If you're looking for a free alternative, explore the beautiful waterfront area surrounding the aquarium. Did you know that it's the largest aquarium in Europe?

19. **Catedral de Valencia**
Explore this iconic cathedral that claims to house the Holy Grail. Entry is free on certain days, so check before your visit. Instead of paying for a guided tour, download a free app for an audio guide! The cathedral's architecture is a blend of styles, reflecting Valencia's rich history.

20. **Museo de Ciencias Príncipe Felipe**
A hands-on science museum with interactive exhibits that are great for families. Tickets are discounted for children and seniors. For a free experience, wander through the beautiful gardens surrounding the museum. The museum is named after the Prince of Asturias, showcasing Valencia's royal connections!

Insider Tips for Valencia

1. **Public Transportation**: Valencia has an efficient public transport system that includes buses, trams, and metro. Invest in a Valencia Tourist Card for unlimited travel and discounts on attractions. It's a great way to explore the city without breaking the bank!

2. **Explore the Turia Gardens**: Once a river, the Turia Gardens are now a sprawling park perfect for walking, cycling, or picnicking. It's a lovely, free escape from the bustling city and a great way to enjoy Valencia's greenery.

3. **Enjoy Free Tapas**: Some bars in Valencia offer free tapas with a drink, especially during happy hour. Be sure to ask where you can find this delightful deal to experience local cuisine without spending much!

4. **Visit Museums on Free Entry Days**: Many museums in Valencia have free entry days, usually on Sundays or specific days of the month. Check their websites for details and plan your visit accordingly.

5. **Book in Advance**: For attractions that charge an entry fee, booking tickets online in advance can often save you money and time, helping you avoid long queues.

6. **Explore Local Markets**: Check out Mercado Central and Mercado de Ruzafa for fresh produce, local delicacies, and vibrant atmospheres. You can grab a quick and cheap meal while experiencing local life.

7. **Enjoy the Beaches**: Valencia's beaches, like Playa de la Malvarrosa, are free to access. Spend a day sunbathing, swimming, or enjoying water sports without any costs!

8. **Use Bicing**: Valencia has a bike-sharing program called Valenbisi. Renting a bike is an affordable and enjoyable way to explore the city at your own pace.

9. **Walk the Historic Center**: Valencia's historic center is compact and pedestrian-friendly, making it easy to explore on foot. Strolling through the charming streets is free and allows you to discover hidden gems.

10. **Check Local Events**: Keep an eye on local event calendars for free concerts, festivals, or exhibitions happening during your visit. These can provide unique cultural experiences at no cost!

Getting Around Valencia Cheaply

1. **Public Transport Pass**: Purchase a Valencia Tourist Card for unlimited access to buses, trams, and metro for 24, 48, or 72 hours. It's economical and convenient!

2. **Walking and Cycling**: Many attractions are within walking distance, and Valencia has a great bike-sharing system (Valenbisi) that allows you to rent bikes cheaply.

3. **Tram System**: The tram is an efficient way to get to various parts of the city, including the beach. Tickets are affordable, and you can use your public transport pass.

4. **Group Discounts:** If you're traveling with friends or family, look for group discounts on public transport and attractions.

5. **Consider Taxis for Groups:** For larger groups, taxis may be more economical, especially when shared among friends.

6. **Use Ride-Sharing Apps:** Apps like Uber and Bolt operate in Valencia and can sometimes offer competitive prices compared to traditional taxis.

Chart of Affordable Luxury Accommodation in Valencia

Hotel Name	Location	Average Nightly Price	Pros	Cons
Hotel Balneario Las Arenas	Near Malvarrosa	€150 - €200	Beachfront, spa facilities	Higher end of the budget
Caro Hotel	Historic Center	€120 - €180	Unique design, great	Limited
Hotel Sorolla Centro	City Center	€100 - €150	Central location, modern	No pool
Hotel Zenit Valencia	Near Turia	€90 - €130	Good transport links,	Basic breakfast
Melia Valencia	Near Convention	€100 - €160	Great views, comfortable rooms	Some areas may be busy
Hotel Ilunion Valencia	Near City of	€90 - €130	Modern, accessible,	Further from
NH Valencia Center	Near Turia	€100 - €140	Comfortable stay,	Can be noisy at
SH Valencia Palace	Near City	€120 - €170	Rooftop pool, elegant	Pricey dining
Hotel Valencia	Near	€90 - €130	Close to attractions,	Limited
Valenciaflats Ciudad de las Ciencias	Near City of Arts	€80 - €120	Apartment-style rooms, family-friendly	Self-catering, no meals

Top 20 Things to Do in Valencia That Feel Luxury But Are Free or Cheap

1. **Stroll Through Turia Gardens**
Enjoy a leisurely walk or bike ride through the lush Turia Gardens. The vast green space is a lovely, free escape, perfect for picnics.

2. **Visit the Valencia Cathedral**
Entry to the Cathedral is around €8, and you can enjoy its stunning architecture. Climb the Miguelete Tower for breathtaking views at €2.

3. **Relax at Playa de la Malvarrosa**
Valencia's main beach is free to access. Rent a sunbed for around €5 or enjoy a stroll along the promenade.

4. **Explore Mercado Central**
Browse through local produce and enjoy free samples. Grab a delicious meal for under €10!

5. **Free Tapas Bars**
Enjoy a drink at certain bars and get free tapas. It's a fantastic way to taste local flavors without spending much!

6. **Wander the Historic Center**
   Exploring the historic streets is free! Take in the beautiful architecture and vibrant atmosphere.

7. **Visit the City of Arts and Sciences**
   Entry to the gardens is free. The complex is stunning, and you can enjoy the views without paying.

8. **Attend Free Events**
   Check local event listings for free concerts or exhibitions happening during your visit.

9. **Explore the Oceanogràfic**
   While entry is €30, consider visiting during discounted days or special promotions.

10. **Visit IVAM for Art**
    Entry to the museum is €6, but free on Sundays. Enjoy contemporary art and culture!

11. **Relax in Parque de la Albufera**
    A day at the natural park is free. Enjoy a boat ride for around €6 if you want a unique experience.

12. **Tour the Lonja de la Seda**
    Entry is around €2, allowing you to explore this UNESCO World Heritage Site.

13. **Enjoy a Picnic at Jardín del Turia**
    Bring your own food and relax in this beautiful park, soaking in the sunshine.

14. **Experience Valencia's Street Art**
    Wander through neighborhoods like El Carmen to see stunning street art for free.

15. **Cycle Along the Coast**
    Rent a bike for around €2 an hour and explore Valencia's coastline at your own pace.

16. **Visit the Museum of Fine Arts**
    Entrance is free, allowing you to enjoy a fantastic collection of Spanish masterpieces!

17. **Explore Ruzafa Market**
    Visit this vibrant market to sample local goods and enjoy a meal for under €10.

18. **Attend the Fallas Festival**
    If you visit in March, enjoy the spectacle of the Fallas festival for free—just grab a drink and soak in the atmosphere!

19. **Visit the Botanical Garden**
    Entry is around €2, offering a peaceful retreat filled with beautiful plants and flowers.

20. **Enjoy Local Parks**
    Parks like Parc Central and Parque de Cabecera are free to access, perfect for a leisurely day outdoors!

Seville

This vibrant Andalusian city is a mesmerizing blend of history, culture, and tradition. Once the capital of the vast Spanish Empire, Seville played a pivotal role during the Age of Exploration as the primary port for trade with the New World. The iconic Giralda tower was originally built as a minaret for the Great Mosque in the 12th century, later transformed into the bell tower of the Cathedral. The city's rich Moorish heritage is evident in its stunning architecture, including the Alcázar Palace, where intricate tilework and lush gardens transport you to a different era.

Flamenco, the passionate dance that embodies the spirit of Andalusia, has its roots in Seville, with its vibrant colors and intense rhythms captivating audiences worldwide. The annual Feria de Abril and Semana Santa are just a few of the lively festivals that showcase the city's deep traditions and sense of community. Today, Seville is a UNESCO World Heritage site that continues to charm visitors with its warm-hearted locals, lively tapas bars, and a magical atmosphere that lingers long after the sun sets.

Top 20 Paid Attractions in Seville

1. **Real Alcázar of Seville**
   This stunning royal palace, originally a Moorish fort, showcases intricate architecture and lush gardens. To save on fees, consider visiting on Mondays or purchasing a combo ticket with the Cathedral. A creative free alternative is to stroll through the nearby Parque de María Luisa, which offers beautiful gardens and fountains. The Alcázar's history is steeped in tales of kings and queens, making it a must-see for any history buff.

2. **Seville Cathedral and La Giralda**
   One of the largest cathedrals in the world, this Gothic masterpiece houses Christopher Columbus's tomb. Save money by visiting during the late afternoon when entry is discounted. Alternatively, enjoy the view of the cathedral from the charming Plaza del Triunfo. Did you know La Giralda was originally built as a minaret? Its tower has become an iconic symbol of the city.

3. **Metropol Parasol (Las Setas)**
   This modern architectural marvel, resembling giant mushrooms, offers panoramic views of the city from its sky terrace. To save, visit during sunset for a breathtaking view and a lower entrance fee. If you're looking for a free alternative, enjoy the vibrant atmosphere of the nearby Plaza de la Encarnación. The Metropol has become a contemporary symbol of Seville, juxtaposing its historic surroundings.

4. **Museum of Fine Arts**
   Housed in a former convent, this museum boasts an impressive collection of Spanish art from the medieval period to the early 20th century. Save by visiting on Tuesday, when admission is free for EU citizens. For a creative alternative, explore the nearby neighborhood of Santa Cruz and admire street art. The museum reflects Seville's rich artistic heritage, including works by Murillo and Zurbarán.

5. **Flamenco Dance Museum**
   Immerse yourself in the passionate world of flamenco through exhibitions and live

performances. Book your tickets online to save and opt for a mid-week visit for lower prices. A great free alternative is to catch an impromptu flamenco performance in the streets of Triana. The museum showcases flamenco's evolution and significance in Andalusian culture.

6. **Torre del Oro**
   This 13th-century watchtower once protected the city from invaders and now houses a maritime museum. Save on fees by taking advantage of the free admission on Mondays. Instead of paying, enjoy a leisurely walk along the Guadalquivir River. The tower's name, meaning "Tower of Gold," is believed to come from the golden tiles that once adorned its exterior.

7. **Parque de María Luisa**
   While entry to the park is free, consider renting a bike to explore its expansive gardens and charming ponds. If you prefer a paid attraction, visit the nearby Plaza de España, which features stunning mosaics and architectural beauty. The park was designed for the Ibero-American Exposition of 1929, showcasing Spain's rich culture.

8. **Palacio de las Dueñas**
   This stunning palace offers a glimpse into the aristocratic lifestyle of Seville's past. Save on admission by visiting during off-peak hours. Alternatively, take a free self-guided walking tour of the historic Santa Cruz neighborhood to admire the architecture. The palace is a treasure trove of art and history, famously linked to the House of Alba.

9. **Casa de Pilatos**
   This Renaissance palace is a beautiful blend of Mudejar, Gothic, and Renaissance styles. Buy tickets in advance for discounts. A creative free alternative is to explore the surrounding streets, filled with charming plazas and historic buildings. The palace's unique architecture reflects the cultural fusion that characterizes Seville.

10. **Catedral de Sevilla – Climbing the Giralda**
    For a small fee, you can climb the ramp to the top of the Giralda for stunning city views. Save by going early in the morning to avoid crowds. A free alternative is to relax in the nearby Plaza del Salvador, a lovely spot for people-watching. The Giralda's unique design allows for a gentle ascent, making it accessible to all.

11. **La Casa de la Memoria**
    This intimate venue showcases traditional flamenco performances in an authentic setting. Save by booking your tickets online in advance. Instead of spending, seek out free street performances in the surrounding Santa Cruz neighborhood. This venue highlights the deep-rooted traditions of flamenco and its emotional storytelling.

12. **Archaeological Museum of Seville**
    Located in the beautiful María Luisa Park, this museum showcases artifacts from ancient Rome and beyond. Save by visiting on free admission days. For a creative free alternative, wander the park and enjoy its beautiful gardens. The museum's collection includes Roman mosaics and treasures from the ancient city of Italica, just a short trip away.

13. **Aquarium of Seville**
   This family-friendly attraction features a variety of marine life and interactive exhibits. Save by visiting during off-peak hours for discounted tickets. Alternatively, explore the nearby waterfront and enjoy a picnic by the river. The aquarium's design reflects Seville's historical ties to the river and its maritime heritage.

14. **Museo del Baile Flamenco**
   Dive deeper into the art of flamenco at this interactive museum dedicated to the dance form. To save, visit during their special promotion days. A great free alternative is to explore local flamenco bars where you can watch talented dancers perform. The museum emphasizes the rich history of flamenco and its emotional expression.

15. **Centro Andaluz de Arte Contemporáneo**
   Housed in a former monastery, this contemporary art center offers rotating exhibitions and a tranquil garden. Save on admission by visiting during free entry days. Alternatively, enjoy the beautiful grounds of the nearby Parque de María Luisa. The center highlights the evolution of modern art in Andalusia, showcasing local and international artists.

16. **Royal Tobacco Factory**
   Once the largest tobacco factory in Europe, this historic building now houses the University of Seville. Save by joining a guided tour for insights into its history. A free alternative is to admire the building's architecture from the outside. The factory was an important site in the industrial era, influencing the city's economy and culture.

17. **Flamenco Shows in Triana**
   Experience authentic flamenco performances in the vibrant neighborhood of Triana. Save by checking for early bird discounts. If you're looking for something free, explore Triana's lively streets and enjoy the local atmosphere. Triana is considered the birthplace of flamenco, and its lively spirit is infectious.

18. **Museo del Automóvil**
   This unique museum showcases an extensive collection of vintage cars and motorcycles. To save, check for special discount days. A creative alternative is to explore the surrounding neighborhood, filled with quaint shops and cafés. The museum tells the story of automotive history in Spain, with vehicles dating back over a century.

19. **Carmona Day Trip**
   While not in Seville proper, a day trip to the historic town of Carmona is a paid excursion worth considering. Save by booking a group tour for discounts. For a free alternative, explore Seville's historic neighborhoods that echo Carmona's charm. Carmona boasts Roman ruins and beautiful architecture, just a short bus ride from Seville.

20. **Horse and Carriage Tours**
   A classic way to explore Seville, these guided tours offer a unique perspective of the city. Save by negotiating prices with drivers. Alternatively, explore the city on foot, which allows for spontaneous discoveries. The tradition of horse-drawn carriages dates back centuries, making it a nostalgic way to experience the city's beauty.

Tips for Seville

1. **Use Public Transport**: Seville's public transport system, including buses and trams, is affordable and efficient. Consider getting a multi-day pass for unlimited travel, which is perfect for exploring the city at your own pace.

2. **Walk and Explore**: Seville's historic center is compact and pedestrian-friendly. Strolling through the narrow streets allows you to discover hidden gems, local tapas bars, and vibrant plazas without spending a dime.

3. **Tapas Hopping**: Embrace the local tradition of tapas by visiting different bars for a small plate at each. Look for places with "tapas specials" or "tapas happy hours" for the best deals.

4. **Free Walking Tours**: Join one of the many free walking tours available in Seville. While tips are appreciated, this is a great way to get an overview of the city and its history without spending much.

5. **Visit During Off-Peak Seasons**: If you can, travel during the shoulder seasons (spring or fall) to avoid crowds and enjoy lower prices on accommodations and attractions.

6. **Local Markets**: Visit local markets like Mercado de Triana for affordable meals and to experience local culture. It's a fantastic way to enjoy authentic food without breaking the bank.

7. **Festival Timing**: If you can time your visit with local festivals like Feria de Abril or Semana Santa, you'll experience the culture at its finest. Many festivities are free to attend.

8. **Look for Free Events**: Keep an eye out for free concerts, art exhibitions, and events at places like the Centro Andaluz de Arte Contemporáneo.

Affordable Luxury Accommodations in Seville

Accommodation Name	Description	Starting Price (per	Notes
Hotel Casa 1800 Sevilla	A beautifully restored boutique hotel with modern amenities and a rooftop terrace.	120 €	Located in the Santa Cruz district.
EME Catedral	Offers stunning views of the Cathedral, stylish rooms, and a rooftop pool.	150 €	Central location with luxurious dining
Hotel Alfonso XIII	A historic hotel with opulent interiors and beautiful gardens, close to major attractions.	180 €	Considered one of the best luxury hotels in
Hotel Palacio de	A stunning 18th-century palace turned hotel, offering a luxurious stay with a spa.	130 €	Located near the city center.
Corral del Rey	A boutique hotel in a restored building, offering a unique and intimate experience.	160 €	Features beautiful design and personalized

Las Casas de la Judería	Combines history and luxury with charming rooms and beautiful patios in the Jewish	140 €	Perfect for exploring Seville's historic sites.
Gran Meliá Colon	Elegant hotel with contemporary decor and luxurious amenities, close to shopping.	170 €	Great for those who enjoy shopping and
Hotel Inglaterra	A historic hotel with a rooftop terrace offering panoramic views of the city.	110 €	Located near the famous Plaza Nueva.
Hotel Palacio de	Combines history and luxury with stunning interiors and a lovely courtyard.	130 €	Located near the Cathedral and Alcázar.
Hotel Doña Maria	Known for its stunning views of the Cathedral and its charming rooftop terrace.	120 €	Great central location.

Getting Around Cheaply in Seville

Getting around Seville is easy and affordable! The city's extensive public transport system includes buses and trams, making it convenient to explore various neighborhoods. A single bus or tram ticket costs around €1.40, but consider purchasing a multi-day pass (like the "Tarjeta del Transporte") for unlimited travel, which can be a great money-saver if you plan to hop around. Walking is another excellent option, as many attractions are within a short distance of each other. Plus, strolling through Seville's charming streets allows you to soak in the local culture, architecture, and vibrant atmosphere.

Free Events or Experiences in Seville

Seville offers a treasure trove of free events and experiences that many visitors overlook. One delightful option is the **Flamenco Street Performances**, particularly in the lively neighborhoods of Triana and Alameda de Hércules. Here, talented dancers often perform in the streets, allowing you to experience authentic flamenco without spending a dime.

Another hidden gem is the **Catedral de Sevilla**, where entrance is free during the last hour before closing. It's a fantastic way to explore this magnificent Gothic cathedral and enjoy a less crowded experience. You can also visit the **Mercado de Triana** to experience the local culture; wandering through this market is free, and you can sample local delicacies at reasonable prices.

Don't miss the **Parque de María Luisa**, where you can enjoy beautiful gardens and tranquil spots for a relaxing afternoon. While entry to the park is free, it's an excellent place to picnic or read a book while taking in the beautiful surroundings.

Practical Tips to Save Money in Seville

1. **Meal Deals**: Many tapas bars offer "tapas specials" during lunchtime (usually from 1 PM to 4 PM), where you can enjoy a range of dishes for around €2–€4 each. This is a fantastic way to try various local dishes without overspending.

2. **Free Museum Days**: Seville has several museums that offer free entry on specific days of the month. For example, the **Museum of Fine Arts** is free every Tuesday. Planning your visits around these days can save you about €8–€12 per museum.

3. **Local Festivals**: Participating in local festivals like **Feria de Abril** or **Semana Santa** is free and offers a vibrant experience filled with music, dance, and culture. Just be sure to check the schedule to plan your visit!

4. **Walking Tours**: Consider joining a free walking tour of the city. While these tours are tip-based, they can be a budget-friendly way to learn about Seville's history and culture without spending much—typically, a tip of €5–€10 per person is sufficient.

5. **Public Transport Passes**: If you plan on using public transport frequently, the "Tarjeta del Transporte" offers unlimited travel for 3 days for about €18. This is a significant saving compared to buying single tickets for each ride.

Historical Facts You Didn't Know About Seville

Seville is steeped in history, and some of its lesser-known facts might surprise you. For instance, the **Giralda Tower**, part of the Cathedral, was originally built as a minaret during the Moorish period. Interestingly, it stands at 104 meters tall, and you can actually climb the ramp to the top instead of stairs, making it unique among bell towers worldwide.

Additionally, Seville was the birthplace of **Christopher Columbus**'s exploration of the New World. In fact, the **Casa de Contratación**, established in 1503, regulated trade between Spain and the Americas, marking Seville as a crucial hub for exploration during the Age of Discovery.

You may also be surprised to learn that Seville is home to the oldest **royal palace** still in use in Europe: the **Real Alcázar**. This stunning palace showcases Mudejar, Gothic, Renaissance, and Baroque architectural styles, reflecting the city's diverse historical influences.

Practical Information for Visiting Seville

1. **Getting There**: Seville is well-connected via the **San Pablo Airport**, which is about 10 km from the city center. You can take a direct bus (EA Line) for about €4. The main train station, **Santa Justa**, offers connections to other major cities in Spain, including Madrid and Cordoba.

2. **Crowd Times**: The best time to visit is during the spring (March to June) or fall (September to November) when the weather is pleasant. Summer can get very hot, and tourist crowds peak during major festivals like Semana Santa and Feria de Abril.

3. **Ticketing Details**: For attractions like the Alcázar and Cathedral, it's wise to book tickets online in advance to avoid long lines. Prices can vary but typically range from €10 to €15.

4. **What to Do There**: Aside from the major attractions, consider visiting lesser-known sites like **Hospital de los Venerables**, an impressive Baroque building that houses art exhibitions.

5. **Secret Spots**: One secret spot is **Las Setas de Sevilla (Metropol Parasol)**, a stunning wooden structure offering panoramic views. It's often overlooked, making it a quieter experience. Additionally, venture to **Calle Alfalfa**, where you'll find quaint shops and local cafés away from the tourist trail.

Granada

Granada is a treasure trove of history, culture, and breathtaking scenery, nestled at the foot of the Sierra Nevada mountains in southern Spain. Its roots trace back to the Romans, but it truly blossomed during the Moorish period, which left an indelible mark on its architecture and culture. The city was the last stronghold of the Moors in Spain until it fell to the Catholic Monarchs, Ferdinand and Isabella, in 1492. This pivotal event not only changed the course of Spanish history but also paved the way for the Renaissance in Spain.

Walking through Granada feels like stepping back in time, especially in neighborhoods like the Albayzín, with its narrow, winding streets and whitewashed houses. The iconic Alhambra, a UNESCO World Heritage site, stands as a majestic testament to the Islamic Golden Age, showcasing stunning palaces, lush gardens, and intricate tilework. As you explore this enchanting city, you'll discover a delightful blend of cultures, from Moorish influences to Spanish traditions, making Granada a must-visit destination for any traveler.

Top 20 Paid Attractions in Granada

1. **Alhambra** The crown jewel of Granada, the Alhambra is a stunning palace and fortress complex that boasts incredible Islamic architecture, lush gardens, and breathtaking views. To save on entrance fees, consider booking your tickets online in advance, as they often sell out. A creative alternative is to stroll through the nearby Generalife gardens, which offer a glimpse of the beauty without the price tag. Don't miss the history of the Nasrid Dynasty, which built this exquisite palace in the 13th century, symbolizing the peak of Islamic art in Spain.

2. **Generalife** The summer palace of the Nasrid rulers, Generalife is a serene escape filled with beautiful gardens and stunning views of the Alhambra. Admission is often bundled with Alhambra tickets, but you can save by visiting early in the morning or later in the afternoon when crowds are lighter. For a free alternative, explore the surrounding hills for panoramic views of the palace complex. Originally built in the 13th century, the gardens served as a retreat for the sultans and are still a peaceful oasis today.

3. **Cathedral of Granada** This grand Renaissance cathedral, built on the site of a former mosque, features stunning altarpieces and chapels. To save on fees, visit during mass for a free glimpse of the interior. If you prefer a free experience, take a stroll around the Plaza de las Pasiegas, where the cathedral's majestic facade is beautifully showcased. Completed in the 16th century, it reflects the city's transition from Islamic to Christian rule and is a symbol of Granada's complex history.

4. **Royal Chapel** The final resting place of the Catholic Monarchs, Ferdinand and Isabella, this chapel houses their ornate tombs. Tickets can be pricey, but purchasing a combined ticket with the cathedral offers savings. For a free alternative, visit the nearby Market of San Agustín for a taste of local life. The chapel, completed in 1521, is a stunning example of Gothic architecture and features magnificent altarpieces that tell the story of the monarchs' reign.

5. **Bañuelo** One of the best-preserved Moorish baths in Spain, Bañuelo offers a glimpse into the lavish lifestyle of Granada's historical elite. Admission is modest, and you can save by visiting during the late afternoon. As a free alternative, explore the nearby Carrera del Darro, a picturesque street lined with charming architecture. Dating back to the 11th century, these baths showcase the sophisticated hygiene practices of the time and are an intriguing stop for history enthusiasts.

6. **Science Park** Perfect for families, this interactive science museum features exhibits on biology, physics, and astronomy. To save on fees, check for family discounts or special days with reduced prices. For a free outing, enjoy the adjacent gardens, which are perfect for a picnic. Opened in 1995, this park aims to make science accessible and fun, with a planetarium that's a hit with kids and adults alike.

7. **Alcaicería** Once the Silk Market, this historic district is a vibrant maze of shops selling textiles, ceramics, and souvenirs. While wandering is free, save on purchases by haggling and looking for less touristy shops. As a free alternative, enjoy a walk along the Carrera del Darro and soak in the local atmosphere. The Alcaicería's origins date back to the 8th century and serve as a reminder of Granada's rich trading history.

8. **Sacromonte Abbey** Nestled in the hillside, this abbey offers stunning views and a glimpse into the region's monastic history. Entry fees are reasonable, but you can save by visiting during the free hours on Sundays. For a unique experience, explore the nearby caves, traditionally inhabited by the Romani community, which are open to visitors. Founded in the 17th century, the abbey is an intriguing blend of history and spirituality, with beautiful gardens to explore.

9. **Carmen de los Mártires** A hidden gem, this beautiful garden is a serene escape filled with fountains, sculptures, and breathtaking views of the Alhambra. Entry is free, making it a perfect alternative for a peaceful afternoon. For a unique experience, bring a picnic to enjoy while soaking in the views. This 19th-century garden was originally part of a 14th-century palace and showcases a mix of Moorish and romantic styles.

10. **Palace of Charles V** Located within the Alhambra complex, this Renaissance palace is known for its impressive circular courtyard. Admission is often included with Alhambra tickets, but you can save by visiting during off-peak times. For a free alternative, explore the surrounding gardens, which offer beautiful views. Built in the 16th century, the palace symbolizes the Catholic Monarchs' desire to assert their power after the Reconquista.

11. **Museum of Fine Arts** Housed in the Palace of Charles V, this museum showcases a rich collection of Spanish art from the medieval period to the 19th century. Admission is often free on Sundays, making it a great time to visit. For a creative free alternative, take a walking tour of the historical center and admire the street art. The museum features works by renowned artists such as Alonso Cano and is a must-see for art lovers.

12. **Carmen de los Abades** This charming garden offers a unique blend of nature and history, with panoramic views of the Alhambra and Sierra Nevada. Entry fees are affordable, and you can save by visiting during the quieter months. For a free

alternative, hike up to the Mirador de San Nicolás for a stunning view of the Alhambra. The garden's history dates back to the 16th century and is a tranquil oasis amidst the bustling city.

13. **Granada Charterhouse** This stunning Carthusian monastery features beautiful architecture and peaceful gardens. Admission is modest, and you can save by purchasing a combined ticket with other attractions. For a free experience, explore the surrounding hills for hiking opportunities. Founded in the 16th century, the charterhouse is known for its exquisite Baroque chapel and serene ambiance.

14. **Fundación Rodríguez-Acosta** This cultural foundation features a unique collection of art and architecture, with stunning views of the city. Entry fees are reasonable, but you can save by visiting on specific days when admission is reduced. For a free alternative, explore the nearby Paseo de los Tristes for a picturesque stroll. The foundation was established in the early 20th century and is known for its fusion of Moorish and modernist styles.

15. **Torre de la Vela** Offering spectacular views of Granada and the Alhambra, this watchtower is a great spot for photography enthusiasts. Admission is included with the Alhambra ticket, but you can save by visiting during sunset for magical views. For a free alternative, hike up to the nearby Mirador de San Nicolás for equally stunning panoramas. The tower dates back to the 13th century and was once part of the fortress' defensive system.

16. **Granada's Flamenco Shows** Experience the passionate art of flamenco in one of Granada's famous tablaos. Tickets can be pricey, but look for dinner-show packages for savings. For a free experience, wander the Sacromonte neighborhood, where you might catch impromptu performances. Flamenco has deep roots in Granada, influenced by the city's diverse cultural heritage, making it a must-see when visiting.

17. **Paseo de los Tristes** This picturesque promenade along the Darro River is a lovely spot for a leisurely walk. While free to stroll, consider stopping at a café for a drink. For a unique experience, visit in the evening when the area comes alive with locals and street performers. The name translates to "Promenade of the Sad," reflecting its historical connection to funeral processions in the past.

18. **Casa del Chapiz** This beautiful building is a blend of Moorish and Renaissance styles, housing the Faculty of Fine Arts. Entry is often low-cost, and saving is easy if you visit during special exhibition days. For a free alternative, enjoy a stroll through the picturesque gardens surrounding the building. Originally built in the 16th century, this casa provides insight into the architectural evolution of Granada.

Insider Tips for Granada

1. **Explore Early or Late**: To avoid crowds, especially at popular attractions like the Alhambra, aim to visit early in the morning or later in the afternoon. The golden hour also offers fantastic lighting for photography!

2. **Local Tapas**: In Granada, many bars offer free tapas with drinks. This is a great way to experience local cuisine without breaking the bank. Order a drink, and enjoy a selection of delicious small plates on the house!

3. **Walking Tours**: Take advantage of the many free or donation-based walking tours available in Granada. These tours are a fantastic way to learn about the city's history and culture from knowledgeable locals.

4. **Public Transport**: Granada has a reliable and affordable public transport system, including buses and trams. Consider getting a travel card for unlimited rides, which can save you money if you plan to explore more distant areas.

5. **Explore the Albayzín**: The Albayzín neighborhood is a UNESCO World Heritage site, full of narrow winding streets and stunning views of the Alhambra. Wander around to soak in the atmosphere, and don't miss the viewpoints like Mirador de San Nicolás.

6. **Local Markets**: Check out local markets like Mercado de San Agustín for fresh produce, local delicacies, and a vibrant atmosphere. You can often sample products for free and find unique souvenirs.

7. **Cultural Events**: Keep an eye out for local festivals and events, which often feature free concerts, art exhibitions, and traditional performances, giving you a taste of the city's vibrant culture.

Affordable Luxury Accommodations in Granada

Accommodation	Description	Average Nightly Price
Hotel Casa 1800	A charming boutique hotel with a rooftop terrace and views of the Alhambra.	120 €
Palacio de Santa	A converted convent offering luxurious rooms in a	150 €
Hotel Villa Oniria	A luxurious hotel with beautifully designed rooms and a	130 €
Hotel Alhambra	Offers stunning views and classic decor, close to the	160 €
Hotel Anacapri	A cozy hotel in a central location with modern amenities.	100 €
Carmen de la	An intimate guesthouse with stunning views and unique	110 €
Hotel Meliá	A stylish hotel in the city center, featuring modern	140 €
Hospes Palacio de	An elegant hotel set in a restored palace with luxurious	190 €
Hotel Palacio de Santa Paula	Offers a blend of history and luxury with beautifully appointed rooms.	160 €
B&B Hotel Granada	A comfortable and affordable option with modern	80 €

Getting Around Granada Cheaply

Getting around Granada is both affordable and convenient. The city has a well-connected public transport system, including buses that can take you to most major attractions. A single bus ticket costs around €1.40, but if you plan to use public transport frequently, consider purchasing a travel card, which offers unlimited rides for a set price, making it more economical for day-long explorations. Walking is also a delightful option in Granada, especially in the historic districts where narrow streets and hidden gems await you at every turn.

Another great way to explore the city is by renting a bike. Many shops offer bike rentals for around €10-15 per day. This not only gives you the flexibility to visit attractions at your own pace but also allows you to discover the city's hidden corners. If you're feeling adventurous, consider walking or biking up to the Sacromonte area, where you can enjoy beautiful views of the Alhambra and the Sierra Nevada mountains.

Free Events or Experiences in Granada

Granada is brimming with free experiences that most visitors overlook. One hidden gem is the **Festival de los Patios**, held in May, where locals open their stunning courtyards adorned with flowers and plants for everyone to admire. While this festival occurs only once a year, many patios remain accessible throughout the year. You can stroll through the **Albayzín** neighborhood, where you'll find beautifully adorned patios and authentic local architecture without spending a cent.

Another lesser-known experience is the **Cueva de la Rocío**, located in Sacromonte. While the caves themselves may have a nominal fee for guided tours, the surrounding area is free to explore. Wander around to enjoy the scenic views and perhaps catch an impromptu flamenco performance from local artists.

Also, look out for local community events at **Calle Elvira** and **Plaza de Bib-Rambla**. These often include free concerts and cultural performances that offer a taste of the local culture without any costs involved.

Practical Tips to Save Money in Granada

1. **Use a Granada Card**: This all-in-one card offers access to numerous attractions and includes public transportation. Prices start at €40 for a 24-hour card, allowing you to save up to 30% on individual entry fees.

2. **Visit Free Attractions**: Many of Granada's stunning sites, like the **Generalife Gardens** and the **Royal Chapel**, offer free entry during certain hours or on specific days. For example, the Royal Chapel is free on Sundays.

3. **Tapas Culture**: Enjoy Granada's famous free tapas with drinks. Order a beer or wine, and you could get a delicious plate of local cuisine at no extra charge. This can save you significantly on meals.

4. **Picnic in Parks**: Instead of dining out, buy fresh produce from local markets and have a picnic in parks like **Carmen de los Mártires** or **Parque de las Ciencias**. This can save you around €15-30 per meal compared to dining in restaurants.

5. **Explore Markets**: Visit the **Mercado de San Agustín** for local delicacies at affordable prices. Sampling local foods here can be a cheap way to experience authentic Granada.

Historical Facts You Didn't Know About Granada

Granada's history is rich and complex, often overlooked by visitors. For instance, did you know that the **Alhambra** was originally built as a modest fortress in the 9th century? It was later transformed into a magnificent palace complex by the Nasrid Dynasty in the 13th century, symbolizing the height of Islamic culture in Spain. The intricate tile work and architecture of the Alhambra reflect a fusion of influences, showcasing not just Islamic art but also Christian and Jewish elements after the Reconquista.

Another fascinating tidbit is that Granada was the last stronghold of the Moors in Spain, falling to Catholic Monarchs Ferdinand and Isabella in 1492. This pivotal moment not only marked the end of Muslim rule in Spain but also set the stage for the Spanish Inquisition and the Age of Exploration.

The **Royal Chapel** is not just a burial site for the Catholic Monarchs; it also houses a wealth of artwork and artifacts from the Renaissance period. The chapel's stunning altarpiece and intricate details reveal the deep connection between the monarchy and the Catholic Church during that era.

Comprehensive Practical Information for Visiting Granada

- **How to Get There**: Granada is accessible by bus and train from major cities like Madrid, Seville, and Malaga. The Granada bus station is conveniently located near the city center, while the train station is a short bus ride away.

- **When to Visit**: Crowds peak in the summer months (June-August) and during major holidays. For a quieter experience, consider visiting in the shoulder seasons of spring (April-May) or fall (September-October). The **Alhambra** is especially crowded, so book tickets in advance to secure your preferred time slot.

- **Ticket Information**: Tickets for the Alhambra should be booked online ahead of time. Prices start at around €14. The Generalife and Nasrid Palaces are included in this ticket. Many attractions offer discounts for students and seniors, so check when purchasing.

- **What to Do**: Beyond the Alhambra and Generalife, explore the historic neighborhoods of **Albayzín** and **Sacromonte**. Visit **Casa del Chapiz**, a beautiful example of Moorish architecture, or take a stroll through the **Carmen de los Mártires** gardens for breathtaking views of the city.

- **Secret Spots**: Look for the **Mirador de San Nicolás** for an iconic view of the Alhambra against the Sierra Nevada backdrop, especially at sunset. Another lesser-known spot is the **Calle de las Teterías** in the Albayzín, known for its tea houses where you can relax with a cup of Moroccan mint tea away from the tourist crowds.

San Sebastián

San Sebastián, or Donostia in Basque, is a gem on Spain's northern coast, renowned for its stunning beaches, culinary scene, and vibrant culture. Founded in 1180, this picturesque city has seen various phases of transformation, from a strategic military outpost to a glamorous resort for European aristocrats in the 19th century. Its famous La Concha beach, often hailed as one of the best city beaches in Europe, became a popular getaway, especially during the summer months. The city's unique blend of Basque culture and Spanish flair shines through in its architecture, local traditions, and, of course, its delectable pintxos. Whether you're exploring the historic Old Town or wandering along the scenic waterfront, San Sebastián's charm is palpable, making it a must-visit destination for travelers seeking beauty, history, and fantastic food.

Top 20 Paid Attractions in San Sebastián

1. **La Concha Beach**
   While technically free to access, renting a sunbed or umbrella can be pricey. To save on fees, bring your own beach towel and snacks. Alternatively, take a stroll along the promenade and enjoy the sunset for a free and beautiful experience. Historically, La Concha has been a favored spot for visitors since the 19th century, attracting the likes of royalty and celebrities alike.

2. **Pintxos Tasting Tours**
   These guided tours through the Old Town offer a delicious way to experience Basque cuisine. To save, join a self-guided tour by researching popular bars and sampling pintxos at your own pace. Creative alternatives include taking a cooking class to learn how to make pintxos yourself. The tradition of pintxos dates back to the 1940s, originally designed to be enjoyed with a glass of wine.

3. **San Telmo Museoa**
   This museum showcases Basque society and culture. Entry is usually around €10, but visiting on Thursdays offers a discounted rate. For a free alternative, explore the museum's exterior, which is a striking mix of old and modern architecture. San Telmo was originally a 16th-century convent and has been a cultural hub since its opening in 2011.

4. **Mount Igueldo**
   The funicular ride to the summit costs about €3.50 one way. To save, consider hiking up the trails for stunning views without the fee. The panoramic vista from the top is perfect for a picnic. Historically, Mount Igueldo has been a lookout point since the early 19th century, providing strategic military advantages during conflicts.

5. **Kursaal Palace**
   This iconic building is home to the San Sebastián International Film Festival. Entry to events can be pricey, so check for free public exhibitions. A lovely walk along the river provides beautiful views of the palace without spending a cent. The Kursaal, designed by architect Rafael Moneo, opened in 1999 and has since become a symbol of modern San Sebastián.

6. **Aquarium**
   The entry fee is around €12, but free admission days are available throughout the year. Alternatively, enjoy a walk along the waterfront, where you can see the exterior and some exhibits through the glass. The aquarium features a fascinating

collection of marine life and pays homage to San Sebastián's fishing heritage, which dates back centuries.

7. **Miramar Palace**
    Once a summer residence for the Spanish royal family, entry to the gardens is free, but guided tours of the palace come with a fee. Save by enjoying a picnic in the gardens and soaking in the views. Built in 1893, Miramar Palace boasts beautiful architecture and stunning views of La Concha Bay.

8. **Catedral del Buen Pastor**
    This neo-Gothic cathedral is a sight to behold. While entry is typically free, donations are appreciated. For a free alternative, take a self-guided walking tour of the area and admire the beautiful architecture from the outside. The cathedral was completed in 1897 and serves as the mother church of the Diocese of San Sebastián.

9. **Culinary Courses**
    Many local schools offer cooking classes focusing on Basque cuisine, usually costing around €70. To save, you can find online tutorials or local food markets where you can learn through experience. Learning about Basque cuisine is not just about food; it's a deep dive into the culture, reflecting the region's rich agricultural history.

10. **Palacio de Aiete**
    This beautiful palace offers tours for a fee. To save, explore the surrounding park, which is free to enter. The park is an excellent spot for relaxation and picturesque strolls. Originally built in 1897 for the royal family, the palace is now a cultural venue hosting various events and exhibitions.

11. **Cider Houses (Sagardotegi)**
    Visiting a traditional cider house can be expensive. Look for special menus or visit during off-peak times for discounts. For a creative alternative, host a cider tasting at home with friends. The cider-making tradition dates back to the 17th century and is a vital part of Basque culture.

12. **Basque Culinary Center**
    Offering workshops and tastings, entry can be pricey. Look for free events or lectures that they occasionally host. Explore nearby local markets for fresh ingredients and get a taste of the culinary scene. This center, founded in 2011, is dedicated to advancing the art of cooking and educating future chefs.

13. **Eureka! Zientzia Museoa**
    This interactive science museum is perfect for families, with an entry fee of around €10. Look for combo tickets that include other attractions for savings. A creative alternative is to enjoy outdoor science experiments with kids. Opened in 2008, the museum emphasizes the importance of science and technology in everyday life.

14. **Basque Coast Geopark**
    Entry fees vary by site, but guided tours can be costly. To save, explore on your own with a map, or participate in free walking tours. The coastline showcases stunning geological formations and rich biodiversity, with origins dating back millions of years, forming a unique landscape.

15. **La Perla**
    This seaside spa offers wellness treatments at a premium price. Look for off-peak discounts or packages for savings. Alternatively, enjoy a free day at the beach, where you can sunbathe and swim. Founded in 1912, La Perla has a rich history as a wellness center, reflecting the city's commitment to health and leisure.

16. **Tabakalera**
    A cultural center housed in a former tobacco factory, entry is free, but some

exhibitions may charge. For creative alternatives, participate in free workshops or attend events. This center has become a hub for contemporary art and culture since its transformation in 2015.

17. **Museo Chillida-Leku**
Dedicated to the works of sculptor Eduardo Chillida, entry costs around €10. To save, visit during special discount days. Explore the surrounding gardens for a beautiful, free experience. Chillida was inspired by the Basque landscape, and his works often reflect the region's natural beauty.

18. **Miramar Palace Gardens**
While visiting the gardens is free, guided tours of the palace incur a fee. To save, take a self-guided tour of the gardens and enjoy a picnic with stunning views. The gardens were designed to blend seamlessly with the surrounding landscape, creating a serene escape for visitors.

19. **Basilica de Santa Maria**
While entry is free, guided tours that delve into its history can cost around €5. Explore the nearby streets to enjoy the charming atmosphere without spending. The basilica, dating back to the 18th century, showcases beautiful Baroque architecture and is steeped in local lore.

20. **Mundaka**
This nearby surf town charges for surf lessons and rentals. To save, rent gear during off-peak times or take advantage of group discounts. Alternatively, enjoy a scenic walk along the coast and watch surfers from the shore. Mundaka is famous for its waves, drawing surfers from around the world, and offers a unique glimpse into the Basque lifestyle.

Insider Tips for San Sebastián

1. **Visit During Off-Peak Season**: If you want to experience San Sebastián without the summer crowds, consider visiting in the shoulder seasons—spring (April to June) and autumn (September to October). The weather is still pleasant, and you'll find fewer tourists, making for a more relaxed atmosphere.
2. **Try Pintxos at Lunch**: Many local bars offer cheaper pintxos during lunchtime than in the evening. This is the perfect time to sample various dishes without breaking the bank. Look for bars that display their pintxos on the counter, which often indicate freshness and variety.
3. **Use Public Transport**: San Sebastián's public transport system is efficient and inexpensive. Buses run frequently, and single tickets cost just €1.50. Consider getting a **Txartela** card for discounted fares if you plan to use public transport frequently.
4. **Explore on Foot**: The city is compact and walkable, making it easy to explore on foot. Strolling through the streets allows you to discover hidden gems, charming cafes, and local shops that you might miss while taking public transport.
5. **Free Walking Tours**: Join a free walking tour to learn about the city's history and culture from knowledgeable local guides. Just remember to tip what you can; it's a great way to meet fellow travelers while getting insider information.
6. **Local Markets**: Check out the **La Bretxa** or **Mercado de San Martín** for fresh produce, local cheeses, and other gourmet items. You can grab a bite at the food stalls without spending much, and it's an excellent way to taste local flavors.

7. **Beach Towels Instead of Rentals**: Instead of renting sunbeds or umbrellas at the beach, bring your own beach towels. This small tip can save you a considerable amount over the course of your stay.
8. **Visit Museums on Free Days**: Many museums have designated free entry days or reduced rates on specific days of the week. Plan your visit accordingly to save on admission fees.
9. **Take Advantage of Discounts**: Look for tourist cards that offer discounts on attractions, transportation, and dining. These cards can be a great way to save money if you plan on visiting multiple sites.
10. **Enjoy the Parks**: San Sebastián is home to beautiful parks like **Parque de la Ciudadela** and **Aiete Park**. These green spaces are perfect for a leisurely walk, a picnic, or simply relaxing without any cost.

Getting Around San Sebastián Cheaply

- **Public Buses**: The Dbus service covers the city extensively, and a single ticket costs around €1.50. Consider getting a **Txartela** card for discounts and ease of travel.

- **Walking**: Many attractions are within walking distance, making it easy to explore on foot and save money on transport.

- **Bicycle Rentals**: Renting a bicycle is a great way to get around and costs about €10 for a day. Look for bike-sharing services for more flexibility.

- **Car Sharing**: If you need to travel a bit further, consider car-sharing services available in the city for short trips.

- **Taxi**: Taxis are available but can be pricey. Use them sparingly for late-night returns or when you're in a rush.

Chart of Affordable Luxury Accommodations in Barcelona

Accommodation Name	Location	Price Range (Approx.)	Key Features
Hotel Neri	Gothic Quarter	€150 - €300	Chic boutique hotel, rooftop terrace
The Wittmore	Gothic	€180 - €350	Stylish decor, close to
Hotel 1898	La	€120 - €250	Rooftop pool, historical
Casa Fuster	Gràcia	€150 - €350	Modernist architecture, stunning views
Hotel Arts	Barceloneta	€250 - €500	Luxury amenities, beachfront location
H10 Casa	Gràcia	€130 - €250	Rooftop pool, great for
Alma	Eixample	€200 - €400	Elegant design,
The One Barcelona	Eixample	€250 - €450	Michelin-star restaurant, luxury

| Hotel Indigo | Eixample | €120 - €200 | Trendy decor, close to transportation |
| Mercer Hotel | Gothic | €250 - €600 | Historical charm, |

Free Events or Experiences in San Sebastián Most People Don't Know About

1. **Cultural Festivals**: San Sebastián hosts numerous cultural festivals throughout the year that are free to attend. One of the highlights is the **San Sebastián Day** on January 20, when locals celebrate their patron saint with parades, music, and traditional dances. This vibrant celebration immerses visitors in local culture and offers a unique insight into the city's traditions.
2. **Open-Air Concerts**: In the summer months, San Sebastián features free open-air concerts at various locations, especially in **La Plaza de la Constitución**. These concerts attract both local and international artists, providing a great atmosphere to enjoy live music without any cost. Keep an eye on local event listings to catch performances during your visit.
3. **The Donostia-San Sebastián International Film Festival**: While many screenings require tickets, there are also free outdoor screenings during the festival, usually held in September. Watching a film under the stars alongside locals is a magical experience that captures the essence of the city's love for cinema.
4. **Art Walks**: Explore the **Gipuzkoa Plaza** and surrounding streets during the summer months when the city hosts free art walks, featuring local artists displaying their work in public spaces. It's an excellent way to experience the creativity of the city while enjoying the outdoors.
5. **Nature Walks at Urgull Hill**: For stunning views of the city and the bay, hike up **Urgull Hill**. While there are some organized tours that may charge a fee, wandering on your own is free. The hill features historical monuments and beautiful landscapes, making it a worthwhile exploration that many tourists overlook.

Practical Things to Remember to Save Money in San Sebastián

- **Pintxos Etiquette**: Enjoying pintxos at bars is a must-do, but prices can vary. Most pintxos cost around €2 to €4 each. To save money, order during lunch when many bars offer special deals or two-for-one offers on pintxos. This can allow you to taste more for less.
- **Visit the Beaches**: Access to the beautiful beaches is free, so pack your own picnic to avoid spending money at overpriced beach bars. A typical beach meal can cost €15 or more, but bringing snacks and drinks from a local grocery store can save you quite a bit.
- **Discounted Museum Days**: Take advantage of free or discounted entry days at museums. Many offer free admission on the first Sunday of the month or reduced rates for students and seniors. This can save you €10 or more per person.
- **Use Public Transport**: Instead of taxis, utilize the local bus system. A single fare is €1.50, and a 10-ride ticket costs about €12.50, saving you money if you plan on using public transport frequently.
- **Happy Hours**: Look out for happy hour deals at bars and restaurants, typically between 5 PM and 8 PM, where you can enjoy discounted drinks and pintxos, potentially saving you 20-30% off regular prices.

Historical Facts You Didn't Know About San Sebastián

1. **A Fortress City**: San Sebastián was originally established as a fortress city by King Sancho VI of Navarre in 1180. Its strategic location along the coast made it a vital military outpost, which played a significant role in various conflicts, including the Spanish Civil War. The remnants of this military past can still be seen in landmarks like **Castle of La Mota** on Urgull Hill.
2. **Home of the Basque Culinary Scene**: San Sebastián has long been regarded as the gastronomic capital of Spain and is home to more Michelin-starred restaurants per capita than any other city in the world. The tradition of pintxos began in the late 19th century and has evolved into a culinary art form that attracts food enthusiasts from around the globe.
3. **Cultural Melting Pot**: The city has been influenced by various cultures throughout its history, including French, Spanish, and Basque. This cultural blending is reflected in its architecture, festivals, and cuisine, creating a unique identity that distinguishes San Sebastián from other Spanish cities.
4. **The Belle Époque Era**: During the 19th century, San Sebastián transformed into a fashionable resort town for the European aristocracy, particularly the Spanish royal family. This led to the construction of elegant buildings and the development of luxury hotels, many of which still stand today, showcasing the city's opulent past.

All the Things You Need to Know to Visit San Sebastián

- **How to Get There**: San Sebastián is easily accessible by train, bus, or car from major cities like Madrid and Bilbao. The **RENFE** train service connects San Sebastián to other Spanish cities. If you're flying in, the nearest airport is in **Hondarribia**, about 20 km away, with shuttle buses available to the city.
- **Crowd Times**: The peak tourist season is during summer (June to August), when the city can become crowded. Visiting in the shoulder seasons of spring (April to June) or autumn (September to October) will allow you to enjoy a quieter experience with pleasant weather.
- **Tickets for Attractions**: Most museums and attractions require tickets, with prices generally ranging from €5 to €15. Consider purchasing combo tickets for multiple attractions, as they often provide savings. For example, the **San Telmo Museum** costs €10, but check for reduced rates on specific days.
- **What to Do There**: Explore the stunning beaches, enjoy pintxos in the Old Town, visit the historic **San Telmo Museoa**, and take in panoramic views from **Mount Igueldo**. Don't miss the vibrant atmosphere of local markets like **La Bretxa**.
- **Secret Spots**: Discover hidden gems like the **Aiete Park**, which offers a peaceful escape from the bustling city, or the **Bateria de las Damas**, a lesser-known viewpoint on Mount Urgull with breathtaking views. The **Basque Culinary Center** also occasionally offers free public events and tastings—keep an eye on their schedule!

Bilbao

Bilbao, the largest city in the Basque Country of Spain, is a captivating blend of old-world charm and modern innovation. Founded in 1300 by Don Diego López de Haro, this vibrant city initially thrived as a port due to its strategic location along the Nervión River. Over the centuries, Bilbao transformed from an industrial powerhouse—primarily known for shipbuilding and iron mining—into a cultural epicenter celebrated for its architecture, gastronomy, and arts. The city's industrial decline in the late 20th century led to a remarkable urban renewal, spearheaded by visionary projects like the iconic Guggenheim Museum, which opened in 1997 and put Bilbao firmly on the international map. Today, the city is known for its lively streets, stunning riverfront, and a rich tapestry of history that beckons visitors to explore its many layers.

Top 20 Paid Attractions in Bilbao

1. **Guggenheim Museum** The star of the city, this architectural masterpiece by Frank Gehry is not just a museum but a work of art itself. Home to contemporary art pieces, it's a must-visit for any art lover. **Save on fees**: Look out for special admission days when entry is discounted. **Free alternative**: Stroll around the museum's exterior to admire its unique structure and the surrounding sculptures. **Tip**: Grab a coffee at the museum café and enjoy the view of the river.

2. **Museo de Bellas Artes** This fine arts museum boasts an impressive collection, including works from the Middle Ages to contemporary pieces. **Save on fees**: Free admission on Tuesdays and reduced rates on weekends. **Free alternative**: Check out the museum's temporary outdoor exhibitions. **Tip**: Plan your visit around the museum's guided tours for deeper insights into the collection.

3. **Bilbao Fine Arts Museum** Nestled in a beautiful park, this museum features an extensive collection from the 12th century onwards, with notable Spanish artists. **Save on fees**: Admission is free on certain days. **Free alternative**: Explore the surrounding Doña Casilda Iturrizar Park, a lovely spot for a picnic. **Tip**: Don't miss the museum shop for unique Basque art-inspired souvenirs.

4. **Casco Viejo** The old town is a labyrinth of narrow streets filled with shops, cafés, and local life. While exploring is free, you can also join guided tours for a fee. **Save on fees**: Self-guided walking tours can be found online for free. **Free alternative**: Enjoy the vibrant atmosphere and local markets without spending a dime. **Tip**: Try the local pintxos in the many bars lining the streets.

5. **Bilbao Arena** This multi-purpose arena hosts concerts and sporting events. Tickets can be pricey, but there are often deals for locals. **Save on fees**: Check the venue's website for discounts on tickets. **Free alternative**: Attend free outdoor concerts held in surrounding parks during the summer months. **Tip**: Arrive early to explore the lively atmosphere before events.

6. **Museum of Basque History** This museum provides insights into the Basque Country's rich culture and history. **Save on fees**: Admission is often reduced for

students and seniors. **Free alternative**: Visit the nearby historical sites around the museum. **Tip**: Engage with interactive displays to make history come alive.

7. **Puente Colgante (Vizcaya Bridge)** A UNESCO World Heritage site, this suspension bridge is an engineering marvel. Take the lift to the top for stunning views. **Save on fees**: Use the bridge's pedestrian walkway instead of the lift. **Free alternative**: Enjoy the riverside park below. **Tip**: Visit at sunset for the best photo opportunities.

8. **Euskalduna Conference Centre** This unique building hosts concerts and events, showcasing the best of Basque culture. **Save on fees**: Look for free performances during festivals. **Free alternative**: Walk around the stunning exterior and gardens. **Tip**: Attend a free guided tour if available.

9. **Alhóndiga Bilbao** A former wine warehouse turned cultural center, this place offers exhibitions, a cinema, and more. **Save on fees**: Look out for free entry days for exhibitions. **Free alternative**: Relax in the rooftop terrace. **Tip**: Check the events calendar for free workshops and talks.

10. **Bilbao Maritime Museum** Dive into the city's maritime history, from shipbuilding to fishing. **Save on fees**: Family tickets often come at a discount. **Free alternative**: Enjoy the riverside area surrounding the museum. **Tip**: Visit during special exhibitions for a unique experience.

11. **Basílica de Begoña** A stunning basilica dedicated to the patron saint of Bizkaia, this landmark is well worth the entry fee. **Save on fees**: Free admission to the basilica itself; there may be a fee for guided tours. **Free alternative**: Explore the surrounding plaza. **Tip**: Visit during a service for a truly local experience.

12. **San Mamés Stadium** Home to the Athletic Club Bilbao, this stadium offers guided tours that include behind-the-scenes access. **Save on fees**: Check for discounts during off-peak times. **Free alternative**: Watch a match outside for a lively atmosphere. **Tip**: Arrive early for a pre-match pintxo crawl.

13. **Bilbao's City Hall** A beautiful example of neo-baroque architecture, you can tour this stunning building. **Save on fees**: Free entrance during public holidays. **Free alternative**: Enjoy the view from the adjacent park. **Tip**: Capture photos from the riverbank for a picturesque backdrop.

14. **El Arenal Park** A lovely urban park perfect for a stroll, El Arenal often hosts markets and events. **Save on fees**: Free access to all park activities. **Free alternative**: Bring a picnic to enjoy in the green spaces. **Tip**: Check out the nearby market for local crafts and food.

15. **Guggenheim Museum Gardens** A hidden gem near the Guggenheim, these gardens are filled with unique sculptures. **Save on fees**: Entry is free. **Free alternative**: Enjoy a leisurely walk around the gardens. **Tip**: Take a guided sculpture tour for insights into the art.

16. **Museo Marítimo Ría de Bilbao** Discover Bilbao's maritime heritage through engaging exhibits and interactive displays. **Save on fees**: Look for combo tickets

with other museums. **Free alternative**: Stroll along the riverside for views of the museum. **Tip**: Plan your visit around special exhibits or workshops.

17. **Palacio de la Diputación Foral** This stunning building houses the Basque government and offers guided tours. **Save on fees**: Free tours are sometimes available on weekends. **Free alternative**: Explore the surrounding square and gardens. **Tip**: Don't miss the impressive interior architecture during your visit.

18. **Centro de Arte Contemporáneo de Málaga** A haven for modern art enthusiasts, this center showcases cutting-edge exhibitions. **Save on fees**: Look for special events with free admission. **Free alternative**: Visit local galleries nearby that often feature free exhibits. **Tip**: Check the schedule for artist talks and events.

19. **Teatro Arriaga** A beautiful theater hosting operas, ballets, and concerts. **Save on fees**: Discounted tickets for students and seniors. **Free alternative**: Attend free events held in the theater's plaza. **Tip**: Arrive early to enjoy a drink at a nearby café.

20. **Mercado de la Ribera** This vibrant market is a feast for the senses with local produce, seafood, and more. **Save on fees**: Entry is free, but budgeting for lunch here is a must! **Free alternative**: Explore the surrounding neighborhood and enjoy street performances. **Tip**: Sample local specialties at various stalls for a culinary adventure.

Insider Tips for Bilbao

1. **Explore the Casco Viejo**: This charming old town is filled with narrow streets, quaint shops, and local eateries. Get lost in the labyrinth and discover hidden gems.

2. **Try Pintxos**: The Basque version of tapas, pintxos are a must-try. Look for bars with a bustling atmosphere where locals gather. The best part? Many bars offer free pintxos with your drink!

3. **Public Transport**: Bilbao has an excellent public transportation system, including the Metro, trams, and buses. Grab a Bilbao Bizkaia Card for unlimited travel and discounts on attractions.

4. **Visit on the Last Friday of the Month**: Many museums and attractions offer free entry during special events like "Bilbao Night" on the last Friday of each month.

5. **Bikes and Walking**: The city is bike-friendly, with many bike lanes. Rent a bike or simply stroll along the riverbanks for a scenic view.

6. **Market Visits**: Don't miss the Mercado de la Ribera. It's not only a place to shop for fresh produce but also a hub for local culture. Sample local foods at affordable prices.

7. **Cultural Events**: Keep an eye out for local festivals and events, often free to attend. The city is known for its vibrant cultural scene, with music, dance, and art festivals throughout the year.

8. **Free Walking Tours**: Take advantage of free walking tours to learn about the city's history and culture. Just remember to tip your guide!

Getting Around Bilbao Cheaply

- **Bilbao Metro**: Efficient and extensive, the metro is the easiest way to navigate the city. A single ticket costs about €1.50, but a 10-trip ticket (BilbaoBizkaia Card) offers better value.

- **Trams and Buses**: Tram and bus fares are similar to the metro. Use the same BilbaoBizkaia Card for discounts.

- **Walking**: Many attractions are within walking distance, especially in the compact Casco Viejo and along the river. Walking is not only free but also a great way to soak in the city.

- **Bikes**: Rent a bike from one of the many rental shops or use the local bike-sharing program. Prices are reasonable, and cycling is a great way to explore.

- **Taxi and Rideshare**: While taxis are available, they can be pricey. Consider using rideshare apps for more competitive rates, especially late at night.

Chart of Affordable Luxury Accommodation in Bilbao

Accommodation	Description	Average Nightly	Pros	Cons
Hotel Gran Bilbao	Elegant design, spa facilities, and great views of the city.	€90 - €150	Spacious rooms, near attractions	Can be busy during peak
Meliá Bilbao	Modern hotel with excellent amenities and riverside	€100 - €160	Close to the Guggenheim,	Limited parking
Hotel Carlton	Historical hotel with classic luxury and central location.	€120 - €180	Beautiful architecture, high-	Higher prices during events
NH Collection Ría de Bilbao	Chic hotel with a riverside terrace and modern decor.	€95 - €145	Stunning views, excellent breakfast	Some rooms can be small
Hotel Ercilla	Contemporary hotel with a rooftop terrace and city views.	€80 - €130	Central location, great for exploring	Parking can be tricky
Silken Gran Hotel	Stylish and modern, located just outside Bilbao.	€75 - €120	Peaceful setting, affordable rates	Not in the city center
Hotel Sercotel Coliseo	A converted theater with a unique atmosphere.	€90 - €140	Central location, interesting design	Can be noisy due to events

Free Events or Experiences in Bilbao That Most People Don't Know About

1. **Bilbao Art District**: Hidden within the city's vibrant streets, the Bilbao Art District hosts various pop-up art exhibitions and events throughout the year. Many of these events are free, showcasing local artists and providing a glimpse into the contemporary Basque art scene. Keep an eye on local listings or follow social media pages dedicated to the district to catch the latest happenings.

2. **Street Performances in Casco Viejo**: While exploring the narrow, winding streets of Casco Viejo, you might stumble upon street performers showcasing their talents. From musicians to dancers, these performances often happen spontaneously and are free to enjoy. Bring some coins to tip the artists as a way to show appreciation for their craft.

3. **Ronda de la Abundancia Festival**: This lesser-known annual festival celebrates the Basque tradition of fishing and is typically held in June. Local fishermen demonstrate traditional techniques, and there are plenty of free workshops and tastings of local fish dishes. It's a fantastic opportunity to immerse yourself in local culture without spending a dime.

4. **Free Guided Tours**: Many organizations offer free walking tours in Bilbao. These tours cover various topics, from history to food. While they don't charge a fee, it's customary to tip your guide at the end if you enjoyed the experience. Look for themed tours, such as "The Hidden Gems of Bilbao," for a unique perspective.

5. **Art Walks**: The city often hosts self-guided art walks that highlight public art installations and murals scattered throughout different neighborhoods. Grab a map from the tourist information center and explore at your own pace—this experience is entirely free and a great way to discover local art.

Practical Things to Remember to Save Money in Bilbao

1. **Public Transport Cards**: Use the **Bilbao Bizkaia Card** for unlimited travel on public transport, which costs around €10 for a day pass. This card offers discounts on various attractions, saving you money on both transport and entry fees.

2. **Eat Like a Local**: Enjoy pintxos during the happy hour (often from 7 PM to 9 PM) when many bars offer discounts or a free pintxo with your drink. Expect to pay around €1-€3 for each pintxo, compared to the €5-€10 in some sit-down restaurants.

3. **Free Museum Days**: Many museums offer free entry on specific days of the month or reduced rates for students and seniors. For example, the Museo de Bellas Artes has free entry on Tuesdays. Planning your visits around these days can significantly reduce your costs.

4. **Tap Water**: Tap water in Bilbao is safe to drink, so carry a reusable bottle. Buying bottled water can add up, costing around €1-€2 per bottle. Refilling will save you money and reduce plastic waste.

5. **Visit During Off-Peak Times**: Crowds tend to gather during weekends and holidays. If you can, plan your visits during weekdays, particularly in the morning or late afternoon to enjoy attractions with fewer visitors.

Historical Facts You Didn't Know About Bilbao

1. **The Origins of the Name**: The name "Bilbao" comes from the Basque words "Bil," meaning "to" and "bao," meaning "confluence." This refers to the city's position at

the confluence of the Nervión River and the Estuary of Bilbao, which was critical for its development as a trading port.

2. **The Oldest Metro in the Basque Country**: The Bilbao Metro, inaugurated in 1995, is often hailed as one of the most efficient metro systems in Spain. What many don't know is that it was designed by renowned architect Sir Norman Foster, who aimed to create a system that blended seamlessly with the city's landscape.

3. **The Iron and Steel Heritage**: Bilbao's industrial heritage is deeply rooted in iron and steel production. In the 19th century, the city was one of the leading iron producers in Spain. This industrial boom transformed Bilbao into a major economic hub, shaping its architecture and urban development.

4. **Bilbao's Transformation**: After a decline in industry, the late 20th century saw a significant urban renewal project, notably the construction of the Guggenheim Museum. This project revitalized the city and transformed its global image, attracting millions of visitors each year.

5. **A Unique Basque Culture**: The Basque Country has its unique language (Euskara) and culture. Did you know that Euskara is one of the oldest languages in Europe and is unrelated to any other known language? This cultural uniqueness is a point of pride for the locals.

Comprehensive Practical Information for Visiting Bilbao

*   **Getting There**: Bilbao is well-connected by public transport. The Bilbao Airport (BIO) is about 12 km from the city center. You can take the Bizkaibus Line A3247 directly to the city, which costs about €3 and takes around 30 minutes. Alternatively, taxis cost approximately €30.

*   **Crowd Times**: The peak tourist season is during summer (June to August), so expect larger crowds. If you prefer a quieter experience, consider visiting in the shoulder seasons of spring (April-May) and autumn (September-October).

*   **Tickets**: Many attractions offer discounts for students and seniors. Check online for combo tickets that include entry to multiple attractions, as this can save you up to 30% on admission fees.

*   **What to Do There**: In addition to the major attractions like the Guggenheim and the Old Town, don't miss the lively atmosphere at the Mercado de la Ribera, where you can taste local delicacies and buy fresh produce.

*   **Secret Spots**: For a quieter experience, visit the **San Juan de Gaztelugatxe**, a stunning islet with a hermitage and beautiful hiking trails. It's a bit outside Bilbao (about 35 km), but the views are worth it. Another hidden gem is **Pikachú**, a quirky little bar in the Old Town known for its creative cocktails and local ambiance.

Santiago de Compostela

Santiago de Compostela, the vibrant capital of Galicia, Spain! This historic city is a treasure trove of culture and spirituality, famously known as the final destination of the Camino de Santiago, a pilgrimage that has drawn wanderers for over a millennium. Legend has it that the remains of St. James the Apostle are buried here, making the cathedral a site of profound significance for Christians.

As you stroll through the city, you'll feel the weight of history in the cobbled streets and magnificent architecture. Santiago was officially declared a city in 1128, and its medieval streets are lined with buildings that tell tales of centuries past. The city flourished in the Middle Ages, becoming a bustling hub for pilgrims, and its UNESCO World Heritage designation highlights its cultural and historical importance. The charming blend of Gothic, Romanesque, and Baroque styles in its architecture is simply mesmerizing! Today, Santiago de Compostela is not only a pilgrimage site but also a lively university town, brimming with youthful energy and delicious Galician cuisine. Let's dive into the top attractions that you won't want to miss while exploring this captivating city!

Top 20 Paid Attractions in Santiago de Compostela

1. **Santiago de Compostela Cathedral** This iconic cathedral is the heart of the city and a must-visit for anyone. Its breathtaking façade and intricate interior will leave you in awe. Admission is free to enter the cathedral, but if you want to climb the towers for stunning views of the city, there's a small fee. **Tip to save:** Visit during the off-peak hours to avoid crowds. **Free alternative:** Enjoy the beauty of the cathedral's exterior and the surrounding Praza do Obradoiro.

2. **Museum of the Galician People** This museum showcases Galician culture and history through artifacts, art, and traditional crafts. The entrance fee is reasonable, and it's well worth it to understand the region's heritage. **Saving tip:** Look for student or senior discounts. **Free alternative:** Stroll through the nearby parks and plazas to enjoy local street performances.

3. **Museum of Sacred Art** Located within the cathedral complex, this museum houses a remarkable collection of religious artifacts and art. Admission fees help maintain this significant site. **Saving tip:** Consider a combined ticket if you're visiting multiple museums. **Free alternative:** Explore the religious art displayed in the cathedral itself.

4. **Casa do Gelato** This quirky ice cream shop is not just about delicious flavors; it also has a small entrance fee for the interactive ice cream museum within. Here, you can learn about the history of ice cream in Galicia! **Saving tip:**Grab a gelato after your visit to cool off. **Free alternative:** Walk along the streets and enjoy people-watching while indulging in your favorite flavors.

5. **Pazo de Raxoi** This historical palace serves as the city hall and features beautiful architecture. While entry to the building is limited, guided tours are available for a fee. **Saving tip:** Look for free guided tours offered by the city on certain days. **Free**

alternative: Take photos of the stunning exterior and enjoy a leisurely walk in the surrounding gardens.

6. **Galicia Contemporary Art Center** A hub for modern art lovers, this center hosts rotating exhibitions from Galician and international artists. Admission fees are modest, and it's a great place to explore innovative works. **Saving tip:** Check for free entry days each month. **Free alternative:** Visit nearby parks that often feature outdoor installations and art.

7. **Botanical Garden of Santiago de Compostela** A beautiful escape into nature, this garden showcases native Galician flora. There's a small entry fee, but the serene surroundings are worth it. **Saving tip:** Pack a picnic to enjoy in the gardens after your visit. **Free alternative:** Enjoy a walk along the riverbanks nearby.

8. **Centro Galego de Arte Contemporánea** This contemporary art center is a testament to modern creativity, showcasing a variety of exhibitions. While there is a fee for special exhibits, many permanent collections are free to visit. **Saving tip:** Attend their workshops for a hands-on experience at no extra cost. **Free alternative:** Take a stroll around the center to appreciate the architecture and outdoor art installations.

9. **Museo do Pobo Galego** This museum celebrates the Galician way of life, featuring traditional costumes, crafts, and historical displays. The entrance fee helps preserve this cultural gem. **Saving tip:** Visit on days with discounted admission. **Free alternative:** Explore the vibrant Mercado de Abastos nearby for a taste of local life.

10. **San Martin Pinario Monastery** This stunning baroque monastery is a hidden gem with an entrance fee to access its beautiful chapel and cloister. **Saving tip:** Join a guided tour to gain more insights into its history. **Free alternative:** Marvel at the monastery's exterior from the adjacent streets.

11. **Café Tertulia** This famous café is known for its delicious pastries and rich coffee, but it also has a small entrance fee for the historical exhibition on its upper floor. **Saving tip:** Enjoy your coffee on the terrace to soak in the atmosphere. **Free alternative:** Visit other nearby cafés with outdoor seating to experience local flavors.

12. **Parque de la Alameda** While access to the park is free, you can pay for guided tours or picnics hosted by local companies. The park offers stunning views of the cathedral and is a perfect spot to relax. **Saving tip:** Bring your own snacks and drinks to enjoy a budget-friendly picnic. **Free alternative:** Just wander through the park and take in the natural beauty.

13. **Castillo de San Antón** This historic castle offers a peek into Santiago's military past. The entrance fee includes a guided tour, making it an informative visit. **Saving tip:** Check for discounts on group bookings. **Free alternative:** Walk around the castle grounds and explore the surrounding area.

14. **Palacio de Fonseca** This stunning palace, now part of the University of Santiago, charges a small fee for guided tours. It's an excellent opportunity to learn about the

university's history. **Saving tip:** Attend special events held at the palace for free entry. **Free alternative:** Explore the university's beautiful courtyard and gardens.

15. **Museo de Historia Natural** Discover fascinating exhibits on natural history, with a modest entrance fee. The museum's collections include everything from fossils to taxidermy. **Saving tip:** Join a tour for a more comprehensive understanding. **Free alternative:** Enjoy a walk in the park nearby, which often features outdoor exhibits.

16. **Estadio Municipal de Riazor** For sports enthusiasts, a tour of this stadium allows you to learn about local football culture. There's a fee for guided tours. **Saving tip:** Attend a local match for an unforgettable experience! **Free alternative:** Check out local bars to catch a game on TV and mingle with fans.

17. **Catedral de Santiago de Compostela Towers** Climb the towers for breathtaking views of the city. There's a fee for this, but the panoramic vista is incredible. **Saving tip:** Visit during sunset for stunning photography opportunities. **Free alternative:** Watch the sunset from Parque de la Alameda for a different perspective.

18. **Museo das Peregrinacións** This museum tells the story of the pilgrims who have traveled to Santiago over the centuries. The small entry fee is well spent on the fascinating exhibits. **Saving tip:** Take advantage of guided tours that include access to multiple attractions. **Free alternative:** Browse the nearby souvenir shops that often sell unique items related to the pilgrimage.

19. **Centro de Recursos para la Sociedade da Información** This center offers insights into the region's digital and technological advancements, with a small entrance fee. **Saving tip:** Look for workshops that are sometimes offered for free. **Free alternative:** Explore the nearby tech shops and cafes showcasing local innovations.

20. **Casa do Cabildo** This historic building has been transformed into a cultural center. While there's a fee for specific exhibitions, many events are free to the public. **Saving tip:** Attend free cultural events for an enriching experience. **Free alternative:** Enjoy the architecture from the outside and engage with locals at nearby markets.

Tips for Santiago de Compostela

1. **Timing is Everything**: If you want to avoid the tourist rush, try visiting during the shoulder seasons (spring and fall). The weather is pleasant, and you'll experience fewer crowds at popular sites.

2. **Pilgrim Passport**: If you're considering walking the Camino, don't forget to get a pilgrim passport! It's a fun way to collect stamps from various locations along the route, and it grants you discounts at certain attractions and accommodations.

3. **Local Cuisine**: Be sure to try Galician specialties like pulpo a la gallega (octopus), empanada, and the famous Tarta de Santiago. For budget-friendly meals, seek out *tapas* bars where you can enjoy smaller dishes at reasonable prices.

4. **Free Walking Tours**: Many local companies offer free walking tours of the city, which can provide you with a rich historical context and insider tips. Just remember to tip your guide based on how much you enjoyed the tour!

5. **Public Transport**: Santiago is quite walkable, but if you need public transport, the bus system is efficient and affordable. Consider getting a refillable transport card for extra savings.

6. **Market Visits**: Don't miss the Mercado de Abastos, where you can taste local products, enjoy fresh seafood, and pick up unique souvenirs. It's a great place to mingle with locals!

7. **Cultural Events**: Keep an eye on local listings for free cultural events, such as concerts and art exhibitions. Many museums offer free entry on certain days, so plan your visits accordingly.

8. **Early Bird Specials**: Some attractions offer discounts for early morning visits or during specific hours, so it's worth checking in advance.

9. **Pack a Picnic**: With so many beautiful parks and gardens, pack a lunch and enjoy a picnic amidst nature or in scenic spots around the city.

10. **Language**: A few phrases in Galician or Spanish can go a long way! Locals appreciate when you make an effort to speak their language.

Free Events or Experiences in Santiago de Compostela

1. **The Daily Pilgrim Mass**: Every day at 12:00 PM, the Santiago de Compostela Cathedral holds a special mass dedicated to pilgrims. While the cathedral is typically a crowded tourist spot, the mass brings a unique atmosphere filled with spirituality. The service often includes traditional music and the presence of the famous Botafumeiro, a giant incense burner that swings dramatically from the ceiling, filling the space with aromatic smoke. Attending the mass is free, and it offers a glimpse into the city's rich pilgrimage tradition that many visitors might overlook.

2. **Art Walks on the Streets**: Santiago is dotted with impressive street art and murals that often go unnoticed. Taking a self-guided art walk through neighborhoods like the historic old town or San Pedro will reveal hidden treasures. Various artists have transformed blank walls into vibrant canvases. You can explore these artworks at your own pace, taking in the stories behind them and enjoying the local vibe. This artistic journey is entirely free and a fantastic way to appreciate the city's creativity.

3. **Local Festivals**: Throughout the year, Santiago hosts various local festivals that often remain under the radar for tourists. Events like the Festival of St. James in July feature parades, traditional music, and performances that celebrate Galician culture. Attending these festivals is free and provides a unique cultural experience. Be sure to check the local calendar for upcoming events during your visit.

4. **Mercado de Abastos**: While it's not a formal event, visiting the Mercado de Abastos (the local market) is an experience in itself. This vibrant market is filled

with local vendors selling fresh produce, cheeses, meats, and seafood. Walking through the market and sampling local delicacies can be a delightful way to spend a few hours without spending much. Grab a few bites or enjoy a meal at one of the small eateries inside for an authentic taste of Galician cuisine.

Practical Things to Remember to Save Money in Santiago

1. **Public Transport**: Santiago de Compostela is a compact city, making it easy to navigate on foot. However, if you need to use public transport, a single bus ticket costs €1.30, and a ten-journey pass is €7.00. Opting for the pass can save you money if you plan to use public transport multiple times during your stay.

2. **Free Museum Days**: Many museums in Santiago offer free entry on the first Sunday of each month. This includes the Museum of the Galician People and the Museo de Historia Natural. Planning your visits around these days can save you around €10-€20 in entry fees.

3. **Discounted Tickets**: If you're visiting multiple attractions, look for combined tickets that offer access to several places at a reduced rate. For example, the ticket for the Cathedral complex includes entry to the museum and the rooftop for around €10-€12, saving you about €5-€7 compared to purchasing individual tickets.

4. **Student Discounts**: If you're a student, always carry your ID. Many attractions offer discounted rates of around 50% off for students. This can significantly lower costs, especially for museums and guided tours.

5. **Dining Deals**: For meals, consider having lunch instead of dinner, as many restaurants offer *menú del día* (menu of the day) for around €10-€15, which includes multiple courses and a drink. Dinner prices tend to be higher, often averaging €20-€30 per person.

Historical Facts You Didn't Know About Santiago de Compostela

1. **The Hidden Tomb of St. James**: Legend has it that the remains of St. James the Apostle were discovered in the 9th century by a hermit named Pelayo, leading to the establishment of Santiago de Compostela as a pilgrimage site. However, what many don't know is that the location of St. James' tomb remained a closely guarded secret for centuries, with various accounts claiming that it was revealed to Pelayo through celestial signs.

2. **Pilgrimage Routes**: The Camino de Santiago has numerous routes that converge on Santiago, with the most famous being the Camino Francés. What's intriguing is that these routes were used not just by pilgrims but also by traders, soldiers, and cultural exchange travelers. The roads have witnessed centuries of history and are considered a UNESCO World Heritage Site, celebrating not only the spiritual journey but also the cultural interactions that occurred along the way.

3. **The Botafumeiro's Origin**: The massive incense burner known as the Botafumeiro is often associated with the Cathedral's liturgical celebrations. While many think it's solely for aesthetic purposes, it was initially used to mask the odor of unwashed

pilgrims during the Middle Ages, making it a practical solution to a rather unpleasant problem!

Practical Information for Visiting Santiago de Compostela

1. **How to Get There**: Santiago de Compostela is well-connected by train and bus. The city's airport has flights from major Spanish cities, and a shuttle bus operates between the airport and the city center for around €3.50. If you're coming from nearby cities, check the Alsa bus service, which offers frequent connections.

2. **When Crowds are Present**: The peak tourist season runs from June to September, especially around the Festival of St. James in late July, when the city is bustling with pilgrims and tourists alike. For a quieter experience, consider visiting in spring (April to June) or fall (September to October).

3. **Ticket Information**: Tickets for the Cathedral complex can be purchased at the entrance or online. The basic ticket includes entry to the cathedral, museum, and rooftop access, costing around €10. It's advisable to book in advance during peak seasons to avoid long lines.

4. **What to Do There**: Besides visiting the cathedral, explore the winding streets of the old town, the Mercado de Abastos, and the beautiful parks such as Parque da Alameda. Don't miss the chance to join a local cooking class or a wine tasting event for a taste of Galician culture.

5. **Secret Spots**: Look for the *Casa de la Troia*, a hidden gem steeped in literary history, where the famous Spanish author Ramón del Valle-Inclán wrote some of his notable works. Another less-known spot is the *Pazo de Xelmirez*, an impressive medieval palace adjacent to the cathedral, which often goes unnoticed by tourists.

6. **Local Apps and Guides**: Consider downloading local apps like "Santiago de Compostela" or "Camino de Santiago" for maps, guides, and event listings. They provide up-to-date information on what's happening in the city and help you navigate effortlessly.

Toledo

Toledo, often called the "City of Three Cultures," is a mesmerizing blend of Christian, Muslim, and Jewish influences that have shaped its rich history over centuries. Situated on a rocky hill overlooking the Tagus River, this ancient city served as the capital of Spain for much of the Middle Ages. It's a place where every street tells a story, and every building whispers secrets from a time when the various cultures coexisted in relative harmony.

The Romans first made their mark on Toledo, but it was during the Visigothic period that it truly flourished, becoming a center of governance and culture. When the Moors arrived in the 8th century, they transformed Toledo into a jewel of Islamic art and scholarship, paving the way for an era of enlightenment that would influence Europe. After the Reconquista in 1085, Toledo became a Christian stronghold, and the city's diverse architectural styles—ranging from Mudejar to Gothic—reflect this fascinating tapestry of history.

Toledo also played a pivotal role in the Spanish Renaissance, producing legendary figures like El Greco, whose vibrant works can still be admired in the city's museums. The winding, narrow streets are lined with impressive monuments, making Toledo a treasure trove for history lovers and a perfect backdrop for anyone seeking to immerse themselves in the charm of old Spain. As you stroll through its ancient walls, you'll find yourself captivated by the magic of this city that once bridged the divides of faith and culture.

Top 20 Paid Attractions in Toledo

1. **Toledo Cathedral (Catedral Primada)**
   A stunning example of Gothic architecture, Toledo Cathedral is a must-visit. Don't miss the breathtaking altarpiece and the famous El Greco paintings. To save on fees, consider visiting during free entry times, usually on specific weekdays. A great free alternative is to enjoy the views from the outside or nearby Plaza del Ayuntamiento. Keep your camera ready for some incredible shots of the exterior!

2. **Alcázar of Toledo**
   This impressive fortress houses the Army Museum, showcasing military history. The entry fee includes access to various exhibits. To save, check for discounted tickets on weekends or during local festivals. If you're looking for a creative alternative, visit the surrounding gardens and enjoy the views from the outside. Don't forget to explore the fascinating history of this site, which has witnessed countless battles!

3. **Museo del Greco**
   Dedicated to the renowned painter El Greco, this museum features an extensive collection of his works. To save on fees, look for combined tickets with other attractions. For a free alternative, stroll around the nearby Jewish Quarter, where you can soak up the historical atmosphere. Learn about how Toledo influenced El Greco's artistry and the unique styles he developed.

4. **Monastery of San Juan de los Reyes**
   A beautiful example of Gothic architecture, this monastery was built to commemorate the victory in the Battle of Toro. To save on fees, visit on the first

Sunday of the month when entry is free. A creative alternative is to explore the tranquil gardens outside. Don't miss the intricate details of the cloister, which tell stories of the city's past.

5. **Church of Santo Tomé**
   Home to El Greco's famous painting "The Burial of the Count of Orgaz," this church is a gem in Toledo. Tickets are affordable, and discounts are available for students and seniors. If you're on a budget, admire the church's exterior and enjoy the surrounding square. The church's history is steeped in legend, making it a fascinating stop for art lovers.

6. **Synagogue of Santa María la Blanca**
   This former synagogue is a stunning example of Mudejar architecture. The entry fee is modest, and it's well worth it for the serene atmosphere. Save on fees by visiting during guided tours offered by the city. A free alternative is to wander around the old Jewish Quarter, rich with history. Discover how this space symbolizes the coexistence of cultures in Toledo.

7. **Mosque of Cristo de la Luz**
   This small mosque is one of the best-preserved remnants of Toledo's Islamic heritage. Tickets are inexpensive, making it a quick and affordable stop. For a creative free alternative, explore the nearby streets to find hidden gems and viewpoints. Learn about how this mosque was later converted into a Christian chapel, reflecting the city's dynamic history.

8. **Toledo City Walls**
   A walk along the ancient city walls offers panoramic views of the city. Entry is often free, but guided tours can provide richer insights. For a creative alternative, bring a picnic and enjoy the scenery. The walls tell stories of sieges and defenses, adding depth to your visit.

9. **Museo de los Concilios y la Cultura Visigoda**
   This museum offers a glimpse into the Visigothic era, with fascinating artifacts on display. The entry fee is reasonable, and discounts are available for groups. A free alternative is to explore the nearby Plaza del Ayuntamiento, where history is palpable. Discover how Toledo was a significant center for the Visigoths, influencing early Spanish culture.

10. **Palacio de Galiana**
    A beautiful Moorish palace with stunning gardens, it offers a tranquil escape. Entry fees are modest, and it's worth visiting in spring when the gardens bloom. To save, check for combined tickets with other attractions. A free alternative is to enjoy the views of the gardens from outside. The palace's history is intertwined with legends of romance and intrigue.

11. **Museum of the Council of Toledo**
    This museum focuses on the important councils that took place in Toledo. Entry fees are quite low, making it accessible. For a free alternative, visit the nearby Plaza de Zocodover, a hub of activity and history. Learn how Toledo was a political center in medieval Spain through its vibrant history.

12. **Casa-Museo de El Greco**
Step into the life of El Greco with this museum dedicated to his work and life. The entry fee is reasonable, with discounts available for students. For a free alternative, explore the surrounding streets of the historic district. The house offers insights into the artist's life, enriching your understanding of his masterpieces.

13. **Toledo's Archaeological Museum**
This museum houses artifacts from Toledo's long history, from Roman times to the Middle Ages. The entry fee is low, and guided tours provide great insights. For a free alternative, explore the ancient streets leading to the museum. Discover how Toledo's rich history is reflected in its archaeological treasures.

14. **Iglesia de San Ildefonso (Jesuit Church)**
A stunning Baroque church with a rich interior, it's known for its beautiful altars. The entry fee is minimal, making it an easy addition to your itinerary. For a creative free alternative, take a moment to admire the building from the outside. The church is named after the patron saint of Toledo and has a fascinating backstory worth learning.

15. **Hospital de Tavera**
This historical hospital is an architectural marvel and houses a great collection of art. Entry fees are modest, and guided tours can enhance your experience. For a free alternative, explore the surrounding area and gardens. The hospital's history as a health institution highlights Toledo's medieval advancements in medicine.

16. **Cerro del Emperador**
This viewpoint offers spectacular views of Toledo, especially at sunset. While there's no entry fee, guided tours are available for those wanting more context. For a free alternative, simply bring a picnic and enjoy the scenery. Learn about how this spot has been a lookout point for centuries.

17. **Plaza de Zocodover**
The main square of Toledo is vibrant with shops and cafés. While exploring is free, consider visiting during local events for an immersive experience. For a free alternative, enjoy a coffee at one of the many cafés and people-watch. The square's history as a marketplace adds to its charm.

18. **Puente de San Martín**
This medieval bridge is a stunning architectural feat. There's no entry fee, making it a lovely stop during your exploration. A creative alternative is to take photos from various angles, especially at sunrise or sunset. The bridge has a history of being a vital crossing point, making it a significant landmark.

19. **Castillo de San Servando**
A castle dating back to the 11th century, it offers great views and a peek into Toledo's past. Entry fees are minimal, and the surrounding area is perfect for picnics. For a free alternative, explore the nearby trails and enjoy the scenic beauty. The castle's role in the defense of Toledo is a captivating part of its history.

20. **Centro Cultural de los Ejércitos**
This cultural center offers exhibitions related to military history and art. The entry fee is affordable, and discounted tickets are available for students. For a free

alternative, visit during open-air events held in the surrounding area. Learn about the military's significant role in shaping Toledo's history, making this a fascinating stop.

Insider Tips for Toledo

1. **Early Bird Gets the Worm**: Visit popular attractions early in the morning to beat the crowds. The peace of the early hours allows you to truly appreciate the beauty of Toledo without the hustle and bustle of tourists.

2. **Walking Shoes are Essential**: Toledo is a city best explored on foot. Wear comfortable shoes, as the cobbled streets can be uneven and steep. Bring a reusable water bottle to stay hydrated while wandering around.

3. **Free Walking Tours**: Take advantage of free walking tours offered by local guides. They provide a great overview of the city's history and culture and often accept tips based on your satisfaction.

4. **Local Cuisine**: Don't miss out on trying local specialties like marzipan and venado (venison). Seek out smaller, local restaurants to avoid tourist traps, and ask locals for their favorite spots.

5. **Visit During Festivals**: If possible, plan your visit during one of Toledo's many festivals, such as Semana Santa (Holy Week) or the Fiesta de San Juan. These events showcase local traditions and can make your experience more memorable.

6. **Explore Off the Beaten Path**: While the main attractions are a must-see, don't hesitate to venture into less-visited areas. The smaller streets often reveal hidden gems, quaint shops, and quieter cafes.

Getting Around Toledo Cheaply

- **Walking**: The best way to explore Toledo is on foot. Most attractions are within walking distance, and the city's layout is designed for pedestrians.

- **Public Buses**: For farther destinations, Toledo has an affordable bus system. Check local schedules for routes that connect you to various points of interest.

- **Bicycle Rentals**: Consider renting a bicycle for the day. There are bike rental shops around the city, and cycling can be a fun way to see the sights.

- **Hop-On Hop-Off Buses**: If you prefer not to walk, the hop-on hop-off bus service offers a convenient way to get around. Tickets are usually reasonably priced and allow you to explore at your own pace.

Chart of Affordable Luxury Accommodations in Toledo

Hotel Name	Price Range (per night)	Features	Location
Hotel Boutique Pintor El Greco	€90 - €150	Charming decor, close to major attractions	Historic Center

Hotel San Juan de	€80 - €120	Beautiful gardens, stunning	Near Monastery of
Eurostars Palacio	€100 - €160	Elegant rooms, swimming pool,	Overlooking the city
Sercotel Hotel Pintor	€80 - €130	Modern amenities, restaurant, close	Central Toledo
Casa de la Mezquita	€70 - €110	Boutique hotel, unique rooms,	Jewish Quarter
Hotel Abad Toledo	€60 - €100	Comfortable rooms, restaurant, great	Near the city walls
Parador de Toledo	€100 - €200	Luxurious stay, fantastic views, historical significance	On a hill overlooking Toledo
Hotel Casona de la Reyna	€70 - €120	Cozy atmosphere, great service	Near Toledo's main attractions
Hotel La Casa del	€60 - €100	Budget-friendly, rustic charm, views	Riverside area
Hotel Hesperia Toledo	€80 - €130	Modern facilities, pool, close to city center	Short distance from attractions

Free Events or Experiences in Toledo

1. **Free Walking Tours**: Many local guides offer free walking tours that provide insights into Toledo's rich history and architecture. While the tour itself is free, it's customary to tip the guide based on your enjoyment. These tours often take you through less-traveled streets and share fascinating anecdotes about the city's past.

2. **Art Exhibitions at La Casa de Cultura**: This cultural center frequently hosts free art exhibitions showcasing local artists. It's a wonderful opportunity to immerse yourself in Toledo's vibrant art scene and discover emerging talent without spending a dime. Check their calendar for upcoming events.

3. **Outdoor Concerts and Festivals**: Throughout the year, especially during the summer, Toledo hosts free outdoor concerts and cultural festivals. These events are usually held in public squares like Plaza de Zocodover. You can enjoy live music, traditional dances, and local food without any entry fee.

4. **Visit the Alcázar Grounds**: While there is a fee to enter the Alcázar of Toledo, you can still enjoy the beautiful grounds surrounding the fortress for free. The area offers stunning views of the city and the Tagus River, perfect for a leisurely stroll or a picnic.

5. **Sunset Views from Mirador del Valle**: While not an event, this viewpoint offers one of the best sunset views of Toledo. It's a little out of the way but worth the trek for breathtaking photographs. Bring a camera and enjoy the peaceful setting as the sun sets over the historic skyline.

Practical Things to Remember to Save Money in Toledo

- **Eat Where Locals Eat**: Avoid tourist traps by dining at local taverns or cafes away from main squares. A meal can cost as little as €10-€15 in a local spot compared to €25+ in tourist areas, saving you a significant amount.

- **Public Transportation**: Use buses instead of taxis to get around. A single bus fare is around €1.50, while a taxi can start at €3.50 plus additional charges. Walking is also a great option, as many attractions are close together.

- **Free Admission Days**: Many museums offer free admission on specific days or times. For instance, the Museo de El Greco often has free entry on Sundays. Planning your visit accordingly can save you up to €12 per person.

- **Use the Toledo Tourist Card**: This card offers discounts on attractions and free public transport for €10 for one day. If you plan to visit several attractions, this could save you money.

- **Picnic in the Park**: Buy fresh produce and local cheeses from markets, such as Mercado de San Agustín, and enjoy a picnic in the beautiful Parque de las Tres Culturas, saving on dining costs while enjoying the scenery.

Historical Facts You Didn't Know About Toledo

1. **The Birthplace of the Spanish Language**: Toledo played a crucial role in the development of the Spanish language. During the 12th century, the city became a melting pot of cultures, leading to the birth of a unique dialect that would influence modern Spanish.

2. **The "City of Three Cultures"**: Toledo was known as the City of Three Cultures due to the harmonious coexistence of Christians, Muslims, and Jews for centuries. This cultural blend is evident in its architecture, art, and culinary traditions.

3. **Toledo's Synagogues**: Despite the expulsion of Jews in the late 15th century, Toledo is home to some of the best-preserved synagogues in Spain, such as Santa María la Blanca. These structures serve as reminders of the city's diverse history.

4. **Famous Sword-Making Tradition**: Toledo has a long-standing tradition of sword-making, dating back to Roman times. The city was renowned for its high-quality steel and craftsmanship, producing swords for notable figures throughout history, including kings and knights.

5. **The Influence of El Greco**: The famous painter El Greco lived in Toledo for most of his life, profoundly impacting the city's art scene. His works reflect the unique cultural blend of the city and can still be seen in various museums and churches throughout Toledo.

Practical Information for Visiting Toledo

- **How to Get There**: Toledo is easily accessible from Madrid, with frequent trains departing from Madrid Atocha station. The journey takes about 30 minutes and costs around €10-€15 for a round trip.

- **Crowd Times**: The best time to visit is during the shoulder seasons (April to June and September to October) when the weather is pleasant, and the crowds are thinner. Summer months (July and August) can be very crowded, especially on weekends.

- **Tickets for Attractions**: Many attractions offer discounted tickets for students and seniors, while some museums provide free entry on the first Sunday of the month. Always check official websites for the latest pricing and offers.

- **What to Do There**: In addition to exploring historic sites, don't miss wandering the narrow streets of the Jewish Quarter, sampling local delicacies, and visiting artisan shops that sell handmade crafts.

- **Secret Spots**: One lesser-known spot is the **Mirador de los Poetas**, a viewpoint that offers stunning panoramic views of Toledo and is often overlooked by tourists. Another hidden gem is the **Museo de los Concilios**, which provides insights into the city's ecclesiastical history and is usually less crowded.

- **Local Events**: Check local event calendars for unique festivals and fairs, such as the Festival of the Virgin of Alcántara, which features traditional music, dance, and food, giving visitors a chance to experience local culture firsthand.

Málaga

Málaga, a vibrant city on Spain's Costa del Sol, is rich in history and culture. Founded by the Phoenicians over 2,800 years ago, it boasts a legacy that includes influences from the Romans, Moors, and Christians. The city was originally known as Malaka, likely derived from the Phoenician word for "salt." It flourished as a trading hub due to its strategic port location. The Romans built significant structures here, including a theater that still stands today.

During the Moorish period, Málaga became a key center for culture and commerce, marked by the construction of the Alcazaba, a magnificent fortress that overlooks the city. The Christian Reconquista in the late 15th century brought significant changes, leading to the construction of the Málaga Cathedral, often referred to as "La Manquita" (the one-armed lady) due to its unfinished second tower.

In the 19th and 20th centuries, Málaga saw industrial growth, especially in the production of sugar and wine, which remains important today. The city is also the birthplace of famous artist Pablo Picasso, and his influence is celebrated through various museums and monuments. Today, Málaga blends its rich historical roots with modern attractions, making it a must-visit destination for travelers.

Top 20 Paid Attractions in Málaga

1. **Alcazaba of Málaga**
    This stunning Moorish fortress dates back to the 11th century and offers breathtaking views of the city. You can save on entry fees by visiting on Sundays after 2 PM when admission is free for EU citizens. For a creative alternative, take a walk around the gardens surrounding the Alcazaba for lovely views without entering. Don't forget your camera; the sunset from the battlements is magical!

2. **Málaga Cathedral**
    Known for its Renaissance architecture, this cathedral is a testament to the city's rich history. To save on fees, consider visiting during Mass, where you can experience the interior without a ticket. A free alternative is to explore the nearby Plaza del Obispo, perfect for people-watching and enjoying a coffee. The cathedral is often called "La Manquita" because of its unfinished tower—perfect for a little historical trivia!

3. **Picasso Museum**
    Celebrating the life and work of Málaga's most famous son, this museum houses an impressive collection of his works. Admission is free on Sundays after 5 PM, so plan accordingly! If you're short on time, check out the outdoor sculpture garden instead for a creative free experience. The museum itself is in a restored palace, adding to its charm.

4. **Carmen Thyssen Museum**
    This art museum focuses on 19th-century Spanish paintings, particularly Andalusian art. On Tuesdays, entrance fees are reduced, making it a great day to visit. A free alternative is to stroll around the Plaza de la Constitucion, where you can appreciate local architecture and street performances. The museum was originally a palatial residence, reflecting the city's artistic heritage.

5. **Castillo de Gibralfaro**
   Perched high above the city, this castle offers panoramic views and a glimpse into Málaga's military past. Save on the ticket price by purchasing a combined ticket with the Alcazaba. For a free alternative, hike up the trails surrounding the castle for equally stunning views. It's said that the castle was built to protect the Alcazaba —an interesting tidbit to share!

6. **Roman Theatre**
   Discovered in 1951, this ancient theatre dates back to the 1st century BC and is one of Málaga's most significant archaeological sites. Entry is free, making it an excellent stop for those on a budget. The theatre is often used for performances, so check for free events during your visit. Its discovery led to the restoration of many other historical sites in the area.

7. **Centre Pompidou Málaga**
   This modern art museum is known for its colorful cube structure and eclectic collection of contemporary works. Discounts are available for students and seniors. If you want to skip the entry fee, explore the surrounding waterfront area, which features public art installations and vibrant street performances. It's a wonderful spot to experience the creative spirit of the city.

8. **Museo del Patrimonio Municipal**
   This lesser-known gem houses artifacts showcasing Málaga's cultural evolution. Admission is often free or low-cost. For a creative alternative, visit the nearby Plaza de la Merced, where you can admire the local street art and enjoy tapas at a café. The museum is housed in a historic palace, adding to its appeal.

9. **Museo de Málaga**
   A combined museum of fine arts and archaeology, it offers a rich collection from different periods. Admission is free on Sundays, making it a perfect day for art lovers. A lovely alternative is to explore the nearby Parque de la Alameda for a leisurely walk and outdoor art installations. The museum's collection includes pieces from the city's Roman past, perfect for history buffs!

10. **Malagueta Beach**
    While the beach itself is free, sunbeds and umbrellas come with a price tag. To save money, bring your own gear for a comfortable day by the sea. A creative alternative is to enjoy a beachside picnic with local delicacies. The beach is a local favorite, and don't miss the chance to try a espetos de sardinas (sardines on a skewer)!

11. **Automobile and Fashion Museum**
    This unique museum features a stunning collection of vintage cars alongside exquisite fashion pieces. Look for discounted tickets on weekdays or combo tickets with other attractions. If you're keen on fashion history, consider browsing the boutiques in the nearby Soho district for a more budget-friendly shopping experience. The museum showcases styles from the 1920s to the present day, making it a visual feast!

12. **Atarazanas Market**
    While not traditionally paid, some tastings and activities can have fees. To save money, sample local olives and cheeses before deciding on purchases. A creative

alternative is to visit the market early in the morning to see the vibrant displays and hustle of vendors. The building itself has a fascinating history, having been a shipyard in the 14th century!

13. **La Concepción Historical-Botanical Gardens**
A beautiful garden featuring diverse plant species from around the world, entry fees apply. To save, visit during the first Sunday of the month when entrance is free. A lovely free alternative is to enjoy a walk in the adjacent parks surrounding the gardens. The gardens were established in the 19th century and are a peaceful retreat from the bustling city.

14. **Museo Carmen Thyssen**
Known for its impressive collection of 19th-century Andalusian art, entry fees are reduced on certain days. If you're looking for a free experience, the plaza outside often hosts events and performances. The museum itself is housed in a stunning 16th-century palace, which is worth seeing in its own right!

15. **Basilica de Santa Maria de la Victoria**
This beautiful church offers a glimpse into Málaga's religious heritage. Entry is typically free, but special tours or events may have fees. For a free alternative, wander the nearby streets and discover charming local shops and cafes. The basilica is notable for its stunning baroque altar, showcasing the city's artistic talent.

16. **Aqualand Torremolinos**
Just outside of Málaga, this water park is a fun family attraction. Discount tickets are available online, especially for early bird purchases. If water slides aren't your thing, head to the nearby beaches for free sunbathing and swimming. Aqualand features numerous slides and pools, ensuring a day full of excitement!

17. **Casa de los Navajas**
This stunning neoclassical building offers beautiful views of the coastline and gardens. Entry is free, but guided tours may have a fee. For a creative alternative, explore the promenade for artistic displays and local vendors. The house was built in the 20th century and is a striking example of architectural beauty in the region.

18. **Museo Picasso**
Dedicated to the works of Pablo Picasso, this museum is a must-visit for art lovers. Look out for discounted tickets on certain days. If you're keen on exploring for free, enjoy the surrounding Plaza de la Merced, filled with vibrant cafés and local life. The museum houses over 200 works, offering a fascinating glimpse into the artist's evolution.

19. **Tivoli World**
This amusement park is a fun day out for families and thrill-seekers alike. Online tickets often come at a discount, especially for group bookings. If theme parks aren't your thing, take a hike in the nearby mountains for stunning views. Tivoli World features a range of attractions from roller coasters to live shows, ensuring fun for all ages!

20. **Fundación Picasso**
This cultural foundation is dedicated to the life and work of Picasso, with various

exhibitions and educational programs. Free admission is offered on the first Sunday of each month. For those interested in more free experiences, stroll around the nearby gardens and enjoy public art installations. The foundation highlights Picasso's influence on contemporary art, making it an insightful visit.

Insider Tips for Málaga

1. **Visit Early or Late**: To avoid crowds at popular attractions like the Alcazaba and the Cathedral, visit early in the morning or later in the afternoon. The golden hour before sunset also offers stunning views and fewer tourists.

2. **Public Transport**: Málaga has an efficient public transport system, including buses and a light rail service. Consider purchasing a Málaga Card for unlimited travel on public transport for a set number of days.

3. **Eat Like a Local**: Skip the tourist traps and dine where the locals do. Check out smaller, family-owned tapas bars for authentic cuisine. Look for "menu del día" options for a cheap and hearty meal during lunchtime.

4. **Free Walking Tours**: Join a free walking tour to get a sense of the city's history and culture. These tours usually operate on a tip-based system, so you can pay what you think the experience is worth.

5. **Explore the Beaches**: Málaga's beaches are public and free. Bring your own towel and enjoy the sun without spending on beach clubs. The Malagueta Beach is particularly popular and has facilities nearby.

6. **Markets and Local Festivals**: Explore local markets like Atarazanas for fresh produce, and check out festival calendars for free events throughout the year. Festivals often feature free concerts and cultural events.

7. **Use Your Feet**: Many attractions are within walking distance of each other in the city center. Strolling around allows you to discover hidden gems and enjoy the city's atmosphere.

8. **Check for Free Days**: Many museums and attractions offer free entry on specific days or during certain hours. Plan your visit around these times to save money.

Getting Around Málaga Cheaply

1. **Buses**: Málaga's bus network is extensive and affordable, with single tickets costing around €1.40. Consider purchasing a multi-trip card to save money.

2. **Metro**: The light rail system connects key areas and is a convenient option for longer distances. Tickets start at about €1.35.

3. **Bicycle Rentals**: Málaga is becoming increasingly bike-friendly, with several rental services available. A typical rental costs around €10 for a day.

4. **Walking**: The city center is compact and pedestrian-friendly, making walking a pleasant and free way to explore. Many of the attractions are within a 20-minute walk of each other.

5. **Car Rentals**: If you plan to explore beyond the city, consider renting a car. Look for deals online to get competitive rates.

Chart of Affordable Luxury Accommodation in Málaga

Hotel Name	Description	Average Nightly	Pros	Cons
Hotel Sur Málaga	Chic hotel with modern amenities near the beach.	80 €	Close to the beach, good breakfast	Can be noisy during peak
Room Mate Valeria	Trendy hotel with stylish decor and rooftop pool.	90 €	Great location, vibrant atmosphere.	Limited parking.
Mariposa Hotel	Boutique hotel with unique rooms and great service.	85 €	Personalized service, central location.	Small rooms in some categories.
Hotel Centro	Comfortable hotel in the	75 €	Walking distance to	Basic amenities.
Salles Hotel Málaga	Modern hotel with a rooftop terrace.	95 €	Fantastic views, gym access.	Slightly higher prices in
Hotel Sur	Affordable hotel with a	80 €	Good for families,	Older building.
Ibis Styles Málaga	Stylish budget option in the city center.	70 €	Clean and modern, good breakfast.	Limited dining options nearby.
NH Málaga	Upscale hotel with	100 €	Excellent service,	Pricey during
Hotel San	Quaint hotel with a	60 €	Budget-friendly,	Limited services.
Hotel La Casa de la Playa	Charming beachside hotel with unique decor.	90 €	Close to the beach, lovely gardens.	Requires booking in

Free Events or Experiences in Málaga That Most People Don't Know About

1. **Art Walks in Soho**: Málaga's Soho district is a burgeoning hub for street art, featuring vibrant murals and graffiti by local and international artists. While many tourists flock to the city center, exploring Soho provides a unique art experience without spending a dime. Keep an eye out for impromptu exhibitions and art installations popping up throughout the area. These walks are especially lively during the first Friday of each month when galleries open their doors for free viewings and events.

2. **Weekly Tapas Tours**: While many guided tapas tours can be pricey, some local organizations and cultural groups offer free tapas walking tours where locals share their favorite spots and dishes. Joining these tours often means you'll get the chance to sample small bites at no cost while learning about the history of Málaga's culinary traditions. These tours typically occur on Friday evenings, allowing you to mingle with locals and tourists alike.

3. **Free Concerts at Parque de la Alameda**: During the summer months, you can often catch free concerts at Parque de la Alameda. Local musicians perform a variety of genres, from flamenco to jazz, making it a fantastic way to immerse yourself in the city's vibrant music scene. The concerts typically start in the early evening, providing a perfect backdrop for a sunset picnic.

4. **Málaga Film Festival Screenings**: The Málaga Film Festival often includes free outdoor screenings of films in various locations across the city. These events usually occur in late spring and offer a chance to watch both local and international films under the stars. Check the festival's schedule online for specific dates and locations.

5. **Local Fiestas**: Málaga hosts numerous local festivals throughout the year that feature parades, music, and dance. Many of these events are free to attend. One notable festival is the Feria de Agosto, held in mid-August, where you can enjoy traditional performances, local food, and cultural exhibitions at no cost. This vibrant celebration offers a great way to experience the local culture firsthand.

Practical Tips to Save Money in Málaga

1. **Utilize the Málaga Card**: Consider purchasing the Málaga Card, which offers unlimited public transport and discounts at several attractions. Prices start around €22 for a day, providing savings on transport and entry fees.

2. **Eat the Menu del Día**: Many restaurants offer a "menu del día" during lunch hours (usually 1 PM to 4 PM), which provides a full meal, including a starter, main course, dessert, and drink, for around €10-15. This is a great way to enjoy local cuisine at a lower price.

3. **Free Museum Days**: Take advantage of free entry days at museums. For example, the Museo de Málaga and the Carmen Thyssen Museum often have free entry on specific days each month. Plan your visits around these days to save on tickets.

4. **Happy Hour Deals**: Many bars in Málaga offer happy hour deals on drinks and tapas. Look for signs advertising "2 for 1" deals or discounts on local wines, which can save you a significant amount on your night out.

5. **Local Markets**: Shopping at local markets, such as Atarazanas Market, allows you to taste fresh produce and local delicacies at affordable prices. You can often find fresh fruit for €1 or less, making it a budget-friendly option for snacks or meals.

Historical Facts You Didn't Know About Málaga

1. **Birthplace of Picasso**: While many know that Pablo Picasso was born in Málaga, fewer know that he was born in the city's Plaza de la Merced, where a museum dedicated to his life and work now stands. The area surrounding his birthplace is rich with history, including the ruins of a Roman theater just a few blocks away.

2. **Málaga's Phoenician Origins**: Málaga is one of the oldest cities in the world, founded by the Phoenicians around 770 BC. It served as a crucial trading port, and archaeological remains from this era can still be found in the city, particularly in the form of ancient pottery and structures.

3. **The Alcazaba's Dual Purpose**: The Alcazaba, which overlooks the city, was not only a fortress but also a palace. It served as a royal residence for Muslim rulers, and remnants of its original gardens can still be seen today, showcasing the city's historical connection to nature and beauty.

4. **Málaga's Maritime Heritage**: In the early 20th century, Málaga was known for its thriving fishing industry, especially the production of anchovies and sardines. The city has a long-standing tradition of espetos (sardines grilled on skewers), a dish that continues to be a local favorite today.

5. **Roman Influence**: The Roman Theatre of Málaga, built in the 1st century BC, was rediscovered in 1951 and is one of the city's key historical landmarks. The theatre could accommodate around 1,500 spectators and hosted various performances, showcasing the importance of arts in Roman culture.

Practical Information for Visiting Málaga

1. **Getting There**: Málaga is easily accessible via the Málaga-Costa del Sol Airport, located about 8 km from the city center. Regular trains connect the airport to the city, with tickets costing around €2. Train services run every 20-30 minutes.

2. **Crowd Times**: The summer months (June to August) are peak tourist season, leading to larger crowds at popular attractions. Visiting during the shoulder seasons (April-May and September-October) can provide a more relaxed experience with fewer tourists.

3. **Tickets and Entry**: Many attractions offer combined tickets, which can save money. For example, a ticket to the Alcazaba can often include entry to the nearby Castillo de Gibralfaro. Always check online for any special discounts or offers available.

4. **Activities**: Besides visiting historical sites, consider taking part in local cooking classes or flamenco dance lessons. Prices for these activities range from €30 to €60, depending on the duration and inclusions.

5. **Secret Spots**: For a hidden gem, visit the little-known Botanical Garden of La Concepción, just outside the city center. It features beautiful tropical plants and stunning views for an entry fee of around €5. Another secret spot is the Mercado de Salamanca, a traditional market where locals shop, offering a more authentic experience than the tourist-heavy Atarazanas Market.

6. **Local Transport**: Use the local buses or trams to navigate the city. A single bus ticket costs around €1.40, while multi-ride tickets offer better value for those planning to explore extensively.

Córdoba

Córdoba, a captivating city in southern Spain, has a rich history that dates back to Roman times. Originally established as a Roman settlement, it flourished into one of the most significant cities of the Roman Empire. The city's true golden age, however, came during the Islamic rule in the 8th century when it became the capital of the Caliphate of Córdoba. This era saw the construction of remarkable architecture, such as the Great Mosque, and the city became a center of learning, culture, and philosophy, attracting scholars from all over the world.

As you stroll through the cobbled streets of Córdoba, you can almost hear the whispers of history. The city is a delightful blend of cultures, reflecting its Roman, Muslim, and Christian past. The Reconquista in the 13th century marked a significant turning point, as Christian kings reclaimed the city, leading to the construction of stunning cathedrals and other monuments atop existing Islamic structures. Today, Córdoba boasts a UNESCO World Heritage status, drawing visitors to its rich tapestry of history, art, and culture.

Top 20 Paid Attractions in Córdoba

1. **Mezquita-Catedral (Mosque-Cathedral)** The crown jewel of Córdoba, this stunning structure is a masterpiece of Islamic architecture, blending elements from both its mosque and cathedral phases. To save on fees, consider visiting on a Monday or during off-peak hours when discounts may be available. A creative free alternative is to explore the surrounding streets for a beautiful view of the exterior. Don't miss the history of the site; it has evolved over centuries, symbolizing the city's complex cultural heritage.

2. **Alcázar de los Reyes Cristianos** This former royal palace features beautiful gardens and fascinating architecture. Entry fees can be reduced by visiting during free hours, typically on Mondays. For a free alternative, the nearby parks offer lovely views. Make sure to learn about the palace's role in the Spanish Inquisition and its connection to Christopher Columbus, who sought royal approval for his voyages here.

3. **Palacio de Viana** Known for its stunning courtyards, this noble house showcases traditional Córdoba architecture. Opt for a guided tour to save money and enhance your experience with fascinating stories. If you're looking for free alternatives, just walking through the historic district offers plenty of beautiful patios. The palace's courtyards reflect the city's Moorish influence and are a perfect example of Andalusian beauty.

4. **Roman Bridge** Dating back to the 1st century BC, this iconic bridge provides stunning views of the city and the Guadalquivir River. While crossing is free, a small fee for the nearby interpretation center can provide a richer understanding of its history. For a creative alternative, enjoy a picnic by the riverbank. The bridge has witnessed many historical events, including battles and festivals, making it a true emblem of Córdoba.

5. **Museo Arqueológico** This archaeological museum showcases artifacts from Córdoba's Roman and Islamic past. Entry fees are often reduced on certain days, so check the schedule! For a free alternative, explore the many archaeological sites

around the city. Each artifact tells a story of Córdoba's ancient civilizations, from Roman mosaics to Islamic pottery, revealing the city's layered history.

6. **Centro de Arte Rafael Botí** Focused on contemporary art, this center hosts a variety of exhibitions. Look for special promotions that might offer free entry during certain events. Alternatively, enjoy the local street art in the city for a creative free option. This center celebrates local artist Rafael Botí and provides insight into Córdoba's modern cultural scene.

7. **Capilla de San Bartolomé** A hidden gem, this chapel is known for its beautiful Baroque architecture. While entrance is usually free, donations are appreciated. Nearby, you can enjoy the vibrant street life for a creative alternative. The chapel is a testament to the city's religious evolution, blending Christian and Moorish styles.

8. **Plaza de la Corredera** This stunning square is lined with lively bars and restaurants, making it a great place to soak up local life. While you can enjoy the square for free, many events take place that might require an entrance fee. For a creative alternative, participate in a local tapas tour. Historically, it was a marketplace and bullring, giving it a unique cultural significance.

9. **Calleja de las Flores** This picturesque alleyway is famous for its vibrant flowerpots. While visiting is free, purchasing local crafts from nearby shops helps support local artists. For a creative alternative, find similar alleys around the city with their own unique charm. The alley's history is tied to the Jewish Quarter and is a popular spot for Instagram-worthy photos.

10. **Museo de Bellas Artes** This fine arts museum showcases works from the Spanish Renaissance to modern art. Look for free entry days to save money! A creative alternative is to explore the local galleries that showcase emerging artists. The museum is housed in a 17th-century convent, providing insight into Córdoba's artistic evolution.

11. **Casa de Sefarad** This cultural center focuses on the Jewish history of Córdoba. Entry is usually free, but donations are welcome for guided tours. A creative alternative is to explore the historic Jewish Quarter. The center reveals the rich contributions of the Jewish community to Córdoba's cultural fabric.

12. **Baños Árabes (Arab Baths)** Experience the relaxation of ancient bathing rituals in these beautifully restored baths. Look for package deals that include treatments for savings. For a free alternative, stroll around the nearby gardens. These baths are a nod to Córdoba's Islamic past, reflecting the importance of hygiene and socialization in Moorish culture.

13. **Córdoba Synagogue** One of the best-preserved medieval synagogues in Spain, this site offers a glimpse into the city's Jewish heritage. Entry fees are low, and free guided tours are sometimes offered. For a free alternative, visit the nearby historic streets. The synagogue's architecture and history highlight the coexistence of cultures in Córdoba.

14. **Puente Romano** A significant historical site, this Roman bridge is a must-visit. While crossing is free, consider stopping at the interpretation center for a small fee. For a creative alternative, enjoy the sunset views from the bridge. It served as a

vital connection in ancient times, demonstrating the engineering prowess of the Romans.

15. **Templo Romano** The ruins of this Roman temple offer insight into the city's ancient past. Entry is typically free, but guided tours can enhance your experience. A creative alternative is to explore other Roman ruins scattered throughout the city. The temple's remnants showcase the grandeur of Córdoba during Roman rule.

16. **Palacio de los Marqueses de Viana** An exquisite noble house featuring a rich collection of art and furniture. Entry fees can be saved by visiting during special promotions. For a free alternative, explore the surrounding gardens. The palace's architecture and history reflect the lifestyles of Córdoba's aristocracy.

17. **Murallas (City Walls)** These ancient walls provide a glimpse into Córdoba's defensive history. While exploring the walls is free, guided tours are available for a fee. A creative alternative is to enjoy the views from the top of the walls. The walls date back to the Roman era and were expanded during the Islamic period.

18. **Catedral de Córdoba** This impressive cathedral, built on the site of the Great Mosque, showcases stunning Gothic and Renaissance architecture. Entry fees are often reduced on certain days, so check ahead. For a free alternative, admire the exterior while enjoying the lively atmosphere of the nearby plaza. The cathedral's history represents the religious transformation of Córdoba.

19. **Museo de los Agustinos** Located in a former convent, this museum showcases religious art and artifacts. Look for discounts or free entry days. A creative alternative is to visit local churches that often feature beautiful art. The museum's collection highlights the importance of religious art in Spanish culture.

20. **Córdoba: A Walk Through History Tour** While this guided tour has a fee, it's worth every euro for the in-depth exploration of Córdoba's historical sites. Check for discounts or group rates. For a free alternative, explore the city with a self-guided walking tour available online. The tour delves into the rich history of Córdoba, making it an enriching experience for any history buff.

Insider Tips for Córdoba

1. **Explore Early or Late**: To avoid the crowds and the heat, especially in summer, explore popular attractions early in the morning or later in the evening. The softer light at these times also makes for fantastic photographs!

2. **Use Public Transport**: Córdoba has an efficient bus network that connects most neighborhoods. A single ticket is inexpensive, and you can buy multi-trip passes for even more savings.

3. **Walking Tours**: The city's historic center is compact and best explored on foot. Free walking tours are available, and tips are appreciated, giving you the chance to learn about Córdoba's rich history while meeting fellow travelers.

4. **Tapas Culture**: Embrace the local tapas culture! Many bars offer free tapas with a drink, making it an affordable way to enjoy authentic cuisine.

5. **Visit During Festivals**: If you can, plan your visit around local festivals, like the Patios Festival in May, when the city's famous patios are open to the public and adorned with flowers, creating a spectacular show without any entry fees.

6. **Stay Hydrated**: Bring a reusable water bottle to refill at public fountains. Córdoba's summers can be scorching, and staying hydrated is essential while exploring.

7. **Seek Out Free Events**: Keep an eye out for free concerts, art exhibitions, and cultural events happening around the city. Many local venues host events that showcase Andalusian music and dance.

Getting Around Córdoba Cheaply

1. **Public Buses**: The local bus system is an economical way to navigate the city. A single ticket typically costs around €1.40, and you can purchase multi-ride tickets for savings.

2. **Walking**: Many attractions are within walking distance of each other, especially in the historic center. Strolling allows you to discover hidden gems along the way.

3. **Bicycle Rentals**: Consider renting a bike for a day. There are several rental shops that offer bikes at reasonable rates, usually around €10 per day.

4. **Taxis and Ride-Sharing**: While taxis can be more expensive, they are relatively affordable for short distances. Apps like Uber are not available, but local ride-hailing apps may offer competitive rates.

5. **Combo Tickets**: Some attractions offer combo tickets that provide entry to multiple sites at a reduced rate. This is a great way to save money if you plan to visit several places.

Affordable Luxury Accommodations in Córdoba

Accommodation Name	Description	Average Nightly	Pros	Cons
Balcon de Cordoba	Boutique hotel with stunning views of the	120 €	Excellent location, rooftop terrace	Limited on-site amenities
Hotel Casa de los Reyes	Charming hotel with traditional Andalusian	85 €	Great service, central location	Can get busy during peak
NH Collection Amistad	Stylish hotel set in a 19th-century mansion.	100 €	Pool, gym, and on-site dining	Higher prices during festivals
Hotel Córdoba Center	Modern hotel near the train station and historic	90 €	Good for business travelers, spacious	Further from the main attractions
Hotel Los Patios	A cozy hotel with a beautiful patio area.	75 €	Affordable, charming atmosphere	Limited dining options nearby
La Hospedería del Monasterio	Converted monastery with a serene atmosphere.	95 €	Unique experience, peaceful surroundings	Some areas may feel remote

Hotel La Llave de la Judería	Elegant boutique hotel in the Jewish Quarter.	110 €	Authentic decor, great breakfast	Smaller rooms
Hotel Eurostars Patios de	Stylish hotel with a beautiful courtyard.	85 €	Central location, free Wi-Fi	Limited parking
Pension La Palmera	Budget-friendly guesthouse with a homely	50 €	Friendly staff, very affordable	Basic amenities
Hotel Villa de Priego	Charming hotel with rustic Andalusian	70 €	Close to attractions, comfortable beds	Limited English-

Free Events or Experiences in Córdoba That Most People Don't Know About

1. **Córdoba Patios Festival**: While many know about the famous patios, few realize the festival occurs every May. During this time, locals open their beautifully decorated patios to the public for free. Each patio showcases unique floral arrangements and traditional Andalusian design, allowing you to experience the city's charm without spending a dime.

2. **Free Concerts in Parks**: Throughout the summer, many local parks host free concerts featuring local bands and artists. These events often take place on Friday or Saturday evenings, providing a great opportunity to relax, enjoy live music, and mingle with locals without any cost.

3. **Art Exhibitions at Local Galleries**: Various art galleries around Córdoba frequently host free exhibitions showcasing local artists. Check out places like the Centro de Arte Rafael Botí, where entry is often free for temporary exhibits. This is a fantastic way to immerse yourself in the local art scene without spending a cent.

4. **Walking Tours**: Some organizations offer pay-what-you-want walking tours that can introduce you to the history and culture of Córdoba. These tours are not only budget-friendly but also provide valuable insights from knowledgeable guides, often revealing hidden gems in the city that many tourists overlook.

5. **Cultural Events at Plaza de las Tendillas**: This lively square often hosts free cultural events, including dance performances and festivals. The calendar of events can be found online or at the local tourist office, offering a chance to experience the city's vibrant culture without any cost.

Practical Tips to Save Money in Córdoba

1. **Visit Museums on Free Admission Days**: Many museums in Córdoba offer free admission on specific days of the month. For example, the Museo Arqueológico often has free entry on the first Sunday of the month. This can save you up to €5 per ticket, making it a perfect day to explore.

2. **Take Advantage of Combo Tickets**: Look for combo tickets that allow entry to multiple attractions at a discounted rate. For instance, a ticket to both the Alcázar and the Cathedral can save you around €5 compared to purchasing individual tickets.

3. **Dine Like a Local**: Instead of eating at touristy restaurants, seek out local taverns or markets where you can enjoy authentic tapas. Many bars offer a free tapa with each drink, which can turn a simple drink into a meal for around €3-5.

4. **Public Transport**: Use public buses instead of taxis to save money. A single bus ticket costs about €1.40, while taxis can easily rack up costs. Consider walking for shorter distances to further save on transport costs.

5. **Shop at Local Markets**: Visiting local markets like Mercado Victoria can be a budget-friendly way to sample local cuisine without spending too much. Grab a plate of tapas or a drink for around €5, which is much cheaper than dining in a sit-down restaurant.

Historical Facts About Córdoba You Didn't Know

1. **A Center of Knowledge**: During the Islamic Golden Age, Córdoba was one of the largest and most advanced cities in Europe, renowned for its libraries and universities. It was home to scholars like Averroes and Maimonides, who contributed significantly to philosophy, medicine, and science, influencing both Islamic and Christian thought.

2. **The Great Mosque's Transformation**: The Great Mosque of Córdoba, or Mezquita, was once the largest mosque in the world. When the Christians took control in the 13th century, they converted it into a cathedral. This unique blend of architectural styles creates a fascinating narrative of cultural and religious transformation in the city.

3. **A Historic Connection to Columbus**: The Alcázar de los Reyes Cristianos served as the royal palace for Ferdinand and Isabella, who famously funded Christopher Columbus's expedition in 1492. The gardens of the Alcázar were a place where Columbus sought the monarchs' approval for his journey to the New World.

4. **A City of Patios**: The tradition of beautiful patios in Córdoba dates back to Roman times. These outdoor spaces were initially designed for cooling off in the hot summer months, and today they reflect the city's rich cultural heritage. The unique style of the patios has been recognized by UNESCO as part of the Intangible Cultural Heritage of Humanity.

5. **Córdoba's Roman Legacy**: The city was originally founded as a Roman settlement known as Corduba in 152 BC. The remnants of Roman architecture, such as the Roman Bridge and Temple, still stand today, showcasing the city's historical depth and influence throughout the ages.

Practical Information for Visiting Córdoba

1. **Getting There**: Córdoba is easily accessible via train from major cities like Madrid and Seville. High-speed trains (AVE) from Madrid take about 1 hour and 45 minutes, with tickets starting at around €25 if booked in advance.

2. **Crowd Times**: The peak tourist season in Córdoba is from April to June and September to October. Visiting during the early morning or late afternoon can help you avoid the largest crowds, especially at popular sites like the Mezquita.

3. **Ticket Information**: Many attractions, like the Alcázar and the Mezquita, offer combined tickets that can save you money. Always check for reduced prices for students, seniors, and free entry days.

4. **What to Do There**: Be sure to explore the Jewish Quarter (Judería), visit the stunning patios, and take time to enjoy local cuisine. Don't forget to check out the local markets for authentic shopping experiences.

5. **Secret Spots**: For a quieter experience, visit **Calleja de las Flores**, an iconic narrow street lined with vibrant flowerpots. Another hidden gem is **Los Patios de la Marquesa**, where you can enjoy a less crowded experience with beautiful floral arrangements.

6. **Public Transport**: Use buses or rent bikes to navigate the city efficiently. Consider purchasing a multi-ride pass if you plan to use public transport frequently.

7. **Free Wi-Fi**: Many cafes and public spaces offer free Wi-Fi. Use this to plan your day or check for local events without incurring roaming charges.

Ibiza

this Balearic Island has a rich history that dates back thousands of years. Initially settled by the Phoenicians around 654 BC, Ibiza quickly became a trading hub, thanks to its strategic location in the Mediterranean. The island's name derives from the Phoenician word *"Iboshim,"* which means "the island of the pine trees," reflecting its lush landscape.

Throughout the centuries, Ibiza has been influenced by various cultures, including the Romans, Moors, and Catalans, each leaving their mark. The island was part of the Roman Empire, serving as a refuge for pirates and traders. Later, during the Islamic period, the Moors introduced advanced agricultural practices, which significantly changed the landscape and economy.

Fast forward to the 20th century, and Ibiza became a haven for artists, musicians, and free spirits, especially in the 1960s and 70s. It transformed into a hub of counterculture, attracting everyone from writers to rock stars, all looking to escape the ordinary. The iconic club scene that we know today began in the 1980s, with venues like Pacha and Amnesia setting the stage for an electric nightlife that continues to pulse through the island. Today, Ibiza is a blend of its historical roots and modern allure, making it a unique destination for travelers from all walks of life.

Top 20 Paid Attractions in Ibiza

1. **Dalt Vila (Old Town)**

   - **Description**: A UNESCO World Heritage Site, this ancient fortress offers stunning views of the island and the sea. The cobblestone streets are filled with history, leading you through charming shops and cafes.
   - **How to Save**: Entry is free, but you can save on guided tours by exploring on your own using an audio guide app.
   - **Creative Free Alternative**: Take a sunset walk around the walls for breathtaking views without spending a dime.
   - **Practical Tips**: Wear comfortable shoes, as the streets can be steep and uneven. Don't forget your camera for those Instagram-worthy shots!

2. **Es Vedrà**

   - **Description**: This iconic rock formation off the west coast is shrouded in myths and legends. Many believe it's the inspiration behind the fabled Atlantis.
   - **How to Save**: Visit during the day for free views from various viewpoints. Boat trips can be pricey, so consider a picnic with a view instead.
   - **Creative Free Alternative**: Hike to the cliffs near Cala d'Hort for incredible photo ops.
   - **Practical Tips**: Bring water and sunscreen, especially in the heat of summer. The sunset views here are simply magical!

3. **Pacha Ibiza**

   - **Description**: One of the oldest and most famous nightclubs in the world, known for its vibrant parties and top DJs.
   - **How to Save**: Look for ticket packages that include drinks or reserve a table in advance to save on entry.

- Creative Free Alternative: Enjoy a night out at one of the beach clubs or bars that don't charge an entry fee.
- Practical Tips: Arrive early to avoid long queues and check the lineup ahead of time to catch your favorite DJs.

4. **Amnesia**

- Description: A legendary nightclub famous for its foam parties and exceptional sound system.
- How to Save: Buy tickets in advance online for discounts and look out for promotional nights.
- Creative Free Alternative: Explore the surrounding San Rafael area for local bars with live music.
- Practical Tips: Dress comfortably but stylishly, as the Ibiza nightlife scene tends to be glamorous.

5. **Ushuaïa Ibiza Beach Hotel**

- Description: Known for its extravagant outdoor parties and incredible pool area, Ushuaïa is a must-visit for party-goers.
- How to Save: Purchase a day pass if you're not staying at the hotel but want to enjoy the pool and parties.
- Creative Free Alternative: Check out the beach outside for a quieter vibe and stunning views.
- Practical Tips: Arrive early to snag a good spot, especially during high season.

6. **Formentera Day Trip**

- Description: A stunning island just a short boat ride from Ibiza, known for its crystal-clear waters and beautiful beaches.
- How to Save: Book your ferry tickets online in advance to get the best rates.
- Creative Free Alternative: Spend the day at the beaches in Ibiza if you're looking to save on transport.
- Practical Tips: Rent a bicycle or scooter upon arrival to explore Formentera easily.

7. **Aquarium Cap Blanc**

- Description: This unique aquarium is set in a natural cave and showcases the diverse marine life of the Mediterranean.
- How to Save: Family tickets are available, offering savings for larger groups.
- Creative Free Alternative: Visit nearby natural caves for free exploration.
- Practical Tips: Combine your visit with a trip to nearby beaches for a full day of fun.

8. **Ibiza Horse Valley**

- Description: An eco-friendly horse riding experience through the beautiful Ibiza countryside.
- How to Save: Group bookings can save you money on individual rides.
- Creative Free Alternative: Take a hike in the hills to enjoy the scenery without the cost.

- Practical Tips: Wear appropriate footwear for riding and bring a camera for picturesque moments.

9. **Cala Comte Beach**

   - **Description**: Famous for its clear waters and stunning sunsets, this beach is a perfect spot for sunbathing and swimming.
   - **How to Save**: Bring your own food and drinks to avoid overpriced beach bars.
   - **Creative Free Alternative**: Enjoy the sunset from the nearby cliffs for a picturesque view.
   - **Practical Tips**: Arrive early to secure a good spot on the beach, especially during peak season.

10. **Sa Talaiassa**

    - **Description**: The highest point in Ibiza offers panoramic views and a great hiking opportunity.
    - **How to Save**: Free access to hiking trails and viewpoints.
    - **Creative Free Alternative**: Pack a picnic and enjoy it at the summit.
    - **Practical Tips**: The hike can be challenging, so bring plenty of water and wear good shoes.

11. **Ibiza Museum of Contemporary Art**

    - **Description**: Showcases a variety of modern art, focusing on Balearic and Mediterranean themes.
    - **How to Save**: Entry is free on certain days, so check their calendar.
    - **Creative Free Alternative**: Explore the nearby streets filled with street art.
    - **Practical Tips**: Combine your visit with a walk around the old town for a cultural day out.

12. **Cascadas de San Miguel**

    - **Description**: A stunning waterfall area ideal for a refreshing dip.
    - **How to Save**: Entry is typically low-cost, but check for any free access days.
    - **Creative Free Alternative**: Explore the nearby hiking trails for free.
    - **Practical Tips**: Go early in the morning for a quiet experience.

13. **Cova de Can Marçà**

    - **Description**: A fascinating natural cave offering guided tours with beautiful stalactites and stalagmites.
    - **How to Save**: Look for combined tickets with nearby attractions.
    - **Creative Free Alternative**: Explore other local caves without a fee.
    - **Practical Tips**: Bring a light jacket as it can be cool inside the caves.

14. **Las Salinas Beach**

    - **Description**: Famous for its salt flats and lively atmosphere, this beach is a great spot for sunbathing and enjoying beach clubs.
    - **How to Save**: Pack a picnic instead of dining at beach bars to save money.
    - **Creative Free Alternative**: Take a stroll along the coast and discover hidden coves.
    - **Practical Tips**: Arrive early to find a good parking spot during peak season.

15. **Es Pujols Beach**

   - **Description**: Known for its vibrant beach clubs and water sports, Es Pujols is a fun place to spend the day.
   - **How to Save**: Rent equipment instead of booking expensive tours for activities like jet skiing.
   - **Creative Free Alternative**: Enjoy a beach day with your own games and snacks.
   - **Practical Tips**: Check the weather before planning a day at the beach.

16. **Sant Antoni Sunset Strip**

   - **Description**: Famous for its stunning sunsets and lively bars, this area is a great place to unwind.
   - **How to Save**: Bring your own drinks and snacks to enjoy while watching the sunset.
   - **Creative Free Alternative**: Visit nearby quieter spots for sunset views without the crowd.
   - **Practical Tips**: Arrive early for the best viewing spots along the strip.

17. **Ibiza Trikes**

   - **Description**: Explore the island in style with a fun trike tour, offering a unique way to see the sights.
   - **How to Save**: Book group tours for a discount.
   - **Creative Free Alternative**: Rent a scooter instead for a more budget-friendly exploration.
   - **Practical Tips**: Wear sunscreen and a helmet, as it can get sunny and hot while riding.

Insider Tips for Ibiza

1. **Visit in Shoulder Season**: To avoid the heavy tourist crowds and inflated prices, consider visiting during the shoulder seasons (late spring or early autumn). The weather is still fantastic, and many clubs have pre-season or closing parties with reduced entry fees.

2. **Use Public Transport**: Ibiza has a decent bus network that connects major areas and beaches. It's a cost-effective way to explore the island. Grab a bus timetable at the airport or your hotel to plan your trips.

3. **Eat Like a Local**: Venture away from tourist spots to find hidden gems where locals dine. Look for "Menu del Día" options at local restaurants, where you can enjoy a full meal for a fraction of the price.

4. **Buy Drinks at Supermarkets**: Instead of splurging at bars and clubs, stock up on drinks at local supermarkets. You can find excellent local wines and spirits at reasonable prices.

5. **Explore Free Beaches**: Ibiza boasts numerous beautiful beaches that are completely free to access. Check out Cala Comte or Cala Bassa for stunning views and vibrant atmospheres without the beach club fees.

6. **Enjoy Free Events**: Many bars and clubs host free events or offer free entry on certain nights. Keep an eye on local event listings for live music and themed nights.

7. **Hike the Island**: Discover Ibiza's natural beauty by hiking its scenic trails, such as the path to Es Vedrà. It's a great way to experience the island without spending a dime.

Getting Around Ibiza Cheaply

1. **Public Buses**: The bus system is reliable and covers most tourist spots, making it the cheapest way to get around. A single fare costs around €1.55.

2. **Bicycles**: Renting a bicycle is an eco-friendly and cost-effective option for exploring the island at your own pace. Prices start at around €10 per day.

3. **Car Rentals**: If you're traveling with friends, renting a car can be economical. Prices vary but can be found starting from €30 per day. Always check for hidden fees!

4. **Shared Taxis**: If you need to take a taxi, consider sharing with other passengers to split the fare.

5. **Walking**: Many attractions are within walking distance of each other, especially in Ibiza Town. Stroll around to discover shops and cafes without spending on transport.

Chart of Affordable Luxury Accommodation in Ibiza

Accommodation Name	Description	Starting Price per	Pros	Cons
Nobu Hotel Ibiza Bay	Upscale beachfront hotel with luxury amenities.	400 €	Gourmet dining, great spa	Pricey, especially in peak season
Hotel Puchet	Chic, modern hotel with	150 €	Close to beach,	Can be noisy at
Ibiza Gran Hotel	Luxury hotel with stunning sea views and a casino.	450 €	Spa, top-notch dining	High price tag
Hotel Cala	Beautiful setting close to	100 €	Affordable,	Limited nightlife
Hard Rock Hotel Ibiza	Family-friendly with a lively atmosphere.	250 €	Entertainment, pools	Can feel crowded during events
Hotel Mirador de Dalt Vila	Stunning views and a historic vibe.	200 €	Unique location, boutique style	Limited amenities
Casa de Hilario	A charming boutique guesthouse in San Antonio.	90 €	Intimate atmosphere, local	Basic facilities
Agroturismo Can Lluc	Eco-friendly hotel with rustic charm.	150 €	Peaceful setting, great service	Far from the nightlife
Pacha Ibiza	Stylish hotel next to the	300 €	Great location,	Noisy during
Hotel Invisa Es Pla	Modern hotel close to the beach.	120 €	Good location, value for money	Older decor

Free Events or Experiences in Ibiza Most People Don't Know About

1. **Local Festivals**: Ibiza hosts various local festivals throughout the year, often featuring traditional music, dance, and food. For example, the Fiesta de San Juan in June is celebrated with bonfires and music on the beach, bringing locals and visitors together. These events are typically free to attend and provide a unique glimpse into local culture.

2. **Sunset at Café del Mar**: While the famous Café del Mar may charge for drinks, watching the sunset here is free. Grab a spot on the rocks outside, and enjoy the stunning views as the sun dips below the horizon. It's a beloved ritual for locals and offers a serene experience away from the bustling nightlife.

3. **Beach Yoga Sessions**: Many beaches, particularly in Santa Eulalia and Talamanca, host free yoga sessions at sunrise or sunset. It's a fantastic way to connect with nature and meet like-minded individuals. Just bring your mat and some water for a refreshing morning workout.

4. **Art Walks**: In the Dalt Vila area, you'll find free art exhibitions and installations. Many galleries hold openings and events throughout the summer months, showcasing local and international artists. Take a leisurely stroll through the cobbled streets, where art often spills out into public spaces.

5. **Street Markets**: Ibiza has several weekly street markets, such as the one in San Juan on Sundays. These markets offer local crafts, food, and live music, creating a vibrant atmosphere that's completely free to enjoy. You can often find handmade souvenirs while soaking up the local culture.

Practical Tips to Save Money in Ibiza

1. **Travel Off-Peak**: Visiting Ibiza during the shoulder seasons (May-June and September-October) can save you a lot. Hotel prices drop significantly, often by 30-50%, and popular attractions are less crowded.

2. **Use Public Transport**: The local bus system is affordable and efficient. A single fare costs around €1.55, while a day pass is about €5. This is a significant saving compared to taxis, which can start at €10 for short rides.

3. **Eat at Local Markets**: Instead of dining at high-end restaurants, explore local markets for fresh produce and prepared foods. You can enjoy a meal for around €5-10 instead of the €20-50 range at touristy eateries.

4. **BYO Drinks**: Buying drinks at supermarkets (where a bottle of wine costs around €5-10) instead of bars and clubs (where cocktails can range from €10-20) will save you a fortune, especially if you plan on having a pre-party gathering.

5. **Free Beach Days**: Many of Ibiza's beautiful beaches are free to access. Instead of paying for a sunbed at beach clubs, bring your towel and enjoy the sun without the extra cost.

Historical Facts About Ibiza

1. **Phoenician Roots**: Ibiza's history dates back to 654 BC when it was founded by the Phoenicians, who recognized the island's strategic location. The remains of their settlement can still be seen today at the Phoenician settlement site of Sa Caleta, a UNESCO World Heritage Site.

2. **Pirate Haven**: In the 16th century, Ibiza became a hideout for pirates and privateers. The island's numerous coves and inlets provided excellent hiding spots. The threat of piracy led to the construction of many coastal defense towers, which can still be seen today.

3. **Hippy Culture**: In the 1960s and 70s, Ibiza became a haven for the counterculture movement. Artists, musicians, and free spirits flocked to the island, drawn by its bohemian lifestyle and beautiful landscapes. The iconic hippy markets and festivals that emerged during this time still reflect this rich cultural heritage.

4. **UNESCO World Heritage**: In 1999, the historic city of Dalt Vila was declared a UNESCO World Heritage Site. The fortified old town showcases the rich history and architectural heritage of Ibiza, featuring structures that date back to the Renaissance.

5. **A Spiritual Center**: Beyond its party reputation, Ibiza has long been considered a spiritual retreat. The island is home to many wellness centers and yoga retreats, attracting those seeking healing and self-discovery.

Practical Information for Visiting Ibiza

1. **Getting There**: Ibiza is accessible by flights from major European cities. Ibiza Airport is located just a few kilometers from Ibiza Town, and taxis or buses are readily available. Expect to pay around €15 for a taxi ride into town.

2. **Crowd Timing**: The peak tourist season runs from June to September. For a more relaxed experience, consider visiting in May or early October when the weather is still pleasant, but crowds are thinner.

3. **Ticketing Information**: Popular attractions like the Ibiza Castle and museums typically charge around €5-10 for entry. Consider buying a combination ticket for multiple attractions to save money.

4. **What to Do**: In addition to nightlife, explore Ibiza's natural beauty through hiking trails like the route to Es Vedrà. Visit traditional villages like Santa Gertrudis for local dining and artisan shops. Don't miss the stunning beaches, such as Cala Jondal and Talamanca.

5. **Secret Spots**: Look for hidden gems like the tranquil beach of Aguas Blancas or the peaceful cove of Cala Xuclar. For an off-the-beaten-path experience, explore the less touristy villages like San Juan, where you can find authentic local culture.

6. **Travel Tips**: Always carry cash, as some smaller shops and restaurants may not accept cards. Sunscreen is a must—consider biodegradable options to protect the environment. Lastly, a reusable water bottle can help save money and reduce plastic waste, with public water fountains available in many areas.

Tenerife

The largest of the Canary Islands, it's a treasure trove of history and culture. This beautiful island was formed millions of years ago from volcanic activity, and today, it's known for its stunning landscapes, from lush forests to arid deserts, and, of course, the iconic Teide volcano. The indigenous Guanches were the first inhabitants, leaving behind a rich heritage that can still be felt in local customs and traditions. When the Spanish arrived in the 15th century, they began to cultivate the land, introducing agriculture and building charming towns that still showcase their colonial past. Over the years, Tenerife has evolved into a vibrant blend of cultures, making it a hotspot for tourists seeking sun, sea, and a bit of history.

Top 20 Paid Attractions in Tenerife

1. **Teide National Park** Teide National Park is home to Mount Teide, Spain's tallest peak. The park offers breathtaking views and hiking trails that lead you through otherworldly volcanic landscapes. To save on fees, consider hiking rather than taking the cable car, and visit early in the morning or late in the afternoon for fewer crowds. A creative free alternative is to explore the nearby towns of Vilaflor and La Orotava, where you can experience local life. Don't forget your camera; the park is a UNESCO World Heritage site!

2. **Loro Parque** This award-winning zoo is known for its extensive collection of parrots and marine life. A visit to Loro Parque can be pricy, but buying tickets online often yields discounts. If you're on a budget, you might enjoy a leisurely stroll along Playa Jardin, a beautiful beach just a stone's throw away. Loro Parque started as a parrot park in 1972 and has since expanded into a conservation hub for various species.

3. **Siam Park** Dubbed the best water park in the world, Siam Park boasts thrilling slides and a lazy river with a tropical theme. Purchase tickets in advance for a discount, and consider visiting during weekdays to avoid the weekend crowds. For a free alternative, head to Playa de Las Américas to enjoy the sun and surf. Siam Park is inspired by Thai architecture and even features a beautiful temple and lush gardens.

4. **Auditorio de Tenerife** This iconic concert hall, designed by Santiago Calatrava, is a masterpiece of modern architecture. While entry is free for some events, performances can be costly. To save on fees, check for free tours offered during specific times or visit the surrounding park for a lovely walk. The auditorium hosts a range of cultural events, from concerts to theater performances, making it a cultural hotspot on the island.

5. **Tenerife Espacio de las Artes (TEA)** TEA is a contemporary art museum that showcases both local and international artists. Admission is often free on specific days, so check their website for details. If you prefer a free alternative, explore the artistic streets of Santa Cruz, where you'll find murals and street art. The museum is not just about art; it also has a fantastic café and a great bookshop, perfect for art lovers.

6. **Pyramids of Güímar** The Pyramids of Güímar are mysterious stone structures that spark curiosity about their origins. Tickets are affordable, but consider visiting during special events for added experiences. For a free alternative, hike the surrounding trails to enjoy stunning views of the coastline. The site features an informative museum that delves into the history and possible purposes of these intriguing pyramids.

7. **Casa de los Balcones** This historic house in La Orotava showcases traditional Canarian architecture and culture. Entrance is usually low-cost, but keep an eye out for free guided tours during cultural festivals. A free alternative is wandering through the picturesque streets of La Orotava, where you can admire beautiful balconies and gardens. This 17th-century house is an excellent spot to learn about Tenerife's history and traditional crafts.

8. **Cueva del Viento** The Cueva del Viento is one of the longest volcanic tubes in the world. Guided tours are available at a reasonable price, but book in advance as they fill up quickly. For a free experience, explore the surrounding natural parks for hiking and picnicking. The cave was formed by a volcanic eruption and offers a fascinating glimpse into the island's geological history.

9. **Parque Nacional del Teide** Not to be confused with Teide National Park, this park offers spectacular views and walking paths around the Teide volcano. Save money by packing a picnic instead of dining at on-site restaurants. You can also explore nearby natural sites like Roques de García for stunning vistas without the cost. It's a fantastic spot for stargazing, as it's one of the best places in the world for clear night skies!

10. **Monkey Park** A smaller zoo that allows visitors to get close to monkeys and other animals, Monkey Park offers an interactive experience. Entry fees are reasonable, but bring your own snacks to save on food costs. As a free alternative, explore the nearby town of Los Cristianos, where you can enjoy local shops and eateries. The park is committed to conservation and rehabilitation, making it a great place to learn about animal welfare.

11. **Lago Martiánez** This stunning pool complex designed by artist César Manrique features seawater pools, gardens, and restaurants. Entrance is a bit pricey, so consider visiting during off-peak hours for discounts. For a free alternative, enjoy a stroll along the nearby coast and marvel at the ocean views. The complex is a beautiful blend of art and nature, perfect for a leisurely day under the sun.

12. **Tenerife Zoo** The Tenerife Zoo offers a chance to see exotic animals up close. Admission prices are reasonable, and buying tickets online often comes with a discount. A creative free alternative is visiting the nearby beaches, where you can relax and enjoy the natural beauty. The zoo focuses on conservation efforts, aiming to educate visitors about the importance of protecting wildlife.

13. **Castillo de San Miguel** This medieval castle offers dinner shows featuring knights in battle, which is quite a spectacle! Tickets can be pricey, so check for deals or group rates. For a free alternative, explore the coastal paths around the castle for stunning sea views. The castle's history dates back to the 16th century, adding a touch of medieval charm to your visit.

14. **Museo de la Ciencia y el Cosmos** This interactive science museum is perfect for families. Admission is affordable, and special exhibitions often have reduced rates. If you want a free alternative, enjoy the science park outside, where you can explore and engage with nature. The museum offers hands-on experiences, making science fun and accessible for everyone.

15. **Basílica de Nuestra Señora de Candelaria** This stunning basilica is dedicated to the island's patron saint. Entrance is free, but guided tours are available for a small fee. A creative free alternative is visiting the nearby beach and enjoying the local market. The basilica's history is rich, with roots dating back to the Guanche culture and the discovery of the island.

16. **Parque Marítimo César Manrique** A beautiful park with pools, gardens, and restaurants designed by César Manrique, it's a great place to relax. Admission is usually low-cost, but bring a picnic to enjoy by the pools to save money. For a free alternative, take a stroll along the promenade. The park celebrates the harmony of nature and architecture, making it a must-visit.

17. **El Teide Observatory** For astronomy enthusiasts, the observatory offers guided tours where you can learn about the stars. Book in advance to secure your spot at a reasonable price. If you're looking for a free experience, hike to one of the nearby viewpoints for breathtaking views of the night sky. The observatory plays a vital role in astronomical research due to Tenerife's clear skies.

18. **Aqualand Costa Adeje** Aqualand is another fantastic water park that promises a day full of fun. Tickets can be pricey, so look out for combo tickets or early bird discounts. If you prefer a free day, the nearby beaches offer sunbathing and swimming without the cost. The park features a variety of water slides and pools, making it a perfect family destination.

19. **Museo de la Naturaleza y el Hombre** This museum in Santa Cruz is dedicated to the natural history of the Canary Islands. Admission fees are affordable, and visiting on Sundays often means free entry! For a free alternative, explore the nearby cultural center, where you can enjoy local art. The museum showcases a wealth of information about the islands' geology and indigenous cultures.

20. **Pico del Teide Cable Car** This cable car takes you near the summit of Mount Teide, providing breathtaking views. Tickets can be expensive, so consider hiking instead if you're up for it! Alternatively, enjoy the views from the base of the mountain or explore the surrounding trails for free. Riding the cable car offers an unforgettable perspective of the island's stunning landscapes.

Insider Tips for Tenerife

1. **Rent a Car**: Renting a car can be an economical way to explore the island at your own pace, especially if you plan to visit more remote areas. Look for local rental companies for better deals.

2. **Public Transport**: Tenerife has a reliable and affordable public bus system (TITSA) that connects major towns and attractions. Consider buying a Ten+ card, which offers discounts on fares.

3. **Free Beaches**: Many of Tenerife's best beaches are free to access. Playa de Las Teresitas and Playa de Benijo are stunning spots to soak up the sun without spending a dime.

4. **Market Days**: Visit local markets, like Mercado de Nuestra Señora de África in Santa Cruz, where you can find fresh produce, souvenirs, and local delicacies at reasonable prices. Plus, it's a great way to experience local culture!

5. **Hiking Trails**: Tenerife offers numerous free hiking trails with spectacular views, especially around Teide National Park. Just pack some water and snacks, and enjoy nature without spending anything.

6. **Cultural Events**: Keep an eye on local cultural calendars for free concerts, festivals, and art exhibitions, particularly during the summer months. These events provide a great way to immerse yourself in local culture.

Getting Around Tenerife Cheaply

- **Bus Travel**: The TITSA bus system is extensive and affordable, with routes covering most tourist attractions and towns. Single tickets start around €1.45, and a day pass costs around €8.
- **Bicycle Rentals**: Consider renting a bike for a day to explore local areas. Many towns offer bike rental services at reasonable rates, around €10-€15 per day.
- **Walking**: Many coastal towns are pedestrian-friendly, making walking a great way to explore without spending money on transport.
- **Shared Rides**: Use ride-sharing apps or local taxi services for short distances, as they can be more economical than renting a car, especially if you're traveling solo or in small groups.

Chart of Affordable Luxury Accommodations in Tenerife

Accommodation Name	Location	Average Nightly Price (€)	Key Features
Hotel La Quinta Park Suites	Puerto de la Cruz	120	Pool, Spa, Family-friendly
Royal River, Luxury Hotel	Adeje	150	Private pool, Spa services
Hotel San Telmo	Santa Cruz	90	Ocean views, Central location
Hotel Jardines de Nivaria	Costa Adeje	180	Beachfront, Pools, Dining
Hotel Gran Tacande	Costa Adeje	200	Luxurious spa, Multiple restaurants
Hotel Puerto Palace	Puerto de la Cruz	130	Pool, near beach, stunning views
Hotel Riu Arecas	Costa Adeje	140	Beach access, All-inclusive options
Iberostar Grand Hotel El Mirador	Costa Adeje	250	Beachfront, Spa, High-end dining
Hotel Bahia del Duque	Costa Adeje	300	Luxury spa, Direct beach

Hotel Meliá Jardines del	Costa Adeje	175	Gardens, Pools, Family-

Free Events or Experiences in Tenerife That Most People Don't Know About

1. **Stargazing in Teide National Park**: Tenerife is renowned for its clear skies and minimal light pollution, making it one of the best places in the world for stargazing. While many tourists flock to the cable car for views, fewer know that you can enjoy breathtaking celestial displays for free. Join local astronomy clubs that often host stargazing events or simply find a quiet spot in the park with a blanket and a thermos of hot chocolate.

2. **Cultural Festivals**: Tenerife hosts a variety of local festivals that are often free to attend. For instance, the Carnival of Santa Cruz is famous worldwide, but smaller, lesser-known celebrations occur in towns like La Laguna or Los Gigantes. These festivals include traditional music, dance, and food, offering a genuine taste of Canarian culture without any entry fees.

3. **Local Artisan Markets**: Many towns in Tenerife have local artisan markets where you can browse handmade crafts, jewelry, and local foods for free. Markets like the one in Santa Cruz, held every Sunday, often have live music and dance performances, creating a vibrant atmosphere. While you might be tempted to buy souvenirs, simply enjoying the atmosphere is a delightful experience.

4. **Exploring Anaga Rural Park**: Anaga Rural Park is a hidden gem with stunning hiking trails and lush landscapes. Many tourists stick to the well-trodden paths, but if you venture deeper, you'll discover secluded trails leading to hidden waterfalls and panoramic viewpoints. Best of all, access to the park is free, making it a perfect spot for a day of adventure without spending a euro.

5. **Hidden Beaches**: While popular beaches like Playa de Las Américas can get crowded, there are countless hidden coves and beaches to discover. One such spot is Playa de Benijo, which offers dramatic cliffs and beautiful sunsets. The walk to these beaches often deters crowds, allowing you to enjoy a more peaceful beach experience.

Practical Things to Remember to Save Money in Tenerife

1. **Eat Like a Local**: Dining at touristy restaurants can quickly drain your wallet. Instead, opt for local eateries, known as *guachinches*, where you can enjoy traditional Canarian food for around €10-€15 per meal. These family-run establishments offer authentic dishes at lower prices compared to tourist spots, often with generous portions.

2. **Discount Cards**: If you plan to visit multiple attractions, consider purchasing a *Tenerife Pass* or *Tenerife Card*, which can offer discounts on various sites and activities. For around €30-€50, these cards can save you up to 30% on entrance fees, making them a worthwhile investment if you plan to be active.

3. **Public Transportation**: Use the TITSA bus system to get around. A single ticket costs around €1.45, while a day pass is about €8. It's a great way to save money compared to taxis, especially if you're planning to explore multiple towns in a day.

4. **Free Tours and Events**: Look for free walking tours available in major cities like Santa Cruz and La Laguna. While the tours are free, it's customary to tip your guide around €10-€15 if you enjoyed the experience.

5. **Pack a Picnic**: Food costs can add up quickly, especially at tourist sites. Bring snacks and drinks when you go out. Local supermarkets sell fresh bread, cheese, and fruit for under €10, perfect for a picnic at one of Tenerife's beautiful parks or beaches.

Historical Facts You Didn't Know About Tenerife

1. **The Guanches**: Before the Spanish conquest in the 15th century, Tenerife was inhabited by the Guanches, a Berber people who had a rich culture and were skilled in agriculture, pottery, and mummification. The Guanches worshipped nature and had a strong connection to the land, which can still be felt in various local customs today.

2. **The First Canary Island to Use Electricity**: In 1893, Santa Cruz became the first city in the Canary Islands to have an electric tram system. The trams connected the city center with the port, revolutionizing transportation on the island long before many European cities.

3. **Mount Teide and Mythology**: Mount Teide, the highest peak in Spain, is surrounded by fascinating legends. It was once believed by the Guanches to be the gateway to the underworld, and the word "Teide" is derived from the word *Echeyde*, which means hell in their language. Today, it stands as a UNESCO World Heritage site, admired for both its natural beauty and cultural significance.

4. **The Role in Space Exploration**: Tenerife played a crucial role during the Apollo missions in the 1960s. The island's unique landscape and climate made it an ideal location for NASA to conduct simulations and training exercises, particularly in preparation for the lunar landings.

Practical Information for Visiting Tenerife

- **Getting There**: Tenerife is accessible by air via two main airports: Tenerife South (Reina Sofía) and Tenerife North (Los Rodeos). Numerous airlines offer flights from various European cities. From the airport, shuttle buses and taxis are available to transport you to popular areas.

- **Best Time to Visit**: The island has a mild climate year-round, but spring (March to May) and fall (September to November) are ideal for fewer crowds and pleasant weather. July and August attract many tourists, especially families, so expect busier attractions.

- **Ticket Information**: Many attractions in Tenerife offer discounted tickets for children, seniors, and families. Look for combo tickets for multiple sites, such as those for Teide National Park and Loro Parque, to save money.

- **Activities to Do**: Beyond the famous attractions, consider joining local cooking classes, visiting local wineries for tastings, or hiking lesser-known trails in Anaga Rural Park.

- **Secret Spots**: One of the best-kept secrets is the little-known Playa de Almáciga, which offers stunning natural beauty and is often overlooked by tourists. Another hidden gem is the town of Garachico, with its historical buildings and natural swimming pools carved from lava.

Ronda

Ronda is a breathtaking gem nestled in the mountains of southern Spain, specifically in the Malaga province. This picturesque town, known for its dramatic cliffs and stunning gorge, has a history as rich as its landscapes. Founded by the Romans as "Acinipo," Ronda later became a significant Moorish stronghold during the Islamic rule of the Iberian Peninsula. It's famously home to one of the oldest bullrings in Spain, a testament to its deep cultural roots in bullfighting.

The town's most iconic feature is undoubtedly the Puente Nuevo, or New Bridge, which spans a staggering gorge and connects the old and new parts of Ronda. This architectural marvel was completed in the late 18th century, making it a vital part of the town's identity. As you wander through Ronda, you'll find cobblestone streets lined with whitewashed buildings, quaint shops, and vibrant gardens, all echoing the town's storied past. Whether you're sipping a glass of local wine or exploring ancient ruins, Ronda offers a unique blend of history, culture, and stunning natural beauty.

Top 20 Paid Attractions in Ronda

1. **Plaza de Toros** The Plaza de Toros is one of the oldest bullrings in Spain and is steeped in tradition. Built in 1785, its neoclassical design is striking. To save on fees, consider visiting during the off-peak season or check for guided tours that include admission. A creative free alternative is to simply stroll around the exterior and admire the architecture. For practical tips, arrive early to enjoy the surrounding gardens and take photos without the crowds. Did you know that this bullring played a pivotal role in the evolution of bullfighting in Spain?

2. **Puente Nuevo** The Puente Nuevo is Ronda's most iconic landmark, spanning a gorge 120 meters deep. While it's free to walk across, the nearby viewpoint requires a small fee. To save on costs, explore the area early in the morning or late in the evening for stunning light and fewer tourists. A free alternative is to hike down to the gorge for a breathtaking view of the bridge from below. Practical tip: wear comfortable shoes, as the terrain can be uneven. The bridge took 40 years to build, reflecting the determination and ingenuity of its creators.

3. **Casa del Rey Moro** This historic house offers a glimpse into the Moorish past of Ronda. The entrance fee grants access to the gardens and the famous staircase leading down to the river. To save on fees, check for combination tickets with other attractions. If you're looking for a free alternative, enjoy the views from the surrounding cliffs. Practical tip: bring water, as the walk can be steep. Legend has it that the house was once the residence of the Moorish king, and it's rumored that the gardens were designed as a retreat from the heat.

4. **Baños Árabes (Arab Baths)** Step back in time at the Arab Baths, one of the best-preserved examples of Moorish architecture in Spain. The entrance fee is minimal, but you can save by visiting during free museum days. A creative free alternative is to explore the nearby gardens, which offer great views. Practical tip: visit early in the day to avoid crowds. The baths date back to the 13th century and provide fascinating insights into the daily lives of the Moors.

5. **Museo Lara** Housed in a charming 19th-century building, Museo Lara showcases an eclectic collection of historical artifacts, including antique firearms and traditional Spanish costumes. Entry is reasonably priced, and you can often find discounts for students and seniors. For a free alternative, explore the nearby streets filled with shops selling local crafts. Practical tip: take your time, as there's plenty to see. This museum is a treasure trove of history, offering a unique look at Ronda's cultural heritage.

6. **El Tajo Gorge** While you can admire El Tajo Gorge for free, guided tours that provide insight into its geological significance come with a fee. To save money, consider joining a group tour rather than a private one. A free alternative is to walk along the paths surrounding the gorge for stunning views. Practical tip: bring a camera—sunset offers spectacular photo opportunities. El Tajo is not just a beautiful sight; it's also an essential part of Ronda's history, separating the old and new towns.

7. **Palacio de Mondragón** This historic palace dates back to the 14th century and offers a glimpse into the lives of Ronda's noble families. The entrance fee includes access to the museum, which showcases local history and art. To save, check for special events or discounts. A free alternative is to enjoy the views from the palace gardens. Practical tip: spend time in the gardens for a peaceful escape. The palace is a beautiful example of Andalusian architecture and was once the residence of the town's Moorish king.

8. **Caminito del Rey** Just a short drive from Ronda, this walkway offers thrilling views of the gorge. While it's a paid attraction, it's worth every euro for the adrenaline rush. To save on fees, book your tickets in advance online. A free alternative is to hike in the surrounding natural park. Practical tip: wear sturdy shoes and arrive early to beat the crowds. The walkway was once considered the most dangerous in the world, but now it's a safe and breathtaking experience.

9. **Iglesia de Santa Maria la Mayor** This stunning church, built on the site of a former mosque, showcases a blend of Gothic and Baroque styles. The entrance fee is minimal, and you can save by visiting during mass or free entry days. A creative free alternative is to explore the surrounding plaza, which often hosts local events. Practical tip: take time to admire the intricate altar and artwork. The church's history is a testament to Ronda's cultural transitions over the centuries.

10. **Cueva de la Pileta** These ancient caves are home to stunning prehistoric paintings and are a UNESCO World Heritage site. Entry requires a ticket, but you can save by booking in advance. A free alternative is to explore the surrounding natural park, filled with hiking trails. Practical tip: guided tours offer the best insights into the cave's history. The paintings date back over 25,000 years, providing a fascinating glimpse into the lives of early humans.

11. **Parque Natural Sierra de Grazalema** While entering the park is free, certain guided tours and activities do come with a fee. To save, consider self-guided hikes that showcase the park's natural beauty. A creative free alternative is to picnic in one of the park's scenic spots. Practical tip: bring binoculars for birdwatching, as the area is home to various species. This natural park is renowned for its breathtaking landscapes and diverse flora and fauna, making it a must-visit for nature lovers.

12. **Bodega La Sangre de Ronda** Explore this local winery and taste some of the finest wines in the region. The entrance fee includes a tour and tasting, but booking in advance often secures discounts. A creative free alternative is to stroll through the vineyards. Practical tip: pair your wine tasting with local cheeses for an unforgettable experience. This winery has a rich history dating back to the 19th century, blending tradition with modern winemaking techniques.

13. **Castillo de la Almoraima** Although it's a lesser-known site, this castle offers stunning views of Ronda. The entry fee is minimal, and guided tours provide insights into its history. To save on costs, visit during free entry days. A free alternative is to hike nearby trails with breathtaking views. Practical tip: check the castle's opening hours, as they can vary. This castle dates back to the 14th century and played a significant role in Ronda's defensive history.

14. **Museo del Bandolero** This quirky museum delves into the fascinating world of bandits in Ronda. Entry is reasonably priced, and discounts may be available for groups. A creative free alternative is to explore the local folklore surrounding bandits by chatting with locals. Practical tip: combine your visit with a walking tour to discover more about Ronda's notorious outlaws. The museum showcases artifacts and stories that capture the spirit of this unique aspect of Spanish history.

15. **Centro de Interpretación del Vino** Wine lovers will appreciate this center dedicated to the history and production of Ronda's wines. The entrance fee covers a guided tour, which is well worth it for the insights offered. To save, look for combo tickets with other attractions. A free alternative is to visit local wine shops for tastings. Practical tip: don't miss the opportunity to buy some local wines to take home. This center provides an in-depth look at the viticulture that has shaped the region.

16. **Casa de Don Juan Bosco** This cultural center is dedicated to the life and work of Saint John Bosco. Admission is typically free, but some special exhibitions may have fees. A free alternative is to explore the nearby gardens and enjoy the tranquil atmosphere. Practical tip: check for workshops or events that might be happening during your visit. The center highlights the importance of education and community in Ronda's history.

17. **El Mirador de Ronda** This viewpoint offers stunning panoramic views of the town and surrounding countryside. While access is free, guided tours that include it may come with a fee. To save on costs, visit during sunset for breathtaking scenery without a tour. Practical tip: bring a camera for unforgettable sunset photos. This spot is perfect for capturing the essence of Ronda's beauty, framed by the mountains and valleys.

18. **Ronda's Water Mine** The ancient water mine, built by the Moors, is a fascinating site to explore. Entry is inexpensive, and guided tours provide historical

Insider Tips for Ronda

1. **Plan Your Visit**: Ronda is best explored in the spring or fall when the weather is mild, and the tourist crowds are smaller. Aim for weekdays if possible.

2. **Wear Comfortable Shoes**: The town's cobbled streets can be uneven, so sturdy shoes are a must for exploring its hilly terrain.

3. **Use Public Transport**: The local bus system is affordable and efficient, making it easy to get to nearby attractions without the hassle of parking.

4. **Sample Local Cuisine**: Don't miss trying Ronda's traditional dishes like *rabo de toro* (oxtail stew) or *pescaito frito*(fried fish). Tapas bars often offer great deals.

5. **Visit Museums on Free Entry Days**: Many museums in Ronda have free entry days, so check their schedules before planning your visit.

6. **Stay Hydrated**: Bring a refillable water bottle, as it can get hot, especially during summer. There are plenty of water fountains throughout the town.

7. **Take Advantage of Walking Tours**: Free walking tours are a fantastic way to learn about Ronda's history and culture. Be sure to tip your guide if you enjoyed the tour!

8. **Explore Beyond the Town Center**: Venture into the surrounding natural parks for hiking and breathtaking views. The scenery is stunning and often less crowded.

9. **Shop at Local Markets**: Check out the local markets for authentic souvenirs and food items. Prices are typically lower than in tourist shops.

10. **Capture the Views**: Ronda is famous for its breathtaking viewpoints. Bring your camera to capture stunning sunsets over the gorge.

Getting Around Ronda Cheaply

1. **Walking**: Ronda is compact and best explored on foot. Most attractions are within walking distance, and strolling through the picturesque streets is part of the experience.

2. **Public Buses**: For trips outside the city center, public buses are a budget-friendly option. They connect Ronda with nearby towns and natural parks.

3. **Bicycle Rentals**: Renting a bike can be an affordable and fun way to explore Ronda and its surroundings. Look for rental shops in the town center.

4. **Taxis**: While more expensive than public transport, taxis can be split among friends or family if traveling in a group, making them a reasonable option for short distances.

5. **Shared Rides**: Apps like BlaBlaCar can connect you with locals offering rides to nearby cities at a fraction of the cost of public transport.

Affordable Luxury Accommodation in Ronda

Hotel Name	Description	Average Nightly	Pros	Cons

Hotel Montelirio	A charming boutique hotel with stunning gorge views.	120 €	Historic building, great location.	Limited parking.
Hotel Ronda	Offers comfortable rooms and a rooftop terrace.	100 €	Central location, good amenities.	Some rooms may be noisy.
La Fuente de la Higuera	An elegant rural hotel with a beautiful garden.	130 €	Peaceful, great for relaxation.	A bit outside the city center.
Hotel Don Miguel	A family-run hotel with traditional decor and local	90 €	Friendly staff, good value.	Basic facilities.
Hotel Rural El Cortijo	Offers rustic accommodation with a tranquil setting.	95 €	Close to nature, beautiful views.	Limited dining options.
Casa Palacio de los Olivos	A boutique hotel set in a former olive mill.	115 €	Unique decor, peaceful	Requires booking in
Hotel Bodega de Jerez	A stylish hotel with a focus on wine and gastronomy.	110 €	Excellent dining options.	Limited English
Hotel La Ciudad	Located in a historic building with modern comforts.	85 €	Budget-friendly, historic charm.	Basic amenities.
Ronda House	Offers spacious rooms and a	75 €	Good location,	Older decor.
B&B La Posada del	A cozy bed and breakfast with a homey feel.	80 €	Personal service, home-cooked	Smaller rooms.

Free Events or Experiences in Ronda That Most People Don't Know About

1. **Ronda's Full Moon Walks**: Each month, Ronda hosts guided walks during the full moon, providing a magical experience as you wander through the town under the moonlight. These walks are free and often led by local enthusiasts who share stories and legends about Ronda's history. The breathtaking views of the illuminated gorge and bridges make this a hidden gem for evening strolls.

2. **Open-Air Flamenco Shows**: During the summer months, various plazas in Ronda come alive with spontaneous flamenco performances. While official shows often require tickets, many locals put on impromptu displays of this passionate art form for free. Just wander through the streets in the evening, and you might stumble upon a mesmerizing performance.

3. **Local Festivals**: Ronda celebrates several lesser-known local festivals throughout the year, including the *Feria de Pedro Romero* in September, which features parades, music, and traditional foods. While some events may have fees, many of the festivities are free to attend, allowing you to experience authentic Andalusian culture without spending a dime.

4. **Free Museum Days**: Many museums in Ronda offer free entry on specific days, such as the first Sunday of each month. Take advantage of these days to explore places like the Museo Lara or the Palacio de Mondragón without any cost.

5. **Secret Viewing Points**: Beyond the popular viewpoints like the Puente Nuevo, there are hidden spots around the town where you can enjoy stunning views of the

gorge and landscape without the crowds. Look for trails leading to the cliffs, or ask locals for their favorite secluded spots to take in the scenery.

Practical Things to Remember to Save Money in Ronda

1. **Accommodation Deals**: Book your stay in advance to secure better rates. Look for hotels or hostels offering discounts for longer stays—many offer up to 15% off if you book for three nights or more.

2. **Eat Like a Local**: Enjoy tapas instead of full meals at restaurants. Many tapas can be found for around €3-€5 each, allowing you to sample various dishes without breaking the bank. Some bars even offer free tapas with your drink!

3. **Free Water**: Ronda has several public fountains where you can refill your water bottle. This can save you around €1-€2 per bottled water throughout your visit.

4. **Public Transport**: Use the local bus system to reach nearby attractions and towns. A one-way ticket costs about €1.50, significantly cheaper than taxi fares, which can start around €10.

5. **Discounted Entry**: Look for combination tickets for attractions like the Plaza de Toros and the Museo Lara, which can save you up to 20% compared to purchasing individual tickets.

6. **Local Markets**: Visit local markets for fresh produce, bread, and cheeses. You can prepare your meals if you have a kitchen, saving on dining costs.

Historical Facts You Didn't Know About Ronda

1. **The First Bullring**: Ronda is home to one of the oldest bullrings in Spain, built in 1785. However, it was also where the modern form of bullfighting was developed. The *torero* Francisco Romero, a native of Ronda, revolutionized the art of bullfighting in the 18th century.

2. **A City of Poets**: Ronda has long been a source of inspiration for poets and writers. Famous Spanish poet Rainer Maria Rilke wrote some of his most renowned works while living in Ronda. The city's stunning landscapes and rich history continue to attract artists and writers seeking inspiration.

3. **Moorish Legacy**: The impressive architecture in Ronda, such as the Casa del Rey Moro, showcases the city's rich Moorish past. The Moors constructed elaborate irrigation systems, which are still in use today, a testament to their engineering prowess.

4. **The Birthplace of Romanticism**: In the 19th century, Ronda became a hub for the Romantic movement in Spain. Writers like Ernest Hemingway and Orson Welles frequented the town, drawn by its beauty and cultural significance, leaving a lasting mark on its history.

Practical Information for Visiting Ronda

1. **Getting There**: Ronda is accessible by train or bus from major cities like Malaga and Seville. The train ride offers stunning views of the countryside and takes about two hours. Bus tickets start around €10, and train fares vary based on the service.

2. **Crowd Times**: The best time to visit Ronda is during the shoulder seasons of spring (April to June) and fall (September to October). During these times, the weather is pleasant, and the crowds are thinner compared to the summer months.

3. **Tickets for Attractions**: Most major attractions, like the Plaza de Toros and the Museo Lara, require tickets ranging from €5 to €15. Be sure to check online for combo·tickets that can save you money.

4. **Activities**: Don't miss hiking the trails around El Tajo Gorge, exploring the ancient ruins, and wandering through the old town's winding streets. Each corner reveals something new and historically significant.

5. **Secret Spots**: One lesser-known spot is the *Caminito del Rey*, a thrilling walkway just outside Ronda. While it requires a ticket, the views and experience are unforgettable. For a free option, seek out *Mirador de Aldehuela*, which offers stunning views of the gorge without the crowds.

6. **Packing Tips**: Bring comfortable walking shoes, a refillable water bottle, sunscreen, and a hat. Even in cooler months, the sun can be strong, and you'll want to be prepared for all-day exploration.

Regions

Spain is a country rich in diversity, boasting a wide range of regions that attract visitors for various reasons, including cultural heritage, natural beauty, and culinary delights. While it's challenging to rank all regions definitively by most visited, as visitor numbers can vary depending on factors such as seasonality and events, here is a list of some of the most visited regions in Spain, based on their popularity among tourists:

- **Catalonia:**
  - Home to the vibrant city of Barcelona, Catalonia is one of Spain's most visited regions. Visitors are drawn to its unique blend of modernist architecture, stunning beaches, and rich cultural heritage. The Costa Brava and Costa Dorada coastlines are popular destinations for sun-seekers, while the region's gastronomy, including Catalan cuisine and world-renowned wines, also attracts food enthusiasts.
- **Andalusia:**
  - Andalusia is famous for its Moorish architecture, flamenco music and dance, and vibrant festivals. The cities of Seville, Granada, and Cordoba are major draws for their historic landmarks such as the Alhambra Palace, the Great Mosque of Cordoba, and the Giralda Tower. The region's picturesque white villages (pueblos blancos), stunning beaches on the Costa del Sol, and natural wonders like the Sierra Nevada mountains further contribute to its popularity.
- **Madrid Community:**
  - As the capital of Spain, Madrid attracts millions of visitors each year. The city is known for its world-class museums, including the Prado Museum, Reina Sofia Museum, and Thyssen-Bornemisza Museum, which house masterpieces by artists such as Velázquez, Picasso, and Goya. Madrid's lively nightlife, gastronomic scene, and cultural events, such as the San Isidro Festival and Madrid Pride, also make it a top destination.
- **Valencian Community:**
  - The Valencian Community, with its capital city of Valencia, is renowned for its futuristic architecture, vibrant festivals, and delicious cuisine. Visitors flock to Valencia to experience attractions such as the City of Arts and Sciences, the historic Old Town, and the lively Central Market. The region's coastal towns, including Alicante and Benidorm, are popular beach destinations offering sun, sand, and sea.
- **Balearic Islands:**
  - Comprising islands such as Mallorca, Ibiza, and Menorca, the Balearic Islands are known for their stunning beaches, crystal-clear waters, and vibrant nightlife. Mallorca attracts visitors with its picturesque villages, historic landmarks like the Cathedral of Santa Maria, and scenic drives through the Serra de Tramuntana mountains. Ibiza is famous for its world-renowned clubs and parties, while Menorca offers a more laid-back atmosphere with tranquil coves and nature reserves.
- **Canary Islands:**
  - Situated off the northwest coast of Africa, the Canary Islands are a popular year-round destination known for their volcanic landscapes, beautiful beaches, and mild climate. Tenerife, with its iconic Mount Teide National Park, is the largest and most visited island. Gran Canaria is known for its

diverse landscapes, from sand dunes to lush forests, while Lanzarote offers otherworldly volcanic scenery and unique attractions like the Timanfaya National Park.

- **Basque Country:**
  - The Basque Country, located in northern Spain, is known for its unique culture, delicious cuisine, and stunning landscapes. The city of San Sebastian attracts visitors with its beautiful beaches, Michelin-starred restaurants, and annual events like the San Sebastian International Film Festival. Bilbao is famous for the Guggenheim Museum Bilbao, a masterpiece of modern architecture, and the nearby coastal town of Getxo offers scenic views and charming seaside promenades.
- **Galicia:**
  - Galicia, in northwestern Spain, is known for its rugged coastline, lush green landscapes, and Celtic heritage. The city of Santiago de Compostela is a major pilgrimage destination, home to the stunning Cathedral of Santiago de Compostela and the end point of the Camino de Santiago pilgrimage route. Visitors also flock to Galicia for its delicious seafood, picturesque fishing villages, and scenic hiking trails along the Costa da Morte and Rias Baixas.
- **Aragon:**
  - Aragon, located in northeastern Spain, is known for its rich history, stunning natural scenery, and outdoor activities. The region is home to the iconic Mudejar architecture of Teruel and the medieval town of Albarracín, both UNESCO World Heritage Sites. The Pyrenees mountains offer opportunities for skiing, hiking, and adventure sports, while the Ordesa y Monte Perdido National Park is a paradise for nature lovers.
- **Murcia:**
  - Murcia, in southeastern Spain, is known for its Mediterranean climate, beautiful beaches, and rich cultural heritage. The city of Murcia boasts impressive Baroque architecture, historic landmarks such as the Cathedral of Murcia, and lively festivals like the Fiestas de Primavera. The Costa Cálida coastline offers sandy beaches, crystal-clear waters, and opportunities for water sports, while the Mar Menor lagoon is a popular destination for relaxation and wellness.

Catalonia

Catalonia, located in northeastern Spain, is a region known for its vibrant culture, stunning coastline, and world-class cuisine. While exploring Catalonia can be luxurious, it's also possible to experience its beauty and charm on a budget.

Here is a list of **20 lesser-known paid attractions** in **Catalonia that we haven't covered**, each offering a unique experience away from the typical tourist spots, along with **money-saving tips** and reasons why you should visit.

1. Sant Pere de Rodes Monastery (Girona)

- **Why Visit**: Perched on a mountain overlooking the Mediterranean, this 10th-century Benedictine monastery offers stunning views and historical insights into medieval Catalonia.
- **Money-Saving Tip**: Visit on the **first Sunday of the month** for free entry.
- **Price**: €6

2. El Call – Jewish Quarter Museum (Barcelona)

- **Why Visit**: Located in Barcelona's Gothic Quarter, this museum delves into the city's Jewish history and the tragic expulsion of Jews from Spain in the 15th century.
- **Money-Saving Tip**: Entry is free on **Sundays after 3 p.m.** and the **first Sunday of the month**.
- **Price**: €3

3. Cardona Castle (Cardona)

- **Why Visit**: One of the most important medieval fortresses in Catalonia, it offers guided tours through its battlements and a fascinating insight into the salt mines below.
- **Money-Saving Tip**: Book online for a **10% discount**.
- **Price**: €8.50

4. Museu d'Art de Girona (Girona)

- **Why Visit**: This museum showcases Catalonia's artistic heritage from the Romanesque to the contemporary period, housed in the former episcopal palace.
- **Money-Saving Tip**: Free entry on the **first Sunday of the month**.
- **Price**: €6

5. Cava Caves of Sant Sadurní d'Anoia (Sant Sadurní d'Anoia)

- **Why Visit**: Explore the underground cellars where Catalonia's famous sparkling wine, **Cava**, is produced, with tastings included.
- **Money-Saving Tip**: Book in advance for **group discounts** or visit during Cava Week in October for special promotions.
- **Price**: €12-€18

6. Museu de les Mines de Bellmunt del Priorat (Tarragona)

- **Why Visit**: Discover the history of mining in Catalonia at this museum, located in the Priorat region, known for its unique wines and landscapes.
- **Money-Saving Tip**: Combine your visit with a wine tour in Priorat for bundled discounts.
- **Price**: €5

7. Santuari del Miracle (Solsona)

- **Why Visit**: A spiritual and artistic retreat with breathtaking views and serene surroundings. The sanctuary is famous for its Baroque altarpiece.
- **Money-Saving Tip**: Entry to the sanctuary is free, but the guided tour costs extra —skip the guide if you're on a budget.
- **Price**: €4 for a guided tour

8. El Celler de Can Roca - Gastronomic Experience (Girona)

- **Why Visit**: The Roca brothers' restaurant is one of the best in the world, offering a unique culinary experience.
- **Money-Saving Tip**: Book well in advance for lunch, which is cheaper than dinner. Or visit their **ice cream parlor**for a more affordable taste of their creations.
- **Price**: Tasting menu from €195

9. Vic Episcopal Museum (Vic)

- **Why Visit**: This museum boasts an impressive collection of medieval art, especially Romanesque and Gothic pieces from the region.
- **Money-Saving Tip**: Entry is free on the **first Sunday of every month**.
- **Price**: €8

10. Montserrat Museum (Montserrat)

- **Why Visit**: Located at Montserrat Abbey, this museum holds works by Dali, Picasso, and Caravaggio, providing a surprising cultural addition to the religious pilgrimage site.
- **Money-Saving Tip**: **Combine your ticket** with a funicular ride to save on transportation costs.
- **Price**: €8

11. Caves Güell (Santa Coloma de Cervelló)

- **Why Visit**: An architectural marvel designed by **Antoni Gaudí** that is lesser-known compared to his Barcelona works, offering a glimpse into his early designs.
- **Money-Saving Tip**: Book online for a **discount** or visit in a group to get reduced rates.
- **Price**: €10

12. Món Sant Benet (Bages)

- **Why Visit**: A historic monastery turned cultural space with immersive exhibitions about the life of monks and the art of food from medieval times to today.
- **Money-Saving Tip**: Look out for special **package deals** combining the monastery visit with local culinary experiences.
- **Price**: €9

13. Santuari de Núria (Pirineu)

- **Why Visit**: Set in the stunning Pyrenees, this sanctuary offers not only religious significance but also mountain trails, a lake, and outdoor activities.
- **Money-Saving Tip**: Take advantage of discounted tickets by purchasing a **combined ticket** that includes the rack railway and museum entry.
- **Price**: €11.50

14. Museu del Cinema (Girona)

- **Why Visit**: One of Europe's most impressive film museums, it offers a deep dive into the history of cinema with hands-on exhibits and original equipment.
- **Money-Saving Tip**: Free entry on the **first Sunday of the month**.
- **Price**: €5

15. Miravet Castle (Tarragona)

- **Why Visit**: A beautifully restored castle overlooking the Ebro River, offering fascinating insights into Catalonia's Templar past.
- **Money-Saving Tip**: Book a **guided tour** in advance to combine with nearby wine tastings for a discounted experience.
- **Price**: €5

16. Estany d'Ivars i Vila-sana (Lleida)

- **Why Visit**: A peaceful wetland sanctuary perfect for birdwatching and nature lovers.
- **Money-Saving Tip**: Entry is free, but for a small fee, you can join a **guided tour** that includes birdwatching equipment.
- **Price**: €3 for guided tour

17. Salt Mountain Cultural Park (Cardona)

- **Why Visit**: Explore the ancient salt mines that have shaped the history of Cardona. Walk inside the mountain and see the spectacular salt formations.
- **Money-Saving Tip**: Book online for group discounts or visit during the **weekdays** for cheaper rates.
- **Price**: €12

18. Sant Cugat Monastery (Sant Cugat del Vallès)

- **Why Visit**: A hidden Romanesque gem near Barcelona with beautiful cloisters and medieval frescoes.
- **Money-Saving Tip**: Free entry on the **first Sunday of the month**.
- **Price**: €4

19. Cap de Creus Natural Park (Cadaqués)

- **Why Visit**: This stunning park offers beautiful hiking trails with access to hidden coves and beaches. The entrance to the **Casa Dalí** is paid, where Salvador Dalí lived and worked.
- **Money-Saving Tip**: Visit in the **off-season** for discounted rates and fewer crowds.
- **Price**: €14

20. Torre de la Creu (Sant Joan Despí)

- **Why Visit**: A lesser-known **Modernist** gem designed by **Josep Maria Jujol**, a close collaborator of Antoni Gaudí, featuring whimsical designs and surreal architecture.
- **Money-Saving Tip**: Check for **group discounts** or local visitor promotions that occur throughout the year.
- **Price**: €5

Money-Saving Strategies for Visiting Catalonia:

1. **First Sundays Rule**: Many museums and historical sites offer **free entry** on the **first Sunday of every month**, so plan visits accordingly.
2. **Combination Tickets**: For some attractions like Montserrat, you can purchase combination tickets that include transportation, access to different areas, and even guided tours at a **reduced rate**.
3. **City Passes**: Look into purchasing city passes like the **Barcelona Card** or **Girona Card**, which offer free or discounted access to multiple attractions, as well as free public transportation.
4. **Online Booking Discounts**: Always book your tickets online in advance, as many places offer **10-15% discounts**for pre-bookings.
5. **Off-Season Travel**: Consider visiting during **shoulder seasons** (spring or fall) when prices for accommodations and tours tend to be lower, and there are fewer tourists.

Andalusia

Andalusia, located in southern Spain, is renowned for its rich cultural heritage, stunning landscapes, and vibrant cities. While the region offers plenty of luxury experiences, it's also possible to explore Andalusia on a budget without compromising on quality. Here's a guide to enjoying Andalusia's top attractions, culinary delights, and accommodations without breaking the bank.

Tips:

- **Visit Free Attractions:** Explore free attractions such as historic neighborhoods, parks, and viewpoints, which offer insight into Andalusia's culture and history without the cost.
- **Enjoy Tapas:** Take advantage of the Andalusian tradition of free tapas with drink orders at local bars and restaurants, offering a budget-friendly way to sample local cuisine.

What to not miss

1. Córdoba's Palacio de Viana

- **Why visit**: This 16th-century palace features 12 spectacular courtyards and gardens, offering a tranquil escape.
- **Money-saving tip**: Visit on Wednesdays between 2:00 p.m. and 5:00 p.m. when some courtyards are free to enter.

2. Setenil de las Bodegas

- **Why visit**: Known for its unique cave houses built into the cliffs, this town is a hidden gem.
- **Money-saving tip**: Avoid paid tours; explore the town independently and enjoy free views.

3. Castillo de Almodóvar del Río

- **Why visit**: This striking medieval castle near Córdoba offers incredible panoramic views and a rich history.
- **Money-saving tip**: Book tickets online in advance to save up to 15%.

4. Cueva de Nerja

- **Why visit**: Famous for its ancient cave paintings and impressive stalactites, it's a must-see.
- **Money-saving tip**: Book combo tickets that include the botanical garden for a discount.

5. Alcazaba of Almería

- **Why visit**: Explore this fortified complex with stunning views of the city and the sea.
- **Money-saving tip**: Entry is free on Sundays after 2:00 p.m. for EU citizens.

6. Medina Azahara

- **Why visit**: The ruins of this Islamic medieval palace-city near Córdoba are a UNESCO site.

- **Money-saving tip**: Free entry on Saturdays after 2:00 p.m. and on Sundays for EU residents.

7. Castillo de Baños de la Encina

- **Why visit**: This well-preserved Moorish castle offers a fascinating glimpse into Andalusia's history.
- **Money-saving tip**: Check for reduced prices during local festivals.

8. Museo del Baile Flamenco, Seville

- **Why visit**: Learn about the history and art of flamenco through immersive exhibitions and live performances.
- **Money-saving tip**: Book online for up to 10% off, or combine with a flamenco show for better value.

9. Doñana National Park

- **Why visit**: One of Europe's most important wetlands, it's a haven for birdwatching and nature lovers.
- **Money-saving tip**: Opt for self-guided hiking rather than paid tours.

10. Monasterio de San Isidoro del Campo

- **Why visit**: This 14th-century monastery near Seville offers remarkable Mudejar architecture.
- **Money-saving tip**: Free entry on Tuesday afternoons for EU citizens.

11. La Rabida Monastery

- **Why visit**: This is where Columbus planned his trip to the Americas; the monastery holds a deep historical significance.
- **Money-saving tip**: Look for combined tickets with nearby attractions like the Muelle de las Carabelas.

12. Jardín Botánico La Concepción, Málaga

- **Why visit**: A peaceful garden oasis featuring rare plants from around the world.
- **Money-saving tip**: Entry is free on Sundays after 4:30 p.m. from April to September.

13. Museo de Bellas Artes, Seville

- **Why visit**: This museum holds a remarkable collection of Spanish art, including works by Murillo.
- **Money-saving tip**: Free entry on Sundays for everyone.

14. Fortress of La Calahorra

- **Why visit**: A lesser-known but stunning Renaissance castle in Granada province.
- **Money-saving tip**: Visit during local festivals when the entry fee is often waived.

15. Molinos de Alcalá de Guadaíra

- **Why visit**: These historic flour mills offer a picturesque and peaceful walk.
- **Money-saving tip**: Free to visit at any time, but there may be a small fee for guided tours.

16. Castillo de Santa Catalina, Jaén

- **Why visit**: A stunning hilltop fortress with panoramic views of the city and surrounding countryside.
- **Money-saving tip**: Combine with a visit to the nearby cathedral for package deals.

17. Museo del Aceite de Oliva, Baeza

- **Why visit**: Learn about Andalusia's olive oil industry with tastings included.
- **Money-saving tip**: Check for discounts on the official website or group tickets for family visits.

18. Casa de Pilatos, Seville

- **Why visit**: A stunning blend of Mudejar, Gothic, and Renaissance architectural styles.
- **Money-saving tip**: Free entry on Mondays from 3:00 p.m. to 7:00 p.m.

19. Castillo de Belmez

- **Why visit**: This ancient fortress offers breathtaking views of the surrounding Sierra Morena mountains.
- **Money-saving tip**: Entry is free on the first Sunday of the month.

20. Centro Andaluz de la Fotografía, Almería

- **Why visit**: A fascinating photography museum showcasing works of Spanish and international photographers.
- **Money-saving tip**: Free entry for all visitors.

Special Foods and Customs in Andalusia

Andalusia is famous for its rich culinary traditions and unique customs that have evolved over centuries. Influenced by Moorish, Roman, and Christian cultures, the region offers a blend of flavors and practices that are deeply rooted in its history.

1. Tapas Culture

- **What it is**: Tapas are small, flavorful dishes meant to be shared, typically served in bars and restaurants. They can be anything from cold appetizers to hot dishes like fried fish or grilled meats.
- **History**: The tradition of tapas is believed to have originated in Andalusia. According to legend, King Alfonso X mandated that taverns serve small portions of food with wine to prevent intoxication. Another story suggests that bartenders used bread or ham to cover (or "tapar") glasses of wine to keep flies out, giving rise to the term "tapas."
- **Custom**: It's common to move from one bar to another, sampling different tapas with each drink. In cities like Granada, tapas are often included for free with a drink.

2. Gazpacho and Salmorejo

- **What it is**: Gazpacho is a cold tomato-based soup with cucumbers, peppers, garlic, and olive oil, perfect for hot summer days. Salmorejo, a thicker version, is made primarily from tomatoes, bread, and garlic, often topped with hard-boiled eggs and ham.
- **History**: Gazpacho's roots date back to Roman times, when a basic mixture of stale bread, garlic, olive oil, and vinegar was consumed. The addition of tomatoes, peppers, and cucumbers came after the Columbian exchange brought these ingredients from the Americas.

- **Custom**: Andalusians enjoy these refreshing soups in the summer months to cool down and rehydrate.

3. Jamón Ibérico

- **What it is**: Jamón Ibérico is a type of cured ham made from Iberian pigs, prized for its marbled fat and rich, nutty flavor. The most famous is **Jamón Ibérico de Bellota**, made from pigs that roam oak forests and eat acorns.
- **History**: The tradition of curing ham dates back to Roman times, but it gained prestige under Moorish rule, where pork consumption was seen as a defiance of Islamic customs. Today, Andalusia produces some of Spain's finest jamón.
- **Custom**: Jamón is a common dish at family gatherings, special occasions, and local festivals. It is typically served thinly sliced with bread or enjoyed alone.

4. Pescaito Frito (Fried Fish)

- **What it is**: A popular dish along the Andalusian coast, **pescaito frito** refers to small fish like anchovies, sardines, and squid, lightly coated in flour and fried in olive oil.
- **History**: The Moors introduced the technique of frying fish, and the abundance of fresh seafood along the Costa del Sol made it a staple in Andalusian cuisine.
- **Custom**: It's often enjoyed with a cold beer or wine while watching the sunset on the coast, especially during summer.

5. Sherry (Jerez)

- **What it is**: Sherry is a fortified wine produced in the "Sherry Triangle" of Jerez de la Frontera, Sanlúcar de Barrameda, and El Puerto de Santa María. Types range from the light and dry **Fino** to the rich, sweet **Pedro Ximénez**.
- **History**: Sherry production dates back to the Phoenicians, who settled in the region around 1,100 BCE. The Moors later refined the process, introducing the method of distillation that would create modern sherry. It gained international popularity during the Age of Exploration when it was exported worldwide.
- **Custom**: Sherry is often served with tapas, and Andalusians celebrate the wine during local **fiestas** like the **Feria de Jerez**.

6. Flamenco and Feria Traditions

- **What it is**: Flamenco is a traditional art form that includes singing (cante), dancing (baile), and guitar playing (toque). Andalusians celebrate their love for flamenco during various **ferias** (festivals), where they dress in traditional costumes, perform, and socialize.
- **History**: Flamenco originated in Andalusia in the 18th century, blending the influences of Gypsy, Moorish, Jewish, and Andalusian cultures. The art form was initially an expression of marginalized communities but has since become a symbol of Andalusian identity.
- **Custom**: During fairs like the **Feria de Abril** in Seville or the **Romería del Rocío**, locals wear flamenco dresses (trajes de flamenca) and suits, sing and dance in the streets, and ride horses or carriages through the town.

7. Turrón and Mantecados

- **What it is**: **Turrón** is a nougat made from honey, sugar, egg whites, and almonds, traditionally eaten during Christmas. **Mantecados** are crumbly, shortbread-like sweets made with lard, often flavored with lemon, cinnamon, or chocolate.
- **History**: Turrón has Moorish origins, brought to Spain during their conquest of the Iberian Peninsula. It became associated with Christmas over time. Mantecados were first made in Estepa, Andalusia, and have become a holiday staple.

- **Custom**: These sweets are exchanged as gifts during the Christmas season and enjoyed at family gatherings.

8. Rabo de Toro (Oxtail Stew)

- **What it is**: A hearty stew made from bull or oxtail, cooked slowly with wine, onions, carrots, and tomatoes.
- **History**: This dish is linked to Andalusia's bullfighting tradition. In the past, the tail of the bull would be given to the matador as a prize, and the meat would be stewed and shared.
- **Custom**: Rabo de Toro is often served in Seville and Córdoba, especially during the bullfighting season.

9. Migas

- **What it is**: A rustic dish made from breadcrumbs fried with garlic, olive oil, and often chorizo or pork belly, with peppers or grapes added for flavor.
- **History**: Originating as a shepherd's meal, **migas** were a way to use up stale bread in Andalusia's rural areas.
- **Custom**: Still enjoyed in many parts of Andalusia, particularly during winter, **migas** are typically served in family-style gatherings or at local festivals.

10. Sardinada

- **What it is**: A local custom along the Andalusian coast, **sardinadas** are communal barbecues featuring freshly caught sardines grilled over open flames.
- **History**: This tradition comes from Andalusia's long-standing fishing heritage and the region's abundant access to fresh seafood.
- **Custom**: Sardinadas are common in seaside towns during summer and are usually accompanied by local wine or beer.

Andalusia's festivals, such as Holy Week (Semana Santa), the Feria de Abril, and the Romería del Rocío, are times when traditional food and customs shine. Tapas culture, the art of sherry-making, and celebrations of music and dance demonstrate the region's unique blend of historical and modern influences. These traditions have not only become a symbol of Andalusian identity but also a major draw for visitors seeking to experience authentic Spanish culture.

Valencian

Valencia has a deep and complex history, shaped by various conquerors and civilizations. Founded by the Romans in 138 BC as **Valentia**, the city was later conquered by the Visigoths and subsequently by the Moors in the 8th century. The Moors' rule had a profound impact on agriculture, architecture, and culture, especially with the introduction of rice, irrigation systems, and spices that are still part of Valencian cuisine today.

In 1238, King James I of Aragon reconquered Valencia, incorporating it into the Kingdom of Aragon. This marked the beginning of Valencia's Golden Age, during which it flourished as a cultural and economic center. During the 15th century, the silk trade brought prosperity, leading to the construction of many of the city's iconic buildings, like **La Lonja**.

Today, Valencia remains a vibrant city with a strong sense of identity, blending its rich past with modernity. Its unique cuisine and traditions are a reflection of its diverse heritage and the lasting influence of the civilizations that once ruled it. What to not miss

1. Cueva de San José (La Vall d'Uixó)

- **Why Visit:** The longest navigable underground river in Europe, this cave offers boat tours with stunning stalactites.
- **Money-Saving Tip:** Visit during off-peak times for discounted entrance fees.

2. Museu de la Pilota (Genovés)

- **Why Visit:** This museum celebrates the traditional Valencian handball game, a unique part of local culture.
- **Money-Saving Tip:** Look for group discounts or combo tickets with nearby attractions.

3. Jardín del Papagayo (Benicarló)

- **Why Visit:** A tropical garden and bird sanctuary where you can interact with exotic birds.
- **Money-Saving Tip:** Book tickets online for a small discount.

4. La Lonja de la Seda (Valencia)

- **Why Visit:** A UNESCO World Heritage Site, this Gothic-style building once housed Valencia's silk market.
- **Money-Saving Tip:** Free entry on Sundays and holidays.

5. Palacio del Marqués de Dos Aguas (Valencia)

- **Why Visit:** Known for its elaborate Rococo-style façade, this palace also houses the National Museum of Ceramics.
- **Money-Saving Tip:** Entry is free on Saturdays from 4 p.m. and all day on Sundays.

6. Museo del Juguete (Ibi)

- **Why Visit:** A nostalgic trip through Spain's toy-making history with unique vintage toys on display.
- **Money-Saving Tip:** Discounts for students and seniors.

7. Ruta de los Molinos (Alborache)

- **Why Visit:** A scenic hiking route that showcases old water mills along the river.
- **Money-Saving Tip:** Parking is free, and you can bring your own snacks to avoid restaurant prices.

8. Museo del Aceite (Segorbe)

- **Why Visit:** Learn about olive oil production in this small museum dedicated to one of Spain's most beloved products.
- **Money-Saving Tip:** Entry is cheaper if combined with a tour of Segorbe Castle.

9. Cuevas de Canelobre (Busot)

- **Why Visit:** A massive cave with fascinating rock formations and stunning acoustics often used for concerts.
- **Money-Saving Tip:** Buy tickets as part of a group to get a reduced price.

10. Museo de la Muñeca (Onil)

- **Why Visit:** Explore the world of doll-making, a traditional industry in this small town.
- **Money-Saving Tip:** Visit during local festivals when admission may be reduced.

11. Castillo de Xàtiva (Xàtiva)

- **Why Visit:** A fortress with incredible views and historical significance, this castle offers a glimpse into Valencia's medieval past.
- **Money-Saving Tip:** Free entry on the first Sunday of each month.

12. Palau Ducal dels Borja (Gandia)

- **Why Visit:** The majestic residence of the Borja family, known for its lavish architecture and rich history.
- **Money-Saving Tip:** Take advantage of free guided tours on select days.

13. La Albufera Natural Park (Valencia)

- **Why Visit:** A vast freshwater lagoon, perfect for bird-watching and boat rides through the wetlands.
- **Money-Saving Tip:** Pack your own lunch and opt for public transport to reach the park.

14. Museo Fallero (Valencia)

- **Why Visit:** This museum showcases the colorful figures from Valencia's famous Fallas festival.
- **Money-Saving Tip:** Free entry on Sundays.

15. Parque Natural de las Hoces del Cabriel (Requena)

- **Why Visit:** Ideal for outdoor enthusiasts, offering hiking, kayaking, and wildlife viewing.
- **Money-Saving Tip:** Entry to the park is free, but bring your own gear for water activities to avoid rental fees.

16. Barranco de la Hoz (Chelva)

- **Why Visit:** A hidden canyon with hiking trails, perfect for a peaceful escape into nature.
- **Money-Saving Tip:** Access is free, but bring water and snacks to avoid buying them at local cafés.

17. Museo de la Imprenta (El Puig)

- **Why Visit:** One of the largest printing museums in Europe, showcasing the evolution of the press.
- **Money-Saving Tip:** Free entry on the first Sunday of every month.

18. Villa Romana de l'Albir (Alfaz del Pi)

- **Why Visit:** A beautifully preserved Roman villa with mosaics and ancient artifacts.
- **Money-Saving Tip:** Reduced prices for students and seniors.

19. Cuevas de la Villa (Requena)

- **Why Visit:** Explore these historical caves beneath the city of Requena, which were used for storage and as hiding places during wars.
- **Money-Saving Tip:** Combine your visit with a wine-tasting tour for a package deal.

20. Aquopolis Cullera (Cullera)

- **Why Visit:** A lesser-known water park that's perfect for a family day out, with fewer crowds than Valencia's bigger parks.
- **Money-Saving Tip:** Get discounted tickets by purchasing online in advance.

Special Foods in Valencia:

1. Paella Valenciana

- **Description:** Arguably the most famous dish from the region, Paella Valenciana is a saffron-infused rice dish traditionally made with rabbit, chicken, and local beans such as garrofó. Paella originated in the fertile area around Albufera, a freshwater lagoon where rice has been grown since Moorish times.
- **History:** The Moors introduced rice cultivation to Valencia in the 8th century, and over time, it became a staple food in the region. The name "paella" comes from the Latin word "patella," meaning pan, which reflects the special wide, shallow pan in which it's cooked.

2. Fideuà

- **Description:** Similar to paella but made with short, thin noodles instead of rice, fideuà is a seafood dish that includes squid, shrimp, and fish. It is typically flavored with saffron and garlic.
- **History:** Fideuà was invented by fishermen in the town of Gandia (south of Valencia) who wanted to prepare a dish similar to paella but with noodles. Legend has it that it was created when a cook ran out of rice while at sea and substituted pasta instead.

3. Horchata de Chufa

- **Description:** A refreshing drink made from ground tiger nuts (chufa), water, and sugar, horchata is a popular summer beverage in Valencia.
- **History:** Tiger nuts were introduced to the region by the Moors in the 8th century. Horchata has long been a part of Valencian cuisine and is often enjoyed with **fartons**, soft, sugar-coated pastries meant for dipping.

4. Esgarraet

- o **Description:** A cold salad made from roasted red peppers, salted cod (bacalao), and olive oil, typically served as a tapa.
- o **History:** Valencia's proximity to the Mediterranean makes fish and seafood staples of the local diet. Salted cod became popular during the Middle Ages when fish needed to be preserved for long periods.

5. **All i Pebre**

- o **Description:** A traditional dish made with eel, potatoes, garlic, and paprika (pebre), usually cooked in a clay pot. It's a classic dish from the Albufera region.
- o **History:** All i Pebre originated around Albufera, where eels are abundant in the wetlands. The dish dates back to the Moorish period when the Arab population introduced the art of cooking with local spices.

6. **Bunyols**

- o **Description:** Deep-fried doughnuts made with pumpkin or potatoes, often enjoyed with chocolate during festivals.
- o **History:** Bunyols are a Valencian tradition, especially during the **Las Fallas** festival, where they are eaten in celebration of the city's patron saints.

7. **Turrón de Jijona**

- o **Description:** A type of nougat made from almonds, honey, and sugar, originating from the town of Jijona.
- o **History:** Turrón has a long history, dating back to the Arab influence in the region. It's traditionally enjoyed during Christmas, though it's available year-round.

8. **Arroz al Horno**

- o **Description:** Baked rice with sausage, black pudding, chickpeas, and potatoes, cooked in a clay dish.
- o **History:** This dish evolved as a way to use leftovers from stews, particularly during times of scarcity in rural Valencia.

9. **Cocas**

- o **Description:** Similar to a flatbread or pizza, cocas are topped with various ingredients like tomato, onion, sardines, and olives.
- o **History:** The tradition of making cocas dates back to Roman times when bread was a staple, and it has evolved over centuries in Valencia to include local ingredients.

Customs in Valencia:

1. **Las Fallas (Falles)**

- o **Description:** One of Spain's most famous festivals, Las Fallas takes place in March to honor Saint Joseph, the patron saint of carpenters. The festival includes the creation and burning of large, intricate satirical sculptures (ninots) made of wood, papier-mâché, and other materials.
- o **Custom:** The festival culminates in the **Cremà** (burning) of these sculptures, accompanied by fireworks, parades, and traditional music.
- o **History:** The origins of Las Fallas date back to the Middle Ages, when carpenters would burn pieces of wood in celebration of the end of winter and in honor of their patron saint.

2. **La Tomatina (Buñol)**

- o **Description:** Held on the last Wednesday of August in the town of Buñol, this is a massive tomato fight, where thousands of people throw overripe tomatoes at each other.
- o **Custom:** Participants throw tomatoes during the one-hour event and then clean off in nearby rivers or showers set up for the occasion.
- o **History:** La Tomatina began in 1945 after a local altercation led to a playful food fight that became an annual event. It was banned for several years during Franco's dictatorship but returned after protests from locals.

3. Noche de San Juan

- o **Description:** Celebrated on the night of June 23rd, Noche de San Juan is a festival marking the summer solstice. People gather on beaches to build bonfires, set off fireworks, and partake in water rituals.
- o **Custom:** One of the main customs involves jumping over a bonfire or running into the sea at midnight, believed to cleanse and bring good fortune.
- o **History:** The tradition has roots in pagan solstice celebrations, which were later Christianized. It remains a deeply ingrained custom in the Valencian region.

4. The Offering of Flowers (La Ofrenda)

- o **Description:** A central part of the Las Fallas festival, this is a religious procession where women in traditional dress carry flowers to create an enormous floral display in honor of the Virgin Mary.
- o **Custom:** The flowers form a giant mantle for the statue of the Virgin, placed in the Plaza de la Virgen.
- o **History:** The tradition of La Ofrenda dates back to the mid-20th century, adding a deeply spiritual element to the otherwise raucous and celebratory Fallas.

5. Moros y Cristianos (Moors and Christians)

- o **Description:** This festival reenacts the battles between Moors and Christians, commemorating the Christian reconquest of the Iberian Peninsula from the Moors.
- o **Custom:** The event includes parades, mock battles, and grand costumes representing both Moors and Christians.
- o **History:** The festival began after the Reconquista in the 15th century and is celebrated in various parts of Valencia, especially in towns like Alcoy.

6. Els Enfarinats (Ibi)

- o **Description:** A lesser-known but fun custom, Els Enfarinats is a flour and egg battle that takes place in Ibi during the Day of the Innocents (December 28th).
- o **Custom:** Participants dressed as soldiers take control of the town in a mock coup, and anyone who challenges them is hit with flour and eggs.
- o **History:** This quirky tradition dates back over 200 years and remains a unique part of the region's holiday customs.

Balearic Islands

The Balearic Islands, including popular destinations such as Mallorca, Ibiza, and Menorca, are renowned for their stunning beaches, vibrant nightlife, and rich cultural heritage. While these islands are often associated with luxury travel, it's possible to experience their beauty and charm on a budget. Here's a guide to enjoying the best of the Balearic Islands without breaking the bank.

Tips:

- **Explore Off-Season:** Visit the Balearic Islands during the shoulder seasons (spring and autumn) to enjoy pleasant weather, fewer crowds, and lower prices on accommodation and activities.
- **Beach Picnics:** Pack your own snacks and beverages and enjoy a day at the beach without spending money on expensive beach bars and restaurants.
- **Free Attractions:** Take advantage of free attractions such as historic sites, scenic viewpoints, and natural parks, which offer a glimpse into the islands' culture and beauty without any cost.
- **Local Markets:** Visit local markets to sample fresh produce, local delicacies, and handmade crafts while experiencing the authentic island culture.
- **Budget-Friendly Activities:** Look for budget-friendly activities such as hiking, cycling, snorkeling, and exploring local villages to experience the islands' natural beauty and cultural heritage without spending a fortune.

Not to miss

1. Ses Salines Natural Park, Ibiza

- **Why Visit**: Discover one of the island's most beautiful coastal landscapes with salt flats, sandy beaches, and birdwatching opportunities.
- **Money-Saving Tip**: Visit during shoulder season for lower entrance fees and fewer crowds.

2. Cabrera Archipelago National Park, Mallorca

- **Why Visit**: This secluded island group offers pristine nature, marine wildlife, and historic ruins.
- **Money-Saving Tip**: Book a combined ferry and park entrance ticket to save on transport costs.

3. Es Baluard Museum of Contemporary Art, Mallorca

- **Why Visit**: An extensive collection of contemporary Balearic, Spanish, and international art in a beautifully restored military fortress.
- **Money-Saving Tip**: Entry is free on Fridays between 3 and 6 pm.

4. Cap de Barbaria Lighthouse, Formentera

- **Why Visit**: Stunning sunset views from the island's southernmost point.

- **Money-Saving Tip**: Rent a bicycle to explore the area instead of using paid guided tours.

5. S'Albufera Natural Park, Mallorca

- **Why Visit**: A haven for birdwatchers, with wetlands and diverse wildlife.
- **Money-Saving Tip**: Visit outside peak hours when parking is cheaper or free.

6. La Mola Lighthouse, Formentera

- **Why Visit**: Panoramic views and a small museum detailing the island's maritime history.
- **Money-Saving Tip**: Entry is cheaper if combined with visits to other lighthouses.

7. Bellver Castle, Mallorca

- **Why Visit**: A unique circular Gothic castle with views of Palma and a fascinating museum.
- **Money-Saving Tip**: Entry is free on Sundays, making it an ideal weekend visit.

8. Drach Caves, Mallorca

- **Why Visit**: Explore an underground world of stalactites and stalagmites with a spectacular underground lake.
- **Money-Saving Tip**: Book tickets online for discounts and avoid same-day pricing.

9. Menorca Horseback Riding Tours, Menorca

- **Why Visit**: Ride along unspoiled beaches and scenic routes, ideal for equestrians of all skill levels.
- **Money-Saving Tip**: Opt for group tours instead of private ones to reduce the cost.

10. Monestir de Miramar, Mallorca

- **Why Visit**: A historical monastery offering beautiful views and peaceful surroundings.
- **Money-Saving Tip**: Buy a multi-site pass for Miramar and other local monasteries to save on individual entrance fees.

11. San Carlos Hippy Market, Ibiza

- **Why Visit**: A vibrant market full of local crafts, food, and music.
- **Money-Saving Tip**: Go near closing time for discounts on goods, as vendors reduce prices at the end of the day.

12. Torre de Canyamel, Mallorca

- **Why Visit**: A medieval defense tower with exhibitions and breathtaking views from the top.
- **Money-Saving Tip**: Combine with nearby attractions like the Canyamel caves for a discounted entry fee.

13. Far de Favàritx Lighthouse, Menorca

- **Why Visit**: Dramatic coastline views and photography opportunities.
- **Money-Saving Tip**: No entry fee for the exterior, and parking is cheaper if you arrive early in the day.

14. Bodegas Macià Batle Winery, Mallorca

- **Why Visit**: Learn about local wine production and enjoy tastings.
- **Money-Saving Tip**: Book a group wine tasting to save on individual rates.

15. Cueva de Can Marçà, Ibiza

- **Why Visit**: A scenic cave experience with a light and sound show.
- **Money-Saving Tip**: Check online for family discounts or combined tickets with other Ibiza attractions.

16. Torre des Molar, Ibiza

- **Why Visit**: A defense tower offering insight into the island's history and fantastic ocean views.
- **Money-Saving Tip**: Skip the guided tour and explore on your own to save money.

17. Santuari de Cura, Mallorca

- **Why Visit**: A peaceful mountaintop monastery with panoramic views and a serene atmosphere.
- **Money-Saving Tip**: Enjoy free entry during religious services or festivals.

18. Museu Etnogràfic, Formentera

- **Why Visit**: Delve into the island's culture and history through traditional exhibits.
- **Money-Saving Tip**: Reduced entry for students and seniors, and free entrance on certain local holidays.

19. Binibeca Vell, Menorca

- **Why Visit**: A charming whitewashed fishing village perfect for a quiet stroll and local photography.
- **Money-Saving Tip**: Visit early morning or evening to avoid parking fees.

20. Finca Can Planes, Mallorca

- **Why Visit**: An open-air museum showcasing traditional Mallorcan life, with local agriculture and crafts.
- **Money-Saving Tip**: Book as part of a group tour to get a discount on the admission price.

Canary Islands

The Canary Islands, located off the northwest coast of Africa, are a paradise for sun-seekers, outdoor enthusiasts, and culture lovers. With their stunning beaches, volcanic landscapes, and year-round sunshine, the Canary Islands offer plenty of opportunities for luxury experiences on a budget. Here's a guide to enjoying the best of the Canary Islands without breaking the bank.

Insider Tips:

- **Off-Season Travel:** Visit the Canary Islands during the shoulder seasons (spring and autumn) to enjoy lower prices on accommodation and flights, as well as fewer crowds at popular attractions.
- **Local Markets:** Explore local markets such as Mercado de la Villa de Teguise in Lanzarote or Mercado de Vegueta in Gran Canaria to sample fresh produce, local delicacies, and handmade crafts at affordable prices.
- **Outdoor Adventures:** Take advantage of the Canary Islands' natural beauty by hiking, cycling, or snorkeling, with many outdoor activities available for free or at low cost.
- **Beach Days:** Spend your days relaxing on the islands' beautiful beaches, such as Playa de las Canteras in Gran Canaria or Playa de las Teresitas in Tenerife, where you can enjoy the sun and sea without spending money on expensive activities.
- **Free Attractions:** Visit free attractions like historic sites, botanical gardens, and scenic viewpoints, such as Teide National Park in Tenerife or Garajonay National Park in La Gomera, for budget-friendly experiences.

Here's a guide to **20 lesser-known paid attractions** in the Canary Islands, along with **money-saving tips** and reasons to visit each location:

1. Cueva del Viento, Tenerife

- **Why Visit**: Europe's longest lava tube, with fascinating geological formations.
- **Money-Saving Tip**: Book online for discounts and avoid peak times for cheaper rates.

2. Palmetum of Santa Cruz, Tenerife

- **Why Visit**: A botanical garden with a vast collection of palm species from around the world.
- **Money-Saving Tip**: Discounts for students, seniors, and families.

3. César Manrique House Museum, Lanzarote

- **Why Visit**: Insight into the life of the famed Canarian artist, with unique architectural design blending art and nature.
- **Money-Saving Tip**: Combine with other Manrique attractions for bundled ticket deals.

4. Jameos del Agua, Lanzarote

- **Why Visit**: An extraordinary volcanic cave system transformed by César Manrique into a cultural center.
- **Money-Saving Tip**: Purchase the island's art, culture, and tourism pass for multiple site access.

5. Cueva de los Verdes, Lanzarote

- **Why Visit**: A stunning lava cave with underground passages and striking lighting effects.
- **Money-Saving Tip**: Visit in combination with other nearby attractions like Jameos del Agua.

6. Las Montañas del Fuego (Timanfaya National Park), Lanzarote

- **Why Visit**: Explore volcanic landscapes and geothermal activities.
- **Money-Saving Tip**: Take advantage of combo tickets to visit other national park sites.

7. Aloe Vera Museum, Fuerteventura

- **Why Visit**: Learn about the history and cultivation of aloe vera, famous for its healing properties.
- **Money-Saving Tip**: Look for discounted entry with museum passes.

8. Pirámides de Güímar, Tenerife

- **Why Visit**: Explore these mysterious step pyramids and ethnographic park.
- **Money-Saving Tip**: Family and group discounts available, or visit during off-peak times for lower prices.

9. Casa de los Coroneles, Fuerteventura

- **Why Visit**: A historic building reflecting the military history of the island.
- **Money-Saving Tip**: Free on certain holidays and reduced prices for specific age groups.

10. La Restinga Diving Center, El Hierro

- **Why Visit**: Explore one of the world's best diving spots with crystal-clear waters and volcanic reefs.
- **Money-Saving Tip**: Book early or off-season for lower rates on diving tours.

11. Museo Canario, Gran Canaria

- **Why Visit**: Offers insight into the history and culture of the indigenous Guanches.
- **Money-Saving Tip**: Combine with other museums in Las Palmas for a museum pass.

12. La Gomera Garajonay National Park

- **Why Visit**: Ancient laurel forests and hiking trails through lush landscapes.
- **Money-Saving Tip**: Entry is free, but guided tours may have fees—book online for discounts.

13. Siam Park, Tenerife

- **Why Visit**: One of the world's largest and most impressive waterparks.
- **Money-Saving Tip**: Buy multi-day or group tickets for discounts.

14. Cueva Pintada Museum and Archaeological Park, Gran Canaria

- **Why Visit**: Fascinating archaeological site showcasing cave paintings and ancient ruins.

- **Money-Saving Tip**: Free entry on specific days or discounted rates for families and students.

15. Lanzarote Aquarium, Lanzarote

- **Why Visit**: Features a large collection of marine life, including species native to the Canary Islands.
- **Money-Saving Tip**: Look for package deals that include other nearby attractions.

16. Teide Cable Car, Tenerife

- **Why Visit**: Offers breathtaking views from the top of Spain's highest mountain, Mount Teide.
- **Money-Saving Tip**: Book in advance for lower rates and combine with nearby Teide National Park tours.

17. Auditorio de Tenerife, Tenerife

- **Why Visit**: A striking modern architectural masterpiece, home to concerts and cultural events.
- **Money-Saving Tip**: Book online and during off-peak seasons for better rates on performances.

18. Bodega Los Berrazales, Gran Canaria

- **Why Visit**: A winery offering tours and tastings in a stunning volcanic valley.
- **Money-Saving Tip**: Opt for small group tours for cheaper rates and combine with nearby attractions.

19. Loro Parque, Tenerife

- **Why Visit**: A highly acclaimed zoo with a focus on animal conservation and a world-class parrot collection.
- **Money-Saving Tip**: Multi-park passes available with Siam Park for combined savings.

20. Mirador del Río, Lanzarote

- **Why Visit**: A spectacular viewpoint designed by César Manrique, offering panoramic views over La Graciosa island.
- **Money-Saving Tip**: Combine with other Manrique-designed attractions for discounted passes.

Special Foods of the Canary Islands

Canarian cuisine is known for its simplicity, freshness, and use of local ingredients. Here are some standout dishes and drinks:

1. Papas Arrugadas (Wrinkled Potatoes)

- **Description**: Small potatoes boiled in heavily salted water until their skins wrinkle, served with traditional sauces called **mojos**.
- **Why Special**: Papas arrugadas are a staple of Canarian cuisine. The potatoes are grown in the rich volcanic soil of the islands, giving them a distinct flavor.
- **Mojo Picon (Red Sauce)**: A spicy sauce made from red peppers, garlic, olive oil, and vinegar.
- **Mojo Verde (Green Sauce)**: A milder sauce made with green herbs, garlic, and olive oil.

2. Gofio

- **Description**: A type of flour made from roasted grains (mainly wheat or maize). Gofio is an ancient food that dates back to the Guanche people.
- **How it's Used**: Gofio is incredibly versatile. It's used in soups, desserts, and as a side dish mixed with water or milk to form a dough. Some Canarians even add it to coffee or use it to thicken stews.
- **Cultural Significance**: It was a staple food of the Guanche and is still an important part of Canarian identity.

3. Ropa Vieja

- **Description**: A stew made from leftover meats (usually beef, pork, or chicken) mixed with chickpeas, vegetables, and spices.
- **Why Special**: The dish reflects the ingenuity of Canarian cuisine, where nothing goes to waste, and traditional flavors are enhanced with time.

4. Sancocho Canario

- **Description**: A hearty stew made with salted fish (usually wreckfish or cherne), potatoes, and sweet potatoes, served with **mojo verde**.
- **Why Special**: This dish reflects the islands' connection to the sea and their reliance on simple, nourishing ingredients.

5. Bienmesabe

- **Description**: A dessert made from ground almonds, honey, sugar, and eggs.
- **Why Special**: Its name means "it tastes good to me," and it's one of the Canary Islands' most famous sweets, often served with ice cream or cake.

6. Queso de Cabra (Goat Cheese)

- **Description**: Canary Islands' goat cheese is known for its distinctive flavor, often smoked or mixed with spices like paprika.
- **Why Special**: The islands have a strong tradition of goat farming, and their cheeses are award-winning, particularly the **Majorero cheese** from Fuerteventura.

7. Almogrote

- **Description**: A spread made from aged goat cheese, olive oil, garlic, and peppers.
- **Why Special**: Almogrote is a specialty from La Gomera and is often served with bread or crackers as a tapa.

8. Miel de Palma (Palm Honey)

- **Description**: A sweet syrup made from the sap of palm trees, particularly from the island of La Gomera.
- **Why Special**: Used as a sweetener and in traditional desserts, palm honey is a unique and important product of the Canary Islands.

9. Carajacas

- **Description**: Thinly sliced liver marinated in a sauce made from vinegar, garlic, paprika, and other spices, then grilled or fried.
- **Why Special**: Carajacas is a hearty and flavorful dish often served as a tapa with bread.

10. Tropical Fruits

- **Description**: The Canary Islands' warm climate makes them ideal for growing exotic fruits like bananas, papayas, mangoes, and avocados.

- **Why Special**: Canarian bananas are particularly famous, and the islands are one of the few places in Europe where tropical fruits are grown.

Canary Islands' Customs and Traditions

1. Carnival

- **What It Is**: The Carnival in Santa Cruz de Tenerife and Las Palmas de Gran Canaria is one of the biggest and most colorful in the world, second only to Rio de Janeiro. It includes parades, floats, music, and elaborate costumes.
- **When**: Held in February, it's a celebration that takes over the entire islands with vibrant parties and shows.

2. Bajada de la Virgen de las Nieves, La Palma

- **What It Is**: A religious festival celebrated every five years where the statue of the Virgin of the Snows is paraded through the streets of Santa Cruz de La Palma. The event includes traditional music, dances, and theatrical performances.
- **Why Special**: It reflects the deep Catholic roots and the importance of religious festivals on the islands.

3. Romerías

- **What It Is**: Religious pilgrimages held throughout the year across the islands, where locals dress in traditional Canarian attire and carry offerings to the saints. The processions are followed by feasts and dancing.
- **Why Special**: These events bring together communities and highlight the strong agricultural traditions of the islands.

4. Belt Wrestling (Lucha Canaria)

- **What It Is**: A traditional Canarian sport where two competitors try to unbalance each other using belts and leg sweeps.
- **Why Special**: Lucha Canaria has its roots in the ancient Guanche wrestling techniques and remains a popular sport on the islands.

5. Traditional Music and Dance

- **What It Is**: Canarian folk music, called **Isa**, is accompanied by traditional instruments like the **timple** (a small guitar). Dances such as **Folia** and **Salto del Pastor** are integral to local festivals and celebrations.
- **Why Special**: These cultural expressions reflect the islands' deep-rooted heritage and are often performed during fiestas and religious celebrations.

Basque Country

The Basque Country, nestled in northern Spain and southern France, is known for its rich cultural heritage, stunning landscapes, and world-renowned cuisine. While the region offers plenty of luxury experiences, it's also possible to explore the Basque Country on a budget without compromising on quality. Here's a guide to enjoying the best of the Basque Country without breaking the bank.

Insider Tips:

- **Pintxos Crawls:** Explore the Basque Country's culinary scene by indulging in pintxos crawls, where you can sample a variety of small bites at local bars for a fraction of the cost of a sit-down meal.
- **Free Attractions:** Take advantage of free attractions such as historic neighborhoods, scenic viewpoints, and cultural events, which offer a glimpse into the Basque Country's rich heritage without any cost.
- **Local Markets:** Visit local markets like La Bretxa Market in San Sebastian or Mercado de la Ribera in Bilbao to sample fresh produce, artisanal cheeses, and regional specialties at affordable prices.
- **Outdoor Adventures:** Explore the Basque Country's natural beauty by hiking in the mountains, surfing along the coast, or cycling through picturesque countryside, with many outdoor activities available for free or at low cost.
- **Budget-Friendly Accommodation:** Look for budget-friendly accommodation options such as guesthouses, hostels, and apartment rentals, which offer comfortable lodging at a fraction of the cost of luxury hotels.

Top 20 Attractions in the Basque Country with Money-Saving Tips:

- **Guggenheim Museum, Bilbao:**
    - Money-Saving Tip: Admire the iconic architecture of the Guggenheim Museum from the outside and explore the surrounding area, including the nearby Zubizuri Bridge and La Salve Bridge, for free. Starting Price: €13 (admission).
- **Old Town, San Sebastian:**
    - Money-Saving Tip: Take a self-guided walking tour of San Sebastian's Old Town to discover its historic architecture, lively plazas, and charming streets for free. Free access.
- **La Concha Beach, San Sebastian:**
    - Money-Saving Tip: Spend a day at La Concha Beach and bring your own towels and beach gear to save money on rentals. Free access.
- **San Telmo Museum, San Sebastian:**
    - Money-Saving Tip: Visit the San Telmo Museum during free admission days or discounted evenings to explore its collections of Basque art and history. Starting Price: €6.
- **Monte Urgull, San Sebastian:**

- Money-Saving Tip: Hike to the top of Monte Urgull for panoramic views of San Sebastian and its coastline at no cost. Free access.
- **Old Town, Bilbao:**
  - Money-Saving Tip: Explore Bilbao's Old Town, known as Casco Viejo, on foot to admire its historic architecture, narrow streets, and bustling markets for free. Free access.
- **Arriaga Theater, Bilbao:**
  - Money-Saving Tip: Attend a free performance or take a guided tour of the Arriaga Theater to learn about its history and architecture. Free access to certain areas.
- **Vizcaya Bridge, Bilbao:**
  - Money-Saving Tip: Cross the UNESCO-listed Vizcaya Bridge, the world's oldest transporter bridge, on foot for a budget-friendly experience. Starting Price: €8 (round trip).
- **Urdaibai Biosphere Reserve, Bermeo:**
  - Money-Saving Tip: Explore Urdaibai Biosphere Reserve's diverse ecosystems and wildlife by hiking, birdwatching, or kayaking for a budget-friendly outdoor adventure. Free access.
- **Santa Maria Cathedral, Vitoria-Gasteiz:**
  - Money-Saving Tip: Visit Santa Maria Cathedral, a Gothic masterpiece, during free admission days or discounted hours to explore its interior and crypt. Starting Price: €6.
- **Chillida-Leku Museum, Hernani:**
  - Money-Saving Tip: Visit the Chillida-Leku Museum during off-peak hours or on free admission days to discover its collection of sculptures and artworks. Starting Price: €12.
- **Txindoki Mountain, Oñati:**
  - Money-Saving Tip: Hike to the summit of Txindoki Mountain for panoramic views of the Basque countryside and surrounding mountains. Free access.
- **Old Port, Getxo:**
  - Money-Saving Tip: Take a leisurely stroll along Getxo's Old Port and admire its historic lighthouse, fishing boats, and waterfront promenade for free. Free access.
- **Albia Gardens, Bilbao:**
  - Money-Saving Tip: Relax in Albia Gardens, a tranquil oasis in the heart of Bilbao, and enjoy its lush greenery and fountains for free. Free access.
- **Akelarre, San Sebastian:**
  - Money-Saving Tip: Dine at Akelarre, a Michelin-starred restaurant, for lunch or during off-peak hours to enjoy a gourmet meal at a reduced price. Starting Price: €180 (lunch menu).
- **San Juan de Gaztelugatxe, Bermeo:**
  - Money-Saving Tip: Visit San Juan de Gaztelugatxe, a scenic island with a medieval hermitage, and explore its winding staircase and coastal views for free. Free access.
- **Cider Houses, Astigarraga:**
  - Money-Saving Tip: Experience a traditional Basque cider house dinner, known as "txotx," during the cider season (January to April) for a budget-friendly culinary adventure. Starting Price: €30-€40.
- **Bakio Beach, Bakio:**
  - Money-Saving Tip: Spend a day at Bakio Beach and bring your own picnic to enjoy a seaside lunch with views of the Basque coastline. Free access.

- **Oma Forest, Kortezubi:**
  - Money-Saving Tip: Hike through Oma Forest, known for its colorful painted trees by artist Agustín Ibarrola, for a unique outdoor experience at no cost. Free access.
- **Atxondo Valley, Atxondo:**
  - Money-Saving Tip: Explore Atxondo Valley's lush landscapes and charming villages on foot or by bike for a budget-friendly day trip from Bilbao. Free access.

Galicia

Galicia, located in the northwest corner of Spain, is renowned for its rugged coastline, lush landscapes, and rich cultural heritage. While the region offers plenty of opportunities for luxury travel, it's also possible to experience the beauty and charm of Galicia on a budget. Here's a guide to enjoying the best of Galicia without breaking the bank.

Tips:

- **Coastal Walks:** Explore Galicia's stunning coastline on foot by hiking along the Camino de Santiago coastal routes or walking trails such as the Ruta da Pedra e da Auga for free or at low cost.
- **Cultural Festivals:** Attend local festivals and events, such as the Rías Baixas Wine Festival or the Festival of St. James in Santiago de Compostela, to experience Galician culture and traditions without spending a lot of money.
- **Tapas Culture:** Embrace the Galician tapas culture by hopping from bar to bar and sampling a variety of small plates, known as "raciones," at affordable prices.
- **Natural Parks:** Visit Galicia's natural parks, such as Fragas do Eume or the Atlantic Islands National Park, for outdoor adventures such as hiking, birdwatching, and kayaking, with many activities available for free or at low cost.
- **Budget-Friendly Accommodation:** Look for budget-friendly accommodation options such as hostels, guesthouses, and rural cottages, which offer comfortable lodging at a fraction of the cost of luxury hotels.

Top 20 Attractions in Galicia with Money-Saving Tips:

- **Santiago de Compostela Cathedral:**
    - Money-Saving Tip: Attend the pilgrim's mass at Santiago de Compostela Cathedral for a spiritual experience and to view the cathedral's stunning interior without paying for a guided tour. Free access.
- **Cíes Islands:**
    - Money-Saving Tip: Take a ferry to the Cíes Islands and spend the day hiking, sunbathing, and swimming at the pristine beaches of Rodas and Figueiras for a budget-friendly island getaway. Starting Price: €18 (ferry).
- **Tower of Hercules, A Coruña:**
    - Money-Saving Tip: Climb the Tower of Hercules, a UNESCO World Heritage Site, for panoramic views of A Coruña and its coastline at a nominal fee. Starting Price: €3.
- **Ourense Thermal Baths:**
    - Money-Saving Tip: Relax in the natural thermal baths of Ourense, such as As Burgas or Outariz, for a rejuvenating experience at no cost. Free access.
- **Praia das Catedrais, Ribadeo:**
    - Money-Saving Tip: Visit Praia das Catedrais, a natural wonder with impressive rock formations and sea caves, during low tide for free access to the beach. Free access.
- **Monte Santa Tecla, A Guarda:**

- Money-Saving Tip: Hike to the top of Monte Santa Tecla for panoramic views of the Minho River estuary and the Atlantic Ocean at no cost. Free access.
- **Ribeira Sacra Vineyards:**
  - Money-Saving Tip: Take a self-guided tour of the Ribeira Sacra vineyards, known for their steep terraces and river views, and sample local wines at affordable prices. Free access to viewpoints.
- **Pontevedra Old Town:**
  - Money-Saving Tip: Explore Pontevedra's charming Old Town, with its cobblestone streets and historic squares, on foot for free and soak up the atmosphere. Free access.
- **Islas Cíes National Park:**
  - Money-Saving Tip: Spend the day exploring Islas Cíes National Park, a protected marine reserve, and bring your own picnic to enjoy a budget-friendly lunch on the island. Starting Price: €18 (ferry).
- **Pazo de Oca, A Estrada:**
  - Money-Saving Tip: Visit Pazo de Oca, known as the "Galician Versailles," during guided tours to explore its gardens and historic architecture at a nominal fee. Starting Price: €5.
- **Pontevedra Pilgrim's Route:**
  - Money-Saving Tip: Walk a section of the Pontevedra Pilgrim's Route, part of the Camino de Santiago, for a scenic hike through rural Galicia at no cost. Free access.
- **As Catedrais Beach, Ribadeo:**
  - Money-Saving Tip: Explore As Catedrais Beach at low tide to admire its natural arches and rock formations for free. Free access.
- **Castro de Baroña, Porto do Son:**
  - Money-Saving Tip: Visit Castro de Baroña, a Celtic hillfort overlooking the Atlantic Ocean, and explore its ruins and coastal views for free. Free access.
- **Muros Fishing Village:**
  - Money-Saving Tip: Wander through Muros, a picturesque fishing village with colorful houses and a lively waterfront, for free and enjoy its authentic atmosphere. Free access.
- **Fragas do Eume Natural Park:**
  - Money-Saving Tip: Explore Fragas do Eume Natural Park on foot or by bike to discover its ancient forests and riverside trails for free. Free access.
- **Carnota Beach, Carnota:**
  - Money-Saving Tip: Spend a day at Carnota Beach, one of Galicia's longest and most pristine beaches, and bring your own snacks and drinks to save money. Free access.
- **Cabo Ortegal Lighthouse, Cariño:**
  - Money-Saving Tip: Visit Cabo Ortegal Lighthouse, perched on a rugged cliff overlooking the Atlantic Ocean, for stunning coastal views at no cost. Free access.
- **Baroña Beach, Porto do Son:**
  - Money-Saving Tip: Relax at Baroña Beach, a secluded cove with golden sands and clear waters, and enjoy a budget-friendly day of sunbathing and swimming. Free access.
- **San Andrés de Teixido, Cedeira:**

- • Money-Saving Tip: Visit San Andrés de Teixido, a charming coastal village with a famous pilgrimage site, and explore its historic church and scenic viewpoints for free. Free access.
- • **Cabo Home Lighthouse, Cangas:**
  - • Money-Saving Tip: Hike to Cabo Home Lighthouse for panoramic views of the Vigo estuary and the Cíes Islands at no cost. Free access.

1. Seafood: Galicia's Culinary Crown

- • **Special Foods**: Galicia is known for its incredible seafood, particularly **percebes** (goose barnacles), **pulpo a la gallega** (Galician-style octopus), and **mejillones** (mussels). The cold Atlantic waters around Galicia provide an abundance of high-quality seafood.
- • **Historical Context**: Galicia's rugged coastline and fishing traditions date back to Roman times. Fishing and shellfish farming have been economic staples, and many coastal towns developed their identity around the sea. Galicia's fishing industry remains one of the most important in Spain.

2. Empanada Gallega

- • **Special Food**: This iconic Galician dish is a large pie typically filled with fish (such as tuna), meat, or vegetables. Each town has its own version.
- • **Historical Context**: The origins of **empanadas** trace back to the need for portable food for travelers, especially those on pilgrimages to Santiago de Compostela. It became a common food for fishermen and farmers, providing a hearty, easy-to-carry meal.

3. Tarta de Santiago

- • **Special Food**: This almond cake, decorated with the cross of Saint James (Santiago), is one of Galicia's most famous desserts. Made with almonds, eggs, sugar, and sometimes a bit of citrus zest, it is a simple yet delicious treat.
- • **Historical Context**: The cake is deeply tied to the **Camino de Santiago**, the pilgrimage to Santiago de Compostela, which has been a spiritual and cultural journey for centuries. **Tarta de Santiago** was created as a tribute to Saint James, whose remains are believed to be in the cathedral of Santiago de Compostela.

4. Queso de Tetilla

- • **Special Food**: This soft, mild cheese is made from cow's milk and has a distinctive conical shape. Its name means "nipple cheese," referring to its shape.
- • **Historical Context**: Cheese-making has been a long-standing tradition in the rural areas of Galicia. **Queso de Tetilla** is a symbol of the region's dairy heritage and reflects the importance of livestock farming in the Galician economy.

5. Caldo Gallego

- • **Special Food**: This hearty soup is made with greens (usually **grelos**, or turnip tops), potatoes, chorizo, and pork. It is considered comfort food, especially during cold winters.
- • **Historical Context**: Caldo Gallego reflects Galicia's rural and agricultural past, where hearty, warming meals were essential for farmers and laborers working the land. Its ingredients are simple and locally sourced, reflecting the Galician reliance on seasonal produce.

6. Albariño Wine

- **Special Drink**: Galicia's Rías Baixas region produces **Albariño**, one of Spain's most celebrated white wines. It has a fresh, fruity flavor, perfect for pairing with seafood.
- **Historical Context**: The **Albariño** grape is native to Galicia, and wine production in the region dates back to Roman times. Rías Baixas became a designated wine region in the 1980s, elevating the global profile of Albariño wines. The local **Fiesta del Albariño** celebrates this wine with food, music, and festivities.

Cultural Customs in Galicia

1. La Queimada: The Ritual of Fire and Spirits

- **Custom**: **Queimada** is a traditional Galician drink made from orujo (a strong spirit), sugar, lemon peel, coffee beans, and sometimes herbs. It is set on fire and recited over with a spell or **conxuro** to ward off evil spirits.
- **Historical Context**: This custom is believed to have its roots in ancient Celtic traditions, as Galicia has a strong Celtic heritage. The ritual and drink symbolize protection and community bonding, especially during **Noite de San Xoán** (St. John's Night), a festival marking the summer solstice.

2. The Pilgrimage to Santiago de Compostela (Camino de Santiago)

- **Custom**: Every year, thousands of pilgrims walk the **Camino de Santiago** to reach the cathedral in Santiago de Compostela, where it is believed that the remains of Saint James the Apostle are buried.
- **Historical Context**: The pilgrimage dates back to the 9th century, when the tomb of Saint James was discovered. The **Camino de Santiago** has been one of the most important Christian pilgrimage routes for centuries and continues to be a cultural, spiritual, and personal journey for many. Along the route, pilgrims experience Galician hospitality through **albergues** (pilgrim hostels) and traditional foods.

3. The Festival of Os Maios

- **Custom**: Held in May, **Os Maios** celebrates the arrival of spring with floral decorations, songs, and processions. People make human-like figures from flowers, leaves, and branches, which are carried through the streets.
- **Historical Context**: This festival has ancient, possibly pre-Christian roots in fertility rites and the celebration of nature's renewal. It is a way for Galicians to mark the changing seasons and express gratitude for the earth's bounty.

4. Romerías: Traditional Pilgrimages and Gatherings

- **Custom**: **Romerías** are religious pilgrimages to shrines and chapels, often located in rural or scenic areas. They combine religious devotion with local festivities, including food, music, and dancing.
- **Historical Context**: These events blend Catholic traditions with older, possibly pagan customs. The most famous romería in Galicia is the pilgrimage to **San Andrés de Teixido**, where legend has it that if you don't visit while alive, you must visit in death.

5. Galician Bagpipes (Gaita) and Music

- **Custom**: The **gaita** (Galician bagpipe) is an essential part of Galicia's musical tradition, often played at festivals, weddings, and public gatherings.

- **Historical Context**: Galicia's Celtic roots are evident in its traditional music, which shares similarities with the folk music of Ireland and Scotland. The **gaita** has been played in the region for centuries and is a symbol of Galician identity.

Aragon

Aragon, located in northeastern Spain, is a region known for its diverse landscapes, rich history, and vibrant culture. From the stunning Pyrenees mountains to the historic cities of Zaragoza and Teruel, Aragon offers a wealth of experiences for travelers on any budget. Here's a guide to exploring the best of Aragon without breaking the bank.

Tips:

- **City Passes:** Consider purchasing city passes or tourist cards in cities like Zaragoza, which offer discounts on attractions, transportation, and dining for budget-conscious travelers.
- **Free Attractions:** Take advantage of free attractions such as historic sites, parks, and viewpoints, which offer insight into Aragon's cultural and natural heritage without any cost.
- **Local Markets:** Visit local markets such as Mercado Central in Zaragoza or Mercado Medieval in Teruel to sample regional specialties, fresh produce, and artisanal crafts at affordable prices.
- **Outdoor Adventures:** Explore Aragon's natural beauty by hiking in the Pyrenees, cycling along scenic trails, or picnicking in parks and gardens, with many outdoor activities available for free or at low cost.
- **Budget-Friendly Accommodation:** Look for budget-friendly accommodation options such as guesthouses, rural cottages, and camping sites, which offer comfortable lodging in picturesque settings at a fraction of the cost of luxury hotels.

Top 20 Attractions in Aragon with Money-Saving Tips:

- **Aljafería Palace, Zaragoza:**
    - Money-Saving Tip: Visit the Aljafería Palace, a UNESCO World Heritage Site, during free admission days or discounted hours to explore its Moorish architecture and gardens. Starting Price: €5.
- **Ordesa y Monte Perdido National Park:**
    - Money-Saving Tip: Explore Ordesa y Monte Perdido National Park on foot or by bike to discover its stunning landscapes, waterfalls, and wildlife for free. Free access to trails.
- **Zaragoza Cathedral:**
    - Money-Saving Tip: Attend a mass or concert at Zaragoza Cathedral to experience its Gothic architecture and interior decoration without paying for a guided tour. Free access during religious services.
- **Albarracín Old Town:**
    - Money-Saving Tip: Wander through Albarracín's medieval Old Town, with its narrow streets and fortified walls, for free and admire its historic architecture and scenic views. Free access.
- **Monasterio de Piedra Natural Park:**
    - Money-Saving Tip: Explore Monasterio de Piedra Natural Park, known for its waterfalls and lush vegetation, during off-peak hours or on weekdays for discounted admission rates. Starting Price: €17.

- **Teruel Mudejar Architecture:**
  - Money-Saving Tip: Take a self-guided walking tour of Teruel's Mudejar architecture, a UNESCO World Heritage Site, to admire its decorative brickwork and Islamic influences for free. Free access to exterior views.
- **Goya Museum, Zaragoza:**
  - Money-Saving Tip: Visit the Goya Museum, dedicated to the works of Francisco de Goya, during free admission days or discounted hours to view its collection of paintings and prints. Starting Price: €4.
- **Huesca Old Town:**
  - Money-Saving Tip: Explore Huesca's historic Old Town, with its Romanesque cathedral and medieval buildings, on foot for free and soak up its cultural heritage. Free access.
- **Loarre Castle:**
  - Money-Saving Tip: Visit Loarre Castle, a well-preserved Romanesque fortress, during guided tours or special events to learn about its history and architecture at a nominal fee. Starting Price: €6.
- **San Juan de la Peña Monastery:**
  - Money-Saving Tip: Explore San Juan de la Peña Monastery, a medieval religious complex, during off-peak hours or on weekdays for reduced admission rates. Starting Price: €5.
- **Daroca Medieval Walls:**
  - Money-Saving Tip: Walk along Daroca's medieval walls, which encircle the historic center, for free and enjoy panoramic views of the surrounding countryside. Free access.
- **Ski Resorts in the Pyrenees:**
  - Money-Saving Tip: Enjoy skiing or snowboarding in the Pyrenees at budget-friendly resorts such as Candanchú or Cerler, which offer affordable lift passes and equipment rentals. Starting Price: €30.
- **Roman Theatre, Zaragoza:**
  - Money-Saving Tip: Visit the Roman Theatre of Zaragoza, dating back to the 1st century AD, for free and explore its archaeological remains and museum exhibits. Free access.
- **Valle de Anso:**
  - Money-Saving Tip: Discover Valle de Anso, a picturesque valley in the Pyrenees, by hiking or cycling along its trails for free and enjoy its mountain scenery. Free access.
- **Calatayud Moorish Walls:**
  - Money-Saving Tip: Walk along Calatayud's Moorish walls, which date back to the 9th century, for free and admire their impressive fortifications and gateways. Free access.
- **Ainsa Medieval Old Town:**
  - Money-Saving Tip: Explore Ainsa's medieval Old Town, with its stone houses and cobblestone streets, on foot for free and immerse yourself in its historic atmosphere. Free access.
- **Santuario de Torreciudad:**
  - Money-Saving Tip: Visit Santuario de Torreciudad, a modern basilica and pilgrimage site, during free admission days or discounted hours to view its contemporary architecture and religious artwork. Free access.
- **Maestrazgo Region:**

- Money-Saving Tip: Discover the Maestrazgo region's rugged landscapes and medieval villages by driving or hiking along scenic routes for free and enjoy its natural beauty. Free access.
- **Parque de la Dehesa de Sástago:**
  - Money-Saving Tip: Spend a day at Parque de la Dehesa de Sástago, a natural park with picnic areas and walking trails, for a budget-friendly outdoor excursion. Free access.
- **Zaragoza Waterfront:**
  - Money-Saving Tip: Stroll along Zaragoza's waterfront, along the Ebro River, for free and enjoy views of the city's landmarks and modern architecture. Free access.

Special Foods of Aargau

1. **Aargauer Rüeblitorte (Carrot Cake)**

   - **Description:** This famous Aargau dish is a moist carrot cake often topped with a sugary glaze and marzipan carrots. Aargau is known as the "Carrot Canton" due to its agricultural heritage, especially the cultivation of carrots.
   - **History:** Aargauer Rüeblitorte originated in the 19th century as a way to use local ingredients like carrots, which grow abundantly in the region. The cake has since become a Swiss classic, symbolizing Aargau's rural charm.

2. **Aargauer Braten (Aargau Roast)**

   - **Description:** A traditional pork roast dish, often slow-cooked with local vegetables like carrots and served with rich gravy.
   - **History:** This dish reflects the farming culture of Aargau, where hearty meals were prepared with ingredients readily available on local farms.

3. **Zwiebelwähe (Onion Tart)**

   - **Description:** A savory pie made with a base of pastry dough and a filling of onions, cream, and eggs. It is sometimes flavored with bacon or cheese.
   - **History:** Originating from German-speaking Switzerland, Zwiebelwähe is a common dish in Aargau and other regions, often served during autumn fairs and family gatherings.

4. **Wurstsalat (Sausage Salad)**

   - **Description:** A Swiss favorite, this dish consists of sliced sausages (often cervelat), onions, and pickles, served with a tangy vinegar-based dressing.
   - **History:** The dish has roots in the rural areas of Switzerland, where sausages were a staple food. In Aargau, it's typically enjoyed during summer months at outdoor gatherings.

5. **Saucisson Vaudois**

   - **Description:** A traditional smoked pork sausage, often served with potatoes and cabbage.
   - **History:** Though more common in the Vaud region, this dish has spread to Aargau and is especially popular in winter.

6. **Aargauer Lebkuchen (Gingerbread)**

- o **Description:** This regional take on gingerbread is less sweet than its counterparts and is often spiced with cloves, cinnamon, and nutmeg. Sometimes filled with nuts or dried fruits, it's a traditional holiday treat.
- o **History:** Gingerbread has been made in Switzerland for centuries, with each region developing its own variety. Aargau's version is a reflection of the simple yet flavorful local ingredients used.

Customs in Aargau

1. Fasnacht (Carnival)

- o **Custom:** Like other parts of Switzerland, Aargau celebrates Fasnacht, a lively carnival with parades, music, and elaborate costumes. Traditionally held before Lent, this festival is marked by masked figures, Guggenmusik (brass bands), and confetti battles.
- o **History:** The origins of Fasnacht date back to the Middle Ages, and it was initially a way to mark the transition from winter to spring. Over the centuries, it became a more elaborate festival, with each region adding its own traditions.

2. Sechseläuten (Spring Festival)

- o **Custom:** In nearby Zurich, but also observed in parts of Aargau, this spring festival involves the burning of the "Böögg," an effigy symbolizing winter. The event also features parades and the ringing of bells to welcome the warm season.
- o **History:** This custom is rooted in medieval times when farmers celebrated the return of longer daylight hours for work in the fields. The festival's modern form developed in the 16th century.

3. Chlausjagen (St. Nicholas Parade)

- o **Custom:** In early December, children participate in a tradition called **Chlausjagen**, where they march through the streets with bells and lanterns to usher in the arrival of St. Nicholas (Samichlaus).
- o **History:** This tradition stems from the Middle Ages and was initially linked to pagan winter rituals. Over time, it became associated with St. Nicholas and is celebrated throughout Switzerland, with regional variations in Aargau.

4. Chilbi (Autumn Fair)

- o **Custom:** A Chilbi is a local fair that takes place in various villages and towns in Aargau during autumn. It features games, food stalls, and rides, often including regional food specialties like Zwiebelwähe.
- o **History:** Chilbi fairs date back to the harvest festivals of medieval times, celebrating the end of the farming season. Today, they are community events focused on fun and local culture.

5. Jodlerfeste (Yodeling Festivals)

- o **Custom:** Yodeling festivals in Aargau celebrate traditional Swiss music, where local choirs and soloists gather to perform folk songs.
- o **History:** Yodeling has been a part of Swiss culture for centuries, initially used as a form of communication in the Alps. These festivals preserve the musical heritage of rural Switzerland, including Aargau.

A Brief History of Aargau

- **Early History:** The Aargau region has been inhabited since prehistoric times, with evidence of Celtic and Roman settlements. Vindonissa, near Brugg, was an important Roman legionary camp in the 1st century AD.

- **Middle Ages:** Aargau was originally part of the Kingdom of Burgundy and later came under the control of the powerful Habsburg dynasty in the 10th century. The region's castles, such as Habsburg Castle and Lenzburg Castle, reflect its medieval importance.

- **Swiss Confederacy:** In 1415, Aargau was conquered by the Old Swiss Confederacy, and its territories were divided among several cantons. The region became a battleground during the Reformation, with both Catholic and Protestant factions vying for control.

- **Modern Era:** Aargau officially joined the Swiss Confederation as a full member in 1803 during the Napoleonic reorganization of Switzerland. Since then, it has developed into a thriving agricultural and industrial region, while maintaining its cultural traditions and historical sites.

Murcia

Murcia, located in southeastern Spain, is a region known for its Mediterranean climate, rich history, and culinary delights. While Murcia offers plenty of luxury experiences, it's also possible to explore the region on a budget without compromising on quality. Here's a guide to enjoying the best of Murcia without breaking the bank.

Tips:

- **Tapas Culture:** Embrace Murcia's tapas culture by hopping from bar to bar and sampling a variety of small plates at affordable prices. Look for "menu del día" offers for budget-friendly dining.
- **Free Attractions:** Take advantage of free attractions such as historic sites, parks, and markets, which offer insight into Murcia's cultural heritage and local lifestyle without any cost.
- **Local Markets:** Visit local markets such as Mercado de Verónicas in Murcia or Mercado de Abastos in Cartagena to sample regional specialties, fresh produce, and artisanal products at affordable prices.
- **Outdoor Adventures:** Explore Murcia's natural beauty by hiking in the Sierra Espuña, cycling along the Via Verde, or picnicking in parks and gardens, with many outdoor activities available for free or at low cost.
- **Budget-Friendly Accommodation:** Look for budget-friendly accommodation options such as guesthouses, rural cottages, and campsites, which offer comfortable lodging in scenic locations at a fraction of the cost of luxury hotels.

Top 20 Attractions in Murcia with Money-Saving Tips:

- **Cathedral of Murcia:**
  - Money-Saving Tip: Visit the Cathedral of Murcia, a masterpiece of Baroque architecture, during free admission days or discounted hours to explore its interior and bell tower. Starting Price: €6.
- **Cartagena Roman Theatre:**
  - Money-Saving Tip: Explore the Cartagena Roman Theatre, dating back to the 1st century BC, for free and admire its archaeological remains and museum exhibits. Free access.
- **La Manga del Mar Menor:**
  - Money-Saving Tip: Spend a day at La Manga del Mar Menor and enjoy its sandy beaches, shallow waters, and water sports activities for free or at low cost. Free access to public beaches.
- **Salzillo Museum, Murcia:**
  - Money-Saving Tip: Visit the Salzillo Museum, dedicated to the works of Francisco Salzillo, during free admission days or discounted hours to view its collection of sculptures and religious art. Starting Price: €3.
- **Sierra Espuña Natural Park:**

- Money-Saving Tip: Explore Sierra Espuña Natural Park on foot or by bike to discover its scenic trails, forests, and viewpoints for free or at low cost. Free access to hiking trails.
- **Cartagena Naval Museum:**
  - Money-Saving Tip: Visit the Cartagena Naval Museum, housed in a historic arsenal building, during free admission days or discounted hours to learn about the city's maritime history. Starting Price: €3.
- **Murcia Old Town:**
  - Money-Saving Tip: Wander through Murcia's historic Old Town, with its narrow streets and picturesque squares, for free and admire its architecture and monuments. Free access.
- **Calblanque Regional Park:**
  - Money-Saving Tip: Spend a day at Calblanque Regional Park, a protected natural area with pristine beaches and dunes, for free and enjoy swimming, sunbathing, and nature walks. Free access.
- **Ricote Valley:**
  - Money-Saving Tip: Discover the Ricote Valley, known for its Moorish heritage and orchards, by driving or hiking along scenic routes for free and enjoy its rural charm. Free access.
- **Los Alcázares Beaches:**
  - Money-Saving Tip: Relax at Los Alcázares beaches and bring your own towels and beach gear to save money on rentals. Free access to public beaches.
- **Archaeological Museum, Murcia:**
  - Money-Saving Tip: Visit the Archaeological Museum of Murcia, housed in a former convent, during free admission days or discounted hours to explore its collections of artifacts and exhibits. Starting Price: €3.
- **Caravaca de la Cruz:**
  - Money-Saving Tip: Explore Caravaca de la Cruz, a pilgrimage town with a medieval castle and sanctuary, for free and soak up its religious atmosphere and historic charm. Free access.
- **Mar Menor:**
  - Money-Saving Tip: Swim in the Mar Menor, Europe's largest saltwater lagoon, for free and enjoy its warm, shallow waters and sandy beaches. Free access to public beaches.
- **Jumilla Wine Route:**
  - Money-Saving Tip: Explore the Jumilla Wine Route, known for its vineyards and wineries, and visit family-owned bodegas for affordable wine tastings and tours. Starting Price: €5.
- **Cabo de Palos Lighthouse:**
  - Money-Saving Tip: Visit Cabo de Palos Lighthouse, perched on a rocky promontory overlooking the Mediterranean Sea, for panoramic views at no cost. Free access.
- **Mula Castle:**
  - Money-Saving Tip: Climb to Mula Castle, a medieval fortress with Moorish origins, for free and enjoy views of the surrounding countryside. Free access.
- **Esparto Grass Museum, Cieza:**
  - Money-Saving Tip: Visit the Esparto Grass Museum in Cieza, housed in a former convent, during free admission days or discounted hours to learn about this traditional craft. Starting Price: €2.

- **Calasparra Rice Fields:**
  - Money-Saving Tip: Explore the Calasparra Rice Fields, known for their terraced cultivation and irrigation systems, by driving or hiking along scenic routes for free. Free access.
- **Lorca Castle:**
  - Money-Saving Tip: Visit Lorca Castle, a medieval fortress with archaeological remains and panoramic views, during free admission days or discounted hours. Starting Price: €6.
- **Santuario de la Fuensanta, Murcia:**
  - Money-Saving Tip: Hike to Santuario de la Fuensanta, a hilltop sanctuary with a Baroque church, for free and enjoy views of Murcia and its surroundings. Free access.

Truly weird and wonderful things to do in Spain

- **Visit the Dalí Theatre-Museum in Figueres:**
  - Immerse yourself in the surreal world of Salvador Dalí at this bizarre museum, which features a collection of the artist's works, including paintings, sculptures, and installations. Don't miss the giant eggs on the roof and the Mae West room.
- **Participate in La Tomatina Festival:**
  - Join thousands of revelers in the small town of Buñol for the world's largest tomato fight. Held annually on the last Wednesday of August, this quirky festival involves throwing ripe tomatoes at each other in a friendly food fight.
- **Explore the Fairy-Tale Village of Setenil de las Bodegas:**
  - Wander through the streets of Setenil de las Bodegas, a picturesque village in Andalusia built into the cliffs. Marvel at the houses and shops carved into the rock formations, creating a magical and surreal atmosphere.
- **Witness the Running of the Bulls in Pamplona:**
  - Experience the adrenaline rush of watching or participating in the famous Running of the Bulls during the San Fermín festival in Pamplona. Brave souls can run alongside the bulls through the narrow streets of the city.
- **Dine at a Medieval Banquet in Toledo:**
  - Step back in time and feast like royalty at a medieval banquet in Toledo. Enjoy traditional dishes served by costumed waitstaff in a historic setting, complete with live entertainment and jousting tournaments.
- **Visit the Museum of Witchcraft in Zugarramurdi:**
  - Delve into the world of witchcraft and superstition at the Museum of Witchcraft in the Basque village of Zugarramurdi. Learn about the infamous witch trials that took place in the region during the Spanish Inquisition.
- **Explore the Capricho de Gaudí in Comillas:**
  - Discover one of Antoni Gaudí's lesser-known works, the Capricho de Gaudí, located in the coastal town of Comillas. This whimsical building features colorful tiles, playful shapes, and ornate details, showcasing Gaudí's unique architectural style.
- **Hike the Caminito del Rey:**
  - Test your nerves by walking along the Caminito del Rey, a narrow and vertigo-inducing footpath attached to the cliffs of El Chorro Gorge. This exhilarating hike offers breathtaking views of the surrounding landscape.
- **Visit the Museum of Automata in Madrid:**
  - Step into a world of mechanical wonders at the Museum of Automata in Madrid, where you can marvel at a collection of vintage automatons, mechanical toys, and elaborate clockwork creations.
- **Attend the Baby-Jumping Festival in Castrillo de Murcia:**
  - Witness a centuries-old tradition known as El Colacho, where men dressed as devils leap over rows of infants to cleanse them of sin and ward off evil spirits. This bizarre festival takes place annually in the village of Castrillo de Murcia.

Best beaches

Spain is renowned for its stunning coastline and beautiful beaches, offering travelers a wide variety of options to choose from. Here are some of the best beaches in Spain, known for their natural beauty, crystal-clear waters, and scenic surroundings:

- **Playa de Ses Illetes, Formentera:**
    - Located on the small island of Formentera in the Balearic Islands, Playa de Ses Illetes is often considered one of the best beaches in the world. Its pristine white sand, turquoise waters, and picturesque setting make it a paradise for beach lovers.
- **Playa de la Concha, San Sebastian:**
    - Situated in the heart of San Sebastian in the Basque Country, Playa de la Concha is known for its crescent-shaped bay, calm waters, and scenic views of the city and surrounding mountains. It's a popular spot for swimming, sunbathing, and water sports.
- **Cala Macarelleta, Menorca:**
    - Tucked away on the island of Menorca in the Balearic Islands, Cala Macarelleta is a secluded cove with pristine white sand and clear turquoise waters. Accessible by boat or a short hike, it's an idyllic spot for snorkeling and relaxation.
- **Playa de Bolonia, Tarifa:**
    - Located near the town of Tarifa on the southern coast of Spain, Playa de Bolonia is known for its wild beauty and natural surroundings. Its long stretch of golden sand and dunes, along with views of the Roman ruins of Baelo Claudia, make it a must-visit destination.
- **Playa de Rodas, Cíes Islands:**
    - Situated in the Cíes Islands off the coast of Galicia, Playa de Rodas is often referred to as the "Caribbean of the Atlantic" due to its pristine white sand and turquoise waters. Accessible by ferry from Vigo or Baiona, it's a protected natural paradise ideal for hiking, snorkeling, and birdwatching.
- **Playa de Maspalomas, Gran Canaria:**
    - Located on the southern coast of Gran Canaria in the Canary Islands, Playa de Maspalomas is famous for its vast expanse of golden sand and iconic sand dunes. It's a popular destination for sunbathing, beach volleyball, and camel rides.
- **Cala Comte, Ibiza:**
    - Situated on the west coast of Ibiza, Cala Comte is known for its crystal-clear waters, rocky cliffs, and stunning sunsets. It's a favorite spot among locals and visitors alike for swimming, snorkeling, and enjoying the island's laid-back vibe.
- **Playa de las Catedrales, Galicia:**
    - Located near the town of Ribadeo in Galicia, Playa de las Catedrales is known for its dramatic rock formations, natural arches, and caves carved by the sea. Its unique landscape makes it a popular destination for photographers and nature lovers.
- **Playa de Zahara de los Atunes, Cadiz:**

- Situated on the Costa de la Luz in Andalusia, Playa de Zahara de los Atunes is known for its golden sand, clear waters, and lively atmosphere. It's a great spot for swimming, windsurfing, and enjoying fresh seafood at beachfront restaurants.
- **Playa de Papagayo, Lanzarote:**
  - Located on the southern tip of Lanzarote in the Canary Islands, Playa de Papagayo is a series of sheltered coves with golden sand and crystal-clear waters. Its natural beauty and tranquility make it a popular spot for snorkeling and sunbathing.

Best public swimming pools with prices

Aside from the beaches Spain has many stunning pools open to the public:

- **Parque del Oeste Pool, Madrid:**
  - Located in the heart of Madrid, Parque del Oeste Pool offers a large outdoor swimming pool surrounded by lush greenery. Admission prices vary depending on age and time of day, but typically range from €5 to €7 for adults and €3 to €4 for children.
- **Piscina Municipal de Montjuïc, Barcelona:**
  - Situated on Montjuïc hill overlooking Barcelona, Piscina Municipal de Montjuïc is an Olympic-sized outdoor pool with stunning views of the city. Prices are around €6 to €8 for adults and €4 to €6 for children.
- **Parc de la Creueta del Coll, Barcelona:**
  - Parc de la Creueta del Coll features a large artificial lake with a swimming area surrounded by grassy lawns and shaded picnic areas. Entry is free for residents of Barcelona with a valid ID card, while non-residents may pay a small fee of €2 to €3.
- **Piscina Municipal de Cartuja, Granada:**
  - Piscina Municipal de Cartuja is a popular public pool complex in Granada, offering multiple pools, water slides, and recreational areas. Prices range from €4 to €6 for adults and €3 to €4 for children.
- **Centro Deportivo Municipal Moratalaz, Madrid:**
  - Centro Deportivo Municipal Moratalaz is a modern sports complex in Madrid with indoor and outdoor pools, as well as other facilities such as gyms and tennis courts. Prices start at around €5 for adults and €3 for children.
- **Piscina Municipal de San Sebastián, Seville:**
  - Piscina Municipal de San Sebastián is a public swimming pool located in Seville's historic center, offering a refreshing escape from the city heat. Prices typically range from €4 to €6 for adults and €3 to €5 for children.
- **Piscina Municipal de Sant Sebastià, Sitges:**
  - Situated in the coastal town of Sitges near Barcelona, Piscina Municipal de Sant Sebastià offers a large outdoor pool with views of the Mediterranean Sea. Prices are around €5 to €7 for adults and €3 to €5 for children.
- **Piscina Municipal de Montemar, Alicante:**
  - Piscina Municipal de Montemar is a popular public pool complex in Alicante, featuring multiple pools, water slides, and sunbathing areas. Prices range from €4 to €6 for adults and €3 to €5 for children.
- **Piscina Municipal de Valencia, Valencia:**
  - Piscina Municipal de Valencia is a large public swimming pool complex in Valencia, offering indoor and outdoor pools, as well as other sports facilities. Prices start at around €5 for adults and €3 for children.

Best Hikes

- **Camino de Santiago (The Way of St. James):**
  - This ancient pilgrimage route spans across Spain and various other European countries, with the most popular route starting in the French Pyrenees and ending in Santiago de Compostela in Galicia. Hikers can choose from multiple trails, each offering stunning landscapes, historic villages, and cultural experiences along the way.
- **Ruta del Cares, Picos de Europa:**
  - Located in the Picos de Europa National Park in northern Spain, the Ruta del Cares is a breathtaking hike along a narrow gorge carved by the Cares River. The trail offers dramatic views of towering cliffs, lush valleys, and crystal-clear streams, with the option to hike the entire 12-kilometer route or shorter sections.
- **Sendero de los Cahorros, Granada:**
  - This exhilarating hike in the Sierra Nevada Mountains near Granada takes you through narrow gorges, across suspension bridges, and along rushing rivers. Highlights include the famous hanging bridges and natural rock formations, offering plenty of opportunities for adventure and stunning views.
- **Monte Perdido, Ordesa y Monte Perdido National Park:**
  - As one of Spain's most iconic peaks, Monte Perdido offers a challenging but rewarding hike through the Ordesa y Monte Perdido National Park in the Pyrenees. The trail takes you through lush forests, alpine meadows, and rugged terrain, culminating in panoramic views of the surrounding mountains.
- **Caminito del Rey, Malaga:**
  - This thrilling hike along a narrow cliffside path offers breathtaking views of the rugged landscape of El Chorro Gorge. Originally built for hydroelectric workers, the restored pathway now attracts adventurers seeking adrenaline-pumping experiences and stunning vistas.
- **Teide National Park, Tenerife:**
  - Explore Spain's highest peak and UNESCO World Heritage Site in the Teide National Park on the island of Tenerife. The diverse landscape includes volcanic craters, lava fields, and unique rock formations, with hiking trails ranging from easy strolls to challenging ascents to the summit of Mount Teide.
- **Montserrat Mountain, Catalonia:**
  - Known for its dramatic rock formations and Benedictine monastery, Montserrat offers a variety of hiking trails suitable for all skill levels. Highlights include panoramic viewpoints, ancient hermitages, and the chance to explore the mystical mountain's hidden caves and grottos.
- **Calanques de Mallorca, Mallorca:**
  - Discover the rugged coastline and hidden coves of Mallorca's Calanques on this scenic coastal hike. The trail takes you through pine forests, limestone cliffs, and turquoise waters, with opportunities for swimming, snorkeling, and beach hopping along the way.
- **Trekking in the Alpujarras, Andalusia:**

- Explore the picturesque villages and terraced hillsides of the Alpujarras region in southern Spain on a multi-day trekking adventure. Follow ancient mule tracks and footpaths, passing through charming whitewashed villages and lush valleys, with stunning views of the Sierra Nevada Mountains.
- **Cumbre Vieja, La Palma:**
  - This challenging hike along the volcanic ridge of Cumbre Vieja offers panoramic views of La Palma's rugged landscape and coastline. The trail passes through pine forests, lava fields, and volcanic craters, culminating in breathtaking vistas from the summit.

What to do at night for free in Spain

Finding free nighttime activities in Spain can be both entertaining and budget-friendly. Here are some suggestions for what to do at night for free:

- **Stroll Through Historic Neighborhoods:** Take a leisurely walk through the historic neighborhoods of cities like Barcelona's Barri Gòtic or Madrid's La Latina. Enjoy the charming ambiance, illuminated streets, and architectural wonders without spending a dime.
- **Explore Night Markets:** Experience the vibrant atmosphere of night markets like Madrid's Mercado de San Miguel or Barcelona's Mercat de Sant Antoni. Browse through stalls selling local crafts, artisanal products, and street food while enjoying live music and entertainment.
- **Enjoy Street Performances:** Wander through bustling pedestrian streets and squares where street performers showcase their talents. From musicians and dancers to magicians and living statues, street performers add to the lively atmosphere of Spain's cities.
- **Attend Free Museum Nights:** Take advantage of free museum nights offered by many museums and cultural institutions in Spain. Check the schedules of museums in your area for special evenings when admission is waived or discounted.
- **Join Nighttime Walking Tours:** Some cities offer free guided walking tours that explore local legends, ghost stories, and historical landmarks after dark. Join a nighttime walking tour to learn more about the hidden mysteries and secrets of Spain's cities.
- **Watch Sunset and Stargaze:** Head to a scenic viewpoint or beachfront to watch the sunset over the horizon. After dark, find a spot away from city lights to stargaze and admire the beauty of the night sky.
- **Picnic in the Park:** Pack a picnic basket with snacks and drinks and head to a nearby park or garden for a relaxing evening under the stars. Enjoy a romantic dinner or a casual gathering with friends while surrounded by nature.
- **Attend Cultural Lectures and Talks:** Look for free cultural lectures, book readings, and talks hosted by libraries, bookstores, and cultural centers. Engage in stimulating discussions and learn about a variety of topics ranging from literature and art to history and current events.
- **Experience Local Nightlife:** While many nightlife activities may come with a cost, you can still experience the lively atmosphere of Spain's nightlife districts without spending money. Take a stroll through popular nightlife areas like Madrid's Malasaña or Barcelona's El Raval and soak up the energy of the city after dark.

Getting Out Cheaply

1. Buses: The Cheapest Option for Intercity Travel

Buses are generally the most budget-friendly way to travel around Spain, especially if you book tickets in advance. The bus network is extensive, connecting major cities and smaller towns.

Major Bus Companies:

- **ALSA:** The largest and most popular bus operator in Spain, ALSA offers routes all over the country, including international trips to nearby countries like Portugal and France.
- **Avanza:** Serves routes between Madrid and coastal cities like Valencia and Málaga.
- **Socibus:** Focuses on routes between Andalusia and Madrid.

Average Prices:

- **Madrid to Barcelona:** €20–€40 (depending on how early you book).
- **Madrid to Valencia:** €15–€25.
- **Barcelona to Seville:** €30–€50.
- **Granada to Málaga:** €6–€10.
- **Seville to Córdoba:** €7–€12.

Practical Tips:

- **Book in Advance:** Like flights, bus tickets are cheaper the earlier you book. ALSA, for example, offers **"Promo"**fares, which are significantly discounted if booked weeks in advance.
- **Night Buses:** For longer trips, consider taking an overnight bus to save on accommodation costs. Night buses often come equipped with Wi-Fi and reclining seats.
- **Discounts:** ALSA offers discounts for students, seniors, and those under 26. Always check their deals page.

Where to Book:

- ALSA Website
- Avanza Website
- Socibus Website

2. Trains: Fast and Efficient, But Vary in Price

Spain's train system, operated by **Renfe**, offers a variety of travel options from high-speed trains (AVE) to cheaper regional trains. While trains are faster than buses, they can be more expensive, particularly on popular routes.

Types of Trains:

- **AVE (Alta Velocidad Española):** High-speed trains that connect major cities like Madrid, Barcelona, Seville, and Málaga. These trains are fast but often pricier.
- **Alvia and Euromed:** Medium-distance trains that connect larger cities at lower speeds than the AVE but are more affordable.
- **Cercanías:** Regional commuter trains that operate in metropolitan areas.
- **Media Distancia and Regionales:** Short and medium-distance trains connecting smaller towns and cities.

Average Prices:

- **Madrid to Barcelona (AVE):** €40–€120 (2.5 hours).
- **Madrid to Seville (AVE):** €40–€100 (2.5 hours).
- **Madrid to Valencia (AVE):** €20–€60 (1.5 hours).
- **Barcelona to Alicante (Euromed):** €25–€55 (5 hours).
- **Regional Trains:** €10–€30, depending on distance and route.

Practical Tips:

- **Look for Promo Fares:** Renfe frequently offers promotional fares on its website, sometimes cutting prices by up to 70%. These fares are usually non-refundable, so plan ahead.
- **Renfe Spain Pass:** If you're planning to travel frequently by train within a short period, consider the **Renfe Spain Pass**, which allows for up to 12 train journeys in a month at a discounted rate.
- **Try Regional Trains:** Regional trains are significantly cheaper than the AVE, though they are slower. For example, the **Media Distancia** from Madrid to Seville costs around €30 but takes 6-7 hours.
- **Youth and Senior Discounts:** Renfe offers special discounts for youth under 26 (with a **Tarjeta Joven** card) and seniors over 60 (with a **Tarjeta Dorada**).

Where to Book:

- Renfe Website

3. Flights: Budget Airlines for Long-Distance Travel

Flying can sometimes be the cheapest and fastest way to travel long distances in Spain, especially between northern and southern cities or to Spain's islands. Budget airlines offer incredibly low prices, particularly if you book far in advance or take advantage of flash sales.

Major Budget Airlines:

- **Vueling:** Spain's largest low-cost airline, flying domestically and to nearby European destinations.
- **Ryanair:** A well-known budget airline that offers domestic flights within Spain and international routes.
- **Iberia Express:** A low-cost subsidiary of Iberia Airlines offering domestic flights.
- **Volotea:** Specializes in routes to and from smaller Spanish cities.

Average Prices:

- **Madrid to Barcelona:** €15–€50.

- **Madrid to Seville:** €15–€45.
- **Barcelona to Bilbao:** €20–€60.
- **Madrid to Palma de Mallorca (Balearic Islands):** €20–€60.
- **Seville to Tenerife (Canary Islands):** €30–€80.

Practical Tips:

- **Check for Extra Fees:** Many budget airlines, like Ryanair and Vueling, charge extra for things like checked baggage, seat selection, and even printing your boarding pass at the airport. Be mindful of these additional costs when booking.
- **Travel Light:** To avoid baggage fees, try to travel with just a carry-on, as most budget airlines include a small bag in the ticket price.
- **Book Early:** Flights are cheapest if booked 1–3 months in advance. Budget airlines frequently offer sales, with one-way tickets as low as €10–€20.

Where to Book:

- Vueling Website
- Ryanair Website
- Iberia Express Website
- Volotea Website

4. Carpooling and Ride-Sharing: Blablacar

If you prefer traveling by road but want to avoid bus schedules or the hassle of renting a car, **Blablacar** is a popular ride-sharing service in Spain. It allows you to share a car with others who are heading in the same direction, making it cheaper and more environmentally friendly.

Average Prices:

- **Madrid to Barcelona:** €25–€35.
- **Madrid to Valencia:** €15–€20.
- **Barcelona to Seville:** €30–€45.

Practical Tips:

- **Read Reviews:** Before booking a ride, read the reviews of the driver to ensure reliability.
- **Flexible Travel:** Blablacar is a great option if you're traveling between smaller towns or want more flexibility in your schedule.
- **Last-Minute Bookings:** If buses or trains are fully booked or expensive at the last minute, Blablacar can offer a cheaper alternative.

Where to Book:

- Blablacar Website

Cheapest Airport lounges in Spain

Finding the cheapest airport lounges in Spain can depend on various factors such as the airport, lounge amenities, and time of visit. Generally, lounges operated by independent companies or those affiliated with low-cost carriers tend to offer more affordable rates compared to premium lounges. Here are some options you can explore along with approximate prices:

- **Plaza Premium Lounge (Barcelona El Prat Airport):**
  - Located in Terminal 1, this lounge offers comfortable seating, complimentary Wi-Fi, snacks, and beverages including alcoholic drinks. Prices start at around €35-€40 for a three-hour stay.
- **Premium Traveller Lounge (Madrid-Barajas Adolfo Suárez Airport):**
  - Situated in Terminal 1, this lounge provides amenities such as snacks, beverages, Wi-Fi, and comfortable seating. Prices typically range from €30-€35 for a three-hour stay.
- **Canary Lounge (Gran Canaria Airport):**
  - Operating in the main terminal, this lounge offers a relaxed environment with amenities like Wi-Fi, snacks, and drinks. Prices start at approximately €25-€30 for a three-hour visit.
- **Puerta del Sol Lounge (Malaga Airport):**
  - Situated in Terminal 3, this lounge provides facilities including Wi-Fi, refreshments, and comfortable seating. Prices usually range from €25-€30 for a three-hour stay.
- **Aena Sala VIP Lounge (Various Airports):**
  - Aena-operated lounges are available at several airports across Spain, including Barcelona, Madrid, Malaga, and Palma de Mallorca. Prices vary depending on the airport and specific lounge location but typically start at around €25-€35 for a three-hour visit.
- **Sala VIP Lounge (Alicante-Elche Airport):**
  - This lounge offers amenities like Wi-Fi, snacks, and beverages in a comfortable setting. Prices typically range from €20-€25 for a three-hour stay.
- **Aerobús VIP Lounge (Barcelona El Prat Airport):**
  - Located in Terminal 1, this lounge is accessible to passengers using the Aerobús shuttle service. It offers amenities such as Wi-Fi, snacks, and drinks, with prices starting at around €20-€25 for a three-hour visit.

Spain's Quirks

Whether you're walking through a small village where everyone knows the local saint by name or wandering the bustling streets of Madrid, you'll quickly realize that many Spanish beliefs and practices are deeply rooted in both religion and folklore. So grab a café con leche, and let's dive into some of the most fascinating superstitions, saints, and cultural quirks that make Spain the uniquely vibrant place it is.

1. Tuesday the 13th – Spain's Unlucky Day

In Spain, Tuesday the 13th is what Friday the 13th is in other parts of the world. It's the day when you might want to think twice about starting any new ventures or, heaven forbid, getting married. The phrase "Martes y trece, ni te cases ni te embarques" ("Tuesday the 13th, don't get married or embark on a journey") is practically gospel here. Why Tuesday? Well, martes (Tuesday) comes from Mars, the Roman god of war, and war doesn't exactly scream good luck, does it?

Many Spaniards genuinely believe that Tuesday the 13th is the unluckiest day of all, and while some just roll their eyes at the notion, others avoid doing anything major on this day. No major purchases, no starting a new job, and definitely no weddings—who wants a war god overseeing their nuptials, right?

2. El Mal de Ojo – The Evil Eye

Ah, **el mal de ojo**, one of the most widespread superstitions not just in Spain but across many cultures. The belief here is that someone can cast a spell on you just by looking at you with envy or ill will, causing you harm or bad luck. But don't worry! Spanish culture has plenty of ways to protect yourself from this "evil eye."

One of the most popular protections is to wear a red string around your wrist. You'll often see this in rural areas or among older generations, but even some fashionable urbanites wear it as a subtle nod to tradition. Another safeguard is the use of an amulet, such as a small blue eye (which is quite common in Andalusia), to deflect the mal de ojo. If you're a baby, your abuela might even tie a red ribbon around your crib to keep the evil eye at bay —because, let's face it, babies tend to attract a lot of attention!

3. Saints and Their Shrines – From Miracles to Matchmaking

Spain is nothing if not devoted to its saints. With over 10,000 canonized saints in Catholicism, many towns and regions have a local patron saint that plays a big role in daily life. Let's talk about a few notable ones.

First up is **San Antonio de Padua**, the saint of lost things—and, intriguingly, the saint you call upon when you're looking for a spouse. In some regions, if you're single and seeking love, there's a quirky little tradition: you can "punish" San Antonio by flipping his statue upside down until he helps you find a partner. Talk about tough love! You'll find these statues everywhere, and while the act might sound sacrilegious, it's done with a playful heart.

Another famous saint in Spain is **Santiago** (Saint James), who has a whole pilgrimage dedicated to him—the famous **Camino de Santiago**. Every year, thousands of pilgrims walk hundreds of kilometers to reach the shrine of Saint James in Santiago de Compostela. Legend has it that St. James's remains were discovered here in the 9th century, and today, people from all over the world make the trek in search of spiritual fulfillment, a new beginning, or even just a great adventure.

4. The Curse of the Gitanas

Gypsies, or **gitanas**, have a strong presence in Spain, particularly in the south. Many Spanish superstitions are linked to these communities, with both admiration and fear tied to their perceived mystical powers. One of the most feared things is the **maldición gitana** —the gypsy curse. While this may sound like something from a gothic novel, many Spaniards genuinely fear being cursed by a gypsy.

How do you avoid it? Well, for starters, if a gitana offers to read your palm or sell you a small trinket in exchange for money, it's best to politely decline but never outright offend her. It's said that angering a gitana could result in her casting a curse on you, leading to all sorts of misfortunes, from bad luck in love to financial woes.

5. Bread – More Than Just a Staple

Bread is sacred in Spain—seriously. Throwing bread away is considered bad luck, and even dropping a piece on the floor might warrant a small apology to the heavens. Spanish bread, whether it's a humble **barra** from the local bakery or a fresh-baked **pan** on the dinner table, is treated with respect.

Here's a quirky tidbit: if you ever find yourself with a loaf that's flipped upside down, it's said to be an omen of bad luck. The fix? Simply turn it right side up, and everything will be fine again. Easy, right? But whatever you do, don't toss it in the trash—give it to the birds or use it for tomorrow's **tostada** instead.

6. El Coco – Scaring Children for Centuries

If you think Santa Claus is a big deal in Spain, wait until you hear about **El Coco**. Spanish parents have been using this monster to keep naughty children in line for centuries. **El Coco** is the Spanish equivalent of the Boogeyman, and he's said to snatch children who misbehave or refuse to go to bed.

There's even a popular lullaby that goes, "Duérmete niño, duérmete ya, que viene el Coco y te comerá" ("Sleep, little child, sleep now, or the Coco will come and eat you"). It's a bit darker than "Twinkle, Twinkle, Little Star," isn't it? But that's Spain for you—where even the bedtime stories come with a warning!

7. Cemeteries and the Importance of Clean Graves

In Spain, the dead are never forgotten. Every year on **Todos los Santos** (All Saints' Day), families flock to cemeteries to clean the graves of their loved ones, leaving fresh flowers and sometimes even picnicking at the gravesite. This tradition is about honoring the dead and keeping their memory alive, and many Spaniards believe that failing to tend to a family grave will bring bad luck to the household.

And speaking of cemeteries, don't be surprised if you see something a little unusual. In some parts of Spain, particularly in Galicia, cemeteries are often located near the ocean, with a direct view of the water. It's said that this helps the souls of the deceased rest in peace, as they are able to "watch" the sea. The symbolism here runs deep—life, like the ocean, ebbs and flows, and so do the spirits.

8. Spanish Weddings – Watch Out for Knives

Spanish weddings are a whirlwind of food, dancing, and joy, but there's a little superstition that might surprise you: knives are a no-no when it comes to gifts. It's said that gifting a knife (or any sharp object) to a newly married couple will sever their relationship. To avoid this bad omen, if you absolutely must give a knife set (hello, modern registries), tradition says the couple should give you a small coin in return, symbolically "purchasing" the knives from you and cutting the curse short.

9. The Midnight Grapes of New Year's Eve

When it comes to Spanish New Year's Eve traditions, there's nothing quite as fun—or as frantically stressful—as **las doce uvas de la suerte** (the twelve lucky grapes). As the clock strikes midnight on **Nochevieja** (New Year's Eve), Spaniards all across the country attempt to eat one grape for each chime of the clock, symbolizing good luck for each month of the coming year.

Sounds simple, right? Wrong. The grapes are often large and filled with seeds, and the chiming of the clock is faster than you'd think! Most Spaniards get a good laugh from watching tourists try to keep up with the tradition, but trust me—after a few New Year's Eves in Spain, you'll be popping those grapes like a pro.

100 useful phrases Spanish with english pronunciation

- Hola (OH-lah) - Hello
- Buenos días (BWAY-nos DEE-as) - Good morning
- Buenas tardes (BWAY-nas TAR-des) - Good afternoon
- Buenas noches (BWAY-nas NO-chess) - Good evening / Goodnight
- ¿Cómo estás? (KOH-moh es-TAHS) - How are you?
- ¿Cómo te llamas? (KOH-moh teh YAH-mahs) - What's your name?
- Me llamo... (meh YAH-moh...) - My name is...
- Mucho gusto (MOO-choh GOOS-toh) - Nice to meet you
- ¿Cómo se dice... en inglés? (KOH-moh seh DEE-seh... en een-GLESS) - How do you say... in English?
- Por favor (por fah-BOHR) - Please
- Gracias (GRAH-syahs) - Thank you
- De nada (deh NAH-dah) - You're welcome
- Lo siento (loh SYEN-toh) - I'm sorry
- ¿Dónde está...? (DOHN-deh ehs-TAH...?) - Where is...?
- ¿Cuánto cuesta? (KWAHN-toh KWEHS-tah?) - How much does it cost?
- ¿Qué hora es? (keh OH-rah es?) - What time is it?
- Necesito ayuda (neh-seh-SEE-toh ah-YOO-dah) - I need help
- No entiendo (noh ehn-TYEHN-doh) - I don't understand
- Sí (see) - Yes
- No (noh) - No
- ¿Puedo usar el baño? (PWEH-doh oo-SAHR ehl BAH-nyoh?) - Can I use the bathroom?
- ¿Dónde está el baño? (DOHN-deh ehs-TAH ehl BAH-nyoh?) - Where is the bathroom?
- Estoy perdido/a (ehs-TOY pehr-DEE-doh/dah) - I am lost (male/female)
- Estoy buscando... (ehs-TOY BOOS-kahn-doh...) - I am looking for...
- ¿A qué hora abre/cierra? (ah keh OH-rah AH-breh/SYEHR-rah?) - What time does it open/close?
- No hablo español (noh AH-bloh es-pah-NYOHL) - I don't speak Spanish

- Hablo un poco de español (AH-bloh oon POH-koh deh es-pah-NYOHL) - I speak a little Spanish
- ¿Cuál es tu número de teléfono? (KWAHL ehs too NOO-meh-roh deh teh-LEH-foh-noh?) - What is your phone number?
- Estoy bien, gracias (ehs-TOY byehn, GRAH-syahs) - I'm fine, thank you
- ¿Qué pasa? (keh PAH-sah?) - What's happening? / What's up?
- Estoy cansado/a (ehs-TOY kahn-SAH-doh/dah) - I am tired (male/female)
- Estoy emocionado/a (ehs-TOY eh-moh-syoh-NAH-doh/dah) - I am excited (male/female)
- ¡Feliz cumpleaños! (feh-LEES koom-pleh-ahn-yohs) - Happy birthday!
- ¿Cuál es tu comida favorita? (KWAHL ehs too koh-MEE-dah fah-boh-REE-tah?) - What's your favorite food?
- ¿Quieres bailar conmigo? (KYEH-rehs bahy-LAHR kohn-MEE-goh?) - Do you want to dance with me?
- ¿Qué recomiendas? (keh reh-koh-MYEHN-dahs?) - What do you recommend?
- ¿Cómo llego a...? (KOH-moh YEH-goh ah...?) - How do I get to...?
- ¿Puedo pagar con tarjeta de crédito? (PWEH-doh pah-GAHR kohn tahr-HEH-tah deh KREH-dee-toh?) - Can I pay with a credit card?
- ¿Cuánto tiempo se tarda? (KWAHN-toh tee-EHM-poh seh TAHR-dah?) - How long does it take?
- ¿Cuántos años tienes? (KWAHN-tohs AH-nohs tee-EH-nehs?) - How old are you?
- ¿Cuál es tu deporte favorito? (KWAHL ehs too deh-pohr-teh fah-boh-REE-toh?) - What is your favorite sport?
- ¿Dónde vives? (DOHN-deh BEE-vehs?) - Where do you live?
- ¿Qué te gusta hacer en tu tiempo libre? (keh teh GOOS-tah ah-sehr ehn too TYEM-poh lee-BRE?) - What do you like to do in your free time?
- ¿Cuál es tu película favorita? (KWAHL ehs too peh-LEE-koo-lah fah-boh-REE-tah?) - What is your favorite movie?
- ¿Te gustaría salir a cenar conmigo? (teh goos-TAH-ree-ah sah-LEER ah seh-NAHR kohn-MEE-goh?) - Would you like to go out to dinner with me?
- ¡Buena suerte! (BWAY-nah SWER-teh) - Good luck!
- ¿Puedo tomar una foto contigo? (PWEH-doh toh-MAHR OO-nah FOH-toh kohn-TEE-goh?) - Can I take a photo with you?

- ¿Qué día es hoy? (keh DEE-ah ehs oy?) - What day is today?
- ¿Cuándo es tu cumpleaños? (KWAHN-doh ehs too koom-pleh-ahn-yohs?) - When is your birthday?
- ¡Salud! (sah-LOOD) - Cheers!
- ¿Cuál es tu color favorito? (KWAHL ehs too koh-LOHR fah-boh-REE-toh?) - What is your favorite color?
- ¿Qué hora cierra el supermercado? (keh OH-rah SYEHR-rah ehl soo-pehr-mehr-KAH-doh?) - What time does the supermarket close?
- ¡Diviértete! (dee-vyehr-TEH-teh) - Have fun!
- ¿Cómo se dice... en español? (KOH-moh seh DEE-seh... en es-pah-NYOHL?) - How do you say... in Spanish?
- ¿Qué tiempo hace hoy? (keh TYEHM-poh AH-seh oy?) - What's the weather like today?
- ¿Qué quieres hacer hoy? (keh KYEH-res ah-sehr oy?) - What do you want to do today?
- ¿Cómo te fue? (KOH-moh teh FWEH?) - How was it? (referring to an experience)
- ¡Qué tengas un buen día! (keh TEHN-gahs oon BWEHN DEE-ah) - Have a good day!
- ¿Cómo se llama esto? (KOH-moh seh YAH-mah EHS-toh?) - What is this called?
- ¿Dónde está la estación de tren? (DOHN-deh ehs-TAH lah ehs-tah-see-OHN deh tren?) - Where is the train station?
- ¿Puedes repetir, por favor? (PWEH-dehs reh-peh-TEER, por fah-BOHR?) - Can you repeat, please?
- ¿Cuál es tu música favorita? (KWAHL ehs too MOO-see-kah fah-boh-REE-tah?) - What is your favorite music?
- ¿Quieres algo de beber? (KYEH-rehs AHL-goh deh beh-BEHR?) - Do you want something to drink?
- ¡Qué bonito/a! (keh boh-NEE-toh/ah) - How beautiful!
- ¿A dónde quieres ir? (ah DOHN-deh KYEH-res eer?) - Where do you want to go?
- ¿Qué estás haciendo? (keh ehs-TAHS ah-see-EHN-doh?) - What are you doing?
- ¿Cuántas personas hay? (KWAHN-tahs pehr-SOH-nahs eye?) - How many people are there?
- ¡Buen provecho! (bwayn proh-VEH-choh) - Enjoy your meal!

- ¿Dónde puedo encontrar un cajero automático? (DOHN-deh PWEH-doh ehn-kohn-TRAR oon kah-HEH-roh ow-toh-MAH-tee-koh?) - Where can I find an ATM?
- ¿Qué opinas? (keh oh-PEE-nahs?) - What do you think?
- ¿Cómo te fue el día? (KOH-moh teh FWEH ehl DEE-ah?) - How was your day?
- ¿Qué te parece? (keh teh pah-REH-seh?) - What do you think about it?
- ¿Cuál es tu libro favorito? (KWAHL ehs too LEE-broh fah-boh-REE-toh?) - What is your favorite book?
- ¿Cuándo llegaste? (KWAHN-doh yeh-GAH-steh?) - When did you arrive?
- ¿Qué quieres ser cuando seas grande? (keh KYEH-res sehr KWAHN-doh sehr-RAHS GRAHN-deh?) - What do you want to be when you grow up?
- ¿Qué te gusta más? (keh teh GOOS-tah mas?) - What do you like more?
- ¿Cuántos años tienes tu hermano/a? (KWAHN-tos AH-nohs tee-EH-nehs too ehr-MAH-noh/ah?) - How old is your brother/sister?
- ¿Te gustaría ir al cine? (teh goos-TAH-ree-ah eer ahl SEE-neh?) - Would you like to go to the movies?
- ¿Por qué hiciste eso? (por keh ee-SEES-teh EH-soh?) - Why did you do that?
- ¿Qué tipo de música te gusta? (keh TEE-poh deh MOO-see-kah teh GOOS-tah?) - What kind of music do you like?
- ¿Dónde trabajas? (DOHN-deh trah-bah-HAHS?) - Where do you work?
- ¿Qué hiciste ayer? (keh ee-SEES-teh ah-YEHR?) - What did you do yesterday?
- ¿Dónde aprendiste español? (DOHN-deh ah-prehn-DEES-teh es-pah-NYOHL?) - Where did you learn Spanish?
- ¿Qué prefieres? (keh preh-fee-REHS?) - What do you prefer?
- ¿Qué te hizo venir aquí? (keh teh EE-soh veh-NEER ah-KEE?) - What made you come here?
- ¿Cuándo es tu cumpleaños? (KWAHN-doh ehs too koom-pleh-ahn-yohs?) - When is your birthday?
- ¿Cuánto tiempo has estado aquí? (KWAHN-toh tee-EHM-poh ahs ehs-TAH-doh ah-KEE?) - How long have you been here?
- ¿Qué hora es en tu país? (keh OH-rah ehs ehn too PAH-ees?) - What time is it in your country?

- ¿Qué te gusta hacer en tu tiempo libre? (keh teh GOOS-tah ah-SEHR ehn too TYEM-poh LEE-breh?) - What do you like to do in your free time?
- ¿Dónde viviste antes de venir aquí? (DOHN-deh bee-VEES-teh ahn-TEHS deh veh-NEER ah-KEE?) - Where did you live before coming here?
- ¿Cuál es tu número de teléfono? (KWAHL ehs too NOO-meh-roh deh teh-LEH-foh-noh?) - What is your phone number?
- ¿Cómo se llega a la estación de tren? (KOH-moh seh YEH-gah ah lah ehs-tah-see-OHN deh tren?) - How do you get to the train station?
- ¿Por qué no puedes venir? (por keh noh PWEH-dehs veh-NEER?) - Why can't you come?
- ¿Cómo puedo llegar a la playa? (KOH-moh PWEH-doh YEH-gahr ah lah PLAH-yah?) - How can I get to the beach?
- ¿Qué día es hoy? (keh DEE-ah ehs oy?) - What day is today?
- ¿Qué deportes te gustan? (keh deh-POHR-tehs teh GOOS-tahn?) - What sports do you like?
- ¿Cómo se escribe tu nombre? (KOH-moh seh ehs-CREE-beh too NOHM-breh?) - How do you spell your name?
- ¿Qué hora es el partido? (keh OH-rah ehs ehl pahr-TEE-doh?) - What time is the game?
- ¿Cuál es tu restaurante favorito? (KWAHL ehs too rehs-tow-RAHN-teh fah-boh-REE-toh?) - What is your favorite restaurant?
- ¿Dónde puedo comprar recuerdos? (DOHN-deh PWEH-doh kohm-PRAR reh-kwehr-DOHR-ehs?) - Where can I buy souvenirs?

Spanish Slang

Starting with **Moorish rule**, Arabic words snuck into daily vocabulary, and some slang still reflects that influence today. For example, "ojalá" (meaning "hopefully") comes from "Inshallah," an Arabic phrase meaning "God willing." After the **Reconquista** (when the Christians took back Spain from the Moors), Spanish began to develop more distinctly, but it was far from unified.

Fast forward a few centuries, and we start seeing **regional slang** emerging. Spain isn't just one language; it's a mosaic of dialects and languages like Catalan, Galician, Basque, and Andalusian Spanish. These regions developed their own sets of slang, many of which have traveled far beyond their borders. For instance, Andalusia gave us **"illo"** (short for chiquillo, meaning "kid"), which is used in the south like "dude" or "man."

Cultural shifts also played a big role in shaping Spanish slang. In the **20th century**, the language absorbed influences from pop culture, especially from Latin America. Spanish soap operas, reggaeton, and globalized media started flooding Spain with slang from places like Mexico, Colombia, and Argentina. This cross-pollination led to fun expressions like "**flipar**" (to freak out) and "**guay**" (cool), which are now common across Spain, though they started in particular areas or contexts.

And of course, Spain's slang has always reflected its **youth culture**. The slang that emerged during Franco's dictatorship, for instance, had to do with rebellion, secrecy, and anti-establishment ideas. Post-dictatorship, the freedom of the 1980s ushered in "La Movida Madrileña," a cultural movement that exploded with new music, art, and, naturally, language. Youth adopted edgy words to express their independence, like "**molar**" (meaning something is cool or you dig it) or "**pasar** de alguien" (to not care about someone).

Today, **social media** plays a huge role in keeping slang fresh. Words like "**postureo**" (posing for Instagram) and "**crush**" (adopted from English for someone you like) show how the language evolves with each generation.

1. ¡Hostia!

- **Meaning:** "Damn!" or "Holy shit!"
- **Pronunciation:** Ohs-tee-ah
- **Usage:** It's used as an exclamation of surprise or frustration. In Andalusia, this is very common.

2. ¡Qué chulo!

- **Meaning:** "How cool!"
- **Pronunciation:** Keh choo-loh
- **Usage:** This can refer to something cool or stylish. In some regions, "chulo" can also mean cocky or arrogant.

3. ¡Coño!

- **Meaning:** "Damn!" or stronger, depending on context (literally "cunt," but commonly used as a general curse word).
- **Pronunciation:** Koh-nyoh
- **Usage:** An expression of surprise, anger, or frustration.

4. ¡Joder!

- **Meaning:** "F*ck!"
- **Pronunciation:** Ho-derr
- **Usage:** One of the most common curse words in Spain, used like the English f-word, for frustration or emphasis.

5. Tío/Tía

- **Meaning:** "Dude" or "chick" (literally "uncle/aunt").
- **Pronunciation:** Tee-oh / Tee-ah
- **Usage:** Used informally to refer to friends or strangers, like "bro" or "man."

6. ¡Vete a la mierda!

- **Meaning:** "Go to hell!" or "Go f*ck yourself!"
- **Pronunciation:** Beh-teh ah lah mee-er-dah
- **Usage:** Said in anger to someone, equivalent to telling them to get lost or worse.

7. ¡Cabrón!

- **Meaning:** "Asshole" or "bastard" (literally "male goat").
- **Pronunciation:** Kah-brohn
- **Usage:** Often used as an insult for someone who has done something bad.

8. ¡Guay!

- **Meaning:** "Cool!" or "Awesome!"
- **Pronunciation:** Goo-eye
- **Usage:** Used to describe something fun, cool, or impressive.

9. Flipar

- **Meaning:** "To freak out" (positively or negatively).
- **Pronunciation:** Flee-par
- **Usage:** Used when something surprises or amazes you, similar to "freak out" or "trip out."

10. ¡Madre mía!

- **Meaning:** "Oh my God!" or "Oh dear!"
- **Pronunciation:** Mah-dreh mee-ah
- **Usage:** Used to express shock or disbelief.

11. ¡Puta madre!

- **Meaning:** "Motherf*cker!*" *or* "*F*cking great!" (depending on tone).
- **Pronunciation:** Poo-tah mah-dreh
- **Usage:** Used both in positive and negative situations, depending on the tone.

12. Majo/Maja

- **Meaning:** "Nice" or "sweet" (describing a person).
- **Pronunciation:** Mah-ho / Mah-ha
- **Usage:** Used to refer to someone who's kind or pleasant.

13. ¡La leche!

- **Meaning:** "The milk!" (slang for "wow!" or "damn!")
- **Pronunciation:** Lah leh-cheh
- **Usage:** Used in a wide variety of situations to express shock or amazement.

14. ¡Me cago en...!

- **Meaning:** "I sh*t on..." (followed by various things).
- **Pronunciation:** Meh kah-goh en
- **Usage:** Used to express frustration, followed by something like "la leche" (the milk) or "Dios" (God).

15. Pringado

- **Meaning:** "Loser" or "sucker."
- **Pronunciation:** Preen-gah-doh
- **Usage:** Used to describe someone who is gullible or always gets the short end of the stick.

Common complaints of tourists visiting

Here's a chart outlining common complaints of tourists visiting Spain along with solutions:

Common Complaint	Solution
Language Barrier	Learn basic Spanish phrases or use translation apps for communication.
High Tourist Crowds	Visit popular attractions early in the morning or late in the afternoon.
Long Lines at Attractions	Purchase skip-the-line tickets online or visit during off-peak hours.
Overpriced Tourist Traps	Research restaurants and shops frequented by locals for better prices.
Pickpocketing and Theft	Keep valuables secure and be vigilant, especially in crowded areas.
Tourist Scams	Be wary of unsolicited offers and always verify prices and services.
Poor Service in Restaurants	Look for well-reviewed restaurants or ask locals for recommendations.
Limited Public Restrooms	Plan restroom breaks strategically and use facilities in cafes or malls.
Overcrowded Public Transportation	Avoid rush hours or opt for alternative transportation like taxis or Uber.
Difficulty Navigating	Use maps apps or carry a physical map, and ask locals for directions.
Noise and Disruptions	Research accommodations away from noisy areas or use earplugs.

Checklist of top 20 things To Do

Here's a checklist of the top 20 things to do in Spain:

- ☑ Visit the Sagrada Familia in Barcelona
- ☑ Explore the Alhambra in Granada
- ☑ Walk along the historic streets of Toledo
- ☑ Experience the vibrant nightlife of Madrid
- ☑ Relax on the beaches of Costa del Sol
- ☑ Wander through the medieval streets of Seville's old town
- ☑ Marvel at the architecture of Park Güell in Barcelona
- ☑ Sample tapas in the bars of San Sebastián
- ☑ Visit the Prado Museum in Madrid
- ☑ Take a flamenco dance lesson in Andalusia
- ☑ Hike the Camino de Santiago pilgrimage route
- ☑ Explore the Guggenheim Museum in Bilbao
- ☑ Relax in the hot springs of Pamplona
- ☑ Tour the Royal Palace in Madrid
- ☑ Discover the historic city of Córdoba
- ☑ Go wine tasting in La Rioja region
- ☑ Watch a bullfight in Seville
- ☑ Take a boat tour of the Canary Islands
- ☑ Visit the ancient Roman ruins of Tarragona
- ☑ Explore the historic fortress of Alcazar in Segovia

History

Ancient Spain: From Iberians to Romans

One of the earliest civilizations to inhabit the Iberian Peninsula were the Iberians, who left behind archaeological remains such as the famous Lady of Elche sculpture. The Phoenicians and Greeks also established colonies along the coast, contributing to trade and cultural exchange in the region. However, it was the Romans who exerted the most significant influence on ancient Spain.

Tourists are often drawn to sites such as Tarragona, where they can explore the well-preserved Roman amphitheater and aqueduct, and Mérida, known for its impressive Roman theater and temple of Diana. These archaeological sites offer insights into Roman life in Hispania, showcasing the grandeur of their architecture and the sophistication of their engineering.

The Moorish Legacy: Islamic Spain

One of the most captivating periods of Spanish history is the era of Al-Andalus, when much of the Iberian Peninsula was ruled by Muslim dynasties. The Moors, as they were known, brought with them a rich Islamic culture and advanced civilization, leaving an indelible mark on Spain's architecture, language, and cuisine.

Tourists flock to cities like Granada to marvel at the breathtaking Alhambra palace, a UNESCO World Heritage site renowned for its intricate Islamic architecture and stunning gardens. The Mezquita-Catedral in Córdoba is another must-visit attraction, with its unique blend of Moorish and Christian elements symbolizing the coexistence of cultures during this period.

The Reconquista and Christian Spain

The Reconquista, or reconquest, refers to the centuries-long Christian campaign to retake the Iberian Peninsula from Muslim rule. This period of conflict and conquest shaped Spain's identity and left behind a legacy of medieval castles, fortresses, and cathedrals.

Tourists often visit iconic landmarks such as the Santiago de Compostela Cathedral, a pilgrimage site that houses the remains of the apostle St. James, and the medieval fortress of Alcázar of Segovia, which is said to have inspired Walt Disney's Cinderella Castle. These sites offer glimpses into Spain's medieval past and the struggles for power and control that defined the era.

The Age of Exploration: Spain's Golden Age

During the 15th and 16th centuries, Spain experienced a period of unparalleled wealth and influence as a result of its exploration and colonization of the Americas. The Age of

Exploration brought vast riches to Spain and ushered in a golden age of art, literature, and innovation.

Tourists often visit Seville's Plaza de España, a stunning example of Spanish Renaissance architecture built for the Ibero-American Exposition of 1929, and the Royal Monastery of San Lorenzo de El Escorial, a grand complex commissioned by King Philip II. These sites serve as reminders of Spain's imperial past and its enduring cultural legacy.

The Spanish Civil War and Franco's Dictatorship

The 20th century was marked by periods of political upheaval and social unrest in Spain, most notably the Spanish Civil War and the subsequent dictatorship of General Francisco Franco. The scars of these turbulent times are still visible today, shaping Spain's modern identity and political landscape.

Tourists interested in this period of history often visit sites like the Valley of the Fallen, a controversial monument built by Franco to honor those who died in the civil war, and the Guernica Peace Museum, which commemorates the tragic bombing of the town of Guernica during the war. These sites offer opportunities for reflection and remembrance, shedding light on Spain's complex and sometimes painful past.

Spain today

The country has emerged as a major player in Europe, known for its thriving tourism, world-class cuisine, and passionate traditions like flamenco and fútbol. Politically, Spain is navigating challenges with Catalonia's push for independence still simmering under the surface, while economic recovery post-pandemic remains a focus. Major events like the **Feria de Abril** in Seville, the **Running of the Bulls** in Pamplona, and the iconic **La Tomatina** festival continue to attract global visitors. Spain's shift toward sustainability is also notable, with renewable energy projects and a push for greener cities.

In daily life, Spaniards are embracing modernity while staying rooted in tradition—whether it's taking part in the timeless **siesta**, enjoying long evenings filled with **tapas**, or packing plazas for political discussions and social gatherings. The country continues to balance the old with the new, making it a fascinating place to visit and explore today!

How to Have a $10,000 Trip to Spain for $500: A Detailed Breakdown

Category	Luxury Value	Budget Hack	Estimated Cost	Tips from Locals
Flights	Regular price: $1,500 round-trip to Spain	Book with **TAP Portugal** for flights under $200, flying into smaller airports like Seville or Bilbao	$200 (round-trip)	- TAP Portugal often offers great deals, especially if you're willing to take a stopover in Lisbon. - Subscribe to fare alerts or use points from frequent flyer programs for even better deals.
Accommodation	5-star hotels: $300/night x 10 = $3,000	Mix **$10/night mountain huts** on hiking trips with occasional day passes to **5-star hotel pools**	$100 for huts + $50 day passes = $150	- Locals often stay in **refugios** (mountain huts) when hiking in places like the Picos de Europa or Pyrenees. - Use **day passes** at luxury hotels to enjoy the pool, spa, and gym without paying full accommodation prices.
Food & Dining	Gourmet restaurants: $200/day x 10 = $2,000	Eat where the locals do: enjoy the **free tapa** with drinks and shop at **local markets**	$100 for 10 days	- In Granada, every drink comes with a free tapa, and in Madrid, you can enjoy budget-friendly **menú del día** for around $10-$12. - Shop for fresh produce, cured meats, and cheeses at **Mercado de San Miguel** or smaller local markets.
Shopping	High-end boutiques: $1,000	Buy **second-hand** and vintage fashion from **markets** like El Rastro in Madrid	$50	- Spanish locals love to shop at **vintage markets** like El Rastro or **Wallapop**, an app for second-hand items. - For souvenirs, browse **local artisans** or regional specialties like **jamón ibérico** or **local ceramics**.
Luxury Experiences	Spa days, high-end tours: $2,000	Use **Too Good to Go** for luxury food at a discount, and mix luxury with free experiences	$50	- Download **Too Good to Go**, an app that lets you buy leftover food from high-end restaurants and bakeries at reduced prices. - Combine free experiences like **beach days** or hikes with discounted day passes to spas.
Transportation	Private cars: $500	Use public transport and **BlaBlaCar**, a ride-sharing service for long distances	$50	- Public transportation in Spain is top-notch and affordable. **Renfe** trains and **Alsa** buses can get you around for a fraction of the price of renting a car. - **BlaBlaCar** offers cheap rides and is a great way to meet locals.

Attractio ns & Tours	$1,000 in museum and tour fees	Use **free museum days**, and hike free trails, plus free walking tours in major cities	$50	- Many museums in Spain are free on certain days or evenings—check schedules for places like the **Prado Museum** and **Museo Picasso**. - Spain's national parks offer countless free hiking opportunities, especially in regions like Asturias.
Daily Expenses	$1,000 for daily miscellane ous costs	Bring **water bottles** to refill, and grab **Too Good to Go**snack bags for cheap eats	$50	- Refill your bottle at public fountains, especially in Madrid or Seville. - Plan ahead with **Too Good to Go** to get bakery or restaurant leftovers at the end of the day for snacks and even meals, saving tons on food costs.

Detailed Recommendations for Luxury on a Budget

1. **Flights:**

   ○ **TAP Portugal** often has sales, and their Lisbon stopover program means you can enjoy two cities for the price of one. Flying into less popular cities like Bilbao, Seville, or even Santiago de Compostela can reduce costs.
   ○ Be flexible with dates to catch better deals, and consider mid-week departures and returns for the lowest fares.
   ○ Pro tip: Use fare aggregators like Skyscanner, and sign up for newsletters from airlines to stay updated on flash sales.

2. **Accommodation:**

   ○ **Mountain huts** (refugios) are hidden gems in Spain's rural hiking regions like the Pyrenees or Picos de Europa. These lodges can cost as little as $10 a night and offer unbeatable views and experiences.
   ○ Splurge occasionally on luxury with **day passes** to 5-star hotels like **Hotel Alfonso XIII** in Seville or **Mandarin Oriental** in Barcelona, where for $50 or less, you can enjoy their pools, spas, and rooftop views without paying the hefty room rates.
   ○ Use **Airbnb** or couch-surfing platforms to connect with locals who can offer budget-friendly accommodation and insider tips.

3. **Food:**

   ○ Spain is known for its **free tapas** culture, especially in places like Granada. Order a drink, and you'll receive a small dish at no extra cost.
   ○ **Too Good to Go** is an absolute lifesaver when traveling on a budget. You can pick up luxury restaurant leftovers for $3-$5, which often include meals that would otherwise cost over $50.
   ○ For a true local experience, hit up **markets** like **La Boquería** in Barcelona or **Mercado de San Antón** in Madrid to buy fresh ingredients and picnic like a local.

4. **Shopping:**

   ○ Second-hand markets like **El Rastro** in Madrid (open every Sunday) or online platforms like **Wallapop** can help you score fashionable pieces for a fraction of the cost.
   ○ Focus on **local artisans** for souvenirs—buying from them is often much cheaper than tourist shops and provides a unique keepsake like hand-painted ceramics or handmade leather goods.

5. **Luxury Experiences:**

   - Want the luxury of a Michelin meal on a budget? Look for special lunch menus at Michelin-star restaurants, where you can dine for around $30-$50, compared to hundreds of dollars for dinner.
   - Mix free experiences like wandering **Park Güell** in Barcelona, enjoying the beaches of **Costa del Sol**, or taking advantage of **free walking tours** in cities like Madrid or Seville.
   - Spain has plenty of free festivals throughout the year, from the **Semana Santa** processions to **local fiestas** in small towns, giving you a taste of the culture without breaking the bank.

6. **Transportation:**

   - Public transportation in Spain is reliable and inexpensive. Use **Renfe's AVE trains** for fast, affordable travel between cities, and **Alsa buses** for routes not covered by trains.
   - **BlaBlaCar** is a popular ride-sharing service where you can book car rides with locals going the same direction for far cheaper than a train or bus ticket.
   - **Walk!** Spanish cities are walkable, and exploring on foot allows you to discover hidden gems that most tourists miss.

7. **Attractions:**

   - Many of Spain's top attractions, like **The Alhambra** and **Sagrada Familia**, have specific days or times when entry is free. Plan ahead to take advantage of these windows.
   - Spain's numerous **national parks** offer free hiking and breathtaking views. Whether you're scaling the peaks of the Pyrenees or trekking through the desert landscapes of **Las Bardenas Reales**, nature's beauty won't cost you a thing.
   - Consider **free walking tours**, which are available in most major cities. They operate on a tips-only basis, so you can enjoy expert guides for as little or as much as you want to contribute.

8. **Daily Expenses:**

   - Always carry a **reusable water bottle**. Most cities, including **Madrid** and **Seville**, have clean, public water fountains where you can refill throughout the day.
   - Use **Too Good to Go** not only for full meals but for snacks and even breakfast the next morning by grabbing bakery leftovers the night before.
   - Set a daily budget and stick to it—spending small amounts on tapas, market snacks, and coffee will go a long way. Opt for street food where locals eat for extra savings.

The secret to saving HUGE amounts of money when travelling to Spain is...

Your mindset. Money is an emotional topic, if you associate words like cheapskate, Miser (and its £9.50 to go into Charles Dickens London house, oh the Irony) with being thrifty when traveling you are likely to say 'F-it' and spend your money needlessly because you associate pain with saving money. You pay now for an immediate reward. Our brains are prehistoric; they focus on surviving day to day. Travel companies and hotels know this and put trillions into making you believe you will be happier when you spend on their products or services. Our poor brains are up against outdated programming and an onslaught of advertisements bombarding us with the message: spending money on travel equals PLEASURE. To correct this carefully lodged propaganda in your frontal cortex, you need to imagine your future self.

Saving money does not make you a cheapskate. It makes you smart. How do people get rich? They invest their money. They don't go out and earn it; they let their money earn more money. So every time you want to spend money, imagine this: while you travel, your money is working for you, not you for money. While you sleep, the money, you've invested is going up and up. That's a pleasure a pricey entrance fee can't give you. Thinking about putting your money to work for you tricks your brain into believing you are not withholding pleasure from yourself, you are saving your money to invest so you can go to even more amazing places. You are thus turning thrifty travel into a pleasure fueled sport.

When you've got money invested - If you want to splash your cash on a first-class airplane seat - you can. I can't tell you how to invest your money, only that you should. Saving $20 on taxis doesn't seem like much, but over time you could save upwards of $15,000 a year, which is a deposit for a house which you can rent on Airbnb to finance more travel. Your brain making money looks like your brain on cocaine, so tell yourself saving money is making money.

Scientists have proved that imagining your future self is the easiest way to associate pleasure with saving money. You can download FaceApp — which will give you a picture of what you will look like older and grayer, or you can take a deep breath just before spending money and ask yourself if you will regret the purchase later.

The easiest ways to waste money traveling are:

Getting a taxi. The solution to this is to always download the google map before you go. Many taxi drivers will drive you around for 15 minutes when the place you were trying to get to is a 5-minute walk... remember while not getting an overpriced taxi to tell yourself, 'I am saving money to free myself for more travel.'
Spending money on overpriced food when hungry. The solution: carry snacks. A banana and an apple will cost you, in most places, less than a dollar.

Spending on entrance fees to top-rated attractions. If you really want to do it, spend the money happily. If you're conflicted, sleep on it. I don't regret spending $200 on a sky dive over the Great Barrier Reef; I regret going to the top of the shard on a cloudy day in Spain for $60. Only you can know, but make sure it's your decision and not the marketing directors at said top-rated attraction.

Telling yourself 'you only have the chance to see/eat/experience it now'. While this might be true, make sure YOU WANT to spend the money. Money spent is money you can't invest, and often you can have the same experience for much less.

You can experience luxurious travel on a small budget, which will trick your brain into thinking you're already a high-roller, which will mean you'll be more likely to act like one and invest your money. Stay in five-star hotels for $5 by booking on the day of your stay on booking.com to enjoy last-minute deals. You can go to fancy restaurants using daily deal sites. Ask your airline about last-minute upgrades to first-class or business. I paid $100 extra on a $179 ticket to Cuba from Germany to be bumped to Business Class. When you ask, it will surprise you what you can get both at hotels and airlines.

Travel, as the saying goes, is the only thing you spend money on that makes you richer. You can easily waste money, making it difficult to enjoy that metaphysical wealth. The biggest money saving secret is to turn bargain hunting into a pleasurable activity, not an annoyance. Budgeting consciously can be fun, don't feel disappointed because you don't spend the $60 to go into an attraction. Feel good because soon that $60 will soon earn money for you. Meaning, you'll have the time and money to enjoy more metaphysical wealth while your bank balance increases.

So there it is. You can save a small fortune by being strategic with your trip planning. We've arranged everything in the guide to offer the best bang for your buck. Which means we took the view that if it's not an excellent investment for your money, we wouldn't include it. Why would a guide called 'Super Cheap' include lots of overpriced attractions? That said, if you think we've missed something or have unanswered questions, ping me an email: philgtang@gmail.com I'm on central Europe time and usually reply within 8 hours of getting your mail. We like to think of our guide books as evolving organisms helping our readers travel better cheaper. We use reader questions via email to update this book year round so you'll be helping other readers and yourself.

Don't put your dreams off!

Time is a currency you never get back and travel is its greatest return on investment. Plus, now you know you can visit Spain for a fraction of the price most would have you believe.

Malaga

Thank you for reading

Dear **Lovely Reader,**

If you have found this book useful, please consider writing a quick review on Amazon.

One person from every 1000 readers leaves a review on Amazon. It would mean more than you could ever know if you were one of our 1 in 1000 people to take the time to write a brief review.

Thank you so much for reading again and for spending your time and investing your trips future in Super Cheap Insider Guides.

One last note, please don't listen to anyone who says 'Oh no, you can't visit Spain on a budget'. Unlike you, they didn't have this book. You can do ANYWHERE on a budget with the right insider advice and planning. Sure, learning to travel to Spain on a budget that doesn't compromise on anything or drastically compromise on safety or comfort levels is a skill, but this guide has done the detective work for you. Now it is time for you to put the advice into action.

Phil and the Super Cheap Insider Guides Team

P.S If you need any more super cheap tips we'd love to hear from you e-mail me at philgtang@gmail.com, we have a lot of contacts in every region, so if there's a specific bargain you're hunting we can help you find it.

DISCOVER YOUR NEXT VACATION

☑ **LUXURY ON A BUDGET APPROACH**
☑ **CHOOSE FROM 107 DESTINATIONS**
☑ **EACH BOOK PACKED WITH REAL-TIME LOCAL TIPS**

All are available in Paperback and e-book on Amazon:
https://www.Amazon.com/dp/B09C2DHQG5

Several are available as audiobooks. You can watch excerpts of ALL for FREE on YouTube: https://youtube.com/channel/UCxo9YV8-M9P1cFosU-Gjnqg

COUNTRY GUIDES

Super Cheap AUSTRALIA
Super Cheap CANADA
Super Cheap DENMARK
Super Cheap FINLAND
Super Cheap FRANCE
Super Cheap GERMANY
Super Cheap ICELAND
Super Cheap ITALY
Super Cheap IRELAND
Super Cheap JAPAN
Super Cheap LUXEMBOURG
Super Cheap MALDIVES 2025
Super Cheap NEW ZEALAND
Super Cheap NORWAY
Super Cheap Spain
Super Cheap SWITZERLAND

MORE GUIDES

Super Cheap ADELAIDE 2025
Super Cheap ALASKA 2025
Super Cheap AUSTIN 2025
Super Cheap BANGKOK 2025
Super Cheap BARCELONA 2025
Super Cheap BELFAST 2025
Super Cheap BERMUDA 2025
Super Cheap BORA BORA 2025
Super Cheap Great Barrier Reef 2025
Super Cheap CAMBRIDGE 2025
Super Cheap CANCUN 2025
Super Cheap CHIANG MAI 2025
Super Cheap CHICAGO 2025
Super Cheap DOHA 2025
Super Cheap DUBAI 2025
Super Cheap DUBLIN 2025
Super Cheap EDINBURGH 2025

Super Cheap GALWAY 2025
Super Cheap LAS VEGAS 2025
Super Cheap LIMA 2025
Super Cheap LISBON 2025
Super Cheap MALAGA 2025
Super Cheap Machu Pichu 2025
Super Cheap MIAMI 2025
Super Cheap Milan 2025
Super Cheap NASHVILLE 2025
Super Cheap NEW ORLEANS 2025
Super Cheap NEW YORK 2025
Super Cheap PARIS 2025
Super Cheap SEYCHELLES 2025
Super Cheap SINGAPORE 2025
Super Cheap ST LUCIA 2025
Super Cheap TORONTO 2025
Super Cheap TURKS AND CAICOS 2025
Super Cheap VENICE 2025
Super Cheap VIENNA 2025
Super Cheap YOSEMITE 2025
Super Cheap ZURICH 2025
Super Cheap ZANZIBAR 2025

Bonus Travel Hacks

I've included these bonus travel hacks to help you plan and enjoy your trip to Spain cheaply, joyfully, and smoothly. Perhaps they will even inspire you to start or renew a passion for long-term travel.

Common pitfalls when it comes to allocating money to <u>your desires</u> while traveling

Beware of Malleable mental accounting

Let's say you budgeted spending only $30 per day in Spain but then you say well if I was at home I'd be spending $30 on food as an everyday purchase so you add another $30 to your budget. Don't fall into that trap as the likelihood is you still have expenses at home even if its just the cost of keeping your freezer going.

Beware of impulse purchases in Spain

Restaurants that you haven't researched and just idle into can sometimes turn out to be great, but more often, they turn out to suck, especially if they are near tourist attractions. Make yourself a travel itinerary including where you'll eat breakfast and lunch. Dinner is always more expensive, so the meal best to enjoy at home or as a takeaway. This book is full of incredible cheap eats. All you have to do is plan to go to them.

Social media and FOMO (Fear of Missing Out)

'The pull of seeing acquaintances spend money on travel can often be a more powerful motivator to spend more while traveling than seeing an advertisement.' Beware of what you allow to influence you and go back to the question, what's the best money I can spend today?

Now-or-never sales strategies

One reason tourists are targeted by salespeople is the success of the now-or-never strategy. If you don't spend the money now… your never get the opportunity again. Rarely is this true.

Instead of spending your money on something you might not actually desire, take five minutes. Ask yourself, do I really want this? And return to the answer in five minutes. Your body will either say an absolute yes with a warm, excited feeling or a no with a weak, obscure feeling.

Unexpected costs

> **"Holding on to anger is like grasping a hot coal with the intent of throwing it at someone else; you only hurt yourself." The Buddha.**

One downside to traveling is unexpected costs. When these spring up from airlines, accommodation providers, tours and on and on, they feel like a punch in the gut. During the pandemic my earnings fell to 20% of what they are normally. No one was traveling, no one was buying travel guides. My accountant out of nowhere significantly raised his fee for the year despite the fact there was a lot less money to count. I was so angry I consulted a lawyer who told me you will spend more taking him to court than you will paying his bill. I had to get myself into a good feeling place before I paid his bill, so I googled how to feel good paying someone who has scammed you.

The answer: Write down that you will receive 10 times the amount you are paying from an unexpected source. I did that. Four months later, the accountant wrote to me. He had applied for a COVID subsidy for me and I would receive… you guessed it almost exactly 10 times his fee.

Make of that what you want. I don't wish to get embroiled in a conversation about what many term 'woo-woo', but the result of my writing that I would receive 10 times the amount made me feel much, much better when paying him. And ultimately, that was a gift in itself. So next time some airline or train operator or hotel/ Airbnb sticks you with an unexpected fee, immediately write that you will receive 10 times the amount you are paying from an unexpected source. Rise your vibe and skip the added price of feeling angry.

Hack your allocations for your Spain Trip

"The best trick for saving is to eliminate the decision to save." Perry Wright of Duke University.

Put the money you plan to spend in Spain on a pre-paid card in the local currency. This cuts out two problems - not knowing how much you've spent and totally avoiding expensive currency conversion fees.

You could even create separate spaces. This much for transportation, this for tours/entertainment, accommodation and food. We are reluctant to spend money that is pre-assigned to categories or uses.

Write that you want to enjoy a $3,000 trip for $500 to your Spain trip. Countless research shows when you put goals in writing, you have a higher chance of following through.

Spend all the money you want to on buying experiences in Spain

"Experiences are like good relatives that stay for a while and then leave. Objects are like relatives who move in and stay past their welcome." Daniel Gilbert, psychologist from Harvard University.

Economic and psychological research shows we are happier buying brief experiences on vacation rather than buying stuff to wear so give yourself freedom to spend on experiences knowing that the value you get back is many many times over.

Make saving money a game

There's one day a year where all the thrift shops where me and my family live sell everything there for a $1. My wife and I hold a contest where we take $5 and buy an entire outfit for each other. Whoever's outfit is liked more wins. We also look online to see whose outfit would have cost more to buy new. This year, my wife even snagged me an Armani coat for $1. I liked the coat when she showed it to me, but when I found out it was $500 new; I liked it and wore it a lot more.

Quadruple your money

Every-time you want to spend money, imagine it quadrupled. So the $10 you want to spend is actually $40. Now imagine that what you want to buy is four times the price. Do you still want it? If yes, go enjoy. If not, you've just saved yourself money, know you can choose to invest it in a way that quadruples or allocate it to something you really want to give you a greater return.

Understand what having unlimited amounts of money to spend in Spain actually looks like

Let's look at what it would be like to have unlimited amounts of money to spend on your trip to Spain.

Isolation

You take a private jet to your private Spain hotel. There you are lavished with the best food, drink, and entertainment. Spending vast amounts of money on vacation equals being isolated.

If you're on your honeymoon and you want to be alone with your Amore, this is wonderful, but it can be equally wonderful to make new friends. Know this a study 'carried out by Brigham Young University, Utah found that while obesity increased risk of death by 30%, loneliness increased it by half.'

Comfort

Money can buy you late check outs of five-star hotels and priority boarding on airlines, all of which add up to comfort. But as this book has shown you, saving money in Spain doesn't minimize comfort, that's just a lie travel agencies littered with glossy brochures want you to believe.

You can do late-check outs for free with the right credit cards and priority boarding can be purchased with a lot of airlines from $4. If you want to go big with first-class or business, flights offset your own travel costs by renting your own home or you can upgrade at the airport often for a fraction of what you would have paid booking a business flight online.

MORE TIPS TO FIND CHEAP FLIGHTS

"The use of travelling is to regulate imagination by reality, and instead of thinking how thin gs may be, to see them as they are." Samuel Jackson

If you're working full-time, you can save yourself a lot of money by requesting your time off from work starting in the middle of the week. Tuesdays and Wednesdays are the cheapest days to fly. You can save thousands just by adjusting your time off.

The simplest secret to booking cheap flights is open parameters. Let's say you want to fly from Chicago to Paris. You enter the USA in from and select Spain under to. You may find flights from New York City to Paris for $70. Then you just need to find a cheap flight to NYC. Make sure you calculate full costs, including if you need airport accommodation and of course getting to and from airports, **but in nearly every instance open parameters will save you at least half the cost of the flight.**

If you're not sure about where you want to go, use open parameters to show you the cheapest destinations from your city. Start with skyscanner.net they include the low-cost airlines that others like Kayak leave out. Google Flights can also show you cheap destinations. To see these leave the WHERE TO section blank. Open parameters can also show you the cheapest dates to fly. If you're flexible, you can save up to 80% of the flight cost. Always check the weather at your destination before you book. Sometimes a $400 flight will be $20, because it's monsoon season. But hey, if you like the rain, why not?

ALWAYS USE A PRIVATE BROWSER TO BOOK FLIGHTS

Skyscanner and other sites track your IP address and put prices up and down based on what they determine your strength of conviction to buy. e.g. if you've booked one-way and are looking for the return, these sites will jack the prices up by in most cases 50%. Incognito browsing pays.

Use a VPN such as Hola to book your flight from your destination

Install Hola, change your destination to the country you are flying to. The location from which a ticket is booked can affect the price significantly as algorithms consider local buying power.

Choose the right time to buy your ticket.

Choose the right time to buy your ticket, as purchasing tickets on a Sunday has been proven to be cheaper. If you can only book during the week, try to do it on a Tuesday.

Mistake fares

Email alerts from individual carriers are where you can find the best 'mistake fares". This is where a computer error has resulted in an airline offering the wrong fare. In my experience, it's best to sign up to individual carriers email lists, but if you ARE lazy Secret Flying puts together a daily roster of mistake fares. Visit https://www.secretflying.com/errorfare/ to see if there're any errors that can benefit you.

Fly late for cheaper prices

Red-eye flights, the ones that leave later in the day, are typically cheaper and less crowded, so aim to book that flight if possible. You will also get through the airport much quicker at the end of the day. Just make sure there's ground transport available for when you land. You don't want to save $50 on the airfare and spend it on a taxi to your accommodation.

Use this APP for same day flights

If your plans are flexible, use 'Get The Flight Out' (http://www.gtfoflights.com/) a fare tracker Hopper that shows you same-day deeply discounted flights. This is best for long-haul flights with major carriers. You can often find a British Airways round-trip from JFK Airport to Heathrow for $300. If you booked this in advance, you'd pay at least double.

Take an empty water bottle with you

Airport prices on food and drinks are sky high. It disgusts me to see some airports charging $10 for a bottle of water. ALWAYS take an empty water bottle with you. It's relatively unknown, but most airports have drinking water fountains past the security check. Just type in your airport name to wateratairports.com to locate the fountain. Then once you've passed security (because they don't allow you to take 100ml or more of liquids) you can freely refill your bottle with water.

Round-the-World (RTW) Tickets

It is always cheaper to book your flights using a DIY approach. First, you may decide you want to stay longer in one country, and a RTW will charge you a hefty fee for changing your flight. Secondly, it all depends on where and when you travel and as we have discussed, there are many ways to ensure you pay way less than $1,500 for a year of flights. If you're travelling long-haul, the best strategy is to buy a return ticket, say New York, to Bangkok and then take cheap flights or transport around Asia and even to Australia and beyond.

Cut your costs to and from airports

Don't you hate it when getting to and from the airport is more expensive than your flight! And this is true in so many cities, especially European ones. For some reason, Google often shows the most expensive options. Use Omio to compare the cheapest transport options and save on airport transfer costs.

Car sharing instead of taxis

Check if Spain has car sharing at the airport. Often they'll be tons of cars parked at the airport that are half the price of taking a taxi into the city. In most instances, you register your driving licence on an app and scan the code on the car to get going.

Checking Bags

Sometimes you need to check bags. If you do, put an AirTag inside. That way, you'll be about to see when you land where your bag is. This saves you the nail biting wait at baggage claim. And if worse comes to worst, and you see your bag is actually in another city, you can calmly stroll over to customer services and show them where your bag is.

Is it cheaper and more convenient to send your bags ahead?

Before you check your bags, check if it's cheaper to send them ahead of you with sendmybag.com obviously if you're staying in an Airbnb, you'll need to ask the hosts permission or you can time them to arrive the day after you. Hotels are normally very amenable.

What Credit Card Gives The Best Air Miles?

You can slash the cost of flights just for spending on a piece of plastic.

LET'S TALK ABOUT DEBT

Before we go into the best cards for each country, let's first talk about debt. The US system offers the best and biggest rewards. Why? Because they rely on the fact that many people living in the US will not pay their cards in full and the card will earn the bank significant interest payments. Other countries have a very different attitude towards money, debt, and saving than Americans. Thus in Germany and Austria the offerings aren't as favourable as the UK, Spain and Australia, where debt culture is more widely embraced. The takeaway here is this: **Only spend on one of these cards when you have set-up an automatic total monthly balance repayment. Don't let banks profit from your lizard brain!**

The best air-mile credit cards for those living in the UK

Amex Preferred Rewards Gold comes out top for those living in the UK for 2025.

Here are the benefits:

- 20,000-point bonus on £3,000 spend in first three months. These can be used towards flights with British Airways, Virgin Atlantic, Emirates and Etihad, and often other rewards, such as hotel stays and car hire.
- 1 point per £1 spent
- 1 point = 1 airline point
- Two free visits a year to airport lounges
- No fee in year one, then £140/yr

The downside:

- Fail to repay fully and it's 59.9% rep APR interest, incl fee

You'll need to cancel before the £140/yr fee kicks in year two if you want to avoid it.

The best air-mile credit cards for those living in Canada

Aeroplan is the superior rewards program in Canada. The card has a high earn rate for Aeroplan Points, generating 1.5 points per $1 spent on eligible purchases. Look at the specifics of the eligible purchases https://www.aircanada.com/ca/en/aco/home/aeroplan/earn.html. If you're not spending on these things AMEX's Membership Rewards program offers you the best returns in Canada.

The best air-mile credit cards for those living in Germany

If you have a German bank account, you can apply for a Lufthansa credit card.

Earn 50,000 award miles if you spend $3,000 in purchases and paying the annual fee, both within the first 90 days.

Earn 2 award miles per $1 spent on ticket purchases directly from Miles & More integrated airline partners.

Earn 1 award mile per $1 spent on all other purchases.

The downsides

the €89 annual fee

Limited to fly with Lufthansa and its partners but you can capitalise on perks like the companion pass and airport lounge vouchers.

You need excellent credit to get this card.

The best air-mile credit cards for those living in Austria

"In Austria, Miles & More offers you a special credit card. You get miles for each purchase with the credit card. The Miles & More program calculates miles earned based on the distance flown and booking class. For European flights, the booking class is a flat rate. For intercontinental flights, mileage is calculated by multiplying the booking class by the distance flown." They offer a calculator so you can see how many points you could earn: https://www.miles-and-more.com/at/en/earn/airlines/mileage-calculator.html

The best air-mile credit cards for those living in Spain:

"The American Express card is the best known and oldest to earn miles, thanks to its membership Rewards program. When making payments with this card, points are added, which can then be exchanged for miles from airlines such as Iberia, Air Europa, Emirates or Alitalia." More information is available here: https://www.americanexpress.com/es-es/

The best air-mile credit cards for those living in Australia

ANZ Rewards Black comes out top for 2025.

180,000 bonus ANZ Reward Points (can get an $800 gift card) and $0 annual fee for the first year with the ANZ Rewards Black
Points Per Spend: 1 Velocity point on purchases of up to $5,000 per statement period and 0.5 Velocity points thereafter.
Annual Fee: $0 in the first year, then $375 after.
Ns no set minimum income required, however, there is a minimum credit limit of $15,000 on this card.

Here are some ways you can hack points onto this card: https://www.pointhacks.com.au/credit-cards/anz-rewards-black-guide/

The best air-mile credit card solution for those living in the USA with a POOR credit score

The downside to Airline Mile cards is that they require good or excellent credit scores, meaning 690 or higher.

If you have bad credit and want to use credit card air lines you will need to rebuild your credit poor. The Credit One Bank® Platinum Visa® for Rebuilding Credit is a good credit card for people with bad credit who don't want to place a deposit on a secured card. The Credit One Platinum Visa offers a $300 credit limit, rewards, and the potential for credit-limit increases, which in time will help rebuild your score.

PLEASE don't sign-up for any of these cards if you can't trust yourself to repay it in full monthly. This will only lead to stress for you.

Frequent Flyer Memberships

"Points" and "miles" are often used interchangeably, but they're usually two very different things. Maximise and diversify your rewards by utilising both.

A frequent-flyer program (FFP) is a loyalty program offered by an airline. They are designed to encourage airline customers to fly more to accumulate points (also called miles, kilometres, or segments) which can be redeemed for air travel or other rewards.

You can sign up with any FFP program for free. There are three major airline alliances in the world: Oneworld, SkyTeam and Star Alliance. I am with One World https://www.oneworld.com/members because the points can be accrued and used for most flights.

The best return on your points is to use them for international business or first class flights with lie-flat seats. You would need 3 times more miles compared to an economy flight, but if you paid cash, you'd pay 5 - 10 times more than the cost of the economy flight, so it really pays to use your points only for upgrades. The worst value for your miles is to buy an economy seat or worse, a gift from the airlines gift-shop.

Sign up for a family/household account to pool miles together. If you share a common address, you can claim the miles with most airlines. You can use AwardWallet to keep track of your miles. Remember that they only last for 2 years, so use them before they expire.

How to get 70% off a Cruise

An average cruise can set you back $4,000. If you dream of cruising the oceans, but find the pricing too high, look at repositioning cruises. You can save as much as 70% by taking a cruise which takes the boat back to its home port.

These one-way itineraries take place during low cruise seasons when ships have to reposition themselves to locations where there's warmer weather.

To find a repositioning cruise, go to vacationstogo.com/repositioning_cruises.cfm. This simple and often overlooked booking trick is great for avoiding long flights with children and can save you so much money!

It's worth noting we don't have any affiliations with any travel service or provider. The links we suggest are chosen based on our experience of finding the best deals.

Relaxing at the Airport

The best way to relax at the airport is in a lounge where they provide free food, drinks, comfortable chairs, luxurious amenities (many have showers) and, if you're lucky, a peaceful ambience. If you're there for a longer time, look for Airport Cubicles, sleep pods which charge by the hour.

You can use your FFP Card (Frequent Flyer Memberships) to get into select lounges for free. Check your eligibility before you pay.

If you're travelling a lot, I'd recommend investing in a Priority Pass for the airport.

It includes 850-plus airport lounges around the world. The cost is $99 for the year and $27 per lounge visit or you can pay $399 for the year all inclusive.

If you need a lounge for a one-off day, you can get a Day Pass. Buy it online for a discount, it always works out cheaper than buying at the airport. Use www.LoungePass.com.

Lounges are also great if you're travelling with kids, as they're normally free for kids and will definitely cost you less than snacks for your little ones. The rule is that kids should be seen and not heard, so consider this before taking an overly excited child who wants to run around, or you might be asked to leave even after you've paid.

How to spend money

Bank ATM fees vary from $2.50 per transaction to as high as $5 or more, depending on the ATM and the country. You can completely skip those fees by paying with card and using a card which can hold multiple currencies.

Budget travel hacking begins with a strategy to spend without fees. Your individual strategy depends on the country you legally reside in as to what cards are available. Happily there are some fin-tech solutions which can save you thousands on those pesky ATM withdrawal fees and are widely available globally. Here are a selection of cards you can pre-charge with currency for Spain:

N26

N26 is a 12-year-old digital bank. I have been using them for over 6 years. The key advantage is fee-free card transactions abroad. They have a very elegant app, where you can check your timeline for all transactions listed in real time or manage your in-app security anywhere. The card you receive is a Mastercard so you can use it everywhere. If you lose the card, you don't have to call anyone, just open the app and swipe 'lock card'. It puts your purchases into a graph automatically so you can see what you spend on. You can open an account from abroad entirely online, all you need is your passport and a camera n26.com

Revolut

Revolut is a multi-currency account that allows you to hold and exchange 29 currencies and spend fee-free abroad. It's a UK based neobank, but accepts customers from all over the world.

Wise debit card

If you're going to be in one place for a long time, the Wise debit card is like having your travel money on a card – it lets you spend money at the real exchange rate.

Monzo

Monzo is good if your UK based. They offer a fee-free UK account. Fee-free international money transfers and fee-free spending abroad.

The downside

The cards above are debit cards, meaning you need to have money in those accounts to spend it. This comes with one big downside: safety. Credit card issuers' have "zero liability" meaning you're not liable for unauthorised charges. All the cards listed above do provide cover for unauthorised charges but times vary greatly in how quickly you'd get your money back if it were stolen.

The best option is to check in your country to see which credit cards are the best for travelling and set up monthly payments to repay the whole amount so you don't pay unnecessary interest. In the USA, Schwab regularly ranks at the top for travel credit cards. Credit cards are always the safer option when abroad simply because you get your money back faster if its stolen and if you're renting cars, most will give you free insurance when you book the car rental using the card, saving you money.

Always withdraw money; never exchange.

Money exchanges, whether they be on the streets or in the airports will NEVER give you a good exchange rate. Do not bring bundles of cash. Instead, withdraw local currency from the ATM as needed and try to use only free ATMs. Many in airports charge you a fee to withdraw cash. Look for bigger ATMs attached to banks to avoid this.

Recap

- Take cash from local, non-charging ATMs for the best rates.

- Never change at airport exchange desks unless you absolutely have to, then just change just enough to be able get to a bank ATM.

- Bring a spare credit card for emergencies.

- Split cash in various places on your person (pockets, shoes) and in your luggage. It's never sensible to keep your cash or cards all in one place.

- In higher risk areas, use a money belt under your clothes or put $50 in your shoe or bra.

Revolut
Revolut is a multi-currency account that allows you to hold and exchange 29 currencies and spend fee-free abroad. It's a UK based neobank, but accepts customers from all over the world.

Wise debit card
If you're going to be in one place for a long time the Wise debit card is like having your travel money on a card – it lets you spend money at the real exchange rate.

Monzo
Monzo is good if your UK based. They offer a fee-free UK account. Fee-free international money transfers and fee-free spending abroad.

The downside

The cards above are debit cards, meaning you need to have money in those accounts to spend it. This comes with one big downside: safety. Credit card issuers' have "zero liability" meaning you're not liable for unauthorised charges. All of the cards listed above do provide cover for unauthorised charges but times vary greatly in how quickly you'd get your money back if it were stolen.

The best option is to check in your country to see which credit cards are the best for travelling and set up monthly payments to repay the whole amount so you don't pay unnecessary interest. In the USA, Schwab[4] regularly ranks at the top for travel credit cards. Credit cards are always the safer option when abroad simply because you get your money back faster if its stolen and if you're renting cars, most will give you free insurance when you book the car rental using the card, saving you money.

Always withdraw money; never exchange.

Money exchanges whether they be on the streets or in the airports will NEVER give you a good exchange rate. Do not bring bundles of cash. Instead withdraw local currency from the ATM as needed and try to use only free ATM's. Many in airports charge you a fee to withdraw cash. Look for bigger ATM's attached to banks to avoid this.

Recap

- Take cash from local, non-charging ATMs for the best rates.
- Never change at airport exchange desks unless you absolutely have to, then just change just enough to be able get to a bank ATM.
- Bring a spare credit card for emergencies.
- Split cash in various places on your person (pockets, shoes) and in your luggage. Its never sensible to keep your cash or cards all in one place.
- In higher risk areas, use a money belt under your clothes or put $50 in your shoe or bra.

---

[4] Charles Schwab High Yield Checking accounts refund every single ATM fee worldwide, require no minimum balance and have no monthly fee.

How I got hooked on luxury on a budget travelling

'We're on holiday' is what my dad used to say to justify getting us in so much debt we lost our home and all our things when I was 11. We moved from the suburban bliss of Hemel Hempstead to a run down council estate in inner-city London, near my dad's new job as a refuge collector, a fancy word for dustbin man. I lost all my school friends while watching my dad go through a nervous breakdown.

My dad loved walking up a hotel lobby desk without a care in the world. So much so, that he booked overpriced holidays on credit cards. A lot of holidays. As it turned out, we couldn't afford any of them. In the end, my dad had no choice but to declare bankruptcy. When my mum realised, he'd racked up so much debt our family unit dissolved. A neat and perhaps as painless a summary of events that lead me to my life's passion: budget travel that doesn't compromise on fun, safety or comfort.

I started travelling full-time at the age of 18. I wrote the first Super Cheap Insider guide for friends visiting Norway - which I did for a month on less than $250. When sales reached 10,000 I decided to form the Super Cheap Insider Guides company. As I know from first-hand experience debt can be a noose around our necks, and saying 'oh come on, we're on vacation' isn't a get out of jail free card. In fact, its the reverse of what travel is supposed to bring you - freedom.

Before I embarked upon writing Super Cheap Insider guides, many, many people told me that my dream was impossible. Travelling on a budget could never be comfortable. I hope this guide has proved to you what I have known for a long-time: budget travel can feel luxurious when you know and use the insider hacks.

And apologies if I depressed you with my tale of woe. My dad is now happily remarried and works as a chef in Spain at a fancy hotel - the kind he used to take us to!

A final word...

There's a simple system you can use to think about budget travel. In life, we can choose two of the following: cheap, fast, or quality. So if you want it Cheap and fast you will get a lower quality service. Fast-food is the perfect example. The system holds true for purchasing anything while travelling. I always choose cheap and quality, except at times where I am really limited on time. Normally, you can make small tweaks to make this work for you. Ultimately, you must make choices about what's most important to you and heed your heart's desires.

'Your heart is the most powerful muscle in your body. Do what it says.' Jen Sincero

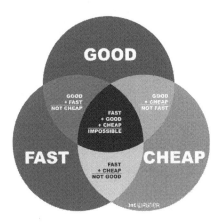

If you've found this book useful, please select some stars, it would mean genuinely make my day to see I've helped you.

Copyright

Published in Great Britain in 2025 by Super Cheap Insider Guides LTD.

Copyright © 2025 Super Cheap Insider Guides LTD.

The right of Phil G A Tang to be identified as the Author of the Work has been asserted in accordance with the Copyright, Designs and Patents Act 1988.

All rights reserved.

Made in the USA
Coppell, TX
24 January 2025

44877157R20180